WITHDRAWN
UTSA LIBRARIES

The Physiology of Truth

The Physiology of Truth

Neuroscience and Human Knowledge

Jean-Pierre Changeux

Translated by
M. B. DeBevoise

The Belknap Press of
Harvard University Press

Cambridge, Massachusetts
London, England / 2004

Library
University of Texas
at San Antonio

Copyright © 2002 by the President and Fellows of Harvard College
Originally published as *L'Homme de vérité,* copyright © Éditions Odile Jacob, 2002

All rights reserved
Printed in the United States of America

Library of Congress Cataloging-in-Publication Data

Changeux, Jean-Pierre.
[Homme de vérité. English]
The physiology of truth : neuroscience and human knowledge / Jean-Pierre Changeux ; translated by M.B. DeBevoise.
p. cm.
Includes bibliographical references and index.
ISBN 0-674-01283-6 (alk. paper)
1. Neurosciences. 2. Brain—Physiology. 3. Knowledge, Theory of. 4. Mind-brain identity theory. 5. Science—Methodology. I. Title.
RC343.C438 2004
612.8—dc22

2003058736

Library
University of Texas
at San Antonio

Contents

The Physiology of Truth

Introduction

What is truth? The question is one of the most ancient in Western philosophy. It was famously posed by Plato, who asked whether there exist eternal truths or whether, to the contrary, man is the measure of all things. Diderot and d'Alembert, in their *Encyclopédie* (1751–1772), proposed a simple and straightforward answer: truth consists in "a conformity of our judgments with things."[1] In other words, something is true when there is a fit between thought and object: *adaequatio rei et intellectus*. This implies not only the conformity of our ideas with external objects, but also the internal consistency of our ideas with one another.

Yet a great many theories that seem to conform to what we see turn out on closer examination to be false. The sun, despite appearances to the contrary, does not in fact revolve around the earth. And many arguments that seem to be sound ultimately are found to be flawed. Does this justify us, then, in placing confidence in astrology, homeopathy, miraculous powers, or supernatural phenomena? Where are we to draw a line between beliefs and established truths, between opinion and scientific knowledge? What are the distinguishing features of the truths produced by science? Do nonscientific truths exist?

These questions lead on to others. Along with error, delusion, and fantasy, there can be conscious falsification—in a word, lying. The person who lies knows it; the person to whom the lie is addressed may not. How is it that we are able to detect deception? Why is the capacity to lie a characteristic trait of the human species? Is it not the counterpart to our ability to tell the truth—something that is impossible for dogs or monkeys?

It may be thought that there is nothing new to be said about truth. But in fact contemporary neuroscience offers a wealth of original observations and bold hypotheses. The sciences of the brain have achieved spectacular advances in recent decades, summarized for general readers in a number of excellent works by authors such as Antonio Damasio, Joseph LeDoux, and Rodolfo Llinás. In February 2002 the first detailed picture of the complete sequence of the human genome was published. Although further clarification is needed, we may confidently look forward to the day when the structure of all the molecules that make up our body—which includes, of course, the brain—will be known. In parallel with these developments, multi-electrode recordings and powerful new methods of magnetic resonance imaging, among many others, have enabled us to objectively examine the higher functions of our brain, opening up new perspectives on our conscious awareness of ourselves and the world. It has now become possible to recast the ancient questions of philosophy in the light of modern neurobiological research.

Certainly there is nothing new about the idea of joining together physiology and philosophy. The earliest philosophers in ancient Greece, notably Democritus and Empedocles, considered only material principles worthy of being considered principles of all things. Nearer to our own time, Spinoza held that "men judge things according to the disposition of their brain." Henri Bergson went so far as to suggest that scientific knowledge of the brain might be expected to have positive consequences for philosophy.[2]

We need to go back and reread Descartes, who remains the pivotal figure of this venerable alliance between philosophy and what today are known as the cognitive sciences. In the fourth part of the *Discours de la méthode* (1637), he asked how we are able to decide whether our ideas are true or false: "It is quite easy to show that the dreams that we imagine while [we are] asleep ought in no way make us doubt the truth of the thoughts that we have when we are awake. For in the end, whether we are awake or whether we are sleeping, we ought always to be persuaded only by the evidence of our reason." The second edition of *L'Homme* (1677) contains an illustration (Figure 2) showing

Figure 1. Detail from Luc-Olivier Merson, *Allégorie de la Vérité* (1901). Truth, shown seated on the edge of the fount of ignorance, is the inspiration of the sciences, the arts, and letters.

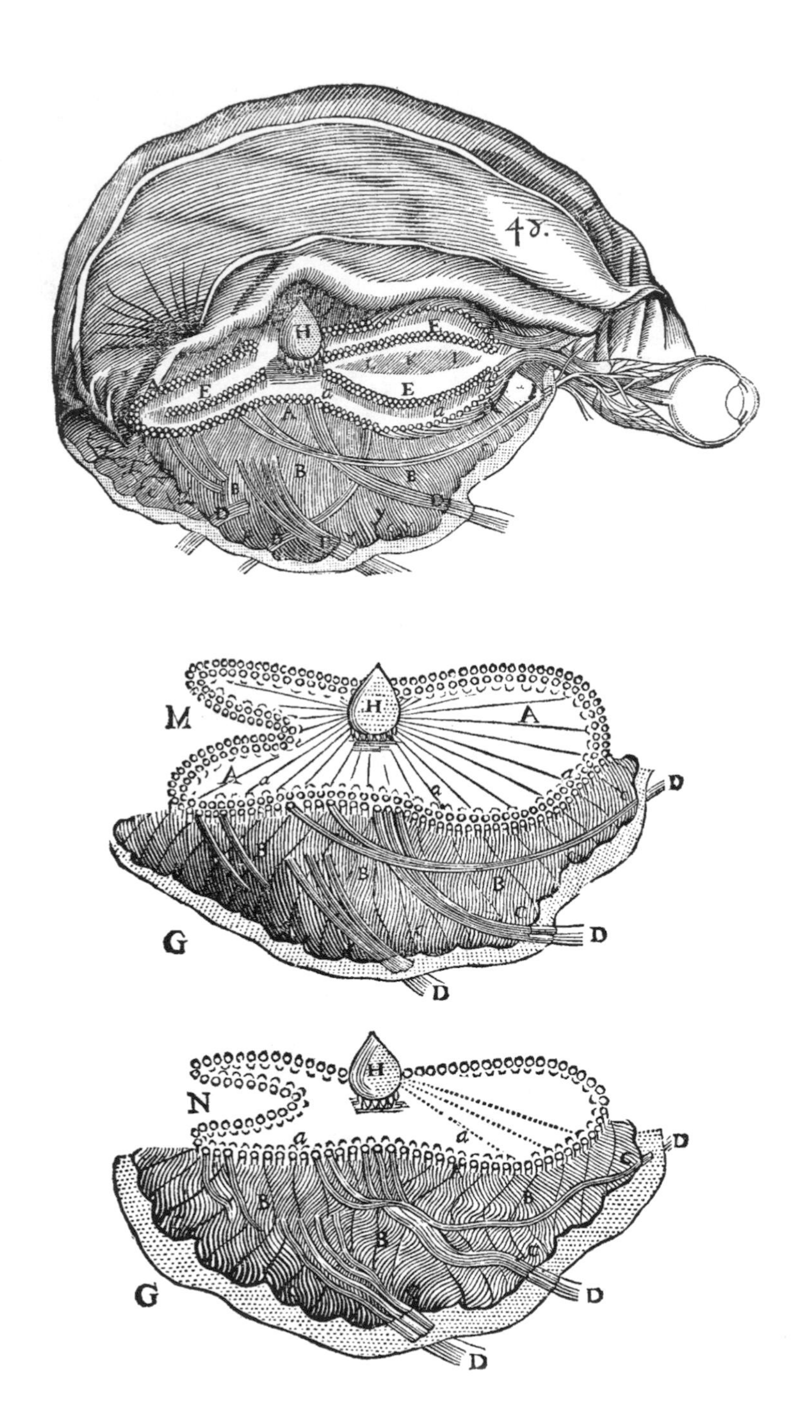
48.
H
E
F
A
B
D
M
A
H
a
D
B
G
D
D
N
H
a
D
B
G
D
D

that the "figures"—or shapes—of the "small tubes by which the animal spirits enter" the brain differ during waking, sleep, and dreaming: "The reasonable soul immediately considers [these figures] when, being united with this machine, it imagines or senses some object." Elsewhere Descartes expressed the opinion that, between *res extensa* and *res cogitans,* there obtains "a unity of composition, insofar as both are met with in the same man, as bones and flesh in the same animal . . . The distinction or difference that I note between the nature of an extended thing and that of a thinking thing does not seem to me to be less than that between bone and flesh." Warned by Père Mersenne of the trial of Galileo, he was never to pursue this line of thought to its logical conclusion.[3]

The Inquisition is no more, but the question posed by Descartes has lost none of its complexity. The obstacles we face today have to do with the difficulty of the question itself: can the anatomical organization and physiological states of activity of the brain be shown to be causally related to the mind's higher cognitive functions and, in particular, to the acquisition of knowledge and the testing of its truth or falsehood? Despite the limited nature of the scientific evidence currently available to us, we are nonetheless in a position to formulate the problems that arise in trying to explain human thought in physical terms with greater precision than ever before. Solving these immensely difficult problems, while frankly acknowledging the provisional character of our present understanding, now stands as the major intellectual challenge of our age.

In embracing this challenge we should nonetheless be modest about what we can reasonably hope to achieve. "Of reality," Democritus said, "we do not grasp anything that is absolutely true, but only that which occurs by chance, in keeping with the momentary dispositions of our body and the influences that affect us or strike us."[4] The repre-

Opposite page

Figure 2. Drawings of the brain from the second edition of Descartes's *L'Homme* (1677), thought to be by Descartes himself. They depict the brain in its entirety *(top),* the brain of a person who is awake *(middle),* and that of one who is asleep and dreaming *(bottom).* The "figures" of the "small tubes" that converge at the pineal gland (H) differ depending on whether the subject is awake or asleep.

sentations that we construct in our brain of our own inner world and of the world around us are themselves, as we shall see, physical objects. They cannot claim to exhaust the reality of the world. There will, moreover, always exist an element of uncertainty in every advance of scientific knowledge. But surely this is no reason to renounce the ambition of knowing more.

Provocation? Perhaps not. No one would deny that the appetite for knowledge lies at the very heart of human nature. What could be more natural than to wish to better understand this very appetite? What dishonor is there in wishing to explain the distinctively human capacity for rational thought? What crime is there in wishing to go beyond a mystical exaltation of human exceptionalism that over the centuries has accumulated an appalling legacy of intolerance, hatred, cruelty, and violence? What grounds are there for fearing that the attempt to naturalize—to materialize—all that traditionally has belonged to the realm of the spiritual and the transcendent will fatally diminish human dignity? Does this attempt really foretell the death of humankind? Hardly. I see it instead as a splendid reaffirmation of human vitality. At the same time, by removing the possibility of appeal to supernatural authority, it places the full burden of moral responsibility on our shoulders as human beings.

The search for the neurobiological bases of consciousness and rationality, far from impoverishing our conception of human integrity, offers an unprecedented opportunity to properly value the multiplicity of personal experience, the richness of cultural diversity, and the variety of our ideas about the world. More than this, by making it possible to regard moral norms as distinctive expressions of a general disposition to ethical behavior, it suggests new ways in which the rights of individuals may be harmonized with their obligations to the social community of which they are members. On this view, the neuroscience of ethics appears as perhaps the most important aspect of the physiology of truth.

Thinking Matter 1

"Science," Gaston Bachelard declared in the introduction to *Le Matérialisme rationnel* (1953), "does not have the philosophy it deserves." Considering the preeminence that idealism has traditionally enjoyed in intellectual life, Bachelard observed, "it should not come as a surprise that materialist arguments have not received sufficient attention from philosophers." Philosophers he found guilty of undue and unwarranted simplification: "They identify materialism with a crude conception of matter, a conception lacking any experimental basis, and thus presume to ignore the various kinds of matter actually treated by science across the ages, even where they treat of matter in general." In short, they set up a straw man—a "matterless materialism."[1]

In their haste to lay a foundation for science once and for all, philosophers fail to grasp the new perspectives revealed by chemistry (which Bachelard saw as the science of the future) and physics. Two centuries of chemical research, from Lavoisier to Mendeleev and the periodic table of elements, and from Berthelot's organic chemistry to contemporary biochemistry and molecular biology, had shown that matter could no longer be conceived as a simple entity reducible to a few external principles: the "receptacle of undefined, undefinable, unsituated irrationalities," the "anti-form," the "simple idea" imagined by a certain tradition. Modern chemistry, Bachelard held, "ushers man into a new world."[2]

In physics the situation had changed even more dramatically. The ancient doctrine of Democritus, for whom atoms were the basic constituents of the material objects apprehended by the senses, was succeeded in modern times by a quantum conception of matter as something distinct from either radiation or the corpuscles governed by the laws of rational mechanics. No longer could the atoms of Rutherford and Bohr be seen as constituting a fixed geometrical arrangement of corpuscles. Matter was now conceived instead as a macroscopic phenomenon formed of elements that are more or less stable from the statistical point of view. The naive materialism that idealist philosophers of earlier times found such an inviting target had therefore to be abandoned. In physics, as in chemistry, a new world demanded a new, more sophisticated materialism—a *matérialisme instruit.*

In the case of the brain, no matter that a great many enigmas and puzzles remain to be solved, modern neuroscience provides no grounds for doubting the existence of what Voltaire, in a letter of 1733, called "thinking matter."[3] Indeed, the chemistry of the brain exhibits not the slightest ambiguity in this regard. It is made up of the same elements as inorganic matter. These elements are assembled in such a way as to form organic molecules, from amino acids to proteins and from nucleotides to DNA. This much we surely know—but it is not enough to explain the origins of thought.

Writing not long after Voltaire, Denis Diderot formulated the problem in quite modern terms. In *Le Rêve de d'Alembert* (1769), Diderot suggested that the formation of a "network" out of what he called "molecules" would produce a "tissue of sensitive matter" that would give rise to actions and reactions. This early instance of an "informed" materialism prepared the way for the idea that our cerebral functions, our sensations and our thoughts, are products of the organization of matter. Understanding the nature of Diderot's "molécules sensibles"—their place and their relationship to one another as well as their integration as part of a whole—ought therefore to make it possible to explain both the unity of the higher functions of the brain and their variation across individuals.[4] At the heart of informed materialism is the notion that the capacity for organization is an essential part of the very definition of matter.

Modern neuroscience, which studies the organization of the brain as a physical object, proceeds by first dividing it into territories, variously known as "organs,"[5] "areas,"[6] "cognitive modules,"[7] or "functional maps,"[8] which jointly constitute a "workspace"[9] (Figure 3). Yet the passage from the atomic scale to cognitive structures is neither simple nor direct. The essential feature of cerebral organization, which may explain the genesis of subjective experience—not only sensory perception and what is commonly called thinking, but also feelings and emotions—is the *architecture* of the brain's cellular and molecular network and the activities that occur within this network.[10] Developed over the course of biological evolution, and established during embryogenesis and postnatal development, this neuronal architecture supports capacities that are peculiar to the human species and allow it to learn, to store information, and to test the truthfulness of the knowledge it has acquired—in other words, to have the intellectual and affective experience that is the hallmark of human life.

Bachelard, regretting the failures of philosophers, called upon scientists to discover and profess "the perspicacious philosophy of their own science."[11] It is part of my purpose in this book, then, to try to give a truer and more complete statement of the materialism that is implicit in what has so far been learned about the origins and development of the brain and, by virtue of this, of thought.

The Elementary Building Blocks of the Brain

I would like to begin by briefly reviewing the basic components of the brain, looking first at neurons and the elementary signals that they generate and propagate among themselves. I will go on to consider two features of cerebral function that are frequently, but in my view mistakenly, considered secondary. The first, which contradicts the standard empiricist conception of the brain as a machine that processes information from sensory input to motor output, is that the brain is the seat of intense spontaneous activity arising independently of interaction with the environment. The second, which disagrees with the nativist view of the brain as genetically determined in all of its aspects, is that the functional properties of nerve cells and of the networks they compose vary according to the pattern of neural activation. A fuller account of these matters may be found in my book *Neuronal Man.*[12]

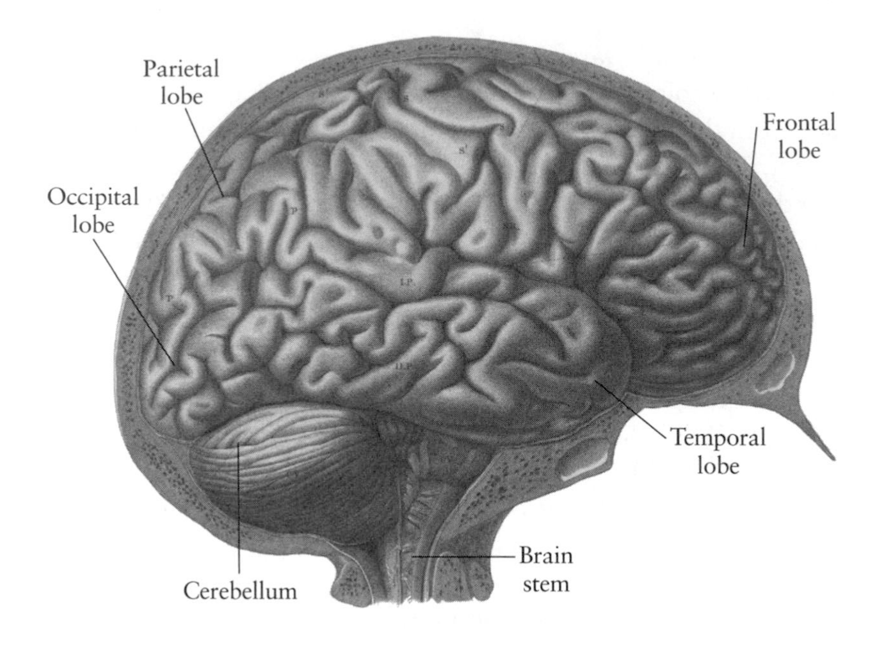
Parietal lobe
Frontal lobe
Occipital lobe
Temporal lobe
Cerebellum
Brain stem

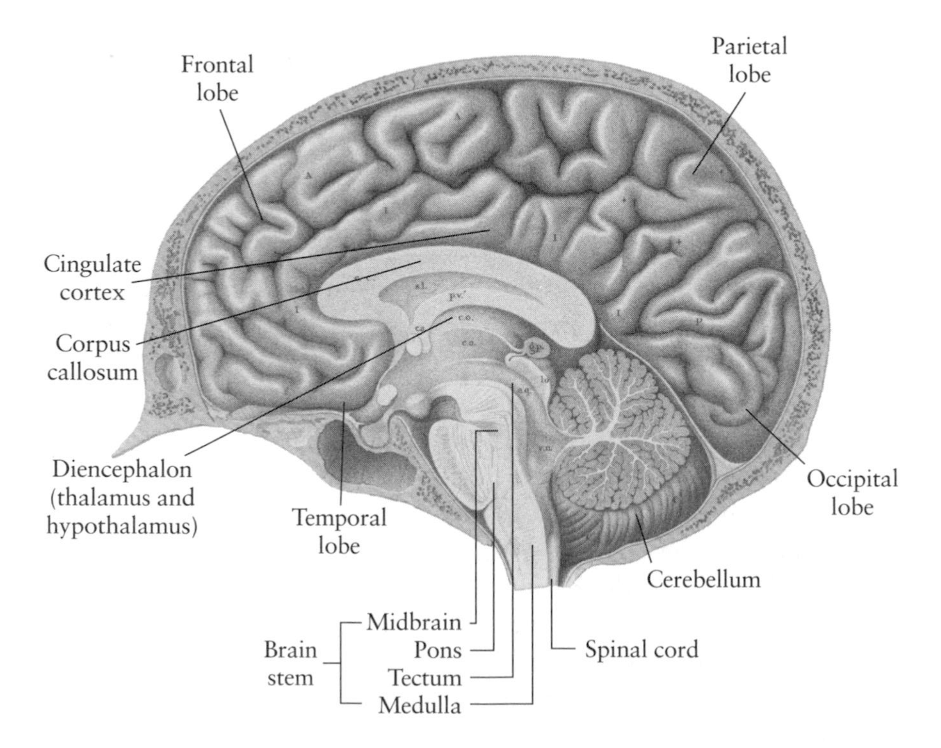
Frontal lobe
Parietal lobe
Cingulate cortex
Corpus callosum
Diencephalon (thalamus and hypothalamus)
Temporal lobe
Occipital lobe
Cerebellum
Brain stem
Midbrain
Pons
Tectum
Medulla
Spinal cord

Neurons and Glial Cells

Thanks to the pioneering neuroanatomist Santiago Ramón y Cajal, whose century-old two-volume work on the histology of the nervous system remains the standard reference for our basic understanding of the structure of the brain,[13] we know that the nerve cell, or neuron, together with its entire system of prolongations—axons and dendritic outgrowths—exhibits both unity and autonomy. Neurons, unlike other types of cells in the human body, form discontinuous networks whose elements are connected to one another by means of junctions known as synapses, which establish fixed, stable bonds with a great many other cells. The human brain contains roughly one hundred billion neurons and on the order of a million billion connections among neurons.

Neurons are divided into distinct categories on the basis of their morphological appearance. In simple nervous systems such as those of the worm, fly, and sea slug, each type of nerve cell is identifiably reproduced from one individual to another. In the nematode *Caenorhabditis elegans,* for example, exactly 302 nerve cells have been distinguished—roughly one-third of the total number of cells in the worm's body. The situation is different in the case of the higher vertebrates, where the number of neural cell types is a thousand or more.[14] These are in all essential respects the same from the mouse to humans, with the exception of a recently discovered category of neuron found exclusively in the cingulate cortex of the large primates and man.[15] In the case of the human brain, the very great number of nerve cells and the variability of their branching patterns pose an obstacle to the precise identification of a given neuron across individuals. It may even be the case that, within a given category, each individual neuron expresses a

Opposite page

Figure 3. These mid-nineteenth-century images of the human brain by Leuret and Gratiolet reproduce its cortical convolutions with rarely equaled precision. If we compare these with the etchings by Vesalius in *De humani corporis fabrica* (1543) and with modern photographic atlases we find that, allowing for differences in technique and style, the structure of the brain has remained essentially unchanged since the sixteenth century in spite of tremendous upheavals in the social and cultural environment. The names of the main components of the central nervous system have been superimposed on the original drawings.

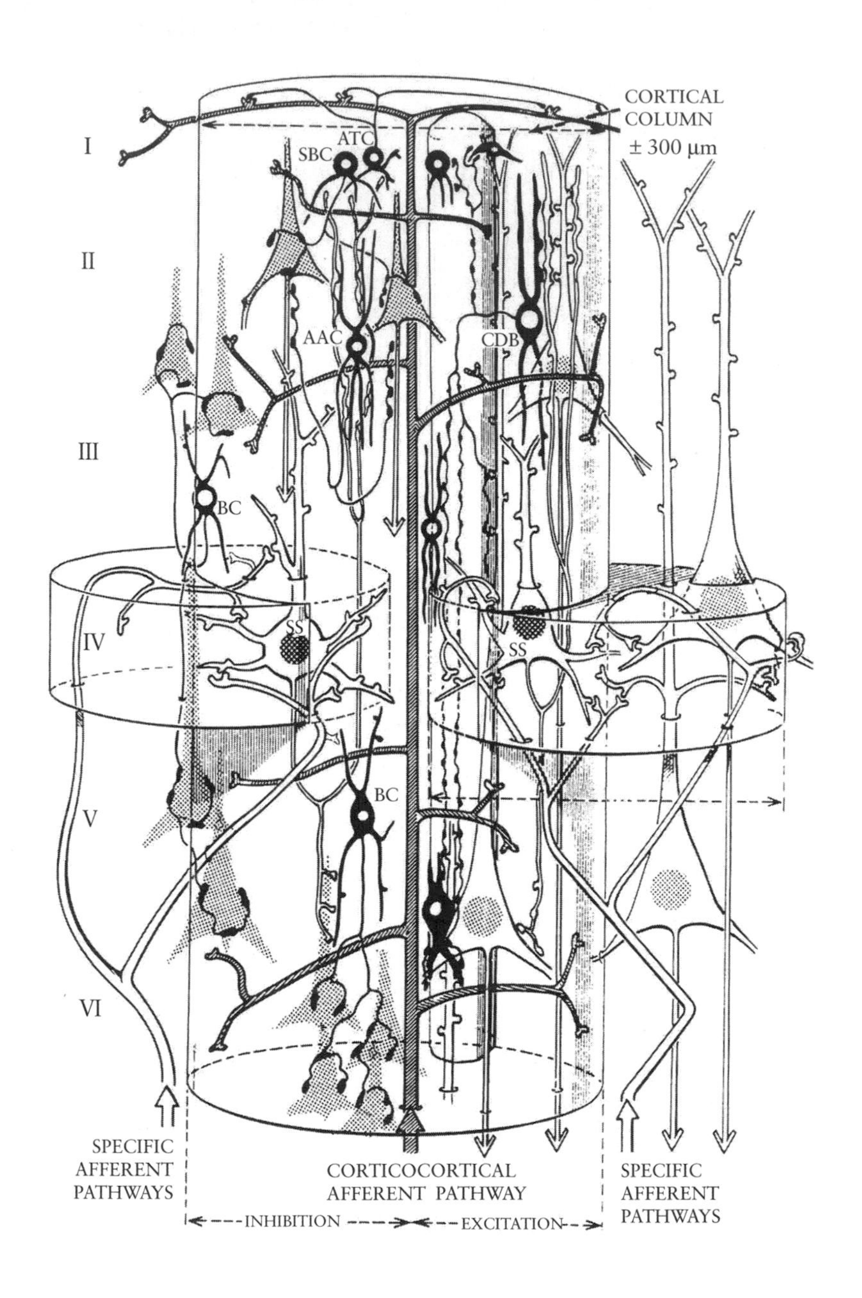

CORTICAL
COLUMN
± 300 μm
I
II
III
IV
V
VI
SBC
ATC
AAC
CDB
BC
SS
SS
BC
SPECIFIC
AFFERENT
PATHWAYS
CORTICOCORTICAL
AFFERENT PATHWAY
SPECIFIC
AFFERENT
PATHWAYS
INHIBITION
EXCITATION

distinctive set of genes,[16] exhibits a distinctive set of connective patterns, and possesses a distinctive set of physiological properties.[17] In other words, although neurons are indeed the main component parts of the human brain, great diversity and variability nonetheless exist among these considered individually, both within a given brain and among individual brains (Figure 4A).

Moreover, the neuronal network of the brain contains a great mass of cells, known as glial cells, which are distinct from neurons and serve to "glue" them together into a compact tissue. These cells come in different types as well and play important supporting and trophic roles, both of which are necessary for normal brain function. The density of synaptic contacts, for example, seems to be related to the number of glial cells. Despite the importance of their function, in normal and pathological states of the brain alike, glial cells are not sufficiently taken into account by neural network models.

Electrical Signals

Philosophers and linguists often neglect another essential aspect of the brain: its physiological activity. In reducing the brain to a compact and immutable tissue of nerve cells and fibers, they fail to pay enough attention to the signals that travel through the pathways linking these cells and that, by mobilizing networks of neurons, establish a fundamental relationship between anatomy and function. Nerve cells and fibers produce both electrical and chemical signals (Figures 4B, 4C,

Opposite page

Figure 4A. A schematic representation of the various categories of neurons present in a column of the cerebral cortex (about 0.4 mm in diameter). Note the excitatory neurons, or pyramidal cells, distinguished by their triangular cell body, apical dendrites, and long axon that goes out from the cortex *(right side);* but also inhibitory neurons exhibiting a great diversity of form (SS, SBC, AAC, CDB, BC, ATC), whose axons do not leave the cortex. Along the center of the figure is an axon that enters from pyramidal cells elsewhere in the cortex and becomes ramified at every cortical level; the other entrant axons that zigzag to the right and left and stop at level IV come from the relay nuclei of the thalamus. There are between 10 and 30 billion neurons in the human cerebral cortex, and the density of synaptic contacts between neurons (abundantly visible in this figure) is roughly 600 million per cubic millimeter, or on the order of 10^{15} for the cortex as a whole.

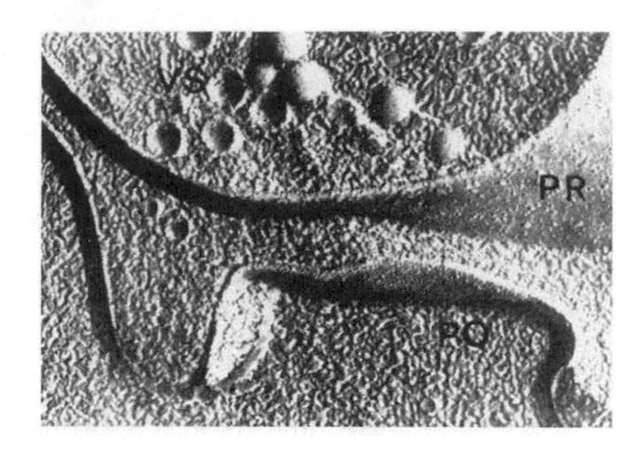

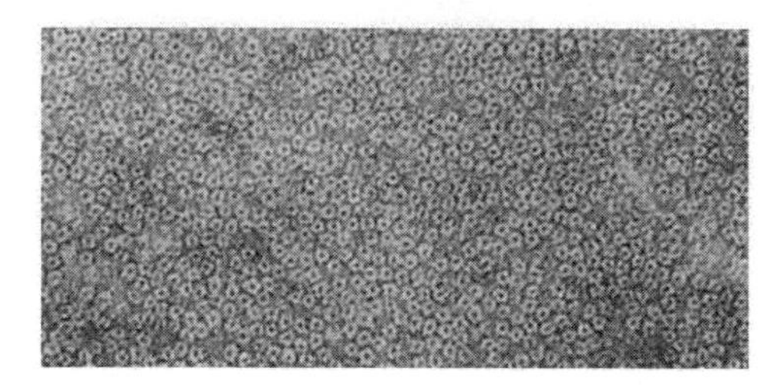

Figure 4B. Electronic microscopy of a chemical synapse *(top)* showing the space separating the nerve ending (with its vesicles filled with neurotransmitter) and the membrane of the adjacent cell, which, in the magnified image *(bottom)*, reveals a bed of particles, each one representing a neurotransmitter receptor molecule. Sizes: synapse, one millionth of a meter; receptor, ten billionths of a meter.

4D). What is more, they are sensitive to these signals and respond to them.

Beginning with the work of Luigi Galvani at the end of the eighteenth century and that of Emil Du Bois-Reymond at the end of the nineteenth, physiologists have long been interested in electrical signals.[18] The global electrical activity of the brain can easily be recorded by means of electroencephalographic techniques. These electrical phenomena result from the summation of elementary microscopic signals, or nerve impulses, that circulate through cellular processes and synapses. The basic nerve impulse is of an all-or-nothing type, with waves roughly a millisecond in length that are propagated at speeds ranging from 0.1 to 100 meters per second, but in any case below the speed of sound. The molecular mechanisms of this elementary signal (or "action potential") are rather well understood today. Its electrical current

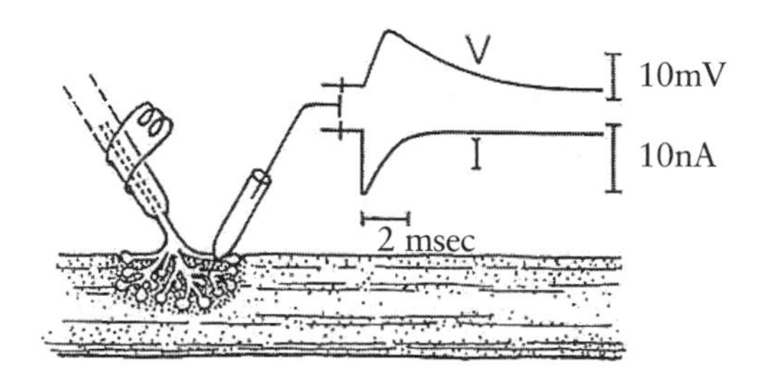

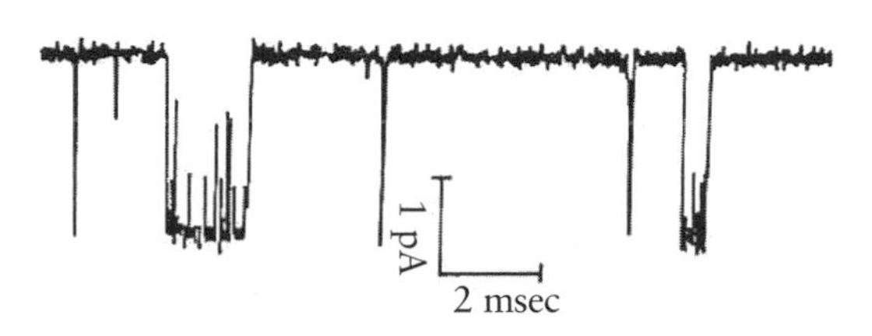

Figure 4C. *Top:* Response of an excitatory synapse (nerve-muscle junction) to a neurotransmitter, in this case acetylcholine, with the change in current (I) conveyed by Na^+ and K^+ ions. *Bottom:* recording of the opening of the ion channel of a single acetylcholine receptor molecule; the average duration of the opening of a single canal is roughly equal to that of the physiological signal (one to two milliseconds).

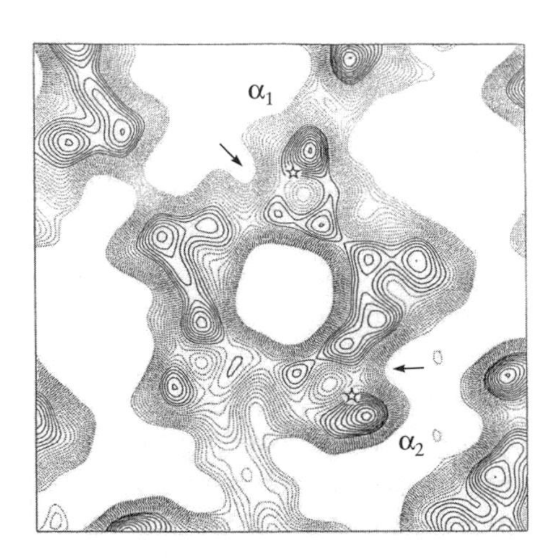

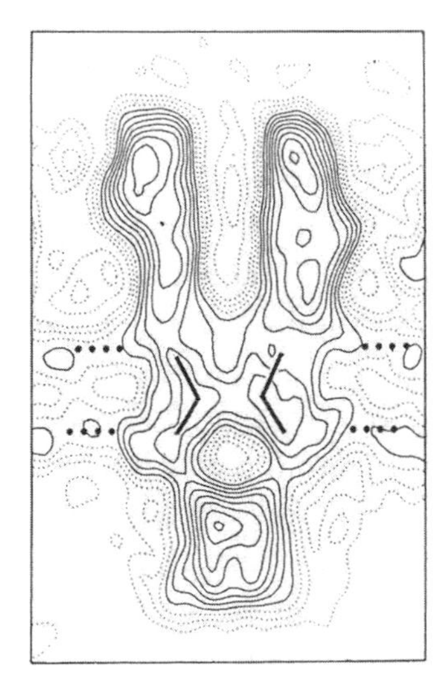

Figure 4D. Acetylcholine receptor molecule from the electrical organ of the torpedo fish *(Torpedo marmorata)*, frontal and profile views.

is generated by the transport through the cell membrane of a class of charged particles called ions that are taken in as part of our daily diet in the form of potassium, sodium, calcium, and chloride. These ions are unequally distributed on either side of the cell membrane. Specialized regulatory molecules in the cell membrane that are sensitive to voltage, known as channel proteins, play a direct role in their passage through the membrane.

Several channel proteins have recently been identified at the molecular level, and it is known that they are traversed all the way through by a microscopic tunnel that contains selective gates for each type of ion.[19] The passage of ions through this channel gives rise to an electrical current whose polarity, or sign, is determined by the positive or negative charge of the ions transported and by their relative concentration inside and outside the cell membrane. The entry of positive sodium and potassium ions produces an excitatory effect giving rise to a nerve impulse, whereas the entry of negative chloride ions is generally inhibitory and blocks the production of a nerve impulse. Conformational changes also cause membrane proteins to open and close the channels with which they are associated. The dynamics of the opening and closing of the gates in these molecular channels, for example under the influence of an electrical field, creates irreducible constraints upon the speed of transmission and propagation of nerve signals (Figures 4 and 5).

Everyday experience leads us to suppose that thoughts pass through the mind with a rapidity that defies the laws of physics. It comes as a stunning surprise to discover that almost the exact opposite is true: the brain is slow—very slow—by comparison with the fundamental forces of the physical world. In fact, the nervous system of all living organisms, including man, propagates electrical signals at a speed well below that of light. This means that neural signaling does not involve electromagnetic waves—a physical limitation inherited from simpler organisms through the evolution of species. In this respect there is little difference between humans, fish, and worms.

The efficient performance of information processing systems depends on the integrity of their weakest—which is to say slowest—links. Human thought, despite the swiftness we are accustomed to attribute to it, does not escape this rule: the processing of information by the brain, from nerve cells and elementary neuronal networks to

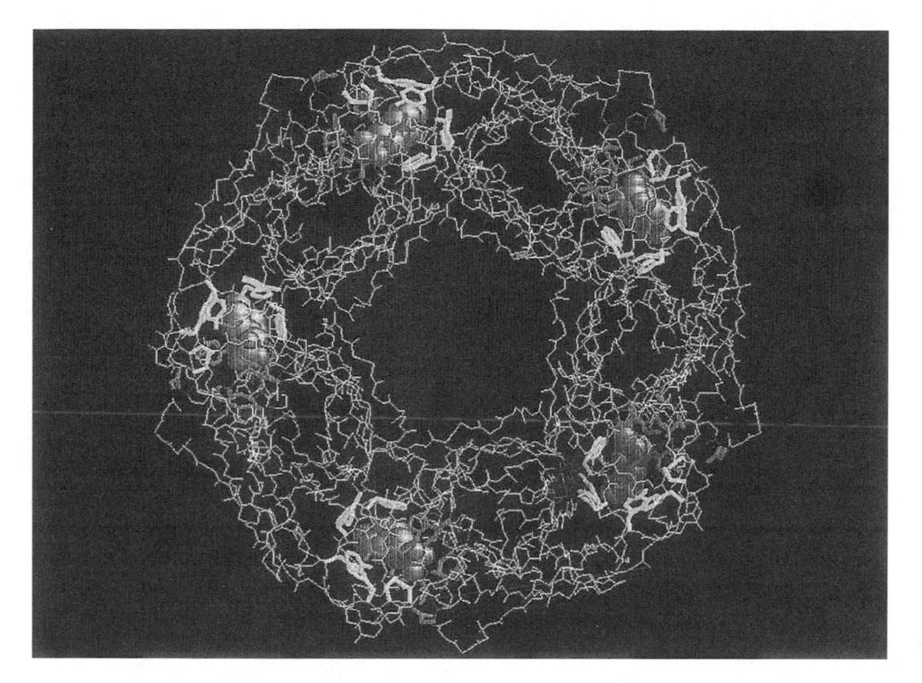

Figure 5A. X-ray diffraction methods reveal the atomic structure of biological macromolecules important for the functioning of the nervous system. Shown here is the crystallographic structure of a molecule of a freshwater mollusk *(Lymnea),* which binds acetylcholine and closely resembles the synaptic domain of the acetylcholine receptor. The positions of the binding sites for the neurotransmitter at the interfaces between subunits are marked by balls, each of which represents an atom.

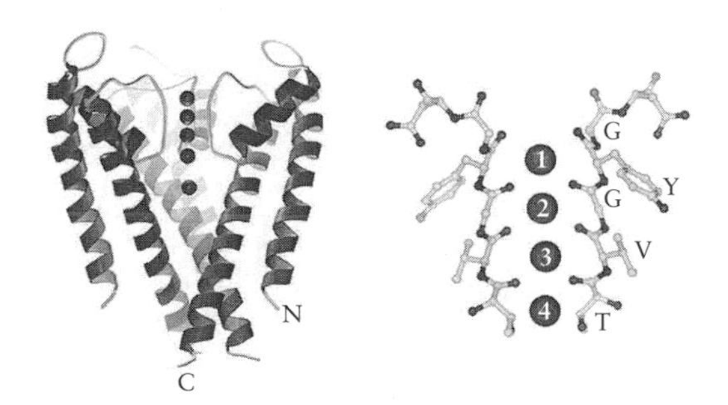

Figure 5B. Crystallographic structure of a bacterial channel permeable to potassium ions (K^+), whose physiological properties are very close to those of the potassium channels in the fly and man. *Left:* Overall structure of the molecule within the lipid layer of the cell membrane. *Right:* Detail of the ion channel, occupied here by four potassium ions (dark balls) during their passage through the membrane.

high-level cognition, ranges from a millisecond to a few hundred milliseconds. Naturally, what neuroscientists call "psychological time" seems instantaneous as a matter of subjective experience. But it is in fact a very long time by comparison with the speeds achieved by computers and Internet communication, which are supposed to represent modest copies of human cerebral performance. The recent discovery of superconductivity at high temperatures holds out the prospect of computers a thousand times faster than the ones we have today. The human brain therefore does not make optimal use of the resources of the physical world; it makes do instead with components inherited from simpler organisms—channel proteins, for example, first emerged in bacteria—that have survived over the course of biological evolution. The question naturally arises, then, in the case of the brain, whether an apparent source of weakness is actually a source of strength.

Chemical Signals

Electrical signals are the simplest of all communication devices. In the human brain they cross the space that separates nerve cells from one another. These spaces are known as gap junctions, or electrical synapses, where the cytoplasmic membranes on either side are juxtaposed closely enough to allow signals to propagate directly from cell to cell. The rapid transmission of electrical signals within and among neuronal networks may contribute to the large-scale synchronization of cerebral activity. During the first half of the twentieth century a good many eminent physiologists, most notably Sir John Eccles, believed that the transmission of physiological signals in the brain was exclusively electrical. Electrical excitation, they held, was sufficient to trigger the firing of the cell at the synapse by a sort of "detonator action."[20] During the same period, however, research in pharmacology and biochemistry, following in the tradition inaugurated by the great French physiologist Claude Bernard (particularly in his 1857 lectures at the Collège de France on "toxic and medicinal substances," which treated peripheral actions such as that of curare on the junctions between nerve and muscle in addition to central actions such as that of strychnine), caused this view to be substantially modified.

Although electrical communication does indeed occur in the brain, in many synapses chemistry takes the place of electricity. Simple chemical substances called neurotransmitters are capable, like electrical impulses, of crossing the synaptic cleft. The brain therefore operates as both an electrical and a chemical signaling machine. Moreover, its wealth of chemical resources, and the diversity of the molecules involved in chemical communication between neurons, are much greater than was initially thought. In the 1930s only a few neurotransmitters were known. The chief one of these, acetylcholine, had first been discovered in connection with the action of the vagus nerve on the heart and also at the junction between motor nerves and skeletal muscle; its action in the rest of the nervous system was detected soon afterward. Several dozen additional neurotransmitters have been identified since, along with an even greater number of peptides serving as chemical messengers. It is now known, too, that an individual nerve cell is capable of synthesizing and releasing more than one neurotransmitter.[21]

Neurotransmitters are synthesized and stored in nerve endings. Released into the space between two neurons, they rapidly diffuse and reach the neighboring cell in a fraction of a millisecond. There they trigger a process of transduction, by which the chemical signal is converted into a new electrical (or chemical) signal. The time it takes to do this varies from a few milliseconds to a few seconds. Sometimes a neurotransmitter overflows the synapse, flooding large adjacent populations of neurons.[22] This phenomenon may be responsible for long-term physiological processes that take place throughout the brain in states of wakefulness or sleep, in reward processes, in tasks requiring mental effort, or in emotional experience.

On reaching their target cells, neurotransmitters are recognized by specialized molecules. In 1905 the English pharmacologist John Newport Langley named these molecules "receptive substances." Receptors, as they are now known, nonetheless remained mysterious for more than a half century. Despite the evident power of their physiological and pharmacological action, they long escaped biochemical identification, chiefly because they are found in very small quantities in neuromuscular junctions. Today it is known that 5 percent of our genes are dedicated to the production of receptors, now understood to be large proteins located in the postsynaptic cell membrane that function as molecular switches, assuring the recognition and transduction of chemical signals.[23]

These membrane proteins are capable of recognizing not only neurotransmitters and neuropeptides but also medicinal substances and drugs that likewise lodge themselves at specialized binding sites (Figure 5A)—like a lock, as it is often said, that recognizes a properly specified key and no other. Receptors also convert the neurotransmitter's signal into biological activity: either the opening of an ion channel or the activation of an enzyme reaction. These "molecular locks" span the cell membrane: on one side they look out upon the synaptic cleft, on the other upon the cytoplasm. They exhibit two distinct and opposed states of molecular activity, active and inactive, and switch back and forth from one to the other—on and off—in an all-or-nothing mode. Depending on the nature of the neurotransmitter "key" and the structure of the receptor "lock," the response of certain receptors is either excitatory (generating an electrical signal) or, by contrast, inhibitory (blocking any excitation). When the receptor is linked to an ion channel, the nature of the response, excitatory or inhibitory, is determined by the selectivity of the channel and the type and charge of the ion passing through the channel.

These receptors are the target of many psychotropic substances, some of which (benzodiazepines, for example, which act as tranquilizers) are currently employed as medicines. These drugs potentiate the receptors of a particular neurotransmitter, gamma-aminobutyric acid (GABA), which are linked to a channel that is permeable to negatively charged chloride ions. The potentiation of chloride ions produces inhibition at the neuronal level and, on the scale of the brain as a whole, regulates subjective states of anxiety.

Receptors thus play an essential role in the cybernetics of the synapse. In fact, they belong to a very large set of proteins that includes cytoplasmic enzymes, factors regulating genetic transcription (hence the name "transcription factors" that is frequently used), ion channels, and a wide variety of signal transducers. Owing to the number of topologically distinct sites that they support, these molecules were named "allosteric proteins."[24] Allosteric locks are nodal points in the networks of signal transduction pathways found in the brain, from the simplest nerve cells to the most complex neuronal assemblies (Figure 6). These pathways mobilize not only neurotransmitter receptors and ion channels but also a considerable number of specialized molecules, among them enzymes involved in biosynthesis and degradation, and membrane transporters. All these molecules work in concert to maintain the stability of the form and function of the organism—what Bernard called "homeostasis."

From the Molecular to the Supramacromolecular

The mathematician René Thom, in a rather controversial book entitled *Paraboles et catastrophes* (1980), quoted the celebrated biologist Francis Crick as describing a bacterium as an "enzyme bag." Whether apocryphal or not, the anecdote furnished Thom with the opportunity to express the view that the essential theoretical problem facing modern biology is to formally specify the relations obtaining between, on the one hand, the molecular (and macromolecular) organization of the cell and, on the other, its larger supramacromolecular structure—and to do so "in such a way as to develop an intuitive feeling for the global constraints" at work in the regulation, or homeostasis, of living organisms.[25] These constraints, Thom believed, are principally topological in character. The topological features that link the molecular with the supramacromolecular are to be found in the nerve cell itself.

Neurons have the cardinal property of conserving their shape, which is to say they exhibit a stable topology of soma, dendrites, axon, and synapse. This shape is due mainly to a complicated and relatively rigid set of tubules and filaments known as the cytoskeleton. The tubular frame is made up of hollow tubes, or microtubules, that are produced by the supramacromolecular assembly of a particular protein called tubulin, together with a set of associated proteins (Figure 7). These rigid tubules are the primary determinants of the morphology of the cell. The filaments of the cytoskeleton, for their part, are quite numerous and of varied composition. Some of them contain contractile proteins, such as actin, along with crosslinking and binding proteins that assemble the contractile proteins in bundles and intervene in intracellular movements as well as activity at the nerve endings. In addition to forming a stable skeleton, these supramacromolecular structures are also responsible for the bidirectional transport of material between the cell body and the extremities of its axonal and dendritic processes. The neuron therefore possesses an internal architecture and a system of

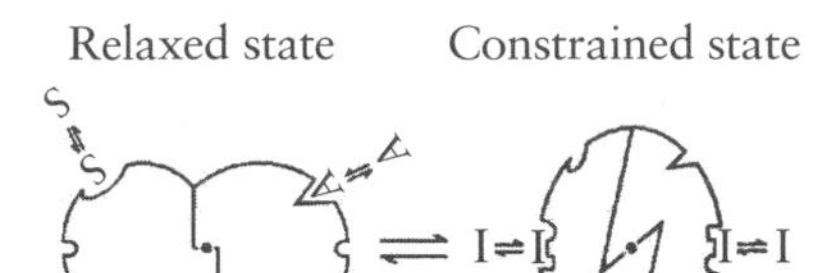
Relaxed state
Constrained state
S ⇌ S
A ⇌ A
I ⇌ I

I

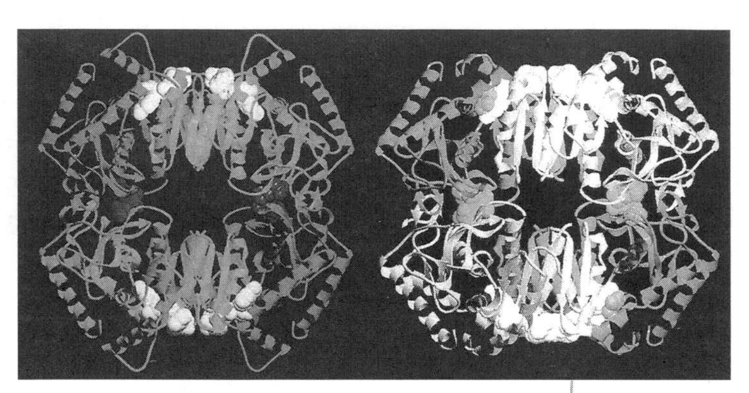

II

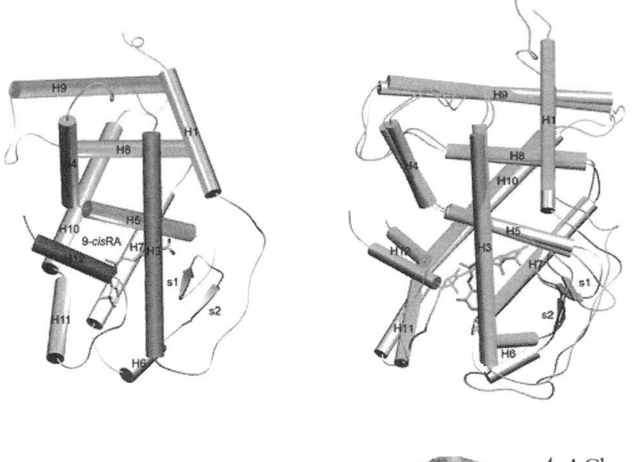
H9
H1
H8
H4
H5
H10
9-cisRA
H7
H3
H12
s1
s2
H11
H6

III

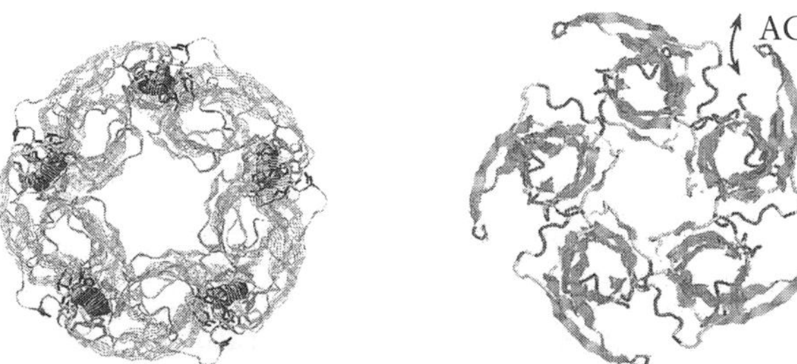
ACh

IV

internal circulation that are constructed from a well-defined set of specialized proteins.[26]

Considering the surface of the nerve cell and the distribution of neurotransmitter receptors from this perspective, the neuronal landscape no longer calls to mind Crick's sack of enzymes. It resembles instead something like a harlequin's costume with its brightly colored patterning. Specific receptors for different neurotransmitters are clustered beneath the sites where the neurotransmitters are released through the nerve endings. The pattern of these clusters varies considerably depending on the specific topology of soma, axons, dendrites, ion channels, and release sites. The cytoskeleton plays a critical role in the positioning of receptors at specific locations on the neuronal surface. Its supramacromolecular assemblies are therefore essential to the establishment and maintenance of the organization of the nerve cell and, as a consequence of this, its ability to establish and maintain a system of neural networks. Little by little the nervous system organizes itself at successively higher levels, constructing cognitive functions on the basis of elementary chemical reactions.

Spontaneous Activity in the Brain

Rather curiously, research in neuroscience has for more than a century been animated by an implicitly empiricist philosophy. This philosophy was already present in the earliest studies of the reflex arc, which led to the identification of the neural pathways that link sensory stimuli with the motor response of the organism.[27] Pavlov produced conditioned responses: the secretion of gastric juices, for example, after hearing a sound

Opposite page

Figure 6. Illustrations of a general mechanism of molecular switching that permits living organisms to regulate the efficiency of their response to surrounding conditions. I. Monod, Wyman, and Changeux's model: the protein is in equilibrium between two different conformations assumed to form "crystalline" microassemblies (in this case two subunits), one active, the other inactive. II. Relaxed state *(left)* and constrained state *(right)* of the molecule of a bacterial enzyme, L-lactate dehydrogenase. III. Bound state *(left)* and free state *(right)* of a fragment of transcription factor acting as a nuclear receptor of the retinoic acid RXR, a powerful chemical differentiation signal. IV. A hypothetical allosteric transition model of the acetylcholine receptor based on structural data about the acetylcholine-binding protein of *Lymnea* (see Figure 5A).

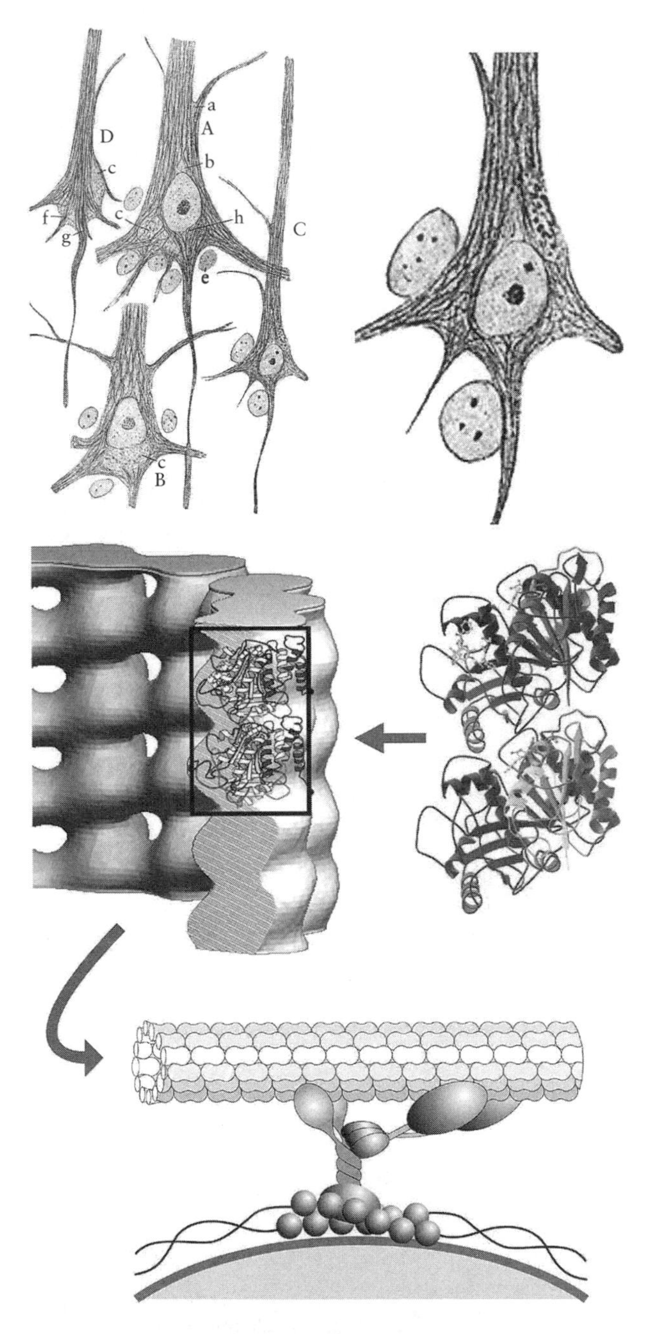

Figure 7. From the molecular to the supramacromolecular: formation of a microtubule. *Top:* Pyramidal cells of the human brain, stained black with concentrated silver nitrate and showing the cytoskeleton, drawn by Ramón y Cajal in the early twentieth century. *Bottom:* Assembly of a tubular frame out of microtubules and the location of the "molecular motor" responsible for intracellular transport.

that previously had been associated in a neutral way with the presentation of food. He even went so far as to claim that, in order to construct a conditioned reflex, the brain has to be free of any other nervous activity.[28] Until not so very long ago, electrophysiological recordings typically consisted of evoked responses, which is to say responses elicited by stimuli from the external world in anesthetized animals.

Today this model seems quite naive and, in any case, much too simple. We now know that the brain naturally behaves as an autonomous system that constantly transmits energy to the outside world, rather than passively receiving the impression of external stimuli.[29] Henri Bergson had earlier made the same point in a quite different context, though without being able to adduce any empirical justification. The intrinsic activity of the brain, manifested through action potentials spontaneously generated by nerve cells, is in fact one of its most characteristic features.[30] These electrical impulses do not differ from ones that are evoked by interaction with the environment. They are produced by special devices known as molecular oscillators, or "pacemakers," which consist generally of two antagonistic, though closely coupled, protein channels.[31] Beyond a certain threshold, the slow fluctuations of the electrical potential of the neuronal membrane generated by these pacemakers trigger spontaneous firings and regular oscillatory activity. Once again, this intrinsic activity can be explained by reference to relatively simple physicochemical mechanisms operating at the molecular level.

Spontaneous electrical activity appears early in the development of the embryonic nervous system.[32] It is responsible for the movements that are observed in the egg after three and a half days of incubation in the chick embryo,[33] and it persists in cultured embryonic neurons as well. In the human fetus, the heart begins to beat three to four weeks after fertilization. Around the tenth week the fetus begins to move, but the mother perceives its movements only seven weeks later.[34] Spontaneous electrical activity is typically registered in the adult brain in the form of complex electroencephalographic waves that vary between sleeping and waking states.[35] An important type of endogenous physiological activity during waking states is known as a "baseline," which may increase (or decrease) in certain regions of the brain during the performance of specific mental operations.[36] As we shall see, this spontaneous activity plays a central role in several mechanisms governing cerebral development and, more generally, in both the acquisition of knowledge and the testing of its truth or falsity.

Neuronal Plasticity

Last but not least, the brain is distinguished by its plasticity.[37] The term "plasticity" designates the general capacity of the neuron and its synapses to change properties as a function of their state of activity. This basic fact contradicts the naive picture of the brain as a sort of rigid automaton, made up exclusively of neuronal cogs and wheels whose operation is wholly determined in advance. Plasticity is already present during early stages of embryonic development: a significant fraction of the nerve cells produced by cell division die before becoming mature neurons. Cell death may be either retarded or accelerated by nervous activity. Similarly, as we shall see, synapses grow and divide during development; but they may also be eliminated and, in some cases, regenerated through new outgrowths from the cell body or from existing dendritic arborizations (a phenomenon that persists, albeit to a lesser degree, in the adult). The release of chemical signals stimulating nerve growth, for example, under the influence of nervous activity, may contribute to synaptic stabilization. Additionally, the efficiency of synaptic contacts in transmitting signals may change over time as a consequence of both the release of neurotransmitters and the behavior of their receptors. For instance, when a neurotransmitter transiently binds to a receptor, it stabilizes an active molecular conformation of the receptor that is favorable to transmission of a signal. If this contact is prolonged, however, the receptor spontaneously switches to an inactive, "desensitized," state (Figures 8A and 8B). The opposite may also occur. This capacity for cellular adaptation is determined by intrinsic physicochemical properties of the receptor molecule. The supramacromolecular assemblies of receptors that I have described, as well as their relationship to the skeletal structure of the cell, may also vary as a function of the state of the cell's activity.

Neural plasticity therefore results from the fact that the various mechanisms for transmitting information in the nervous system are themselves regulated by the physiological activity, whether spontaneous or evoked, that they mediate. It is this property that confers upon

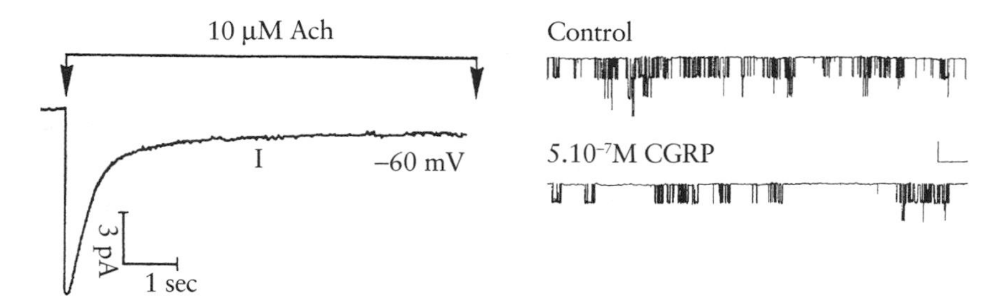

Figure 8A. Plasticity of the acetylcholine receptor at the molecular level. *Left:* Rapid repetition of electrical impulses or the prolonged application of a neurotransmitter, in this case acetylcholine (ACh), leads to a fall in amplitude of the response to the neurotransmitter on time scales of a second to a minute—a phenomenon known as "densensitization." *Right:* Desensitization may also be triggered by other substances, such as neuropeptides. Here the calcitonin gene-related peptide (CGRP), acting indirectly upon its specific receptor, modifies the allosteric equilibrium between the resting (potentially active) state and the inactive (densensitized) state of the acetylcholine receptor, a change manifested here by a reduction in the frequency of the opening of its channel by acetylcholine.

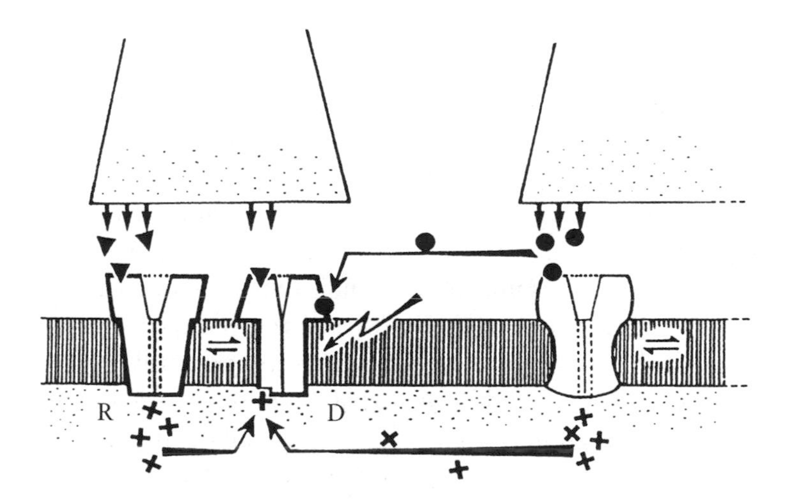

Figure 8B. A schematic and still hypothetical model of the rapid learning that is assumed to take place at the level of neurotransmitter receptors as a function of their desensitization. The synapse on the left is strengthened when its own firing nearly coincides with that of the synapse on the right. The neurotransmitter receptor on the left "reads" the temporal coincidence between the signals emitted by the two synapses by means of a desensitizing transition from a resting activable state (R) to a desensitized state (D). Each receptor is an allosteric protein capable of responding to at least two kinds of signals, electrical signals (zigzag line) and diffusible chemical signals (dot or cross).

neuronal networks at once their functional flexibility, their ability to store information, and their capacity for self-organization. Any attempt to model the functions of the brain—in particular, the storing of information in memory that makes the acquisition of knowledge possible—will have to take into account these elementary processes of plasticity at the molecular and cellular level.

The Architecture of Neural Networks

In order to understand how the great medieval cathedrals were constructed, it is not enough to have a detailed description of each of the stones used. One must also know their relationship to one another, and the general plan according to which the pillars, vaults, and spandrels are arranged. In the same way, the attempt to reconstruct a neurobiological function—and, ultimately, a behavior—on the basis of the elementary components of the brain identified over recent decades requires an understanding of the rules of organization that determine the general architecture of its constituent neuronal networks.

The neuron is distinguished from a liver or a skin cell chiefly by its ability to create a great many stable and well-defined connections with other neurons. These connections are not established at random. The branching and ramification of axonal and dendritic processes, as well as the highly variable length of the connections among neurons, cause a variety of distinct territories to be differentiated within the brain. Two main forms of organization are intertwined with each other. In addition to hierarchically organized structures that over time develop into vertically nested networks, neuronal maps and pathways multiply horizontally in tandem with larger-scale interconnected systems. It is not enough merely to note the complexity exhibited by this system of interrelated hierarchical and parallel networks. In order to understand the architecture and the function of the human brain, we need to know how these networks emerged in the course of biological evolution and embryonic development.

Hierarchy

The notion of hierarchical organization goes back to Aristotle, but its modern formulation in terms of mental "faculties" is due to Kant, who distinguished three such faculties: first, what he called intuition, defined as the capacity of sense organs to receive "sensible impressions" from the external world; second, understanding, which permits the synthesis of concepts out of sensible elements; third, reason, which contains the principles by which we know things and organize the concepts spontaneously produced by the understanding.[38]

These functional levels do not agree with the familiar tripartite description of information processing, which distinguishes between a physical machine ("hardware"), itself likened to a neural network; the programs the machine runs ("software") and the algorithms that define the relation between input and output, imagined to reproduce the physiological activity of an organism; and the computational principles implemented by the machine, replicating the organism's intentionality or capacity for planning. Nor do they correspond to the dimensional scale of neurophysiological analysis, which moves from the molecular level to complex systems of neural networks. The levels of organization that I wish to consider are at once anatomical *and* functional, and so make it possible in principle to establish a causal link between anatomy and function.[39]

The functional organization of the visual system constitutes an excellent example in this regard: it relies on fourteen superimposed levels, from the retina to the prefrontal cortex; at least six of these are situated among the thirty-two visual areas of the cerebral cortex (in the case of the monkey) and contribute to the simultaneous processing of the form, color, and motion of three-dimensional objects, from their sensory perception as objects of the external world to their conscious apprehension and manipulation in the brain as mental representations (Figure 9).[40] One of the most remarkable aspects of all this is that it functions not only from the bottom up, so to speak, in the case of the perception of a visual object; but also, in the case of retrieval from memory of an image of this object, from the top down.

Parallelism

In addition to this vertical stratification of hierarchically interlocking levels, parallel processing systems develop across the brain as well. We owe to Franz Josef Gall the idea that the cerebral cortex is not a sort

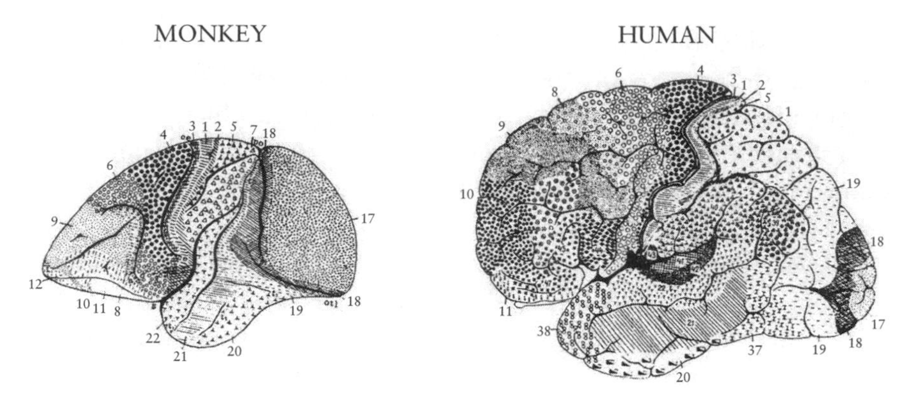

Figure 9. Expansion of the surface of the cerebral cortex and proliferation of the cortical areas from the rhesus monkey (macaque) to man. The development of cognitive functions and the acquisition of language are accompanied by a spectacular increase in the number of cortical areas of the prefrontal region (10, 11, 44, 45) and of the parieto-temporal region (37–43).

of seamless cloak but a mosaic of distinct territories that he called "organs," each of which was seen as the seat of innate, essential, and irreducible faculties. Simplistic though this notion appears today, a careful examination of the anatomy of the vertebrate cerebral cortex unmistakably reveals a distribution of cortical areas having specialized functions that is peculiar to each species. The growth in the number of hierarchical levels over the course of vertebrate evolution was accompanied by an increase in the number of parallel maps at each level, with the result that the total number of neural representations increased as well (Figure 9). In the case of vision, for example, the number of retinal representations does not exceed 3 or 4 in primitive mammals; in primates and carnivores it ranges between 15 and 20, reaching 32 in the macaque; in humans it is still higher.[41] From monkey to human the number of anatomically distinct areas in the frontal lobe grows in a spectacular way (see Figure 41 in Chapter 5). This part of the brain developed exceptionally rapidly in humankind's primate ancestors. As we shall see, the frontal lobe plays an essential role in cognitive functions.

Integration

Gall's localizing and nativist conception of the brain has recently been made fashionable again by cognitive psychology (though it now speaks of "modules" instead of organs) and by magnetic resonance imaging. As it turns out, control centers do not exhibit such sharply defined differences in functional anatomy as Gall supposed. Nor do Kant's hierarchical levels—intuition, understanding, reason—correspond to wholly distinct entities from either an anatomical or a functional point of view. As Auguste Comte argued in the *Cours de philosophie positive* (1830), integrative mechanisms are needed to bind together the activity of these separate territories "in a concerted manner," thus assuring the coordinated operation of the "higher social functions" of the brain.[42] Certain specialized elements of neuronal architecture help account for this functional integration. In addition to short-range reciprocal connections between neighboring nerve cells, long-range connections between distant nerve cells had already been detected by Ramón y Cajal at the turn of the century. In the 1930s certain authors spoke of "reverberating circuits" in this regard;[43] cybernetics later popularized "feedback loops," now known as "reentrant connections."[44] These connections operate not only vertically between superimposed levels but also horizontally between parallel maps. In the visual cortex of the monkey, for example, 305 types of pathway linking its 32 visual areas have been identified. This figure represents only 40 percent of the total number of possible connections.[45]

Other specialized architectural components, which we shall study in Chapter 3, are involved in large-scale integrative processes that link the results of local processing throughout the brain as a whole, for example by means of extended horizontal connections between distinct cortical areas in one or both hemispheres,[46] or else through the long-range diffusion of chemical signals.[47]

Simple rules of network architecture therefore make it possible to combine a great variety of signal-processing structures with the capacity to integrate and globalize local activities of the brain, both from the top down and from the bottom up. It is clear that these integrative components of neural architecture of the brain must be taken into consideration in any attempt to reconstruct cognitive functions. But this is hardly enough to create a machine that will be in all respects similar to the human brain. The problem is still more complicated.

An Open, Motivated, and Self-Organizing System

Artificial neural networks are seldom described as open and motivated systems. The term "open" must be understood here in both a psychological and a thermodynamic sense for two reasons: first, the brain is not a black box whose internal states can be neglected; and second, the fact that the brain is the seat of a considerable amount of spontaneous activity does not mean that it constitutes an independent and autonomous system functioning under conditions of thermodynamic equilibrium. Because the brain is constantly exchanging energy and information with the outside world, it produces stable internal thermodynamic states—patterns of oscillation, for example—under conditions that are very far from equilibrium. The reciprocal exchange of signals with the environment through the sense organs and via motor actions helps establish what the physical chemist Ilya Prigogine calls "dissipative structures." The relevance of such states to the higher functions of the brain—consciousness, in particular—may seem rather far-fetched. Nonetheless, as we shall see later on, the brain's sustained openness to external events enables it to generate the global states required for conscious perception to occur, which suggests a natural connection between neurobiological research and philosophical inquiry into the phenomenology of consciousness.[48]

In addition to its outward-looking character, the nervous system displays motivated behavior. For the operation of the brain is not limited to processing information from the outside world; it also actively produces representations that it then projects onto the outside world. The spontaneous activity of specialized sets of neurons causes the organism to constantly explore and test its physical, social, and cultural environment, to capture and register responses from it, and to compare them with its inner repertoire of stored memories. In consequence, the brain develops a striking capacity for "autoactivation," and, by virtue of this, of self-organization.[49] It is in this sense that I apply the term "motivation" to a network of neurons. The brain needs to be seen, then, as an open, motivated, and self-organizing system continually engaged in the exploration of its environment—a quality that recalls Bergson's theme in *La Pensée et le mouvant* (1934), except that in this work I make no reference to any spiritualist metaphysics whatsoever.[50] The properties of openness and motivation I have described are physical properties of the structure and function of the neuronal networks that make up the human brain.

The Synthesis of Evolutionary Processes

The pre-Socratic philosophers long ago discovered a way to avoid having to choose between saying, on the one hand, that everything concerning the organism's relations with the external world is innate and, on the other, that everything is acquired. The solution they proposed amounted to saying that the rigidity of genetic determinism could be escaped by introducing an element of random variability while at the same time maintaining constraints and limits in learning processes. Before Democritus and the atomists, Empedocles had imagined a "genesis" of living species that, despite its metaphorical cast, strikingly prefigured our current understanding of biological evolution. Empedocles argued that the "elements" out of which the world is made are randomly mixed together and exchanged through the action of attractive and repulsive forces. Monstrous forms of animal life, for example, were formed from the assembly of "members" brought together by "chance encounters." Some elements resisted incorporation in this way while others disappeared. Those elements that were left over combined to form living creatures: "Thus the human race came about."[51] This idea (today one speaks of genesis by variation and selection) was later taken up by Diderot.

Almost two millennia passed before an evolutionary theory of natural selection was formulated in biologically acceptable terms by Charles Darwin, working within the "transformist" framework of the living world elaborated earlier by Jean-Baptiste de Lamarck. Darwin's theory rests on two fundamental ideas. The first is the concept of heritable variation, which appears spontaneously and at random—blindly, as it were—in individual members of a population and is immediately transmitted through descent. The second is the idea of natural selection, which results from a "struggle for life." Only individuals whose hereditary endowment enables them to survive and reproduce in a particular environment can multiply and perpetuate the species.

Following Darwin, the notion of evolution by selection was very quickly extended to include "epigenetic" processes that take place within the organism without modifying the genome. In the late nineteenth century the great English neurologist John Hughlings Jackson made use of this idea to explain the development of multiple levels of hierarchical organization in the human brain.[52] Hippolyte Taine had similarly proposed, in *De l'intelligence* (1870), that "images" are produced in consciousness and enter into competition with one another through trial and error, until only the most robust among them remains. It is precisely this random variability, together with the brain's capacity to evaluate the adequacy of the images it produces, that enables us to represent the outside world to ourselves in increasingly diverse and precise ways.

In the 1970s Jacques Monod suggested extending Darwin's model to cultural evolution and the evolution of ideas. Related arguments were also developed by Karl Popper, which I shall consider in the final chapters of this book. The proposition separately advanced by these authors is that cultural evolution arises from the externalization of the inner representations of the brain, the sharing of these representations among the brains of individual members of a social group, and ultimately their storage in extracerebral memories.[53]

The human brain's success in accurately and objectively representing the world has depended on its ability to incorporate and synthesize the results of a series of nested evolutionary processes, each of which involves variation and selection. In this way the genetic evolution of species is amplified by more rapid processes that do not require (or are not necessarily accompanied by) large changes to genetic material in the short term.

This hypothesis imposes severe constraints from both the theoretical and experimental point of view. The recognition that networks of neurons are organized in distinct functional levels of organization constitutes a theoretical claim that needs to be made explicit, for example by taking the comparative anatomy and physiology of the brain into account from an evolutionary perspective. The notions of random variation, evaluation, selection, and amplification also require that variability be carefully examined and defined at each level of organization, from the molecular to the cognitive and social.

The purpose of approaching the study of the brain in this fashion, as I have said, is to establish pertinent causal links between structure, physiology, and behavior. One of the chief obstacles to demonstrating the existence of such connections arises from the contextualized character of neuronal activity, itself a consequence of the exceedingly complex ways in which the hierarchical and parallel structures of the brain are functionally related to one another.[54] Accordingly, the physiological and behavioral significance of any one of the component parts of this system, whatever the level of organization, cannot be understood without analyzing its relationship with the other elements of the system and, more generally still, the ways in which individuals communicate and interact with one another.

To more precisely describe this type of constraint, it will be useful to broaden the concept of "relevance," first introduced in connection with language by the cognitive anthropologists Dan Sperber and Deirdre Wilson, to include all aspects of the organism.[55] The basic idea is that there is an analogy between the communication that occurs *between* organisms and that which occurs *within* the organism, particularly in the course of development. In what follows I take the liberty of generalizing this idea to include the mechanisms of gene expression and the development of neuronal networks. Initially—and this is another point to which I shall return later—Sperber and Wilson were interested in a type of linguistic communication, distinct from usual forms of information processing, in which the intentions of speaker and listener are preponderant. For example, the phrase "How are you?" is to be interpreted, not only as communicating a simple message, but also as conveying a number of implicit (and ordinarily uncontroversial) assumptions about everyday life. When a new piece of information is introduced that cannot be deduced from prior assumptions, Sperber and Wilson call it "relevant" if it serves to increase and multiply the meaningfulness of the concepts involved and thereby enriches the semantic context in which speaker and hearer interact. The more meaningful an additional piece of information, the greater its relevance.

This notion of hierarchical contextual interaction may be extended by analogy to include the expression of a gene or the state of activity of a neuron within an interactive network. The introduction of a new element in a gene network or in a neuronal network amounts to much more than simply adding an isolated component to the system or making a local modification. The action of an additional gene or neuron may instead have an amplifying effect, with dramatic consequences for the system as a whole. The greater the repercussions for the phenotype (in this case the function of a network of genes or nerve cells), the greater the relevance of the new element.

No reasonable person would deny that a reductionist approach to the study of the human brain that lays emphasis on its component parts is a first and necessary step toward understanding human cognition. But it is no less clear that structural description must be supplemented by an exhaustive account of the various interactions that are relevant—in the special sense I have just described—to the function of an efficient and an autonomous organism.

From Matter to Conscious Thought

In principle, then, it ought to be possible to describe the constitutive elements of the brain—neurons, their connections with one another, the signals they produce and propagate, their plasticity, and the architecture and the evolutionary dynamics of these components within an open and motivated system—in molecular terms. The language of physics and chemistry (what Rudolf Carnap famously called "the language of all science")[56] should also be adequate to describe the higher functions of the brain and, in particular, those functions which support learning and the acquisition of knowledge—on the condition, as Diderot stressed long ago, that their mutual relationships be explicitly taken into account. Perhaps the most remarkable property of matter, as we have seen, is its capacity for spontaneous self-organization into interlocking neuronal assemblies, whose joint and coordinated evolution over time ultimately gave rise to conscious thought—Voltaire's "thinking matter."

The theory of evolution offers a way out, it seems to me, from the paradox apparently posed by the ability of the brain to understand the world. Einstein, like many other physicists, found it "mysterious" that nature should be comprehensible to human beings and its laws knowable by them.[57] The answer to this riddle is to be sought not in some special a priori property of the external world—as though the world were designed to be understood by the human brain—but in the contingent properties of the brain itself. What need to be understood are the fundamental dynamics that enabled the brains of those species which came before us to explore the world in progressively more comprehensive and precise ways during the course of biological evolution. At the most elementary level, unicellular organisms such as bacteria or paramecia are dissipative structures (in Prigogine's sense) that preserve their form and reproduce themselves. The eminent zoologist J. Z. Young, developing an idea originally due to Claude Bernard, suggested half a century ago that living organisms are "homeostats"—that is, that they must be able to devise a representation of the world around them that favors their survival. In unicellular organisms this requires molecular structures capable of capturing and metabolizing the chemical substances present in the immediate environment. With the advent of multicellular organisms a specialized organ came to be differentiated that served to regulate the internal functions of the organism, its representations of the external world, and the agreement of these representations with the facts of the world: the nervous system.[58]

Over time this system came to be organized in increasingly complex ways, operating in both hierarchical and parallel fashion. Its capacities for investigating the surrounding world and picturing this world to itself likewise evolved, moving from the physical and biological environment to take in the social and (in the case of human beings) cultural environment. This process of evolution was accompanied by an increase in the plasticity of the brain's neuronal network, which led in turn to a heightened capacity for learning. The world that the fly pictures to itself differs from that pictured by the mouse, monkey, or human being. With the emergence of humankind, innate dispositions became enriched by the exploitation of epigenetic rules arising from interaction with the world, enlarging the brain's power to understand and act upon it, and ultimately creating a culture that could then be propagated and transmitted from one generation to the next. In this way differences in the experience of the world at the individual level came to create cultural diversity among human populations.

Lamarck, in the *Philosophie zoologique* (1809), long ago called attention to "a singular faculty with which certain animals and man himself are endowed," which he called "inner feeling."[59] The properties and functions of this faculty are the same as those we customarily attribute to consciousness. Yet despite the unique character of each person's subjective experience of the world, the brain is capable of producing objective knowledge—a sort of universal framework of thought—that permits communication among individuals by means of language.

The cerebral functions that developed originally in response to the individual's struggle for survival eventually came to operate at the level of the social group, whose collective interest in the benefits of an exact and accurate understanding of the world caused habits of learning and education to be formalized. Cultural evolution, having taken over from biological evolution, gave rise to scientific inquiry and the search for truth, both distinctive aspects of modern societies. The mystery of the brain's capacity to understand the world and to act upon it is therefore to be explained not by appealing to some higher, supernatural authority but by examining the natural history of the origins of the brain and its subsequent evolution.

The Acquisition of Knowledge 2

In the *Abhandlung über den Ursprung der Sprache* (1772), Johann Gottfried Herder argued that language flows from a fundamental cognitive property—a desire for knowledge that he named *appetitus noscendi.*[1] This instinct is not peculiar to human beings, Herder held, though it is especially developed in them. It is roughly equivalent to the architectural principle I mentioned earlier in describing the brain as a motivated neural system, genetically equipped with a predisposition to explore the world and to classify what it finds there. Owing to the plasticity of its neural network, the human brain has developed additional, epigenetic capacities for acquiring knowledge of the world that were added to the initial stock of innate elementary rules and behaviors inherited from man's nearest ancestors. The question nonetheless arises whether a correspondence exists between objects of the external world and the mental objects produced by the brain in a state of wakefulness—between the facts of the world and our ideas of them. As Spinoza expressed the point, "A true *idea* must agree with the *object* of which it is the idea."[2] This much seems clear enough. Less clear are the answers to a further set of questions: What does it mean to say that an idea agrees with an object—with external reality? How is this agreement established? How is it verified?

One reply is that the brain generates thought objects, or beliefs (in the Anglo-American sense of the term), and that these beliefs are true when what Bertrand Russell called *congruence* obtains between object and belief—an "isomorphism" between the structure of thought and reality.[3] On this view, true beliefs fit facts in the same way that a glove fits the hand. The simplicity of the metaphor is appealing, but to the neurobiologist it is implausible, or at least insufficient. For the purposes of scientific research it is necessary to ask: what is the physical basis for this congruence between thought and object? How does the brain establish an appropriate causal relation between ideas and the facts of external reality to which they refer? What are the specific mechanisms that enable the brain to determine whether the information that it stores in memory is accurate?

Many of these questions were debated at the end of the nineteenth century in the context of comparative psychology.[4] The challenge brought by Darwin and his followers against the dominant empiricist tradition of associationism laid stress on the "instinctive behavior" specific to each species, transmitted hereditarily and refined by natural selection. This approach left untouched, however, the problem of "learned behavior." There thus developed two opposed schools of thought based on contrasting styles of theory and experiment that, surprisingly, are still current today. On the one hand, there was the theory of classical conditioning, illustrated by Pavlov's experiments on the conditioning of salivation in dogs; on the other, the theory of operant conditioning, which grew out of Edward L. Thorndike's work on cats.[5] Pavlov's 1897 experiments purported to show that a relationship was established in the animal's brain, independently of its actual behavior, between two events originating in the external world: an unconditioned stimulus (the presentation of a piece of meat, triggering salivation) and a novel stimulus (the ringing of a bell), which conditions the reflex, so that the dog salivates in response to the sound of the bell, now associated with the presentation of food.

As against this paradigm, which inspired a great many psychological and behavioral studies of various animal subjects, from the sea slug *(Aplysia californica)* to the rat and the mouse,[6] Thorndike's experiments suggested a more complicated set of relationships. On placing a cat in a "puzzle box," he noticed that it moves about in a random way at first, then by chance comes across the device that locks and opens the box, escape from which gives access to food and freedom. The number of successful escapes, Thorndike found, increases with the number of trials. From this he concluded that there exists a causal relation between spontaneous behavior, the action of the organism on its environment, and a given event: action may be shaped and reinforced by means of positive rewards (what he called a "satisfying state of affairs") received from the outside world; or it may be suppressed and redirected by punishment (an "annoying state of affairs"). Thorndike's analysis of trial-and-error learning through reward was subsequently extended by Clark Hull, who used food-deprived rats to enhance the reward in maze-learning experiments, and by B. F. Skinner in related studies of pigeons.[7] In all these experiments, the learning process depends in part on a large repertoire of instinctive impulses (or "reflexes") peculiar to a given species. But, as we shall see later, it also exploits epigenetically established behaviors that have been selectively stabilized in the course of development.

The argument I wish to make here concerns the broader problem of accounting for knowledge acquisition. It extends Thorndike's conception to the neural bases of what I have called learning by selection,[8] which Thorndike himself had even more specifically described, with reference to cognitive tasks, as a struggle for existence among neuronal connections.[9] I shall begin by reviewing the experimental evidence in favor of a set of instinctive mechanisms that lead us to seek knowledge, by means of three examples: thirst, self-stimulation, and drug addiction. I shall also consider the treatment of error during cognitive learning in the monkey, which will lead to an important distinction between motivation toward the environment and the reward received from it.

I shall then take up the difficult question of the physical representation of mental objects: What do we know—or think we know, on the basis of our present understanding of the brain—about the neural bases of meaning? Finally, I shall examine the quite speculative suggestion that knowledge acquisition may in some way be a consequence of cognitive games played by the child, primarily in the earliest stages of development (Figure 10).

Motivation and Reward

It may seem premature to inquire into the neuronal bases of the *appetitus noscendi* in man. Other species exhibit analogous behaviors, how-

Figure 10. Detail from Jean-Honoré Fragonard, *L'Heureuse Fécondité* (ca. 1774). This drawing nicely captures the spirit of the cognitive games that infants and small children learn to play at home.

ever, which have been carefully studied and which may serve as models for explaining this characteristically human predisposition.

Both humans and animals spontaneously explore their environment to satisfy basic needs essential to their survival: eating, drinking, and sexual activity. Both humans and animals readily seek out more favorable surroundings as circumstances require. Both are subject to inner urges, or drives, that motivate them to act upon the outside world in ways that depend on their changing physiological states and individual histories. A number of students of animal behavior (notably Nikolaas Tinbergen, Peter Marler, and Charles Gallistel) have insisted upon the existence of an innate predisposition to acquire knowledge—an "instinct to learn"[10]—in many animal species.

Thirst

With the first signs of dehydration, humans and animals alike begin actively to search for water. Often they return to nearby sources whose location they have committed to memory, but they may also venture farther afield in the hope of discovering new ones. The primary motivation is physiological, namely to increase the intake of liquid. But this requires that the organism experience a subjective sensation that will cause it to seek, find, and drink water. That sensation is thirst. Its principal determinant is the osmotic pressure of the blood serum. Homeostatic mechanisms regulating the onset of thirst include osmoreceptors located in the anterior wall of the third cerebral ventricle; other regulatory structures are found in the anterior cingulate gyrus, the temporal gyrus, and a region of the midbrain adjacent to the reticular formation known to be involved in arousal and vigilance.[11] Once a thirsty animal—or human being—has had its fill of water, between three and ten minutes, both thirst and the desire to drink disappear. In fact, a sense of satiation is felt long before the absorbed liquid is able to restore the normal osmotic equilibrium of the body's fluids. Other studies confirm that the neural pathways mobilized by the desire to drink are distinct from those involved in the satisfaction of this desire. Like hunger, sexual desire, and the instinct to migrate, thirst activates inborn neural mechanisms that underlie basic survival behaviors.[12]

Self-Stimulation, Drug Addiction, and Mental Reward

Reward mechanisms are typically triggered by signals from the outside world that stimulate an internal reaction of either desire or aversion. Certain neural circuits built into the brain almost automatically determine a positive or negative sensation, or "feeling," depending on the type of stimulus received from the environment.

In 1954, in an ingenious experiment, James Olds and Peter Milner permanently implanted electrodes in specific areas of the brain of a rat. In moving about its cage the rat chanced to step upon a pedal that discharged an electrical current into its brain.[13] In such experiments, once the rat has accidentally administered and received an initial stimulus, it continues to press down upon the pedal, as often as several

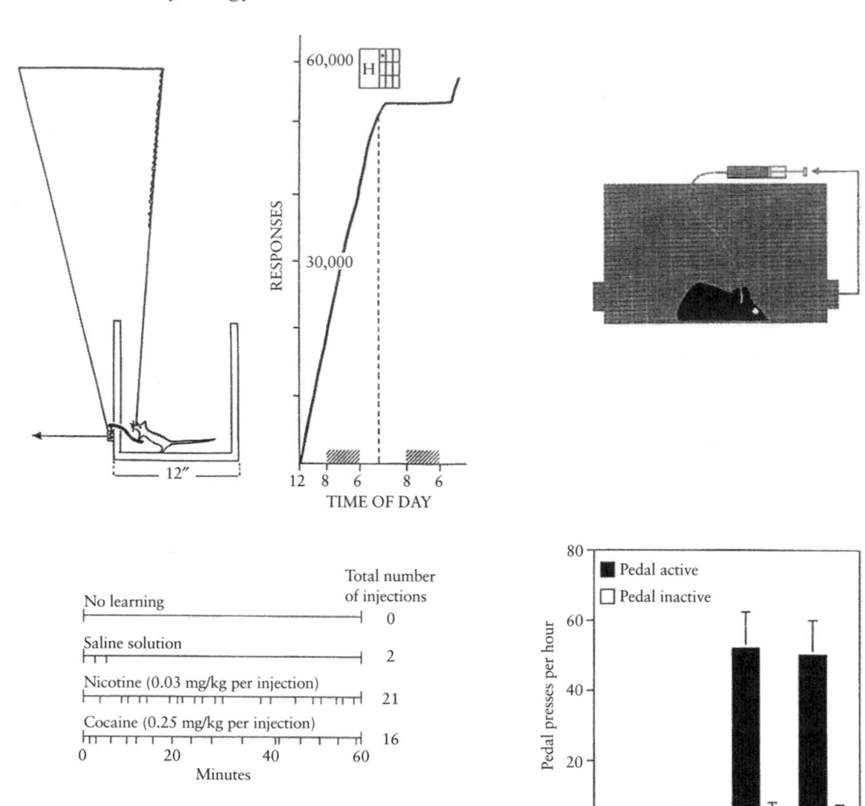

Figure 11A. Reward neurons. Electrical self-stimulation and chemical self-administration of cocaine and nicotine in the rat and the mouse. *Top:* The animal is implanted with either an electrode *(left)* or an intravenous catheter connected to a syringe containing a solution of cocaine or nicotine *(right).* In either case it activates the self-stimulation device by pressing on a pedal in its cage. Once the animal discovers that pressing the pedal yields an electrical or chemical reward, it continues to do so indefinitely. *Bottom:* Self-administration of nicotine (Nic) and cocaine (Coc) recorded in a mouse. The mouse injects itself with these drugs virtually to the exclusion of the saline solution (Sal).

thousand times an hour for several hours, thus becoming a prisoner of its own behavior (Figure 11A). This loss of self-control is similar to what one finds in drug addiction. Several distinct neuronal networks are involved in both cases. The pathways of the reward system mobilized in Olds's experiment run roughly parallel to the ones followed by

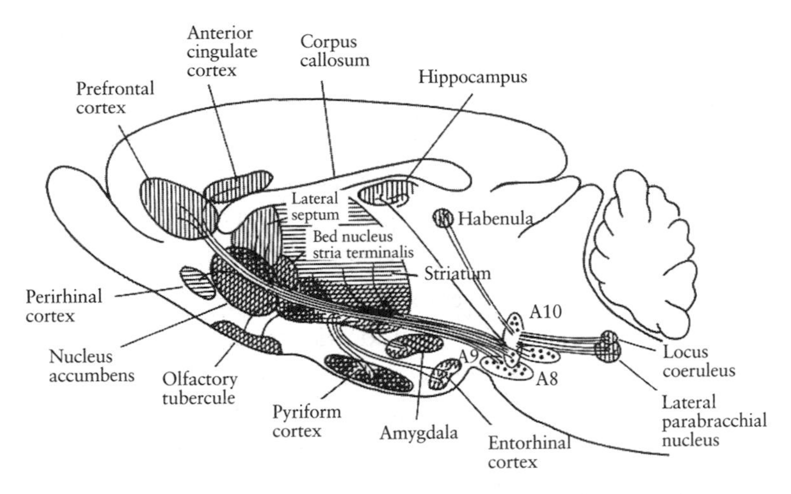

Figure 11B. The system of dopamine neurons involved in the reward process.

neurons in the midbrain that synthesize and release a neurotransmitter called dopamine. Their cell bodies, located in the brain stem, project to various regions of the brain, in particular a concentration of gray matter located at the base of the brain, the nucleus accumbens, and the anterior region of the cerebral cortex (known as the prefrontal cortex).

Compulsive behavior similar to that observed by Olds with electrical stimuli has been produced using chemical substances such as morphine, cocaine, and even nicotine (Figure 11A). It is now recognized that the condition of dependence that arises from drug abuse is associated with the release of dopamine through the projection of neuronal pathways from the brain stem to the nucleus accumbens (Figure 11B). The dopamine-stimulant effects of addictive drugs are localized more specifically in a particular area of the nucleus accumbens called the "shell." This area is primarily involved in emotion (owing to its links with the amygdala and the limbic system), whereas the "core" that it envelops is more directly involved in motor control.[14] The nucleus accumbens acts as an intermediary between motivation and action: by detecting the release of dopamine it works to regulate the selective contacts of the brain with the external world.

Detailed analysis of the psychostimulant effect of drugs such as cocaine and amphetamines (which are often considered "reward" substances) has revealed a neurochemical substrate for the distinction between appetitive and hedonic behaviors, that is, between *wanting* a drug and *enjoying* the pleasurable effects it produces. There is often a tendency to think of the drug addict as a perverse sort of hedonist, constantly seeking to maximize his pleasure. This notion is probably mistaken. The compulsive use of drugs is likely to have a different origin that is related, at least in part, to motivation.

Most addictive drugs possess a chemical structure similar to that of endogenous neurotransmitters and, like these substances, bind to specific receptors. In effect they act as surrogates for neurotransmitters involved in reinforcement. Consumed regularly over long periods, their presence in the organism creates adaptive changes in the brain's circuits, with the result that these circuits can function normally only in the presence of the drug. In its absence the adaptive neural trace persists, however, and sudden deprivation causes major disturbances. Withdrawal is marked by feelings of physical discomfort and pain, and, more generally, by negative affective states such as dysphoria, depression, irritability, and anxiety. Experimental studies with animal subjects show that these symptoms are motivational rather than hedonic in nature, arising from the disruption of the habitual urge to engage in self-stimulation and a lasting reduction in the reinforcing properties of rewards. Deprivation is accompanied by a decrease in dopamine transmission in the shell of the nucleus accumbens.

The biochemical disturbance to the appetitive system caused by drug taking leads to a loss of control, compulsive use, and, ultimately, addiction. Repeated consumption—abuse—of the drug converts harmless recreational indulgence into a downward spiral of suffering and distress. The negative effects of withdrawal are therefore not due to a simple absence of pleasure, but to a suffering similar to that created by intense thirst or hunger. This is what produces the craving typical of addiction—the irrepressible motivation to have more of the drug.[15] Motivational states mobilize a number of specific circuits in the brain, particularly (though not exclusively) the system of dopamine neurons that, as we have seen, regulates the interaction of the organism with the external world.

The analysis of pathological cases is often helpful in explaining normal behavior.[16] Certain aspects of the spiraling cycles of addiction and suffering associated with drug abuse can also be found in patterns of reinforcement that do not involve drugs.[17] The list of behaviors over which control may be lost is long: gambling, eating, exercise, sex, and shopping are only a few of many examples. Disturbances to the function of dopamine neurons, among others, probably contribute to compulsive behavior. The chemical trace of such behavior can even be visualized through cerebral imaging of subjects operating electronic slot machines. When the subject wins money, dopamine is observed to be released in the corpus striatum (which includes the nucleus accumbens)[18] together with the activation of neurons in the midbrain and the frontal (dorsolateral and orbital) cortex. It is not unreasonable to suppose that scientific inquiry gives rise to similar patterns of neural activity—money reward being replaced by the pleasure of acquiring knowledge.

Anticipation of Reward and Processing of Error

Humans, like animals, take pleasure in being rewarded. As a consequence, both learn to predict reward and to search for the conditions in which it can reliably be obtained. This capacity to anticipate reward seems to me to represent an essential mechanism of the predisposition to acquire knowledge, even if, in many situations, it happens that reward is deferred. The anticipation of reward has been recorded by electrophysiological methods at the level of dopamine neurons in the midbrain of the monkey. When a trained monkey succeeds in grasping a peanut hidden in a box, the inside of which it cannot see, the activity of dopamine neurons increases at precisely the moment when the animal recognizes the food with its fingers. The activation of these neurons coincides, then, with the reward. In a second phase of the experiment, the monkey rapidly learns, when the door of the box opens, that it will subsequently have access to the food inside. Dopamine neurons become active the moment the door opens, before the monkey seizes the food. In this case the activation of dopamine neurons no longer coincides with the reward itself: as a result of learning, the reward is anticipated.[19]

But what happens if the expected reward is not obtained? The activity of these neurons then suddenly decreases. The error in prediction leads to a disturbance. One might say, somewhat loosely, that the monkey possesses neural structures (including the midbrain dopamine neurons) responsible for producing plausible hypotheses and testing their validity.

Apart from the nucleus accumbens, one of the principal targets of innervation of dopamine neurons is the prefrontal cortex (especially in its medial areas). These areas, as we shall see, are directly involved in the planning of actions. Instead of pairing an unconditioned stimulus (such as food) with a neutral stimulus, as Pavlov did with the sound of a bell, researchers have paired an unconditioned stimulus with a painful electrical discharge, which, when transmitted to the feet of a laboratory rat, produced a marked increase in the amount of dopamine released in the animal's medial prefrontal cortex.[20] Dopamine, in addition to its role in the anticipation of reward and the processing of error, may also be involved in the adaptation of higher cortical structures to new conditions. Ultimately, dopamine neurons not only are a source of motivation in familiar situations but also help to resolve problems posed by new situations and to devise new concepts based on this experience.

Mental Objects

Ludwig Wittgenstein, in the *Philosophical Investigations,* asked how human beings are able to understand one another despite differences among languages. It is probable that there exists a basic set of concepts, or representations, common to all human brains. Wittgenstein argued that the decisive criterion for knowing whether or not another person understands something is "what he says and what he does."[21] An internal representation that picks out a particular object of the external world must, by definition, produce the same behavior—or action on the world—in every individual who possesses this representation.[22] A representation is thus defined by its causative effect on behavior (and even on internal mental states). Some authors have challenged the very concept of representation, arguing that no object of the external world has ever been present inside the brain, or can ever be represented to it in any form whatever. On this view, there is an immaterial aspect of common meanings, and knowledge in general, that will forever escape scientific explanation.[23]

I wish to argue for the opposite thesis, namely that it ought to be possible to identify the element common to human brains that, as Wittgenstein held, leads individuals to behave in the same way. Later on I shall review the debate that has arisen from the fact that connections among neurons vary considerably from one brain to another, even in identical twins. Because these different connective systems nonetheless produce the same actions, the problem is therefore to determine how common mappings between neural structure and behavior are established—how the same meanings, and the same pieces of knowledge, are registered in quite different individual brains. It is necessary first to examine the empirical neurobiological data in order to discover how such constant features of mental activity come to be established.

Neurosemantics

Studies of cerebral lesions, supplemented in recent years by analysis of healthy brains using powerful new imaging techniques, supply persuasive evidence of a neural basis of semantic knowledge. The study of disorders in object recognition began in the second half of the nineteenth century with the work of Heinrich Lissauer and Sigmund Freud, aimed at describing and classifying patients who had lost the ability to perceive or identify the objects they saw.[24] These patients were said to suffer from "mind blindness" (or, to use the modern term, agnosia). In the meantime further research based on observation of a large number of patients and a great variety of lesions has been conducted on this question.[25]

Several kinds of deficit in the recognition of objects may be distinguished. The visual recognition of objects can be altered by brain lesions that compromise sensory processing (acuity, shape recognition, color perception). Other lesions affect the perception of objects: patients are incapable of recognizing incomplete drawings or silhouettes presented from an unusual angle. A third type of disorder specifically concerns the identity of objects: familiar objects are perceived as though they have never been seen before. Certain patients preserve the ability to make fine distinctions at certain levels of classification (for example, recognizing the image of a mammal from among three different animals), but they are no longer capable of recognizing more specific attributes (knowing if the animal belongs to a nonnative species, for example, or if it is dangerous). Still more surprising, and of great interest, is the fact that certain patients exhibit recognition deficits for certain categories of objects but not others. This implies that distinct regions of the cerebral cortex are specialized in the recognition of different categories of objects.

J. M. Nielson was the first, in the late 1930s, to report these strange cases of patients suffering deficits of visual recognition restricted to living creatures, their knowledge of other objects being unaffected.[26] One of his patients suffered from a severe impairment of the ability to recognize animals: he confused, for example, images of a squirrel with those of a cat, believing that both were cats because they had whiskers. Yet he had no difficulty telling apart different trees, flowers, and other ordinary objects. Since then a great many patients have been discovered who exhibit disorders in the recognition of animals, foods, and plants, but not of inanimate objects.[27]

These data need to be interpreted with caution. It can be argued that the recognition deficit does not depend on the particular identity of a given object, but on the sensory modalities through which one has access to them: for example, in the case of an animal, by seeing its image or hearing or reading its name. Brain imaging gives a preliminary answer to this difficult question. The problem is to distinguish the cerebral pathways and territories associated with seeing, reading, and hearing that give access to meaning from those which hold particular shared meanings. Several independent brain imaging studies have succeeded in distinguishing the pathways peculiar to the modalities for hearing words and seeing images, each of which mobilizes different parts of the brain, and a common semantic network for both words and images. The imaging data clearly show that a particular semantic network is activated by a particular semantic category in the left superior occipital gyrus, the middle and inferior temporal cortex, and the inferior frontal gyrus, irrespective of the means of access.[28]

It follows, then, that different semantic categories mobilize different neural activation patterns. This can be verified by the use of functional imaging to examine the brain of a subject who is shown images of tools, houses, animals, and faces (Figure 12). When the subject is asked to look at an image, to use it in a memorization task, and to name it,[29] the same patterns of cortical activation are consistently registered for a given object, regardless of the task, but distinct territories situated in the posterior temporal lobe are differentially activated by images of tools, animals, and faces. The neural activation patterns are similar from one subject to another, whether the stimuli are pictures of objects or the written names of these objects, and whether they are recognized or mobilized for further action.

I emphasize that these are only preliminary observations. More detailed study will be required of the topology and the dynamics of the processes involved. In the meantime, debate over their proper interpretation continues. Nonetheless the results so far obtained by neuropsychological investigation converge with respect to several points: on the one hand, semantic knowledge is stored in dispersed (or "distributed") form throughout a network of neurons clustered in several distinct areas of the brain; on the other hand, the location of these areas is not random, but mirrors the organization of sensory and motor systems[30] and their respective contributions to the representation of meanings in the brain. Finally, simpler but very closely related patterns of activation in the cerebral cortex have been discovered in certain primates. The monkey, like many other animals, "knows" very well how to distinguish fruits from stones and snakes and how to make use of this knowledge in order to act upon the world. The presence of more elaborate patterns in the human brain is therefore the result of a long evolutionary and genetic history.

We now find ourselves in a position to sketch the outlines of a plausible interpretation of the neural bases of meaning. The naive view that the neural representation of a complex meaning—a yellow Renault, for example—is located in a single, hierarchically prominent nerve cell (the so-called pontifical neuron) has been found to be unjustified for the most part. It is generally accepted today that distinct populations of neurons in sensory, motor, associative, and other territories are linked as part of a distributed network that the psychologist Donald Hebb called a "cell assembly."[31] Each component neuron of the assembly possesses its own distinctive patterns of connectivity, amounting to a kind of "singularity" or individuality.[32] On this view, different meanings mobilize different populations of neurons situated in various cortical territories corresponding to particular features, or traits, of an object, each of which has a different "weight" (Figure 13). The word

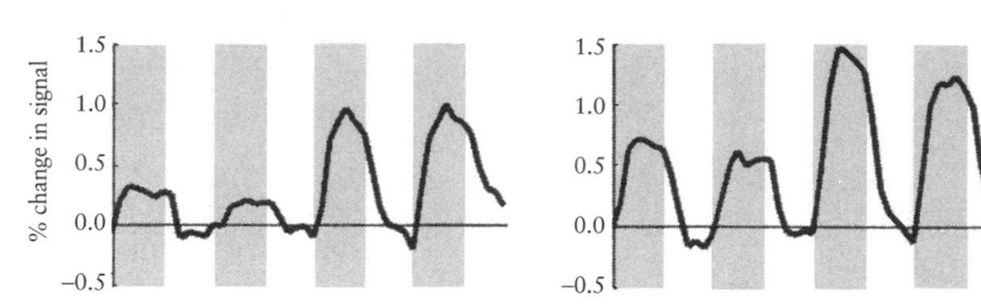
a
LEFT
RIGHT
Lateral fusiform gyrus (A > T)
% change in signal
1.5
1.0
0.5
0.0
−0.5

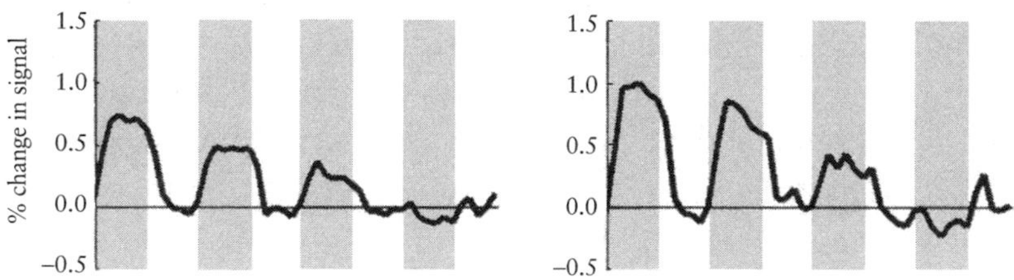
b
Medial fusiform gyrus (T > A)
% change in signal
1.5
1.0
0.5
0.0
−0.5

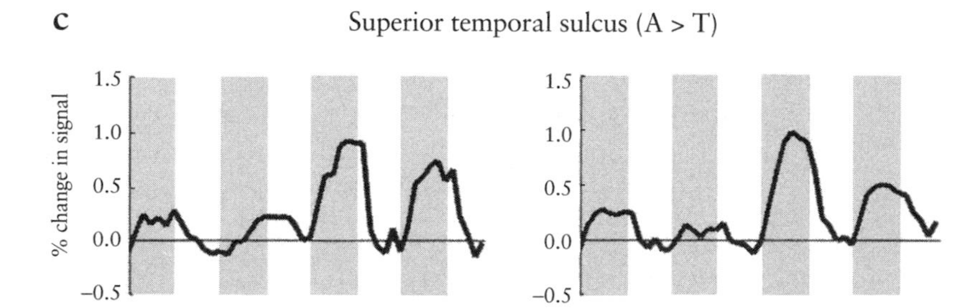
c
Superior temporal sulcus (A > T)
% change in signal
1.5
1.0
0.5
0.0
−0.5

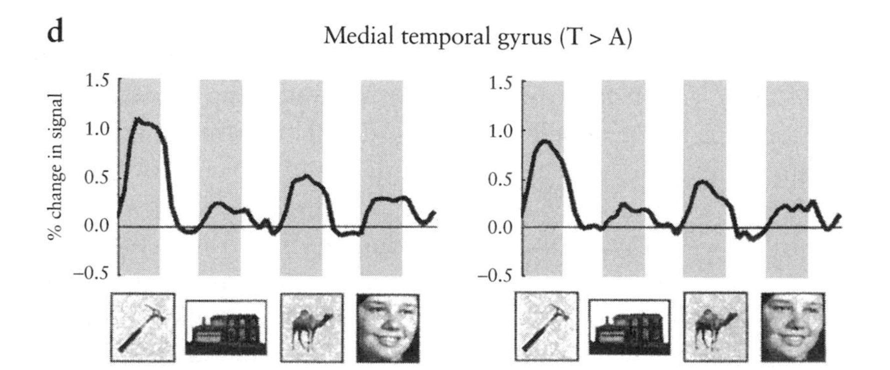
d
Medial temporal gyrus (T > A)
% change in signal
1.5
1.0
0.5
0.0
−0.5

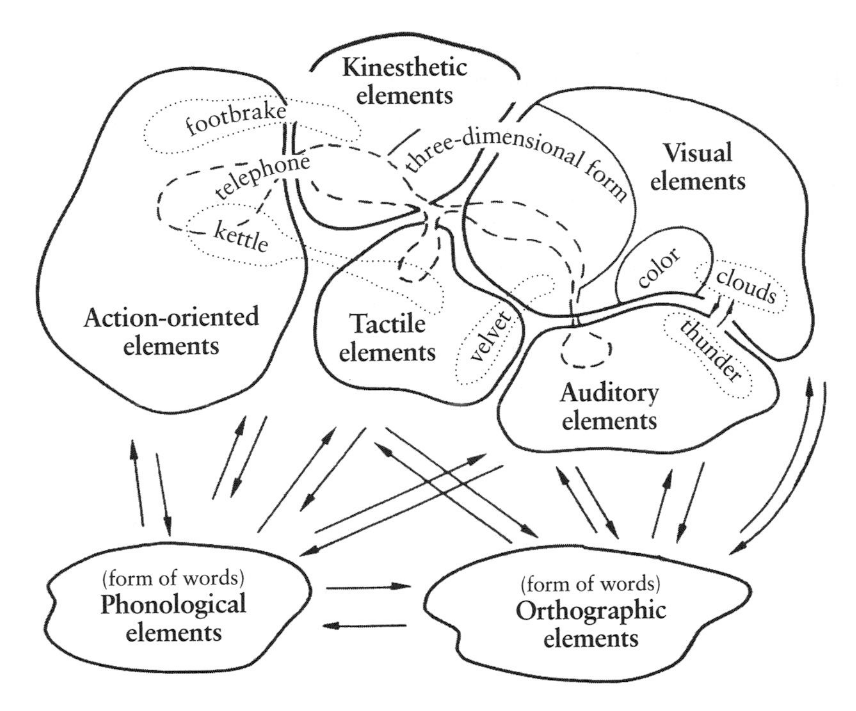

Figure 13. Theoretical neurosemantics: The presentation of a word mobilizes several distributed sets of neurons corresponding to features, or traits, that characterize its meaning. Here, for example, the word "telephone" is supposed to activate neurons in areas specialized in motor action, tactile and kinesthetic sensation, form, and, of course, hearing.

(or image) of a kangaroo, for example, mobilizes populations of neurons distributed among the areas activated by animals (temporal cortex) and by the perception of the color brown (visual cortex), as well as those involved in the perception of movement (visual and parietal cortex), which detect a characteristic trait of kangaroos, namely that they jump rather than gallop.[33] The pattern of selected traits—John

Opposite page

Figure 12. Experimental neurosemantics: Tools, houses, animals, and faces evoke different patterns of activity in the cerebral cortex (here the temporal cortex) in perceptual experiments, delayed-response (memory) tasks, and name-response tasks. Note the differential activations in (a) the lateral fusiform gyrus, (b) the medial fusiform gyrus, (c) the superior temporal sulcus, and (d) the medial temporal gyrus.

Locke's "bundle of qualities"[34]—mobilizes several distinct and functionally specific territories of the brain in a discrete manner, thus constituting a neural embodiment of meaning.[35] Note that this assumption does not require that an exact topology of anatomical connections be constructed that is reproducible across individual brains in every detail, only that a map of functional relations be established—patterns of common semantic features—whose content is determined by the functional specificity of the relevant cortical areas. The implication of such a map is that anatomically variable networks can register and store the same meanings from one individual to another. I will come back to this point later.

Synchronization

By hypothesis, then, the particular characteristics or traits that constitute a given piece of knowledge are distributed over different regions of the brain. What is the mechanism that links them together to form a uniquely meaningful entity? This question—known among neurobiologists as the binding problem—is far from being settled.[36]

In 1919 the zoologist Yves Delage speculated that each individual neuron in the cerebral cortex has a characteristic "vibratory mode," and that the vibration of neurons "in unison" accounts for the "representation of an idea." Their "coaction," he suggested, suffices to make them vibrate in a synchronous fashion.[37] Delage's proposal recalled Hume's notion of the role of "contiguity in time or place" in the association of ideas[38] and anticipated by thirty years a concept that is now usually attributed to Hebb.[39] Today we have solid evidence that the temporal synchronization of neuronal firing serves to integrate and coordinate the action of mutually connected populations of neurons (Figure 14A). This hypothesis, though not unanimously accepted, has given rise to a number of experimental studies.[40] Multi-electrode recordings of activity in the frontal cortex of a monkey performing a spatial delayed-response task show a strong correlation between neuronal firings in direct response to a given behavioral event, for example the triggering of rapid low-amplitude eye movements (or saccades).[41]

Researchers have also investigated the binding problem in the cat by examining the neural correlates of the visual perception of two gratings, moving in different directions, which may be seen either as two

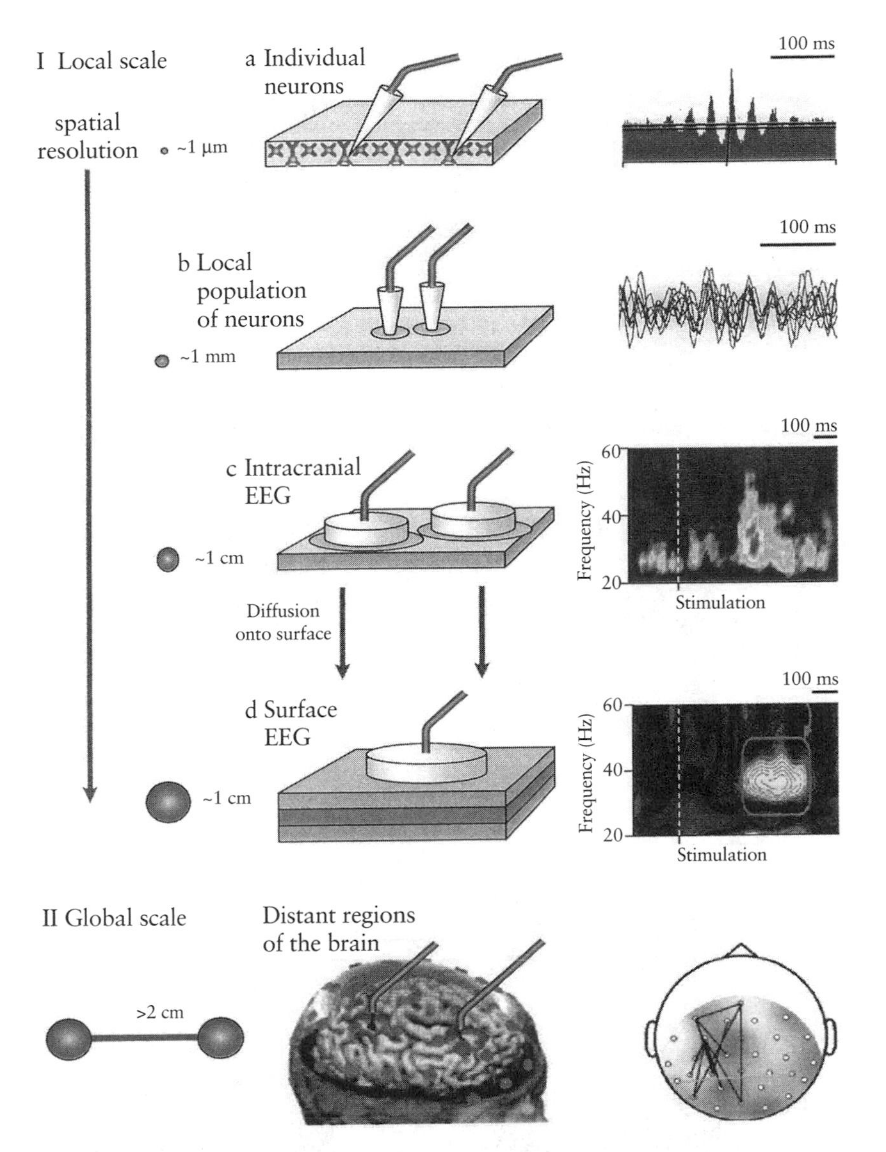

Figure 14A. Methods of recording synchronization between neurons from the cellular level to the global level of the brain. *From top to bottom:* I. Local recordings of (a) individual neurons and (b) a small local population of neurons using eight electrodes (LFP), and of large local populations of neurons by (c) intracranial electroencephalography (IEEG) and (d) surface electroencephalography (EEG). II. Global recordings by comparative electroencephalography of populations in distant regions of the brain.

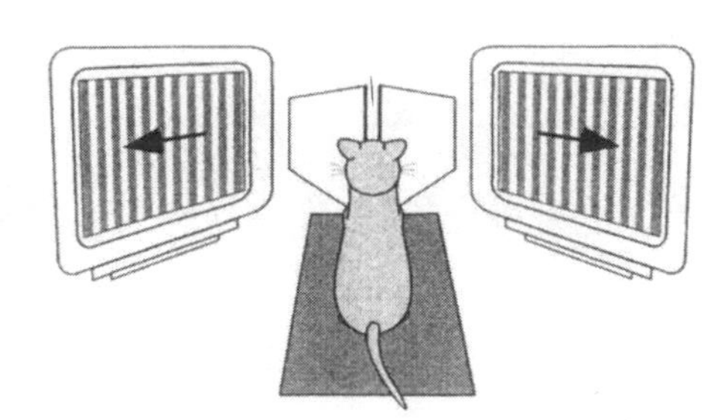

a

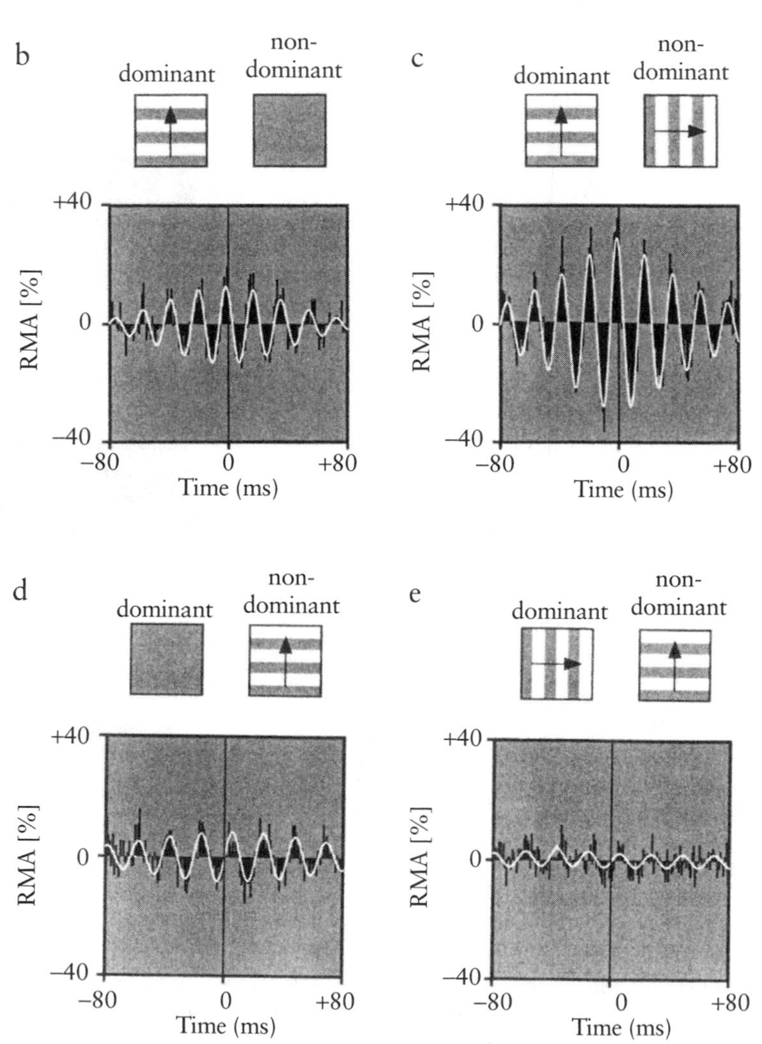

b
dominant
non-dominant
+40
0
−40
RMA [%]
−80
0
+80
Time (ms)
c
dominant
non-dominant
+40
0
−40
RMA [%]
−80
0
+80
Time (ms)
d
dominant
non-dominant
+40
0
−40
RMA [%]
−80
0
+80
Time (ms)
e
dominant
non-dominant
+40
0
−40
RMA [%]
−80
0
+80
Time (ms)

distinct surfaces or as a single surface (Figure 14B).[42] Electrophysiological recordings of individual neurons in two separate areas of the visual cortex reveal that their firings are synchronized in response to the contours of a single surface but not in response to the contours of different surfaces. Nonetheless, the fact that the dynamic changes observed in the synchronization of neuronal firings are correlated with differentiation between a single surface and two overlapping surfaces does not mean that one is the cause of the other. Critics of the temporal binding hypothesis do not deny the experimental record. They argue instead that the fact of synchronization does not explain how it is produced; moreover, they point out, binding can occur without synchronization.[43] In other words, synchronization may reveal binding between neurons without necessarily causing it. Synchronization also raises the issue of boundaries: how does it happen that neuronal grouping changes abruptly when visual attention shifts, for example, from a figure to the background?[44] More puzzling still, synchronous phenomena may spontaneously appear in certain populations of neurons for no apparent reason.

Spontaneous Activation

In Chapter 1 I briefly referred to the spontaneous firing of neurons as one of the fundamental properties of the human brain. The existence of sustained cortical activity in the absence of sensory input is a well-established phenomenon, even in primary sensory areas.[45] But recent studies using both optical techniques and single-neuron electrophysiological recordings show that it amounts to something far more than simple "noise." The spontaneous activity of neurons in a given region of the brain such as the visual cortex is, in fact, coordinated with the firing of many other neurons.[46] Compared to the activity evoked by

Opposite page

Figure 14B. Correlation between local neuronal synchronization and perception of a pattern of dark and light bands in a cat suffering from squint (strabismus). Only the dominant eye gives rise to a synchronization of neuronal activity in the primary cortex that corresponds to the perception of the object. The degree of synchronization is represented by the amplitude of the recorded wave. This amplitude is diminished in the eye that does not perceive the image.

sensory stimulation, the dynamics of spontaneous activity are considerably more variable. Nonetheless, its extent can be half as great as that of the visually-evoked response. These studies clearly demonstrate, then, that in the absence of stimulation the cortical network passes through various states marked by the coherent activation of distinct neuronal assemblies.[47] But the import of such experiments is limited by the fact that they have been conducted on anesthetized animals. One would like to know what goes on in alert human subjects under conditions favorable to the acquisition of knowledge. The available evidence, although still fragmentary, is sufficiently suggestive to generate a working hypothesis.

Cognitive Games

Wittgenstein suggested that children learn their native language through experiments that he called "language games."[48] I will address this particular point a bit later; for the moment I would like to extend the notion to prior episodes of knowledge acquisition that take place before or at the very onset of language learning. From birth the infant constantly explores the external world, ceasing only to sleep. This exploratory activity is accompanied by, and indeed organized around, the spontaneous production in the infant's brain of hypotheses about the world that I call pre-representations, as well as their testing by means of what might be called, by analogy with Wittgenstein's phrase, cognitive games. These games, prominent in the first phases of development, prepare the way for the more elaborate games involving the understanding and production of words that come later.

Pre-Representations

The action of the environment on the organism should not be thought of as the direct and unbiased instruction of a passive brain through evoked activity, as the classical associationist model supposes.[49] I wish to argue, to the contrary, that knowledge acquisition is indirect and results from the selection of pre-representations.[50] Spontaneous activity plays a central role in all this, acting as a Darwinian-style generator of neuronal diversity.[51]

Pre-representations (known also as "neural schemas"[52] or preliminary categories) may be defined as dynamic, spontaneous, and transient states of activity arising from the recombination of preexisting populations of neurons. The introduction of a critical element of variability invites comparison with Darwinian genetic variations, only now it operates at the level of the phenotype (population) rather than, as in the evolution of species, at the level of the genotype (individual). This perspective represents in any case a break with the rigid and deterministic view of the organism as being strictly controlled by its genes. The intrinsic variability of neuronal networks results in part from epigenetic development—a point that will need to be developed later in some detail. For the time being I would like to suggest additional sources of variability associated with the ways in which already existing networks are activated.

Variability may arise from the random behavior of neuronal oscillators, but it may also be caused by transmission failures across synapses—evidence that they do not function in an all-or-nothing manner. A nerve impulse does not always produce a response in the postsynaptic neuron, which has only a certain probability of occurring.[53] Variability in the spatio-temporal patterns of activation leads in turn to "chaotic" behavior among variable and hierarchically organized groups of synchronous cell populations.[54] On this view, different patterns of activity develop as a function of variable initial conditions. The coordinated behavior of neuronal populations exploits reciprocal[55] (or "reentrant")[56] connections among excitatory neurons in the cerebral cortex. Networks of inhibitory neurons may also play a crucial role in the genesis of pre-representations. These transient states of activity combine and mobilize innate structures (including various sensory pathways and motor territories) as well as neuronal patterns established epigenetically by prior experience.[57]

The hypothesis that pre-representations arise from the joint and synchronized action of neuronal networks meets at once with a serious objection, however, namely that the number of possibilities created by a generator of diversity over the scale of the entire brain would rapidly become too large to be efficiently tested in a limited time. One reply is to say that no pre-representation is fully autonomous. As we saw in Chapter 1, mental objects are embedded within the hierarchical and parallel organization of neural networks in such a way that they are constrained by the particular context in which they appear. Another possibility is that the orientation of motivation and selective attention constrains the variation of pre-representations, limiting the number of actual combinations that occur. Or it may be that pre-representations are formed from previously stabilized "categories" or "prototypes" within an established conceptual space, shifting its boundaries or merging it with immediately adjacent spaces, or both.[58] In the chapters that follow (especially Chapter 4) I shall consider the problem of combinatorial explosion, as it is known, in greater detail.

The genesis of pre-representations by a combinatory mechanism of the type I have described constitutes a simple neuronal implementation of the "productivity"[59]—even, if I may use the term, the creativity—of cognitive processes. This hypothesis carries with it a decisive implication: pre-representations unite a variety of distinct patterns of neural activation, harnessing multiple sources of sensorimotor information in functionally distinct territories of the brain.[60] In other words, pre-representations form the basis of the brain's ability to make sense of the world. They are, in short, the source of imaginative activity.

Confronting Reality

The first test of truth, as it may well be called, occurs early in life. From birth, and even prior to birth, the infant's brain is the seat of intense spontaneous activity. The pre-representations to which this activity gives rise are manifested externally by movements of the arms and hands, by cries and wailing and screams, by tears and smiles. The baby tries to sit, then to move forward by crawling, and finally to walk. Gradually she manages to coordinate her movements with greater precision, ceaselessly exploring the immediate environment. She seizes objects, looks at them carefully, and then casts them aside, relaxing her attention only once this process of examination is complete.[61] She spends a considerable amount of time engaged in play.[62] In this way the infant—and later the child and the adult—projects pre-representations onto the surrounding world, overtly at first, through motor actions, and later, tacitly, through the manipulation of mental objects. These activities constitute what I referred to earlier as cognitive games. Proceeding empirically, by trial and error, the infant tries to recognize, identify, and categorize objects and phenomena of the world around her. But what, it may be asked, is the response of the outside world to the transient neural states that elicit these behaviors?

Evaluation

Whether or not a given pre-representation is stabilized depends on the nature of the signal received from the outside world. This external response constitutes a test of what has variously been called the "agreement" (in the sense given this term by Diderot and d'Alembert in the article on truth in the *Encyclopédie*), "saliency,"[63] or "adequacy"[64] of the pre-representation vis-à-vis the environment. The test is decisive, for the result will determine whether a pre-representation is meaningful—whether it "makes sense."

Two main types of mechanism have been suggested. The first, selection by reward, is hypothesized to be responsible for the evaluation of actions. The signals received from the environment recruit some of the neuronal pathways that are involved in motivation or pleasurable reward, or both. Positive reward from the external world results in the widespread release of neurotransmitters such as dopamine, norepinephrine, or acetylcholine, sometimes several at once. Directly or indirectly, these neurotransmitters stabilize a given pre-representation by strengthening (in some cases by weakening) the synaptic connections between the neurons of the relevant networks. In other words, the coincidence of the internally generated pre-representation and the externally evoked positive response has the effect of storing the adequate "hypothesis" in memory. A negative response ("punishment") has the opposite effect: it destabilizes the tested pre-representation, prompting the diversity generator to search for a more adequate alternative.[65]

It may be, however, that an alternative neural mechanism, which I have called selection by resonance, is better suited to explain sensory perception.[66] This mechanism rests on a correspondence between the perceptual activity aroused by sensory stimulation and the pre-representation present in the brain at the moment of stimulation: the precise matching of evoked and endogenous activity results in changes of synaptic strength and thus selective storage.

These two modes of selection bring about the stabilization, or retention, of salient and meaningful knowledge in the form of maps of *functional relations* embodied in a distributed neuronal network. Though the precise patterns of connectivity in the network may vary from individual to individual, its functional relationships (or stabilized meanings) remain constant. In this way a simplified "scale model" of external reality—one that, since it is neuronal, is therefore a physical model as well—is selected and stored in memory in the brain. Memory objects enjoy a genuine existence, then, as latent "forms" composed of stable neuronal traces. One would expect, as a consequence of selection, that the number of pre-representations ought to decrease as a function of experience, which is to say of performing thought experiments upon the world. To repeat the formula I employed in an earlier book, "To learn is to eliminate."[67]

Tests and Limits

The hypothesis of selective stabilization of semantic knowledge by means of cognitive games operating on variable neuronal networks is not wholly "constructivist" in spirit, since it rejects the view of knowledge as nothing more than the neutral stamp of the external world upon the brain, which passively receives it.[68] Nor does it accord with the "nativist" view that our true ideas (in the Cartesian sense) have a strictly innate or endogenous origin, and that the enrichment of conceptual resources is due to maturation rather than to learning.[69] The view I present here is that internally generated pre-representations assume a variety of transient forms, and that these forms are novel by comparison with the inborn endowment of the species to the extent that they mobilize not only elements specific to it but also elements that have been epigenetically stabilized in the course of development. The development in the child of the capacity for face recognition furnishes a good illustration of this point. This capacity includes traits shared by all members of the human species as well as ones that are peculiar to the individual and learned by a process of selection.[70]

Next, the interaction with the external world that leads to the selection of pre-representations through reward or resonance, depending on the effect produced, makes it possible to assess what John Locke called the "reality" of knowledge. Before Diderot, in the *Essay Concerning Human Understanding* (1690), Locke had argued that "our knowledge is real only so far as there is a conformity between our ideas and the reality of things."[71] The mechanism I have proposed here satisfies this condition. From a theoretical point of view, it gives a preliminary answer to the difficult problem of explaining the constancy of stored knowledge despite the variability of neuronal networks from one individual to another. Nonetheless, it is not a wholly satisfactory answer. I shall come back to this point in a later chapter.

Stanislas Dehaene and I sought to test the plausibility of the theory from the neuronal and behavioral point of view by constructing a neural network model capable of carrying out simple cognitive tasks.[72] The tasks selected belong to the large class of delayed-response tasks, initially developed to test the capacity of monkeys (and other species) to solve problems on the basis of memorized information.[73] The animal must concentrate its attention on different aspects of the environment—the identity or position of a particular object, for example, that serves as a cue—and store this information in its working memory. After a variable delay, during which the scene is covered up, the animal is presented with two objects and asked to apply a memorized rule: "Choose the object identical to the cue," or "Choose the position identical to that of the cue." When it succeeds, the animal is rewarded with a sip of orange juice. Certain lesions of the prefrontal cortex selectively modify the animal's performances.[74] Piaget adapted this task to human infants by presenting them with stuffed animals in various positions.[75] Children between the ages of seven-and-a-half and nine months, which is to say at a stage of intense maturation of the prefrontal cortex, are able to carry out this task.[76]

The artificial neural networks we designed to perform delayed-response tasks—and also more elaborate ones such as the Wisconsin card-sorting task (Figures 15A and 15B) and the Tower of London test—incorporate a generator of diversity and a reward system for the purposes of selection. While all of the models were successful, none of these tasks directly involved the acquisition of knowledge or the creation of new concepts. They are restricted to the implementation of pre-programmed rules for classifying a set of elements (as in the Wisconsin card-sorting test) or for mentally solving complex planning problems by trial and error (as in the Tower of London test). Successfully carrying out each of these tasks, as I have noted, requires the integrity of the prefrontal cortex.

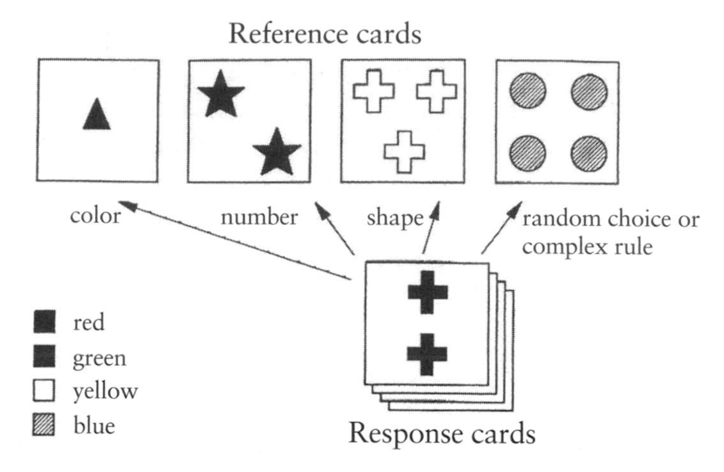

Figure 15A. The Wisconsin card-sorting test, commonly used to detect lesions of the prefrontal cortex. The task is to discover the rule according to which a pile of cards is sorted. Four reference cards, which differ with respect to the color, number, and shape of the figures they display, are placed next to a pile of response cards. The subject is asked to take response cards from the pile and put each one next to the appropriate reference card. After each response, the examiner tells the subject that the response is "right" or "wrong," using an implicit classification rule (having to do with the color, number, or shape of the figures). The subject tries to discern the rule so as to give as many "right" responses as possible. Then, without warning, the examiner changes the rule. The subject must first detect the change and then discover the new rule.

In all these cases, the generator of diversity consists of only a few clusters of excitatory neurons displaying a high degree of synergy, each autoexcitatory cluster being linked to the others by long-range inhibitory connections. The state of spontaneous activity of each cluster—amounting to a very simplified sort of pre-representation—serves to encode a rule whose activation regulates the operation of lower-level sensorimotor networks. Lateral inhibition is built into the network in such a way that only one cluster of excitatory neurons can be active at any given moment. In the case of a positive reward, the activated cluster is stabilized, blocking the diversity generator. In the case of error, by contrast, punishment causes the diversity generator to resume operation. A diversity generator of this type exhibits the main features of Turing's model of morphogenesis, which I shall describe in detail later on; for the moment it can be thought of as a mechanism for generating patterns of neuronal activation. In formal terms the diversity generator serves its purpose, even if the postulated mechanism is too

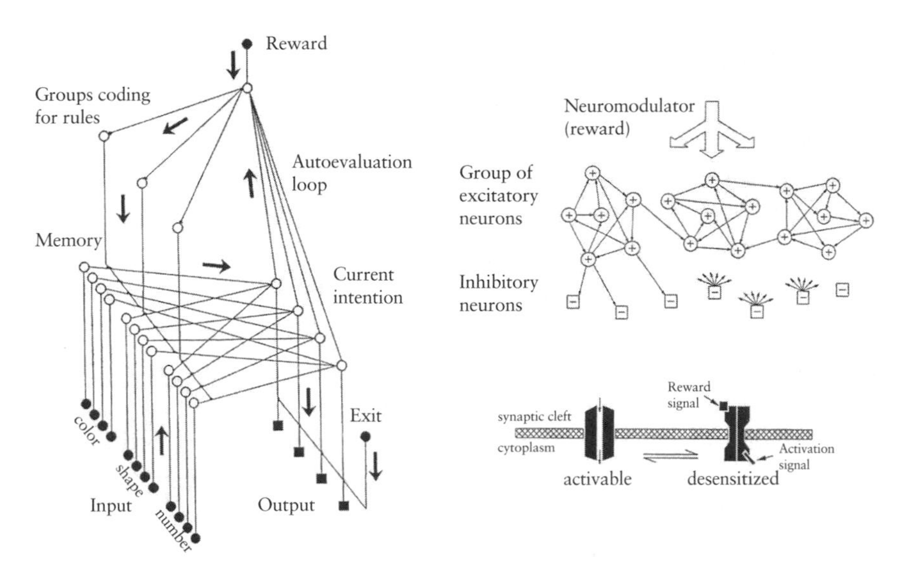

Figure 15B. A neuronal model of the Wisconsin card-sorting test, proposed by Dehaene and Changeux. *Left:* Schematic neuronal architecture with several superimposed levels of organization: input and output, memory and present intention, rules, and reward or error. Each level is implemented by groups of neurons, represented here by circles. *Top right:* The relation between rule neurons and reward system. Each group of excitatory rule neurons may be active in a discrete all-or-nothing manner at any given moment. But so long as one is active the others are suppressed by long-range inhibitory neurons. The system serves as a "diversity generator" for testing various possible hypotheses (here limited to three). When the reward response is positive, the released neuromodulator (dopamine or acetylcholine, for example) changes—directly or indirectly—the synaptic strengths of the group of rule neurons that has won. *Bottom right:* The selection of the correct hypothesis exploits the plasticity of the network: for example, the neuromodulator stabilizes an allosteric state of the receptor directly (here the desensitized state) or indirectly (through phosphorylation).

simple to be fully realistic, in part because the range of variability to which it has access, consisting only of a few groups of neurons, is very narrow. However, as we shall see in the next chapter, this range has been considerably enlarged in a revised version of the model, which introduces the hypothesis of a neuronal workspace.[77]

The constantly changing cognitive games to which the infant devotes itself are embedded in the waves of synaptic development that follow one upon another after birth (see Chapter 6). Lower-level representations, immediately involved in the perception of external objects and action upon the outside world, become incorporated into higher-level representations. In other words, the child works out basic categories of the outside world that are progressively "nested" within more global categories.[78] As these categories come to be informed more by the internal states of the brain itself than by external reality, they gradually acquire a more abstract, or conceptual, character.

The computer models I have just discussed have a very simple neuronal architecture. This is enough to pass the Tower of London test. But what about the more difficult case of mathematical problems? Alain Connes and I have distinguished three functional levels in the operation of computing machines that carry out mathematical operations by means of nested evaluation systems.[79] In the most elementary case, the machine is able to play chess, for example, which requires it simply to determine in the course of the game how far away it is from winning. At the second level, it is capable of developing novel strategies through the use of methods of evaluation corresponding to a definite plan of action. At the third and final level, no plan has been fixed in advance: the machine exhibits genuine creativity, having the power to devise new plans and to develop methods of evaluation capable of recognizing the novelty of these plans and determining whether or not they are consistent with the structure of external reality. This will be my subject in the next chapter.

At the molecular level, for example, the mechanism of selection by reward operates through the direct (or indirect) action of the reward signal on postsynaptic neurotransmitter receptors. As we saw in the last chapter, these receptors—known as allosteric proteins—function as simple molecular locks that are able simultaneously to recognize one or more keys on both sides of the membrane. Moreover, allosteric receptors are capable of detecting the coincidence of the reentrant reward signal and the activity of the postsynaptic cell by means of discrete conformational changes of the receptor molecule.[80] They sense, as it were, the success (or failure) of a given motor strategy. Studies have been made of transgenic animals in order to determine the actual contribution of these receptors to the storage of learning traces. For example, a mouse in which the gene that codes for a sub-unit of the acetylcholine receptor (referred to as βz) has been deleted finds it difficult to carry out passive-avoidance learning tasks. It also loses the ability to administer nicotine to itself.[81] Of course, other synaptic mechanisms based on specific properties of particular receptors or ion channels may also contribute to changes in synaptic strength.[82] For example, in the case of glutamate receptors, the ion channel may be blocked by a magnesium ion, but the electric potential of the postsynaptic membrane generated by a conditioned stimulus forces the ion across the channel activated by the unconditioned stimulus, creating an alternative mechanism for detecting whether the activation of the receptor by the neurotransmitter coincides with the state of activity of the postsynaptic cell.

The anticipation of reward—variously known as "value prediction,"[83] "reward expectation,"[84] or simply "self-evaluation"[85]—has been extensively studied in the monkey. A simple mechanism of self-evaluation has been implemented in neural network models by the incorporation of an internal device that predicts future rewards from the outside world. Such a self-evaluation loop accelerates learning and suggests a tentative approach to the exceedingly difficult problem of modeling the confidence attached to beliefs about future outcomes: each action, and each plan of action, is immediately associated with an increase (or decrease) in the probability of subsequent rewards.[86] Moreover, it gives the organism access to an internal mode of reckoning in which various courses of action can be tacitly evaluated without having to be tried out in the external world.[87] Unlike Piaget's sensorimotor experiments, the cognitive games I have in mind are not restricted to the child's actual experience of the external world, but can rapidly develop internally through the evaluation of stored memories, as we shall shortly see.

Until quite recently only a limited amount of electrophysiological data was available concerning cortical neuronal activity during learning. The model I have described, it will be recalled, has a crucial consequence: learning ought to lead to a decrease in the range of variability of spontaneous activity. In the rat, the neuronal activity of the sensorimotor cortex during the course of learning a motor task exhibits a remarkable pattern of evolution. Single-neuron recordings do not reveal significant change. But recordings of neuronal populations show that average firing rates, the precise distribution of firings over time (intervals of more than 10 milliseconds), and the coordination of individual firings increase with the prediction of the learned response.[88]

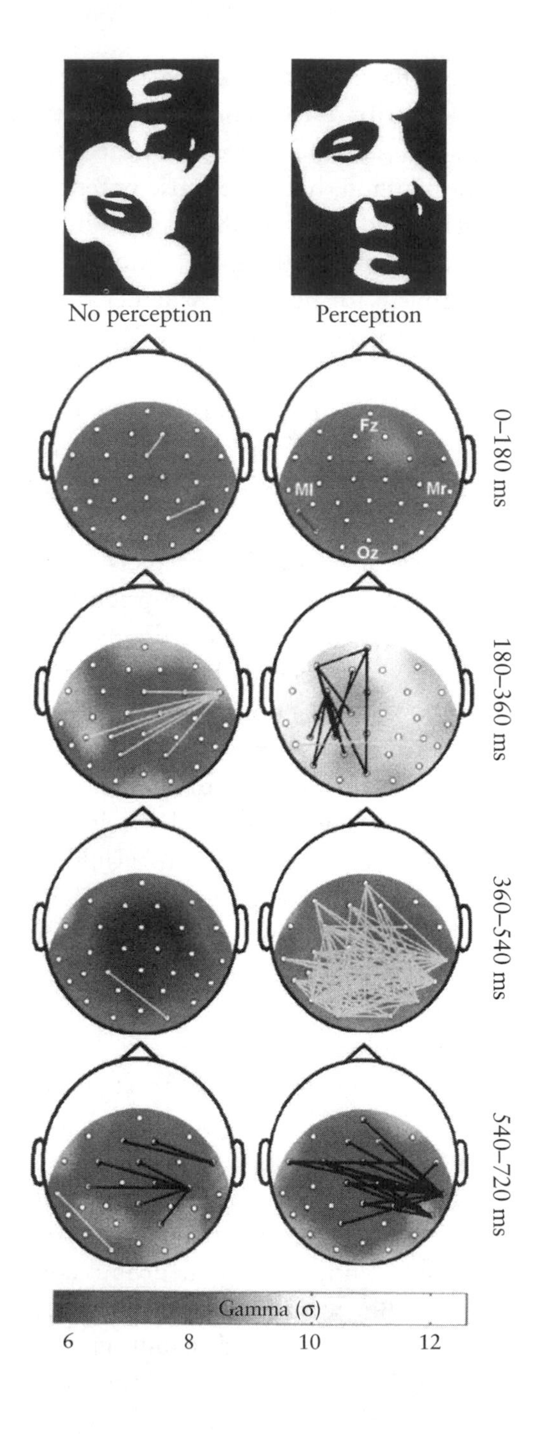
No perception
Perception
0–180 ms
Fz
Ml
Mr
Oz
180–360 ms
360–540 ms
540–720 ms
Gamma (σ)
6
8
10
12

Single-neuron recordings in humans are rare, for obvious ethical reasons; but electroencephalographic and magnetoencephalographic recordings of neuronal populations yield similar evidence of large-scale synchronization during the performance of recognition tasks.[89] In the case of recognition of simplified ("moony") faces, for example, a consistent pattern of synchronization between the occipital, parietal, and frontal areas is observed about 250 milliseconds after the presentation of the stimulus. Neither recognition nor synchronization takes place, however, when the faces are presented upside down (Figure 15C).[90] This type of measurement is still very crude, but the results agree with the model I have just described. It is expected that more direct experimental tests of these specific hypotheses will be possible in the near future.[91]

Earlier I mentioned Russell's claim that, in the case of true beliefs, there exists a congruence—an analogy of form, or isomorphism—between a belief (or category) and its object. Patterns of activation in neuronal networks do not, as it happens, exactly reproduce the features of an object of the outside world. Imaging studies done in the rat of the primary visual areas of the cerebral cortex have revealed patterns of neuronal activity in which the object perceived by the retina can actually be recognized, allowing for some small degree of deformation. But it is generally the case that, in passing through the hierarchy of visual areas, retinal images are drastically altered.

Another way of posing the question is to ask if the retrieval of traces from memory, for example of a visual object, in the form of a mental image mobilizes the same pathways and the same territories as those involved in the direct perception of the object. The matter is still undecided. Yet imaging studies of the human brain reveal a great similarity

Opposite page

Figure 15C. *Right:* Correlation between global synchronization (black lines) and recognition of a stylized "moony" face. The strongest synchronization, which involves the fronto-temporal and parieto-occipital regions, occurs between 200 and 260 milliseconds and is followed by a general desynchronization (white lines), after which a new parietal and occipito-temporal synchronization occurs, at the moment when the subject presses a button to signal that he has recognized the face. *Left:* When turned upside down, the face is not recognized.

between the two, with the primary visual areas playing a dominant role when memory seeks a finer resolution of the details of the image.[92] One interesting experiment involves asking subjects to mentally rotate images of hands and feet. Transcranial magnetic stimulation (a method that transiently inactivates the underlying neural structure) of the primary motor cortex affects the performance of this task, demonstrating the causal role played by the activation of this part of the brain.[93]

Knowledge acquisition by the child has been extensively and elegantly investigated, though until now mostly by behavioral methods.[94] These methods do not suffice to test the neurobehavioral conjectures that I have advanced here. It nonetheless seems likely that the early acquisition of physical knowledge about fluids and solids, and the continuity of material objects, proceeds through a constant testing of "hypotheses"[95] formed by the child at definite moments of development.[96] Further study of the physiology of these early stages of knowledge acquisition is needed in order to identify the neural mechanisms underlying the cognitive games involved. The importance of this work is all the greater since the attempt to place the inquiry into the nature of human knowledge on secure physical foundations is no longer an impossible dream, but a well-defined program of ongoing research in cognitive neuroscience and psychology.

3 States of Consciousness

"The most important problem in the biological sciences," in the view of the philosopher John Searle, "is one that until quite recently many scientists did not regard as a suitable subject for scientific investigation at all. It is this: How exactly do neurobiological processes in the brain cause consciousness?"[1]

We possess knowledge of the world and of ourselves, and we know that we are the authors of this knowledge. We do not for a moment suppose that knowledge, in its many and varied facets, is the same thing as consciousness, which is distinguished above all by its unity and the subjective sense of identity it supports. Yet identifying the neurobiological processes that are at the root of consciousness—what the cognitive neuroscientist Antti Revonsuo calls "this real, natural, biological phenomenon, literally localized in the brain"[2]—is now seen as a decisive step in understanding the nature of knowledge and how it is obtained. In all of this the question of truth is central, since what seems true to one person often does not appear so in the eyes of another, though both testify to their opinion in good faith.

The terms of the modern debate about the origins of consciousness were already set by the beginning of the nineteenth century. In France, Étienne Bonnot de Condillac, a dominant figure of the Enlightenment, upheld an extreme empiricism, even more radical than that of David Hume in Britain. In the *Traité des sensations* (1754), Condillac argued that the edifice of mental life was constructed entirely of sensations. He asked his readers to imagine themselves as "statues," devoid of all psychological content, and to reconstruct their actual mental life on the basis of elementary sensations. The consciousness the statue has of itself, Condillac asserted, is nothing more than "the collection of the sensations which it experiences, and those which memory recalls to it."[3] But how could unity and identity result from so diverse a collection of sensations? After all, I remain the same person over time—whether I am eating an apple, looking at a painting, remembering my first course in biology, or cloning a gene.

Kant sought to expose the fallacy of empiricist reasoning. In *Anthropologie in pragmatischer Hinsicht* (1798) he showed that the consciousness of oneself cannot result from a simple succession of sensations—that, indeed, it actually precedes them.[4] But where then did this consciousness come from, this "I" that seems immediately given? Kant lacked the means to explain it in natural terms. The position of the first evolutionary theorists, in particular Jean-Baptiste de Lamarck and, later, Herbert Spencer, differed from both that of Condillac and that of classical rationalism, inherited from Descartes. No matter that their views on the mechanisms of evolution were subsequently shown to be mistaken, notably by Charles Darwin, they correctly recognized that the nervous system had developed over time, passing from simple to more complex organisms by means of what Lamarck called "gradual and imperceptible formation and development."[5]

Lamarck, in the *Philosophie zoologique,* distinguished a "singular faculty with which certain animals and man himself are endowed" that he called "inner feeling."[6] We receive emotions, he held, both through the operation of the intelligence and through sensations and needs. Inner feeling integrates the higher level of the will, which results from judgments produced by the organ of intelligence. On Lamarck's view, the outside world impinges upon the brain in such a way as to excite consciousness, though not to create it. Almost half a century later, Herbert Spencer, in *Principles of Psychology* (1855), tried to retrace the evolutionary development of the nervous system through the progressive integration of new "grouped states" (today one would say "clusters") of neurons alongside preexisting ("primitive") grouped states. A process of evolution from "simple to composed," marked by the "convergence and divergence of fibers" establishing higher levels of integration, thus gave rise to a consciousness independent of the immediate environment.[7] Contemporary neuroscience, though it does not entirely endorse these arguments, has adopted from Lamarck and Spencer the idea that the development of consciousness is related to the complexity of the nervous system.[8] Nonetheless, a simple increase in complexity would not by itself suffice to explain the development of consciousness. The mystery of its origin remains complete.

Most neuroscientists regard consciousness as a property or function of the brain, comparable to breathing or digestion, that in principle should be explicable in terms of the activity of neurons and synapses and their regulation by chemical signals. But consciousness exhibits unique characteristics. For the philosopher it involves a "phenomenal level of organization" that corresponds to a "world of inner, subjective, qualitative states and of processes of sentience or awareness"—of data reported by the subject in the first person.[9] For the neuroscientist it is a sort of "open-loop phenomenon with entries and outlets in constant mutation";[10] for the psychologist and psychiatrist, a complex "structure" endowed with self-referential properties whose organization "links the subject to others and to his own world."[11] On all of these views there is anatomical, physiological, and behavioral evidence for the thesis that I wish to argue for here, namely that consciousness arises from the operation of specific neural networks in the brain. The chief problem facing neuroscience today, in my view, is to identify these specialized structures and to determine to what extent, in making the acquisition of knowledge a conscious activity, they help decide its truth or falsity.

The neuroscientific investigation of consciousness is only in its infancy. Philosophers, writers, and theologians, on the other hand, have produced a very rich literature on the "phenomenon" of consciousness. Let us begin, then, by examining at least a few of the problems that have preoccupied these thinkers for centuries—problems that are directly related to the question of how reliable knowledge about the world can consciously be obtained.

Philosophical Problems

A number of contemporary philosophers interested in consciousness have suggested that it involves qualitative subjective states that they call "qualia."[12] When I look, for example, at Nicolas Poussin's painting *Et in Arcadia ego*, how can my personal feeling, which I experience directly, be exactly the same as that of another person looking at the same work? It has long been supposed that such qualia are not amenable to scientific examination. And indeed so long as consciousness is defined as a sort of inner awareness that is the unique property of the person who experiences it, only introspection can give access to its states. To be sure, my experience of this painting will not be exactly the same as that of someone who has not studied the many other paintings by Poussin in the Louvre or traced the genesis of these works from drawings and literary and historical sources. Nonetheless we will agree about many of its aspects—its figures, forms, colors, the overall composition of the work, and so on. Surely it would be useful to investigate such first-person reports by exploiting the most advanced technologies and scientific methods in order to establish their neural correlates, and to compare them with the subjective states experienced by other persons under similar conditions that have produced similar reactions.

It seems reasonable to expect that these shared qualia may be correlated with physical brain states despite the fundamental variability that exists between brains and between individual experiences. The vivid reds in Rothko's *Black over Reds*, for example, are perceived in a constant and common—if not exactly identical—manner by different viewers under different lighting conditions, whether natural or artificial. (If this were not the case there would no longer be art critics—we would no longer agree about the quality of any piece of art.) The constancy of qualia very likely implies the constancy of their corresponding neural states, but establishing this experimentally remains a critical task in the study of consciousness. It involves a central biological question, which I will take up in greater detail in the following chapter in connection with the neuronal basis of the sharing of knowledge within a social group.

Another important problem has to do with the unity of consciousness. When we are awake, we "live" the subjective experience of a scene in a unified and global way. Within this inner world a sort of synthesis takes place, with the result that various modes of perception, memories of previous experiences, emotions, and feelings, as well as of plans of action, are subjectively unified in what the neuroscientist

Rodolfo Llinás calls a "conscious milieu," or, as the psychiatrist Henri Ey called it, "field of consciousness."[13] On the one hand, the flow of consciousness is dynamic and continually changing—like a bird that, no sooner than it has perched, takes wing again, as William James put it.[14] But this flow is anything but chaotic. It is, as Alfred Fessard remarked, "at once one and many in each of its moments."[15] William Faulkner's *The Sound and the Fury* gives a wonderful sense of what this dynamic synthesis of consciousness involves. In the first part, the unfolding drama of a family is seen through the eyes of Benjy Compson, a mentally retarded man. Even though Faulkner describes the sensations, emotions, and images that present themselves to Benjy's consciousness as a chaotic succession of events, rather like those of a dream, the overall effect is one of organization and unity, the like of which we experience every moment we are awake. We need, then, to attempt to define the neuronal architecture that gives consciousness both its coherence and its variety.

Consciousness displays a third important aspect that philosophers and moralists usually call autonomy. The capacity to make judgments with regard to truth and other values depends on the autonomy of the person. The conscious milieu opens not only upon the external, physical, and social world; it can also be accessed by introspection and personal judgment, which includes the making of predictions and anticipation of the likely consequences of possible actions. These predictions are evaluated with reference to the "I," the self, which may be the self that acts and is the "owner" of actions,[16] or else the narrative self of experience and personal history, which includes long-term memory.[17] This autonomy of judgment agrees with the projective style of brain function that I discussed earlier, and with the arguments developed by Llinás, who sees consciousness as being modulated, rather than generated, by the senses. It is also consistent with the conception of the conscious brain as a "symbolic simulator"[18] or a "self-organizing" system.[19] These thought experiments all refer to a coherent, stable, self-generated image—a "personal model"[20] or a "conception of the world."[21] Once again, the task of the neurosciences is to discover the neuronal structures that make the autonomy of consciousness possible.

Finally, and notwithstanding the unity and autonomy I have just mentioned, there exists a multiplicity of levels of consciousness corresponding to the states of sleeping, dreaming, and wakefulness, and of hierarchies among these levels. Pierre Buser has distinguished two main types of consciousness in the waking state: passive (or perceptual) primary consciousness, and attentive (or reflective) secondary consciousness, which includes organizing and planning, reasoning, and solving problems with the aid of effortful introspection.[22] This distinction captures the fact that the direct experience of feeling is readily distinguished from the knowledge that one has a feeling. Levels of consciousness may be progressively destructured or "dissolved,"[23] causing clinical manifestations: hallucinations, oneiric states, depersonalization, emotional disturbances, epilepsy. It is important to note that consciousness emerged by successive stages in the course of the evolution of species,[24] as it does during the postnatal development of the human newborn.[25]

No set of models based on our current understanding of the brain is capable of accounting for the whole of conscious experience. In this chapter I will be chiefly concerned with the unifying and synthesizing activity of consciousness, which stands in contrast to the diversity and multiplicity of its underlying levels. In combination these things constitute a "conscious workspace,"[26] as the psychologist Bernard Baars calls it, on which the heightened alertness and attention required by difficult tasks requiring effort are brought to bear. I would like first to briefly present some empirical data about this workspace and then discuss the conscious and nonconscious cognitive operations that take place within it, the multidimensional character of the conscious workspace, the genesis of intentional behavior, and the neural basis for the sense of self. I shall then go on to sketch the outlines of a neural network model that could account for conscious activity, examine the implications of the model in four domains, and consider future directions for research on consciousness.

The Conscious Milieu: Empirical Data

Electrophysiological recordings of cerebral activity suggest an approximate neuronal correlate of the milieu within which conscious experience is unified. The intrinsic electrical activity of the cerebral cortex can change dramatically as a function of the level of arousal and attention. The measurement of electroencephalographic (EEG) waves obtained by placing electrodes on the scalp, as well as single-neuron recordings in animals, reveal distinct patterns of spontaneous and evoked activity in different states of sleep and wakefulness, including paradoxical or rapid-eye-movement (REM) sleep and attentive states (Figure 16).[27]

Electroencephalograms of awake and alert subjects display rapid and irregular low-amplitude waves. When the subject closes his eyes and becomes drowsy, the activity becomes regular and rhythmic, with a frequency of about 10 cycles per second. Falling asleep, with loss of consciousness, is accompanied by a gradual transition to much slower waves (1 to 5 cycles per second) having very large amplitude. From time to time these waves are disrupted by sudden high-frequency bursts of low-voltage electrical activity. The slow waves correspond to the phases of REM sleep, which ordinarily are associated with a unique state of consciousness—dreaming. Local high-frequency firings (about 40 cycles per second) are also recorded in alert subjects in attentive states related to the processing of representations in the brain.[28] In recent years there has been a suggestion that these 40 Hz oscillations represent the neuronal correlate of consciousness.[29] Half a century of careful research has shown, however, that much more is involved than this.[30]

Despite the fact that these electrical activities occur in or near the cerebral cortex, they involve populations of neurons located in nuclei relatively far away from the cerebral cortex, though these neurons are strongly and reciprocally associated with it. The thalamic nuclei play a strategic role in the brain, serving both as generators of internal electrical activity and as relay stations for signals arriving from the external world. Two types of thalamic nuclei are distinguished, corresponding to each of these functions.

The neurons of the "specific" nuclei receive afferent inputs from the environment through sensory (and motor) pathways and establish connections with a particular layer of the cerebral cortex, layer IV (see Figure 4A in Chapter 1). This cortical layer is the main gate, or point of entry, for external signals. Moreover, these signals are received by excitatory neurons that are in contact with neighboring inhibitory neurons, with which they begin to oscillate. These cortical oscillations re-

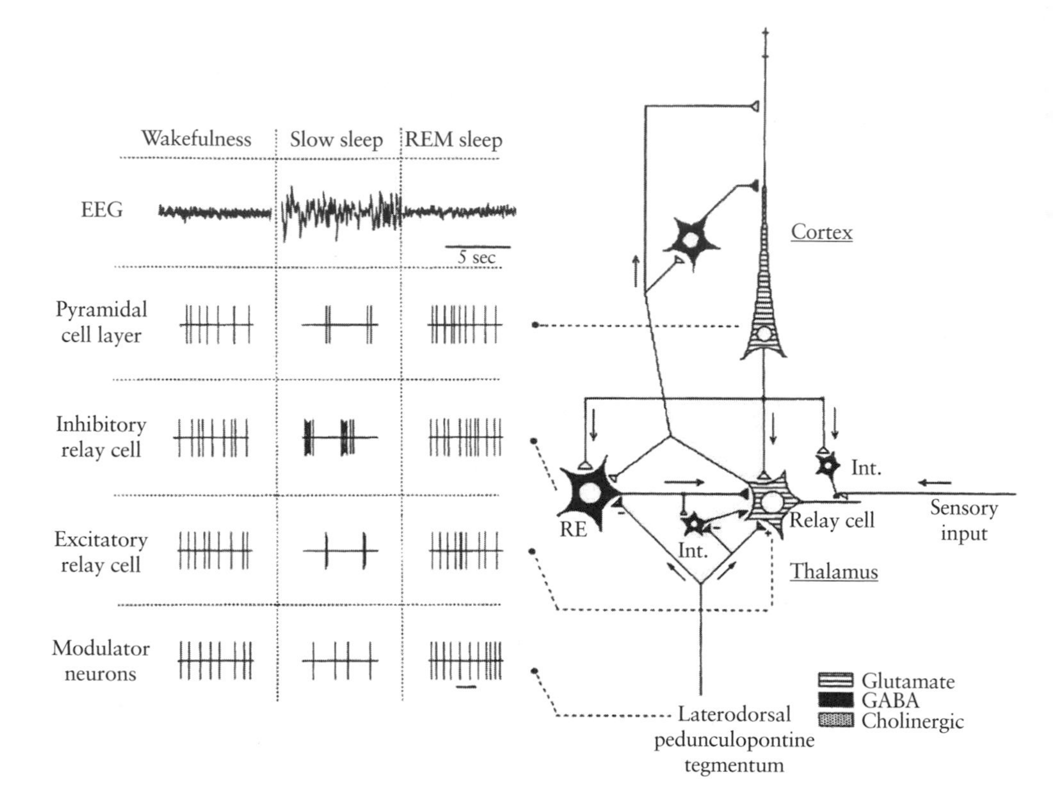

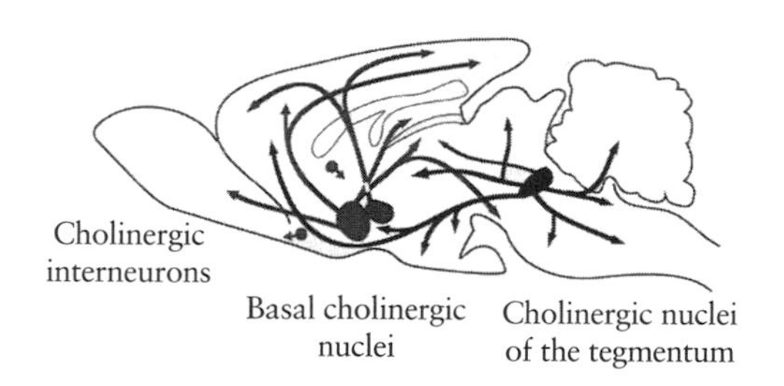

Figure 16. Neuronal circuits involved in waking, sleeping, and dreaming. *Top right:* An extremely simplified diagram of the cerebral cortex and the various thalamic nuclei that are interconnected with it. *Top left:* The activity of the thalamocortical loops in the cortex (EEG) differs in waking, slow sleep, and REM sleep (dreaming). The principal categories of neurons of the oscillatory circuit are the pyramidal cells of the cortex and the relay neurons of the thalamus, both of which are excitatory and release glutamate. But inhibitory GABA neurons also play a role, both in the cortices and in the thalamus. Recordings of individual neurons in each of the principal cell types reveal resemblances between the waking state and REM sleep. The circuit receives two principal inputs: sensory inputs that are largely (but not totally) disconnected during sleep; and regulatory cholinergic inputs from the pedunculopontine nuclei and the tegmentum. *Bottom:* A simplified rendering of the system of cholinergic neurons, which, together with noradrenaline neurons, control the states of waking and sleeping in the rat.

enter the thalamus, creating a specific oscillatory loop between the thalamus and the cortex.

The neurons of the "nonspecific" nuclei, by contrast, are not connected to the external world via sensory or motor systems. These neurons project in a diffuse way to all the layers of the cerebral cortex, mobilizing a distinct set of thalamocortical loops. Damage to the nonspecific thalamic system produces sleep disorders, lethargy, and coma. A mild form of epilepsy known as petit mal is accompanied by an abnormally low frequency of this thalamocortical activity. It seems probable that the access of sensory stimuli to consciousness arises from interaction between the specific (sensory) thalamocortical loop and the nonspecific loops,[31] which produce temporal coherence, or resonance. The specific system furnishes the *content* of the inner world of consciousness, through its contact with the outside world, and the nonspecific system gives it *context.*

The electrophysiological properties of thalamic neurons have important implications. Recordings of individual neurons show that the depolarization of the cell membrane suffices to generate the rapid oscillations of 40 cycles per second that characterize the conscious state and the phases of REM sleep. Their hyperpolarization, on the other hand, is associated with slow-wave sleep. Waking and REM-sleep states are similar from the electrical point of view, but their modulation by sensory inputs displays an essential difference. In awake and alert subjects, sensory stimuli reset, or renew, the rapid thalamocortical oscillations—the first stage of the processing of sensory information by the brain. During REM sleep, sensory inputs reach the cerebral cortex without, however, resetting the thalamocortical resonance loop. During slow-wave sleep, by contrast, sensory inputs are blocked from reaching the cerebral cortex and so do not modify the loop at all. There are thus good reasons for thinking that the corticothalamic system that receives and processes information from the outside world functions differently depending on the state of consciousness. It is interesting to note that these state-transitions occur rather abruptly for the most part, sometimes in an all-or-nothing fashion, as in the case of petit mal epilepsy. Significantly, the reciprocal circuits established within the thalamocortical loops display a considerable degree of nonlinearity.

We are now in a position to identify the molecular mechanisms that turn oscillatory activity on (or off) in the corticothalamic system. For more than half a century the complex groups of specialized neurons responsible for regulating such activity have been the object of very active research focusing on the *reticular formation,* a nonspecific activation system distinct from the thalamic pathways. Giuseppe Moruzzi and H. W. Magoun, who discovered this system in the late 1940s, emphasized the decisive role played by reticular neurons in regulating states of consciousness.[32] These neurons form a complex interconnected set of nuclei situated in the brain stem, between the spinal cord and the thalamus. Morphologically, they are very unusual. Although their cell bodies are located in the brain stem, in groups of several thousands, their axons are widely dispersed in fanlike patterns throughout the brain, on account of which they exercise an extensive modulatory influence. Moreover, by means of reciprocal connections they establish large-scale mechanisms of reverberation and integration that, combined with top-down connections from the cerebral cortex, form a vast feedback system that creates a further degree of nonlinearity in the transitions between states of consciousness.[33]

More recent studies have shown that the reticular neurons of the brain stem exhibit great biochemical and topological diversity. They contain well-defined sets of neurotransmitters (such as acetylcholine, noradrenaline, and serotonin) and, through the massive release of these chemicals, exert differential control over the various states of consciousness.[34]

Experiments conducted by Herbert Jasper and his colleagues in the early 1960s highlighted the role played by the neurotransmitter acetylcholine in the sleep-waking cycle. The level of acetylcholine released in the cerebral cortex changes from one moment to the next, reaching its highest point in two very different situations: the activation of the cerebral cortex by sensory (or electrical) stimulation during the waking states and during REM sleep. Electrophysiological recordings reveal that the arousal of the brain to a state of full consciousness begins with the activation of the brain-stem neurons, which include acetylcholine neurons. These neurons release a "fountain of neurotransmitters"[35] that creates a chemical link with the loop between the thalamus and the cortex I have just described. Receptors for these neurotransmitters, in particular for acetylcholine, are present in thalamic neurons.[36] Stimulation by these neurotransmitters causes the electrical state of the thalamic neurons to switch back and forth from the oscillatory mode associated with sleep to the rapid waves characteristic of waking. These chemicals may even be able to reorient the flow of information within the circuits of the cerebral cortex.[37]

Consciousness therefore mobilizes autonomous processes that are endogenous to the brain. Its various states are controlled by long-range chemical signals, chiefly ones triggered by neurons in the brain stem. Consciousness arises from intrinsic and spontaneous activity generated by neuronal oscillators—one of the many processes that illustrate the projective character of brain function. This activity is modulated—rather than constructed, as Condillac would have said—by signals evoked by the senses.[38]

Conscious and Nonconscious

During slow-wave sleep we are not conscious. Often, however, we have a limited, though usually fragmentary, recollection of the dreaming episodes experienced during REM sleep. When we are awake and alert, we are seldom aware that our brains are the seat of intense nonconscious activity. When we are walking or running, for example, we are not usually conscious of the precise position of our feet and joints; nor are we usually aware of the beating of our hearts or of the rhythm of our breathing. At any given moment we consult only a small fraction of our repertoire of long-term memories. Whether or not the "unconscious" operates in the manner described by psychoanalysis remains a matter of debate; but its existence is not in doubt, nor that it arises from nonconscious operations of the brain that are intertwined with those of our conscious inner life.

This idea is by no means new. The German philosopher Johann Friedrich Herbart, in *Psychologie als Wissenschaft* (1824–1825), introduced the notion of a threshold of consciousness beyond which "inhibited" or unconscious ideas become "real" or conscious.[39] About a century later, with the work of Pierre Janet and Sigmund Freud, the question aroused intense speculation, but only recently has it become the object of scientific study.

Cerebral lesions reveal that certain measurable cognitive processes can occur without the subject being aware of them. Consider, for example, the phenomenon known as "blind sight." A lesion of primary visual area 17 produces a scotoma, which is to say a loss of vision in certain regions of the visual field. Nonetheless, if a flash of light is presented in the patient's blind field and he is asked to move his eyes[40] or to point his finger in the direction of the flash,[41] he is able to do so—while denying that he has seen a flash of light. Of course we have no choice but to accept the testimony of such patients. Yet the phenomenon of blind sight is easily reproduced: it has also been demonstrated in the monkey by a series of elegant behavioral experiments.[42] In patients suffering from blind sight produced by the lesion of primary visual areas, the processing of visual information appears to borrow noncortical pathways. This observation suggests, on the one hand, that the cerebral cortex contributes to conscious vision and, on the other, that visual information can be efficiently conveyed along noncortical pathways without the subject being aware of it. Significant differences in this respect may therefore exist between humans and the lower mammals (and, to a greater degree, between man and reptiles or birds). In 1881 Hermann Munk removed the visual cortex of a dog and observed that it continued to see and to avoid obstacles.[43] Was it still conscious, or did it have a spontaneous form of blind sight almost as effective as conscious sight?

Another line of experimental evidence attesting to the nonconscious character of certain cognitive operations involves the phenomenon of "semantic priming."[44] The subject is presented with a series of written words in such rapid succession that, by his own account, he does not consciously perceive them. Nonetheless this rapid presentation does not prevent the subsequent processing of related words. Brain imaging techniques show that stimuli presented for only a very brief time measurably influence the activation patterns of several cortical areas, in particular (though not exclusively) patterns involved in motor programming that are activated nonconsciously. Quite different areas are mobilized, however, when the subject perceives the visual stimulus in a fully conscious manner. The activation of prefrontal and parietal areas, negligible during the nonconscious processing of masked words, increases spectacularly during conscious perception (Figure 17). The neural structures that account both for conscious perception and the

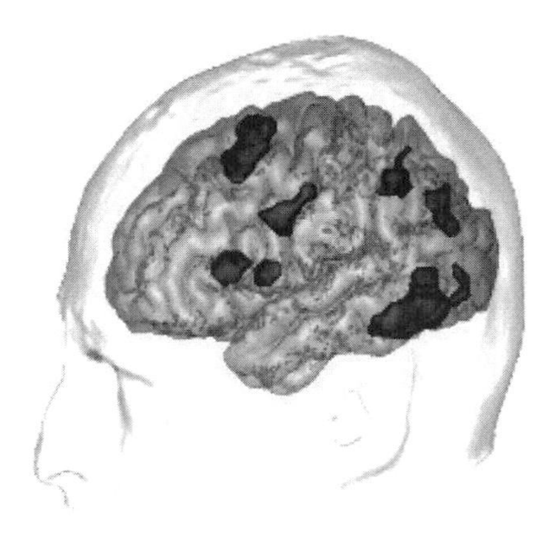

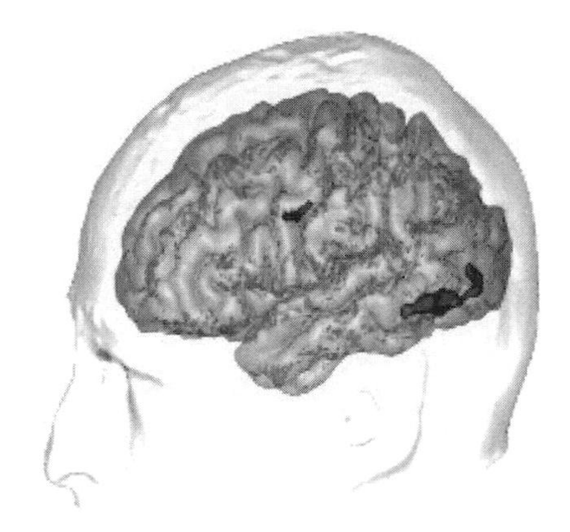

conscious visible words　　　　nonconscious masked words

Figure 17. Functional magnetic imaging of conscious perception and nonconscious processing of written words. The difference between the two cases has to do with the sequence of images rapidly presented to the subject. The presentation of a complex image (a mask) immediately before and after a word prevents the word's conscious recognition but allows it to be used later in a semantic priming task. If the mask is replaced by a blank image, the word is perceived consciously. Conscious processing activates the occipital areas (vision), fusiform areas (form of words), and, above all, areas of the frontal cortex.

conscious processing of information are clearly distinct from those involved in the nonconscious processing of information.[45]

Mental Syntheses

Paul Ricoeur, like other philosophers in the phenomenological tradition, stresses the extreme complexity and hierarchical organization of conscious experience.[46] At an elementary level there is what may be called daily experience, which includes the use of language. At higher levels, in addition to scientific activity and the practical applications of knowledge (which I shall discuss later), one finds the social and political dimensions of life, as well as poetry, the arts, and religion—in short, what Ricoeur calls the "totality" of human experience. This extraordinary diversity is nonetheless subjectively perceived and experienced as a unified and global mental process.

Working out plausible models of this total experience is not yet within the reach of the neurosciences. But much simpler experimental situations may help us understand how operations that simultaneously involve several distinct modalities—visual perception, semantic memory, motor action—are unified in the execution of a given task. This is the case, for example, with a famous cognitive test of color-naming known as the Stroop task. The subject is asked to name the color of the ink with which a color term is written. Responses are rapid when the word and color coincide; they are slower and require more effort when, for example, the word "blue" is written in red ink. The neural pathways that lead from the written word to its meaning are passed through more rapidly and more automatically than those which lead from the perceived color to the naming of the color. Instinctively, one reads "blue" even if the word is written in red. The like of this happens very often in daily life.[47] Errors are frequent, but with concentrated effort it is possible to avoid them. One quickly learns to say "red" when the word "blue" is written in red ink. The interference of color with meaning requires that distinct modalities be linked together in unanticipated ways in order to produce the correct motor action.

More generally, both monkeys and humans are capable of simultaneously holding different kinds of sensory information in working memory, independently of interfering stimuli. In all such tasks, including Stroop's, the subject makes a conscious effort of synthesis that is sustained for several seconds, even longer. Certain cerebral lesions are known to selectively affect this kind of parallel processing, which requires the integrity of the dorsolateral prefrontal cortex. This set of specific areas within the system of corticothalamic connections and modulatory neurons of the reticular formation is responsible for one of the most characteristic aspects of consciousness, namely the capacity to create a unified synthesis of inner and outer worlds. The prefrontal cortex is therefore essential to the conscious acquisition of knowledge.[48]

Monitoring, Testing, Planning

When we are awake, we pass a great part of our conscious life remembering the past and speculating about the future. This is true of all human beings, no matter what their education or social position. Consciousness gives access to the past, present, and future though two sorts of cognitive process: simulation, by means of which internal models of external reality are generated, and testing, by which their adequacy, or fit with reality, is judged. This test of truth, as it may well be called, engages neural systems that monitor the flow of information, supply context, and detect inconsistencies with stored memories.[49] These two processes—the simulation and testing of reality—can be seen more generally as supervisory[50] or executive functions that include decisionmaking, goal-directed behavior, and planning. As one might expect, lesions of the frontal lobe have grave consequences for these functions. Three examples will serve to illustrate this point.

Certain patients suffering from neurological disturbances exhibit bizarre deficits. Presented with objects such as a fork, a knife, a glass, and a bottle of water, they seize them at once and use them without being asked to do so. François Lhermitte, the neurologist who discovered this phenomenon, named it "utilization behavior."[51] The patient imitates the experimenter even when his behavior is socially inappropriate—going to sleep upon entering a bedroom in the middle of the day, for example. These subjects have lost the ability to consciously simulate and check reality with reference to a definite plan.

Certain lesions of the frontal lobe can disorganize daily behaviors, such as preparing breakfast or brushing one's teeth. Consider the example of preparing coffee, a task that involves several levels of control.[52] Patients suffering from frontal lesions consistently make errors, typically omissions (they forget to add milk or sugar) and inappropriate substitutions (they put butter or salt in the cup rather than coffee); what is more, they persevere in these things, repeating earlier mistakes. Failing to select actions suited to the end in view, they are unable to translate a deliberate plan into reality.

Certain frontal patients also display a remarkable incapacity to explain the sources of their memories. Factual information is correctly recalled, but frequently in an inaccurate context. Unable to distinguish plausible memories from implausible ones, the patient makes things up. ("In the mountains there was a shipwreck," one such patient claimed, "which despite the avalanche welcomed the snow like a dog, so much so that it resembled a naval helicopter in the middle of the ocean.")[53] Here again, the ability to make coherent use of stored knowledge is severely impaired.

Both elements of conscious experience—synthesizing different kinds of sensory information and actively testing the result against reality—require the integrity of the cerebral cortex and, more specifically, the prefrontal areas.

The Neuronal Self

The synthesis and testing of sensory information depends not only on the outside world but also on the inner world of recollections stored in memory. Subjective experience makes constant reference to an "I" that is constructed out of the ongoing perception of one's own body and recollection of one's own past. Certain specialized neural structures selectively take part in maintaining the awareness of self. In 1914 the neurologist Joseph Babinski discovered the remarkable case of a patient suffering from a lesion of the right hemisphere covering the somatosensory areas that had left him hemiplegic. Quite astonishingly, however, the patient refused to admit the reality of his paralysis. Babinski coined the term "anosognosia" to denote the denial of a severe loss of bodily control. Not only did the patient not notice the peripheral incapacity resulting from the lesion, he actually claimed it did not exist, reproaching his doctor for exaggeration and accusing him of lying. In some patients there is evidence of interference with the normal function of perceptual pathways as a result of sensory deficits that may explain this phenomenon. An alternative explanation is that damage to the pathways connecting the left and right hemispheres of the brain via the corpus callosum prevents the one from learning of an injury to the other. Other interpretations are possible as well.[54]

Lesions of the parietal lobe have been discovered that cause the opposite dissociation. In this case the "egocentric" perception of one's own body is preserved, but the "allocentric" perception of one's body in extrapersonal space is disturbed. Recent research has uncovered persuasive evidence that there exists a neural basis for self-awareness.[55]

Behavioral evidence of a subjective sense of self in monkeys can be confirmed only indirectly and will, in any case, always be open to doubt. But even here a considerable amount of experimental evidence points to the existence of neural correlates of self-awareness. Recordings of individual cells in the superior temporal sulcus show that these neurons are activated by gestures and sounds produced by another monkey (or by the experimenter), but are not activated by the same stimuli when these are produced by the monkey itself.[56] Similarly, in the rear part of the anterior cingulate cortex and adjacent medial prefrontal areas, cells have been discovered that become active immediately *before* the production of movements initiated by the monkey.[57] These cells may be involved in the neuronal representation of self-determined goals in the planning of actions in primates and humans.[58]

The Neuronal Workspace

The foregoing makes it clear that Condillac's conception of the self as a "collection of sensations" acquired exclusively through experience must be abandoned. A more promising alternative is to look for evidence of the "grouped states" of neurons postulated by Spencer and the neural bases of what Lamarck called "inner feeling."

The theory that Stanislas Dehaene, Michel Kerszberg, and I have proposed, which I shall refer to here and in what follows as the neuronal workspace hypothesis,[59] does not aim at solving the problem of consciousness. Nor does it pretend to account for all of the experimentally identified characteristics of consciousness. In its present form the hypothesis deals with neither the conscious milieu nor the multiple states of consciousness, although investigation is already under way in both these directions. Instead it constitutes a modest attempt, using a very simple network architecture, to model the independent processing of a great variety of signals passing through distinct parallel pathways as well as their integration in a "unified field" (in John Searle's phrase) or a common "workspace" (Bernard Baars's term). Searle has distinguished two different approaches to the study of consciousness: models based on fundamental physiological elements (or "building blocks") and unified-field models. My colleagues and I have sought to reconcile the two by accounting for the integrative aspects of Ey's "field of consciousness" on the basis of elementary building blocks. Rather than concentrate on the biophysics of the conscious milieu alone, the model we have proposed treats both the integration and the differentiation of consciousness.

This novel formulation belongs to the tradition of neuronal models described earlier in connection with delayed-response tasks that mobilize the prefrontal cortex. Nonetheless, it incorporates several new structural elements. On the one hand, the neuronal workspace hypothesis differs from the rather abstract approach based on complexity theory that Giulio Tononi and Gerald Edelman have developed.[60] On the other, it diverges from the somewhat simplistic reductionism of Francis Crick and Christof Koch, who have argued that 40 Hz waves constitute the neural correlates of consciousness. Neither of these models (nor, as far as I am aware, any other model) specifies a detailed neuronal network architecture capable of carrying out cognitive tasks (such as the Stroop color-naming task) that require a conscious effort. The one we have proposed is simple yet realistic.

The central proposition of the already quite venerable workspace hypothesis, recently revived and modified by Baars, is that two main computational spaces can be distinguished in the brain. The first is a processing network composed of parallel, distributed, and functionally specific processors. These processors are in competition with one another and exhibit a great diversity, operating upon primary sensory and motor stimuli, the contents of long-term memory (including a semantic database), the self and subjective personal experience, and systems of attention and evaluation involving motivation, rewards, and, in a general way, the emotions.

The second computational space corresponds to a global workspace consisting of a distributed set of excitatory cortical neurons that are very richly interconnected. These neurons, with their long axonal processes, establish horizontal connections within the same cerebral hemisphere and, through the corpus callosum, between hemispheres. The cerebral cortex, as we have seen, has a stratified structure whose neuronal composition varies from one layer to another. The pyramidal cells of layers II and III (together with some neurons in layers V and VI) possess particularly long axons that fan out within one or both hemispheres (Figures 18A and 18B).[61]

By hypothesis, these neurons play a privileged role in the workspace. The fact that the pyramidal neurons of layers II and III are particularly

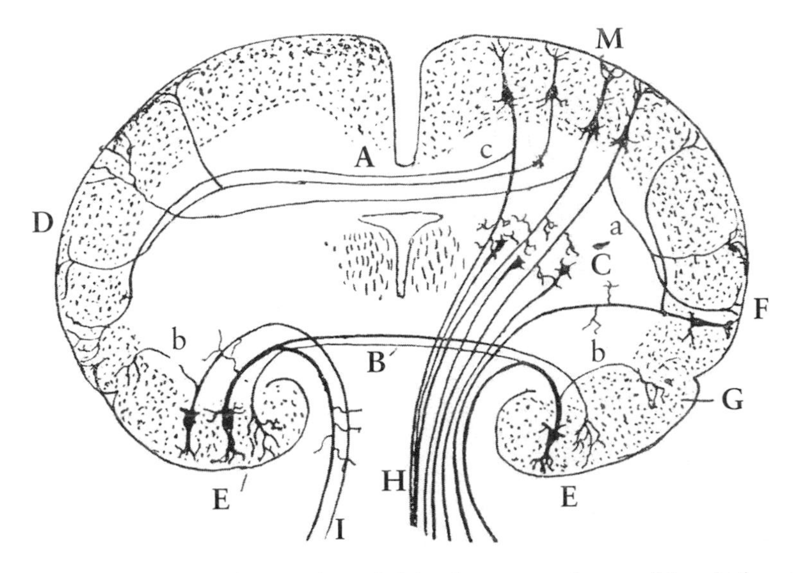

Figure 18A. A diagram by Ramón y Cajal, who suggested a possible role for what he called "association fibers" in "higher mental phenomena." These fibers connect different territories of the cerebral cortex, not only within a single hemisphere (a, b) but also between hemispheres (A, B).

abundant in the prefrontal, dorsolateral, and inferoparietal cortical areas makes it possible to establish a topology of differential patterns of regional activation that, in principle, can be detected using brain imaging techniques. And owing to the vertical interconnections that I mentioned earlier among cortical neurons, principally those of layers V and VI, and the neurons of the thalamus, this long-range intracortical connectivity may be further reinforced by long-range connections among the thalamic neurons themselves.

The model suggests, moreover, that within the corticothalamic system, during a task requiring conscious effort and sustained attention, the workspace neurons are spontaneously and jointly activated, forming discrete but variable spatiotemporal patterns. These global prerepresentations, as we call them, create mutual interconnections between multiple cerebral processors throughout the workspace that are modulated by attention and vigilance signals, and selected as representations by reward signals (Figure 19).

The workspace and processor neurons are postulated, then, to be reciprocally linked with each other, exhibiting both top-down and

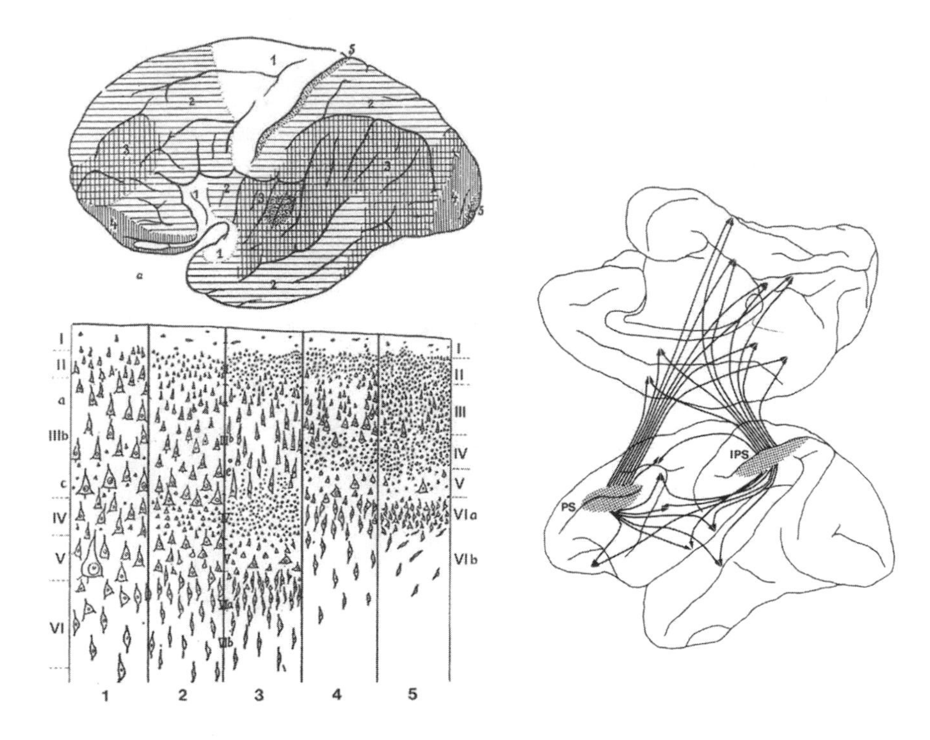

Figure 18B. *Left:* C. F. von Economo distinguished five types of cellular organization in the cerebral cortex, noting different proportions of pyramidal cells and granular (inhibitory) cells in the six cortical layers. Type 2, extremely rich in pyramidal neurons in layers II and III, is widely distributed throughout the frontal and parietotemporal areas. *Right:* Reciprocal long-range connections issuing from the principal sulcus of the frontal cortex (PS) and of the intraparietal sulcus (IPS) and their various projections.

Opposite page

Figure 19. Schematic representation of the neuronal workspace hypothesis. *Top:* Five principal types of relatively autonomous and specialized processors involved in perception, motricity, attention, evaluation, and long-term memory are shown as connected throughout the brain by the long-axon neurons of the workspace. *Bottom:* During an effortful conscious task, an association between the groups of neurons in the various processors operates in a top-down manner through the activation of a specific population of workspace neurons—principally, but not exclusively, from layers II and III of the frontal cortex.

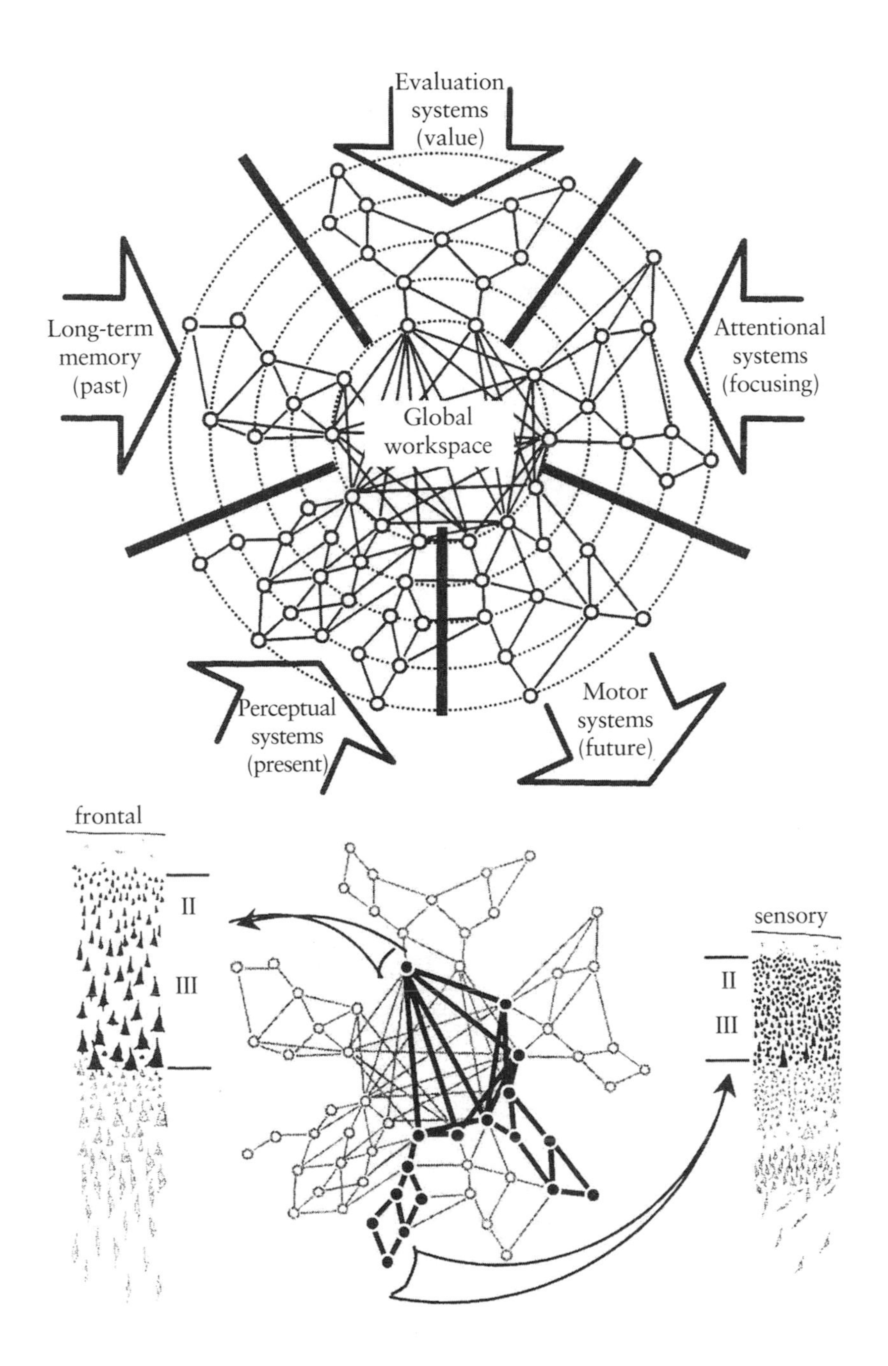

Evaluation systems (value)
Long-term memory (past)
Attentional systems (focusing)
Global workspace
Perceptual systems (present)
Motor systems (future)
frontal
II
III
sensory
II
III

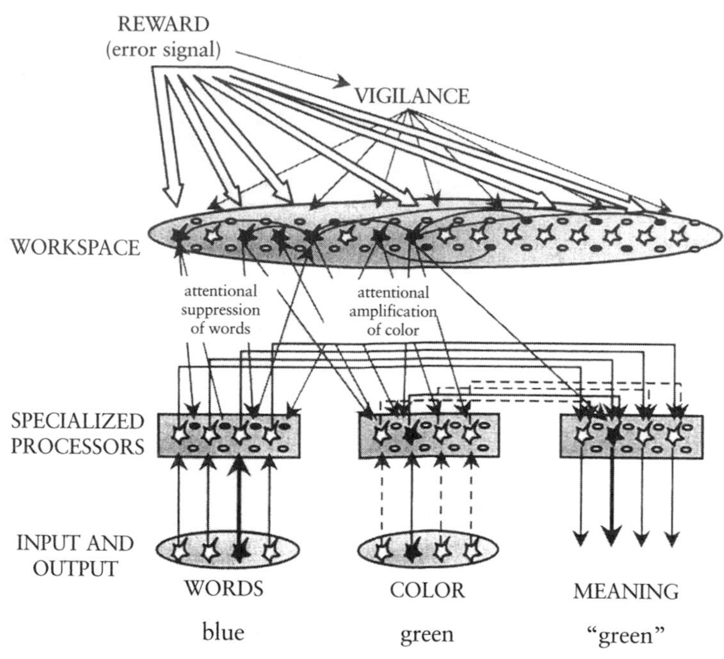
REWARD
(error signal)
VIGILANCE
WORKSPACE
attentional suppression of words
attentional amplification of color
SPECIALIZED PROCESSORS
INPUT AND OUTPUT
WORDS
COLOR
MEANING
blue
green
"green"

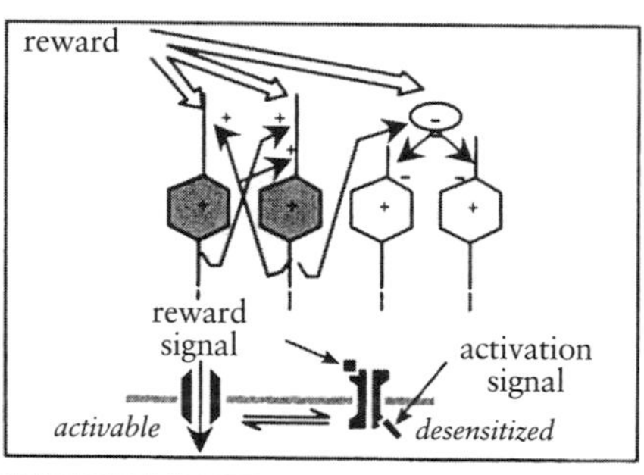
reward
reward signal
activation signal
activable
desensitized

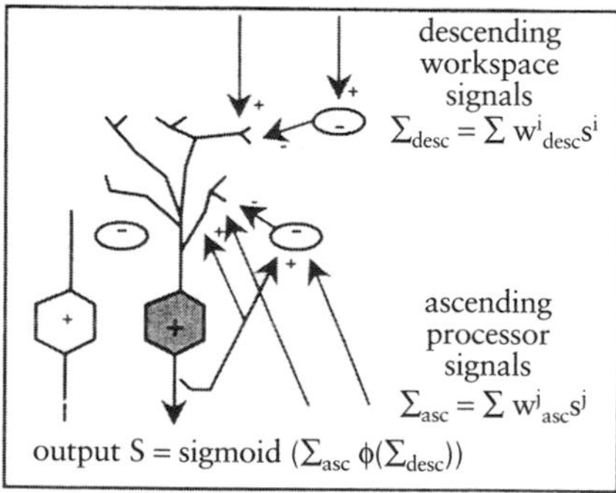
descending workspace signals
$\Sigma_{desc} = \Sigma w^i_{desc} s^i$
ascending processor signals
$\Sigma_{asc} = \Sigma w^j_{asc} s^j$
output S = sigmoid $(\Sigma_{asc}\ \phi(\Sigma_{desc}))$

bottom-up connectivity (though not symmetry). The processor neurons—like those which mediate sensory inputs—project upward to the interconnected sets of neurons that make up the global workspace. Conversely, at any given moment, though solely in a downward direction, the representations of the workspace selectively channel the activity of a subset of processor neurons (Figures 19 and 20). By hypothesis, this top-down control is modulated by descending projections linking workspace neurons to more peripheral processor neurons (which may be cortical, or thalamic, or both).[62] These projections may selectively amplify (or arrest) the ascending inputs of the processor neurons, thus mobilizing at any given moment a specific set of processors in the workspace, while inhibiting the contribution of others (Figure 20).[63]

A pre-representation that has been selected as a representation within the workspace may remain active, in an autonomous manner, and resist changes in peripheral stimulation so long as it receives positive reward signals. If, however, signals are negative or attention is no longer sustained, this pre-representation can be revised or replaced, through a process of trial and error, by another discrete combination of workspace neurons. Nonselected patterns are suppressed by long-range inhibitory connections; but they can be reactivated if circumstances change, either independently or as part of a new combination of neurons. Computer simulations of the dynamics of neuronal activity in the workspace (Figure 21)[64] produce a constant flow of coherent individual episodes, of variable duration, that serve to test new combinatory hypotheses. These episodes may constitute a neural embodiment of what the cognitive scientist Zenon Pylyshyn calls "compositional" or "creative" activity.[65] They also constitute a short-term mechanism of epigenetic neuroselection, or "mental Darwinism" at

Opposite page

Figure 20. Neuronal network model of the Stroop task. Each unit represents a group of neurons, for example a cortical column of about 100 neurons (see Figure 4A). The Stroop task consists in naming the color of the ink in which a color word is written. Here "blue" is written in green. The subject instinctively says "blue" and must then make an effort to correct the error. To say "green" he must first identify the error through the reward system and then mobilize workspace neurons that, by means of a descending (top-down) signal, will select a specific group of neurons mobilized by the correct ascending (bottom-up) signal.

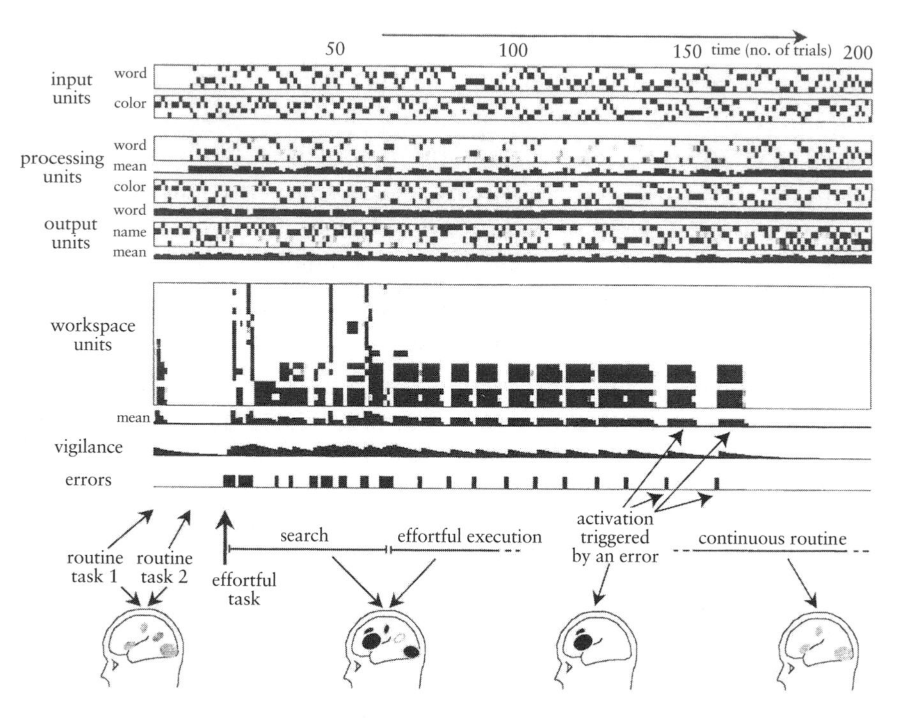

Figure 21. Simulation of the activity of workspace neurons and processors involved in the Stroop task. The simple task of naming the color of the ink when the ink matches the meaning of the word (routine 1) mobilizes word and color processors but very few (if any) workspace neurons. When the word and the ink do not match, these neurons are mobilized by a task requiring effort that is carried out by trial and error until the word processor is suppressed in favor of the color processor. The schematic drawings illustrate the possible distribution of cortical areas activated in the different stages of learning.

the level of the brain, by variation and selection.[66] The neuronal architecture we have suggested includes, as I noted earlier, a Darwinian-style diversity generator that operates within the unified field of the conscious workspace.

Attentional circuits play an essential role in exploratory behavior and in the search by trial and error for positive rewards from the external world. They have far-reaching consequences for the survival of a given animal species to the extent that they serve to select and amplify a relevant input channel under certain critical circumstances.[67] In the neuronal workspace model, attentional circuits are assigned a crucial supplementary role in the spontaneous production and selection of workspace representations on the basis of long-term memories.

Additional circuits could be added to the neural architecture I have described, forming an autoevaluation loop of the sort already contained in models of two well-known cognitive tasks that involve the prefrontal cortex: the Wisconsin card-sorting task and the Tower of London test.[68] The neurons constituting this internal loop would be tacitly—but nonetheless consciously—activated by the actual contents of the workspace, without requiring direct interaction with the external environment. Switching internal attentional circuits on (or off) would thus selectively amplify (or eliminate) signals from certain subsets of memories stored in processor neurons. In combination with evaluation systems, they would generate high-level intentional representations within the workspace that might support an elementary kind of voluntary behavior. In this case voluntary decisionmaking would result from the synthesis of autoevaluations of concurrent, if not also alternative, programs of action. The day when the autonomy of consciousness can be given a neuronal interpretation may not be as far off as is generally supposed.

Experimental Predictions

Anatomy

The anatomical foundation of the neuronal workspace hypothesis is a dense horizontal network of corticocortical connections, interhemispheric connections passing through the corpus callosum, and possibly long-distance intrathalamic connections. In the monkey there is direct anatomical evidence for the existence of reciprocal connections linking the dorsolateral prefrontal cortex with the premotor cortex, superior temporal, inferior parietal, anterior and posterior cingulate cortices, as well as with more deeply embedded structures that include the neostriatum and the parahippocampal formation.[69] A similar, still richer connectivity exists in humans.

Lesions of the prefrontal cortex do not give rise to losses of consciousness as striking as those created by thalamic lesions, but they do seriously affect, as I have said, the coherent and sustained ordering of information as well as the production of new strategies, planning, and intentional behavior. The prefrontal cortex is therefore postulated to contain a large population of workspace neurons. With regard to anosognosia, the deficit described at the beginning of this chapter, and to the disconnection syndromes discovered by the neurobiologist Roger Sperry in patients exhibiting interhemispheric lesions of the corpus callosum,[70] a simple interpretation may be proposed: in these subjects, the connections between workspace neurons have been interrupted, thereby destroying the unity of conscious experience. Brain imaging studies of such patients could be used to test a critical prediction of the neuronal workspace hypothesis, namely that the contribution of the prefrontal cortices of each hemisphere in relevant cognitive tasks is altered as a consequence of the injury.

Workspace neurons, which unify conscious representations through the long-range horizontal prolongations of their axons, are also postulated to mobilize vertical corticothalamic loops throughout the cerebral cortex.[71] Electrophysiological recordings may therefore be expected to demonstrate the contribution of these loops to conscious processing of stimuli, by contrast with the nonconscious propagation of signals by processor neurons within the loops.[72] In all these cases, nonlinear processes underlie the discontinuous character of both workspace representations and the various states of the conscious milieu. The challenge to experimental neuroscience will be to distinguish the activation patterns typical of neuronal populations involved in creating the representations of the workspace from those involved in maintaining the stability of the conscious milieu and regulating its state transitions. It may plausibly be conjectured that the phase synchronization over long distances that I discussed in the last chapter is responsible for orchestrating this large-scale integration, but there is not yet any direct proof that the selective alteration of synchronization produces changes in conscious behavior.[73]

Cerebral Imaging and States of Consciousness

The neuronal workspace model was designed to account for tasks that require a conscious effort on the part of an awake and alert subject. Arousal and vigilance are marked by major changes in brain function that control the subject's capacity to respond to internal and external events. Cerebral imaging studies[74] now confirm indications of the central role played by the thalamus, the reticular formation (pontomesencephalic tegmentum), and the anterior cingulate cortex, whose global activity decreases in passing from a state of relaxed wakefulness to slow-wave sleep. (A similar correlation is observed in subjects placed under general anesthesia: progressively deeper states first extinguish the activity of the cerebral cortex, causing disturbances to speech; and then that of the thalamus, resulting in complete loss of consciousness.)[75] Conversely, the transition from sleep to waking is marked by activation of the prefrontal cortex and of the parietal cortices.[76] Focusing attention over short periods of time—on auditory stimuli, for example—leads to increased activity in the prefrontal cortex (frontopolar, dorsolateral, and orbitofrontal), the parietal cortex, and the secondary auditory cortex (superior temporal gyrus), without producing any significant interference with the operation of the arousal network, which has its principal source in the thalamus. The control of sleep and waking and the regulation of attention involve different sets of processors.

The neuronal workspace hypothesis yields a critical prediction in the domain of brain imaging, namely that areas activated in the course of performing tasks requiring conscious effort are correlated with areas possessing a sizable share of neurons having long-range connections that link distinct cortical areas within a single hemisphere or between hemispheres. As we have seen, the cell bodies of these long-axon neurons are present in particularly dense concentrations in the dorsolateral prefrontal cortex. Indeed, brain imaging experiments reveal that the dorsolateral prefrontal cortex and the anterior cingulate cortex are activated during effortful cognitive tasks such as the Stroop task, and that the degree of activation varies as a function of the difficulty of the operation.[77] When the performance of the task becomes routine, the activity in these two areas decreases, but it immediately reappears if a new situation presents itself.[78] The anterior cingulate cortex is also activated when the subject makes a mistake.[79] These spatio-temporal patterns of activity agree with computer simulations of the neuronal workspace model.[80]

The model makes the further claim that a selection takes place among workspace neurons and among the specialized processors that they mobilize. In confirmation of this prediction, brain imaging demonstrates that when a subject brings his attention to bear on a given sensory channel (hearing, for example), neural activity increases in this channel but decreases in parts of the brain responsible for processing information from other channels.[81]

Yet another critical prediction of the neuronal workspace model turns out to be consistent with the experimental evidence. If one compares the cerebral images of subjects performing cognitive tasks requiring conscious effort, with reference to different aspects of executive control involving perception, the selection of responses, working memory, and problem solving, one finds very similar patterns of activation in the frontal lobe and especially the cingulate cortex, the remaining zones (medial and orbital) being largely unaffected (Figure 22).[82] On the other hand, more detailed analysis using functional imaging of the territories involved in tasks mobilizing working memory has made it possible to distinguish the selection of responses (area 46 of the dorsolateral prefrontal cortex) from the maintenance of items in working memory (prefrontal area 8).[83]

While the available imaging data largely agree with the neuronal workspace hypothesis, they also illustrate its limits and the need for more careful investigation of the neural territories usually subsumed under the umbrella term "frontal lobe," as well as a closer examination of the precise groups of neurons, particularly workspace neurons, that are mobilized by a particular task.

The Chemistry of Consciousness

From the point of view of pharmacology and molecular biology, the model we have proposed makes the interesting prediction that workspace neurons are the direct (or indirect) targets of neuromodulatory systems that globally monitor the inputs associated with vigilance, sleep, attention, and reward. As we have seen, several modulatory neurotransmitters (acetylcholine, noradrenaline, and serotonin) are crucially involved in the regulation of states of consciousness of the brain, as well as the classical excitatory and inhibitory neurotransmitters (glutamate and GABA, respectively). In the waking state, levels of glutamate, noradrenaline, and acetylcholine are high. Conversely, the onset of sleep is facilitated by GABA and accompanied by a decline in

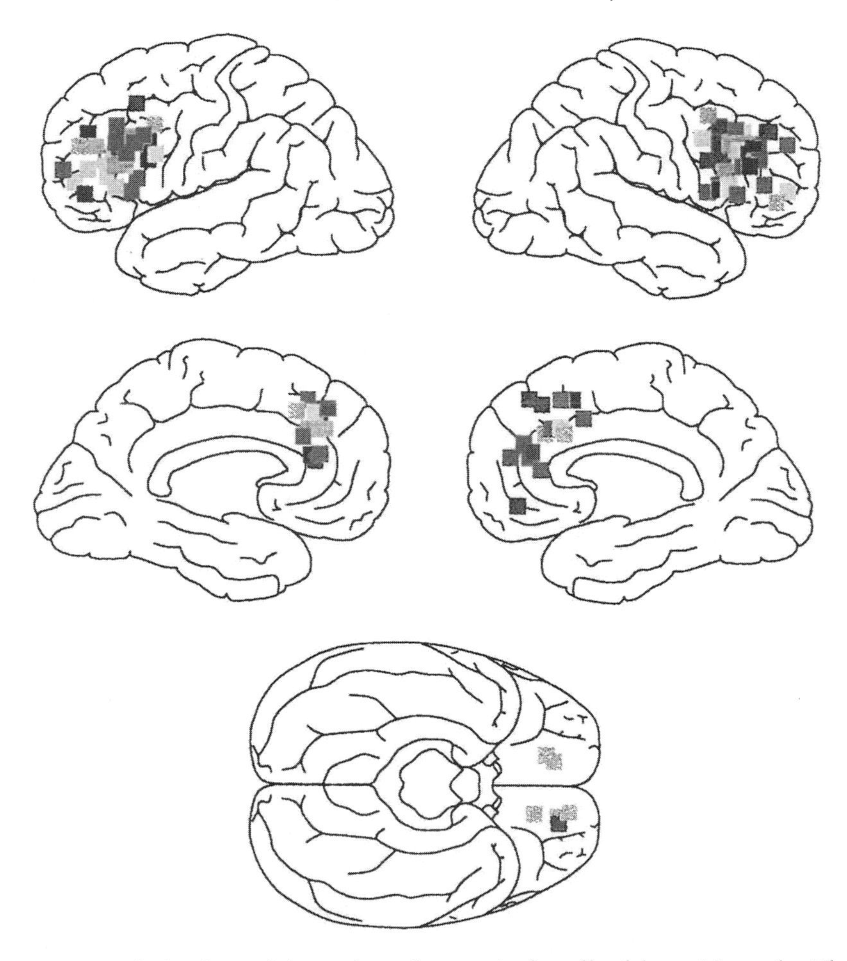

Figure 22. Activations of the prefrontal cortex in five effortful cognitive tasks. The peaks of activity recorded in each of the tasks studied—response conflicts, novelty, capacity and duration of working memory, perceptual difficulty—are shown by squares in different shades of gray.

the levels of these neurotransmitters, with the exception of a sudden increase in acetylcholine in the early phases of REM sleep. Attention also selectively mobilizes the noradrenaline neurons of the locus coeruleus.

A peptide called hypocretin has recently been shown to play a critical role in the regulation of the waking state by stimulating the firing of nerve cells in the locus coeruleus. Its absence—as a consequence, for example, of a genetic defect (in mice and dogs)—produces behavioral disturbances that resemble the illness that in humans is called narcolepsy, in which wide-awake patients suddenly fall asleep.[84]

Another dramatic switch from wakefulness to a nonconscious state is caused by general anesthesia. Surgical concentrations of anesthetic agents such as N_2O, halothane, ketamine, and propofol are thought to alter the transport of ions through channels whose gates are controlled by neurotransmitter receptors for glutamate, GABA, and even acetylcholine. Ketamine, for example, is supposed to block the excitatory receptor channel for glutamate, and halothane to potentiate inhibitory currents from particular potassium channels or GABA receptors. It is not yet known if these very general effects on the receptors and channels of the brain as a whole are responsible for the loss of consciousness, or if these pharmacological agents act more specifically on molecular targets present in neuromodulatory neurons, for example in the brain stem.[85]

Dopamine neurons, as we saw in the last chapter, play an essential role in reward systems and in the selection of workspace representations. Pharmacological agents that bind to specific receptors for dopamine (and acetylcholine) affect—both in the monkey[86] and in the rat[87]—the performance of effortful tasks that mobilize the prefrontal cortex in a way analogous to what occurs in the Wisconsin card-sorting test and the Stroop task.

Similarly, current research on pathological mutations in humans (as well as in genetically modified animals in which, for example, the functional—notably allosteric—properties of certain subtypes of neurotransmitter receptors have been modified) may help identify the cerebral circuits and molecular mechanisms involved in conscious awareness. To take an example related to our work on nicotinic receptors,[88] the contribution of acetylcholine to the modulation of consciousness is suggested by a consistent and detailed set of experimental observations. These include the regulation of attention by nicotine; the regulation of rapid eye movements (during sleep or dreaming) by cholinergic neurons;[89] and the stimulation of hallucinations (which typically gain access to the workspace by escaping the mechanisms that selectively regulate attention) by muscarinic antagonists of acetylcholine.[90] Similarly, certain substances having a modulating effect on the cholinergic system also make it possible to alleviate the deficits in the conscious retrieval of recent memories that accompany aging and Alzheimer's disease.[91]

A very specific and particularly revealing example involves a genetic, autosomal, nocturnal, and dominant form of epilepsy that affects the frontal lobe. One of its characteristic features is an abrupt change in the state of consciousness during sleep. The subject suddenly awakes and violently tosses and turns, exhibiting facial expressions of intense fear—and then falls back to sleep again. Teams led by the neurologist S. F. Berkovic and the molecular biologist Ortrud Steinlein have recently discovered that this very particular kind of epilepsy is caused by discrete mutations occurring within two distinct genes that code for subunits ($\alpha 4$ and $\beta 2$)[92] of a neuronal receptor for nicotine that possesses a very high affinity for acetylcholine.[93] As a consequence of these mutations, the conformational transitions of these allosteric receptors are modified. The loss of consciousness that occurs during episodes of frontal lobe nocturnal epilepsy seems to be directly or indirectly linked to the modulation of these receptors by endogenous acetylcholine. It seems plausible to suppose that the nocturnal occurrence of such epileptic fits, after the patient falls asleep, may be related to variations in the level of endogenous acetylcholine during the transitions between waking, slow-wave sleep, and REM sleep—a chemical change first noticed by Herbert Jasper in the 1960s.[94]

Hallucinations and Retrieval of Memories

Another element of the neuronal workspace hypothesis, which has not yet been formalized, has to do with the reportability of conscious experience. The ability to explicitly refer to personal subjective experience is an essential aspect of the definition of consciousness and has particular relevance for the experimental investigation of subjective states, which the subject can describe in one way or another—the simplest being to press a button. The possibility of giving such an account depends on the retrieval of memories of past events.

Hallucinations differ from the conscious recollection of the past in that they spontaneously and involuntarily occur without specific external stimulation. Hallucinations are frequent in schizophrenic patients, and often contribute to the diagnosis of this condition. In the case of one patient who had never undergone pharmacological treatment and who suffered from both auditory and visual hallucinations (he reported seeing heads detached from bodies rolling about in space, talking to him, and giving him orders),[95] brain imaging revealed the activation of areas responsible for visual association and for the hearing of spoken language, as well as a complex set of subcortical networks. Quite interestingly, though not surprisingly, the prefrontal cortex—generally supposed to be the principal target of schizophrenia—remained silent. On this point as on many others, hallucinations differ from the conscious voluntary retrieval of long-term memories. Conversely, they exhibit similarities with certain aspects of REM sleep, raising the possibility that hallucinations amount to uncontrolled intrusions of REM sleep into the conscious workspace of the alert subject.

The voluntary and conscious retrieval of long-term memories has been the object of intense research since the end of the nineteenth century and the first attempts by Hermann Ebbinghaus, in 1885, to apply the experimental method to the analysis of human memory.[96] In these early experiments (of which he was the first subject), Ebbinghaus presented a series of items to be memorized, for example a series of nonsense syllables. He was able then to quantitatively measure the number of items memorized. Frederic C. Bartlett, in his classic monograph *Remembering* (1932), went further in this direction. He read his subjects a story (one was an old Indian legend known as "The War of the Ghosts") and then asked them to try to tell the story in their turn, at fixed intervals of time. Bartlett noted that the recollection of the story varied with the number of retellings. He concluded from this that recollection is an imaginative reconstruction of past events, which may include false memories.[97] The occurrence of inaccuracies and distortions suggests that memory is not a simple matter of retrieval, of direct recall, but the result instead of internal testing and selection among alternative accounts, in the course of which reactivated memories may be unconsciously biased by preexisting knowledge or by the emotional resonance of actual memories of past experience. Memories may even be deliberately modified—revised—through the incorporation of new information meant to strengthen their plausibility. We know, moreover, that lesions of the frontal lobe alter the capacity for conscious recollection. All this is consistent with the neuronal workspace model.

Recent brain imaging studies confirm the essential role of the frontal lobe in memory recall. A great many experimental observations had pointed to the involvement of a very old region of the cerebral cortex called the hippocampus. Early imaging studies yielded conflicting results, however, revealing variable and nonreproducible patterns of activation that involved the prefrontal cortex as well as the hippocampal formation. In some cases no activation of the hippocampus was recorded; in others the prefrontal cortex remained silent. Daniel Schachter and his colleagues then realized that the brain images differed depending on whether or not memory retrieval had been successful.[98] From this they concluded that intentional recollection—the effort to search for explicit memories—consistently activates the prefrontal cortex (especially in the right hemisphere), whereas the hippocampus is activated only if conscious recollection has been successful.

The neuronal workspace hypothesis suggests a possible interpretation of these observations. The workspace neurons located in the prefrontal cortex test internal hypotheses, or pre-representations, that furnish a context for the reactivation by the hippocampus of memories stored in areas of the cerebral cortex directly (or indirectly) linked to sensory perception and motor action.[99] When suitable memories are found—that is, when internal evaluation yields a positive reward—they are then integrated as part of the representations of the workspace via the hippocampus. This interpretation is consistent with Bartlett's view that retrieving a memory trace involves "an effort to understand"—a reconstruction of a past event that consists in testing hypotheses about information that has only partially been retained. In other words, the recall of stored knowledge is never complete, but is systematically biased by the process of recollection itself.

An animal model of the top-down search for memory traces has been devised in the monkey.[100] Electrophysiological recordings of individual neurons in the inferior temporal cortex show that they are activated by signals descending from the prefrontal cortex as part of executive control of memory retrieval, in the absence of ascending inputs (Figure 23). Moreover, these descending signals are not transmitted

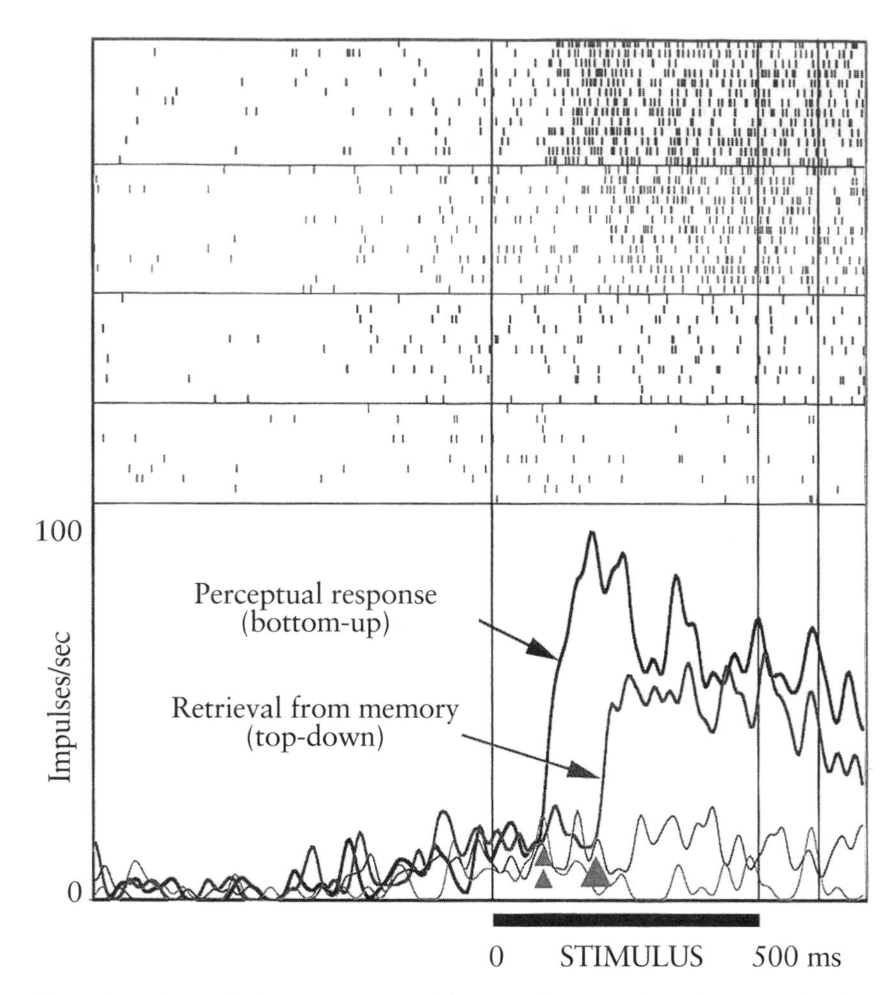

Figure 23. Control of memory retrieval by a monkey's prefrontal cortex. The four panels in the upper part of the figure correspond to cellular recordings of activity in the inferior temporal cortex, midway between the visual areas and the prefrontal cortex. The lines at the bottom represent the same results in impulses per second. The monkey carries out a task under two different conditions: (1) perceptually, in close contact with the external world (bottom-up response), and (2) by retrieval from memory under the control of the prefrontal cortex (top-down response). Note that the same neuron may be activated in both a top-down and a bottom-up manner, and that the top-down response involves a delay of about 100 milliseconds.

through a subcortical—for example, thalamic—pathway. In keeping with the neuronal workspace hypothesis, these signals propagate horizontally through long-range connections that link distinct areas within and across hemispheres.[101]

Finally, the successful retrieval of long-term memories requires, at some stage, a decision. How the brain arrives at a decision concerning an evoked memory or even a perceived event, and how it acts upon it, is still barely understood. But recent recordings in alert monkeys reveal that simple perceptual decisions about, for example, tactile stimuli or sounds or ambiguous images (such as the image in which either the profile of Freud or a naked woman can be discerned) activate particular sets of neurons known as "decision cells." Interestingly, again, these cells belong principally to the prefrontal cortex.[102]

Conscious Melody

Delayed-response tasks, memory retrieval experiments, and other cognitive tests involving conscious planning unfold sequentially over time and give rise to fairly brief and simple temporal sequences that may be thought of as melodies. While it is true that certain tasks (such as Stroop's color-naming test) can be modeled by computer simulations,[103] it nonetheless must be admitted that we are still a long way from having a neural model of the conscious organization of knowledge—of what is ordinarily called thinking or reasoning. We do know, however, that the brain is capable of producing, selecting, and retaining items of knowledge, and that in principle it can also perform computations on these mental representations, evaluating them and linking them together in a sort of melody that is constantly tested by comparing inner and outer worlds—the reality of present, past, and future events—with reference to a neuronal self. I shall develop this notion of a workspace melody further in the final two chapters.

Brain imaging studies have shown that a dramatic change occurs when, in the course of carrying out a given task, the subject shifts from a perceptual mode that is undemanding but prone to error to a more accurate deductive mode requiring greater effort. The psychologist Olivier Houdé and his colleagues have observed that the switch to logical thought is accompanied by a very clear swing from a posterior

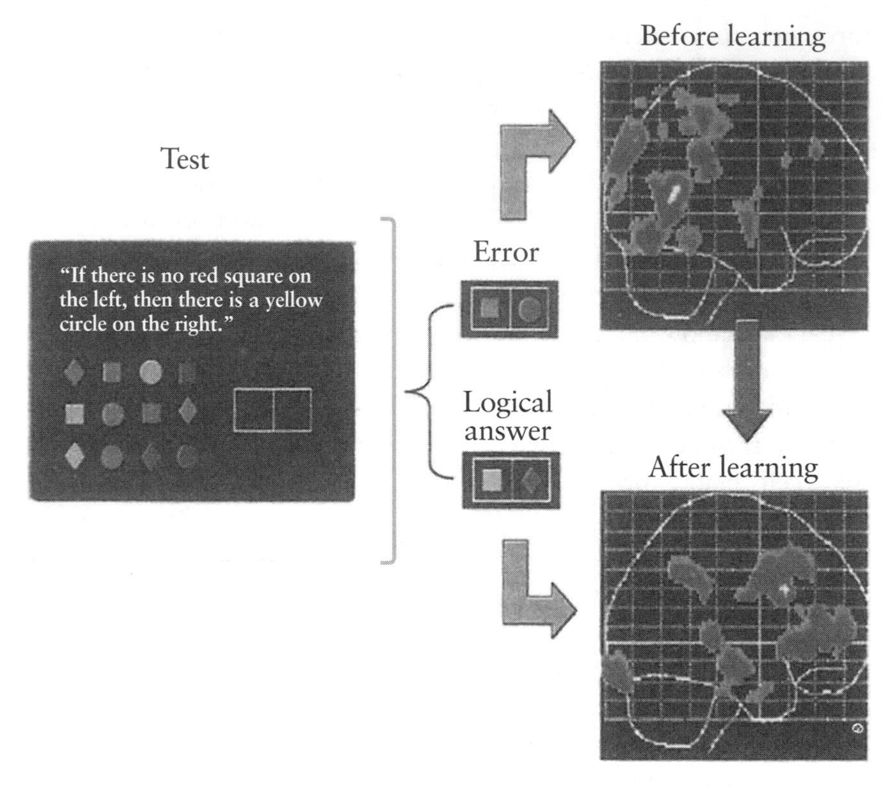

Figure 24. Brain images obtained during the performance of an effortless perceptual task and an effortful logical task. The logical task consists in responding "true" or "false" to the question: "If there is no red square on the left, then there is a yellow circle on the right." In passing from the perceptual to the logical mode, a mostly posterior pattern of activations (visual area) is replaced by a mostly anterior pattern including the left prefrontal cortex (Broca's area), the insula, and the supplementary motor area.

pattern of activation in the brain including ventral and dorsal visual pathways to a left prefrontal pattern involving notably the medial frontal gyrus, Broca's area, the anterior insula, and the presupplementary motor area (Figure 24).[104]

Any serious theory of consciousness must undertake to explain how this coherent flow of sensations and ideas comes to be orchestrated in such a way that propositions can be rationally examined and access obtained to formal truth (described by Kant as consisting in the agreement of knowledge with itself, through abstraction from differences among individual mental objects).[105] We are still far from knowing the answer to this question.

Looking to the future, scientific research on the neural architectures underlying consciousness and the testing of reality will profit from further study of behavioral development from birth through early childhood. Several successive steps have been distinguished in the appearance of consciousness in the human infant.[106] An initial state of minimal consciousness in the newborn is characterized by first-person representations and expectations concerning objects (pacifiers, for example) that make no reference to an explicit sense of self, even if the distinction between oneself and others is clear in the case of imitation behaviors. The newborn is conscious of what he sees, but in an unreflective manner that is oriented toward the present. He is already capable of storing visual images in memory, but he does not remember seeing what he has seen. He immediately engages, however, in the cognitive games that I discussed in the last chapter, and he already shows signs of initiating action.

At the end of the first year, the infant's behavior undergoes profound changes. He is now able to point his finger in the direction of objects and to search for objects that are hidden from view. He is also capable of delayed imitation and of joint attention. What is more, he can now associate two distinct mental representations and simultaneously hold them in working memory, and, more generally, free himself from the repertoire of basic automatic reflexes of early infancy. These things constitute what may be called recursive consciousness. At this stage, the architectures of the neuronal workspace that I have described are established and functional. The child is now capable of successfully performing delayed-response tasks.

An authentic self-consciousness—awareness of an "I"—appears only toward the end of the second year of life, and the use of rules characteristic of a more elaborate reflective consciousness still later, between two and a half and three years.[107] The acquisition of a theory of mind marks the final stage in the development of consciousness in the child.

The neural networks associated with these interlocking phases of the development of consciousness are established in the course of the first years of postnatal life, then, beginning with minimal consciousness, which arises in tandem with the development of closely interconnected processor neurons. This state gives way to recursive consciousness, which is formed when the workspace neurons become integrated with the processors; then to reflective consciousness, which becomes functional with the establishment of autoevaluation networks; and, finally, to a theory of mind, which appears with the development of higher-level autoevaluation networks that incorporate representations of oneself and of others. Plainly these are nothing more than crude hypotheses—but they are a start.

The comparative study of animal behavior suggests that the biological evolution of consciousness may to some extent resemble its development in humans.[108] Animals that are incapable of imitation, such as rats and mice, nonetheless display expectations and are amenable to classical (or instrumental) conditioning. They are capable, albeit with difficulty, of successfully carrying out delayed-response tasks. May they therefore be said to possess a rudimentary consciousness? As the philosopher Thomas Nagel pointed out in a famous article, it will always be difficult—perhaps impossible—to objectively evaluate the subjective states of a bat or a hummingbird.[109] Yet, as we shall see in the next chapter, some insight can be had into the differentiation of conscious space in the course of evolution from the lower mammals to humans by examining the relations among individuals within a social group. In packs of mammals such as wolves and monkeys, for example, imitation may exist in a momentary way without understanding. These animal species may be seen, then, as manifesting a minimal consciousness comparable to that of the human newborn. Chimpanzees, on the other hand, exhibit mutual understanding, recursive consciousness, and, as the mirror test demonstrates, signs of self-consciousness (they are capable, for example, of recognizing that they have a red mark on their forehead when they look at themselves in a mirror).[110] But a theory of mind, together with the recognition of false beliefs, seems to be solely the property of human beings.

There remains, in any case, a very clear difference between these higher primates and man with regard to the quantity of knowledge that they are capable of holding in working memory for purposes of evaluation and planning, which requires the activation of the workspace neurons of the prefrontal cortex. The surface of the prefrontal cortex as a proportion of the neocortex is 7 percent in the dog, 8.5 percent in the lemur, 11.5 percent in the macaque, 17 percent in the chimpanzee, and 29 percent in *Homo sapiens* (see Figure 41 in Chapter 5).[111] It is very tempting to relate this anatomical expansion to the development of consciousness that distinguishes modern humans from their closest living relatives. From chimpanzee to man one observes an increase of at least 70 percent in the possible connections among prefrontal workspace neurons—undeniably a change of the highest importance. As we shall see in connection with the human genome, this expansion may have required only the modification of a limited set of developmental genes active during the formation and differentiation of the neural plate in the first embryonic stages of life.

The evolutionary development of consciousness made it possible to relate new experience to a subjective sense of self and to stored memories of the past. In other words, consciousness integrates the day-to-day flow of information, not only with acquired social and cultural knowledge, but also with the basic behaviors characteristic of the human species that have developed within the constraints of its genetic endowment. It offers the individual an additional way of evaluating truth that is particularly useful for the survival of the species. The organism's ability to test the reality of current "on-line" information against knowledge stored in long-term memory, and to compare recollections with one another, permits the tacit simulation of contemplated behaviors and decisions about future courses of action—all in the space of real psychological time (as little as 100 milliseconds). This makes it possible in turn to avoid behaviors that are often dangerous for the individual and for the species, and leads to the extremely rapid epigenetic acquisition of validated knowledge. In order to achieve maximum efficiency, of course, conscious knowledge must be free of all traces of false memory, errors of recollection, dreams, and hallucinations. Above all, in order to cope with new and unanticipated situations, it must be imaginative.

The imagination introduces an element of novelty in the pre-representations that the subject forms about the world and, by improving the chance of predicting successful outcomes, favors the survival of individuals—and so of the species as well. It needs to be kept in mind that human beings are not only rational individuals. They are also social creatures. As we shall see in Chapter 4, social intercourse offers new possibilities for still more efficiently testing the truth of acquired knowledge.

Knowledge and Social Life 4

The acquisition of knowledge in the earliest stages of human life takes place by means of what I have called cognitive games with the external world. In the course of development these games progressively expand until they fill the part of the brain concerned with the conscious manipulation of mental objects. The child's conception of physical reality is tested through comparison of preliminary internal models ("pre-representations") with the information supplied by the outside world: those models which are confirmed by both external evidence and internal processes of evaluation within the neuronal workspace itself are stabilized as permanent features ("representations") of the developing cognitive apparatus. As we saw in the last chapter, the conscious processing of external information assumes an increasingly reflective character during the course of childhood. Automatic actions are gradually replaced by delayed simulations that depend on tacit computations carried out within individual brains.

How, then, do we decide whether what we perceive and internally represent to ourselves constitutes a faithful and accurate description of the world? Opinions are apt to differ with regard to the nature and significance of common objects and the ordinary events of daily life. I have already mentioned the hallucinations and delusions experienced (even in the absence of external stimuli) by schizophrenics. These persons hear voices that speak to them and about them—the emanations of extraterrestrial powers or supernatural beings, they suppose, the veracity of which it does not occur to them to doubt. They are also susceptible to visual hallucinations of chimerical or monstrous beings. Schizophrenics believe that the voices they hear and the images they see are real and express the truth. How are such claims to be verified? Very often these delusory beliefs are so strong that they resist any attempt at critical examination, either by friends and family or by physicians. Patients not only resist persuasion; they may actually try to conceal their hallucinations in order to avoid being thought mad.

An effective (even if not altogether satisfactory) way of determining the truthfulness of these reports of subjective experience is to refer them to the judgment of a third party, who then moderates a discussion with the others. The usefulness of verbal communication between conscious subjects in helping to resolve such questions highlights the decisive role that language plays in testing the correctness of individual perceptions of the world.

Comparing subjective experience raises another major difficulty of a different sort. I have already mentioned—and I will come back to this point at greater length in a later chapter—the anatomical variability of the brain that exists even among genetically identical individuals. I have furthermore suggested that it may be helpful to conceive of neuronal coding not in terms of precisely reproducible patterns of connectivity, but in terms of functional mappings common to distinct populations of nerve cells distributed throughout the cerebral cortex. Once again we are faced with the old problem: How is it possible for two persons to understand each other despite substantial differences in cerebral organization? How can individuals who have had different experiences in early childhood draw upon the same patterns of functional relationships, or even similar qualia, in such a way that they can efficiently achieve mutual understanding?

In evolutionary terms the price to be paid for the epigenetic development of neuronal networks seems rather high. Moreover, the use of spoken language to communicate representations, meanings, and thoughts, and to test their truth at the social level, raises yet another issue: the diversity of languages. No matter that spoken language is a distinctive characteristic of the human species, the sound patterns employed for purposes of communication may differ strikingly from one community to another. Wittgenstein, in the *Philosophical Investigations,* argued that the use of a word determines its meaning.[1] Is this a sufficient criterion? More generally, can the neurosciences help us understand how knowledge is communicated and how conjectures about the reality of the external world are tested at the social level?

I would like to argue that the use of language in the acquisition and communication of knowledge depends on much more than a simple link between sound and meaning. It involves a pooling of neuronal workspaces and the contextualized sharing of the representations that are created there, as well as their joint selection by the members of the social group.

The Triangle of the Sign

At the turn of the twentieth century two original thinkers profoundly altered our understanding of how human beings communicate by means of spoken language: the American philosopher Charles Sanders Peirce and the Swiss linguist Ferdinand de Saussure. Both reexamined the classical Aristotelian distinction between external object, the mental image that it evokes, and the communication of this image by words.

For Aristotle, the link between thing and concept was natural, being founded on imitation, whereas the relation between sound and concept was arbitrary, the result of tradition. Peirce sought to develop a general theory of signs, or semiotics, that would account for the acquisition and communication of knowledge. The essential problem in his view was to explain how one person can create in the mind of another something equivalent to—or still more complicated than—what is found in his own mind, whether or not this refers to something real. Peirce postulated that there exists a triadic relation between an object of the external world, the interpreting subject or mind (which he called the *interpretant*), and the acoustic (or visual) image of the object formed by the interpretant (the *representamen*).[2]

Saussure, in his famous *Cours de linguistique générale* (1916), agreed with Peirce (though he was unfamiliar with the philosopher's work) regarding the definition of the linguistic sign. On Saussure's view, the sign is a mental representation that links not a thing and a name, but a concept and an acoustic image. In Peirce's terms, the sign corresponds to the base of the triangle and connects interpretant and

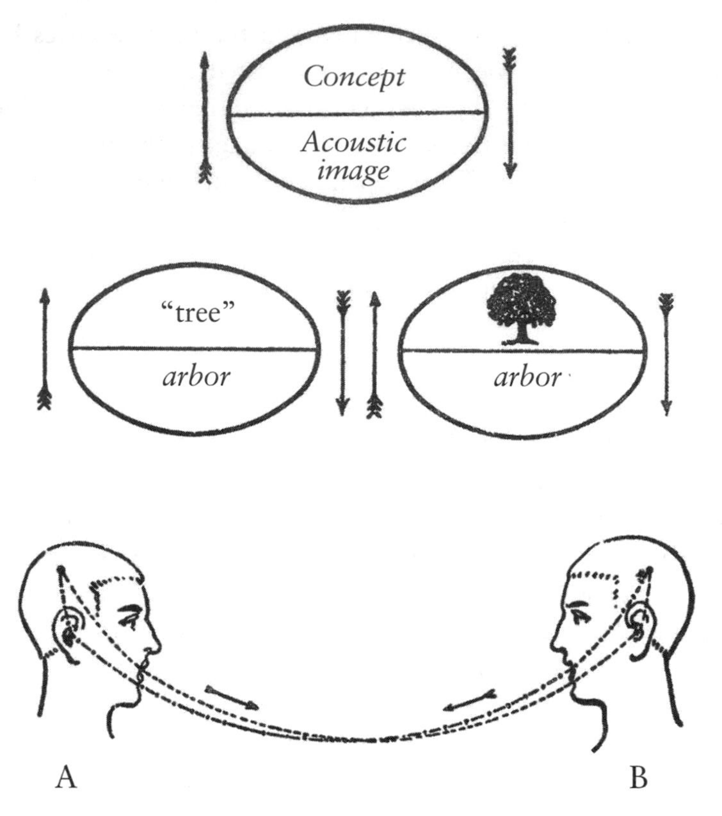

Figure 25. The linguistic sign: Saussure's model of interpersonal communication.

representamen. Saussure pushed this idea further, proposing that the sign is a two-sided mental entity that may be likened to a sheet of paper: on one side is thought (the *signified*) and on the other, sound (the *signifier*).[3] I would say that the signified refers to the knowledge that a subject has of an object: the selected neural pattern of features, or traits, that corresponds to it. The sole purpose of the signifier, then, is to establish a mechanism for the transmission of knowledge between individuals. Saussure claimed that the *designation*—the union of signifier and signified—is the result of a process of learning in each individual brain (Figure 25). I would say that it results from the epigenetic stabilization of common neural networks.

Peirce had already gone beyond Wittgenstein, so to speak, in distinguishing three main aspects of mental interpretation: *affective,* which refers to the "feeling" associated with the understanding of a given sign; *energetic,* or the physical "effort" required by understanding; and *logical,* or the psychological "effect" of communication that leads to a change in habit. In other words, communication between individuals occurs when the acoustic image produces a change in the listener's state of consciousness and, in particular, in his plans of action and his actual behavior.

Saussure made another important point, namely that the linguistic sign, which produces these changes in a person's state of consciousness, is "unmotivated," having "no natural point of attachment" to the signified reality—no mimetic reference that creates a resemblance between the acoustic image and the idea with which it is associated. As a result, the connection between signifier and signified is "arbitrary": there exists no intrinsic relation between a sequence of sounds and the concept represented.[4] It is merely a convention adopted by society and ratified by the collective consent of individual speakers. The sum of the imprints registered in the brains of the members of a community constitutes the language of this community. Consequently, the link between signifier and signified requires a long epigenetic learning process that infants spontaneously undergo during postnatal development in interaction with their social environment.

Neither the brain nor its physiology was of direct interest to Peirce and Saussure. Saussure unambiguously asserted that the connections between signifier and signified took place in the brain, and that language was the sum of the "impressions laid down in each brain,"[5] but he did not go further than this.

Alongside these linguistic approaches there were many attempts during the nineteenth century, especially in France and Germany, to directly explore the relationship between brain structure and language. Franz Joseph Gall's phrenology, laid out in *Sur les fonctions du cerveau et sur celles de chacune de ses parties* (1822–1825), located moral and intellectual faculties in specific parts of the brain; though later much criticized on account of the doubtful character of its cranioscopy, it furnished a useful preliminary model that inspired fruitful clinical research into the disturbances of spoken language produced by cerebral lesions.[6] Jean-Baptiste Bouillaud, and later Paul Broca, presented the first convincing clinical cases of a correlation between the loss of specific language functions and lesions of the anterior lobe of the brain. Monsieur Le Borgne, Broca's first patient, exhibited difficulties in uttering simple words and sentences, though he was still capable of understanding them. Broca argued that this kind of language disorder was due to a lesion of the third frontal convolution (or gyrus) of the left hemisphere, subsequently known as "Broca's area."[7] In Saussure's terms, the capacity to produce signifiers was affected, but the patient's understanding of the signified was in large measure (though not totally) preserved.

A few years later Carl Wernicke described patients exhibiting rather different deficits.[8] These patients were capable of speaking in a fluent (indeed effusive) manner, but their speech was virtually unintelligible, filled with neologisms and inappropriate or meaningless words bearing no relation to one another. The result was an incomprehensible sort of jargon. One aphasic patient studied by Wernicke described a picture as showing "broaking little costles, a holyene here, two footled enforks, two soab zanes, a candlesite putting on the cliston."[9] At the same time, these aphasics were incapable of understanding correct language. A lesion was discovered, again in the left hemisphere, but at the level of the temporal lobe, slightly behind the primary auditory cortex. This disorder may be interpreted in Saussurean terms as an incapacity to produce relevant signifieds, or concepts, which is to say a disturbance of the classificatory function of language processing.

Shortly afterward a third category of patients was discovered that exhibited signs of aphasia different from those described by Broca and Wernicke. They were capable of using spoken language and of perceiving objects visually, but had lost the ability to connect sounds with the objects they conventionally represent. The existence of such "agnosic" patients argues in favor of the idea that there is a neurally based stock of signifieds in the brain.

A diagram contained in an article published in 1885 by Ludwig Lichtheim summarizes these classic data (Figure 26).[10] This schema may be considered the first neuronal interpretation of Peirce's and Saussure's linguistic sign, only on a much more macroscopic scale involving cortical "centers" or, as we would say today, "regions" of the cerebral cortex. Moreover, Lichtheim's model had novel implications with respect to neural connectivity. The underlying assumption

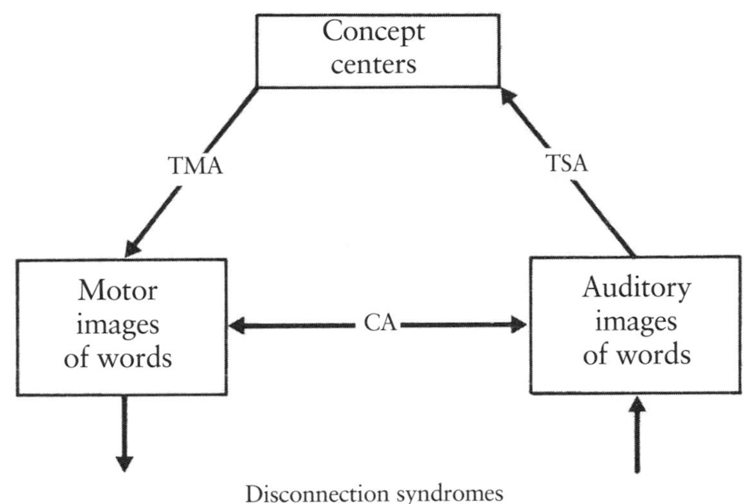

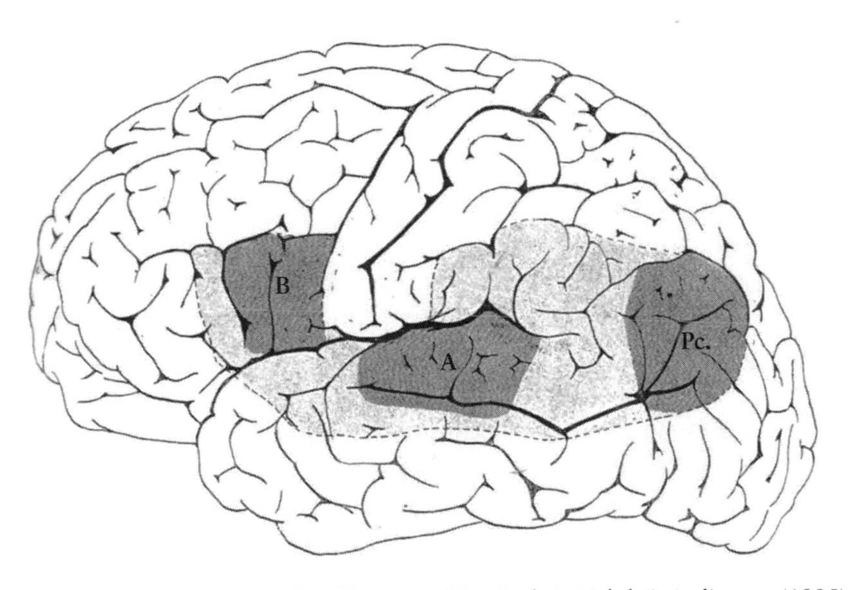

Figure 26. Neuronal networks of language. *Top:* Ludwig Lichtheim's diagram (1885) distinguishing "centers" of concepts (or signifieds) and of motor and auditory images of words (or signifiers). The connections between these centers can be interrupted by lesions creating "disconnection" syndromes: conduction aphasia (CA), transcortical motor aphasia (TMA), and transcortical sensory aphasia (TSA). *Bottom:* Joseph-Jules Déjerine's map (1901) of cortical localizations of language. B = Broca's area; A = Wernicke's area; Pc = center of visual images of words. This third center in the left hemisphere is specifically concerned with the reading of written words. Injury to it produces a "pure verbal blindness," that is, an inability to read, though not to write.

is that the relations between signifier and signified (to use Saussure's terms once more) can be placed in correspondence with a system of anatomic connections among groups of cortical neurons. Thus Lichtheim postulated the existence of "concept centers" responsible for processing the meanings of words (signifieds) that are distinct from centers involved in the production and perception of speech. These territories are associated with one other by bundles of fibers that create pathways through the brain. One neural link in particular, a transcortical pathway, connects the auditory image center and the concept center. It is when the latter center is injured that the deficit known as agnosia appears.

The system that connects the processing of images with that of concepts can therefore be thought of as a neural implementation of the arbitrary link between signifier and signified in Saussure's sense. In the brains of individuals speaking the same language, common pathways exist between the concept center and the word-production center and between the concept center and the auditory image center. It may plausibly be supposed, then, that the diversity of human languages arises in the first instance from the plasticity of the transcortical motor and sensory pathways.

Human beings are able to understand one another despite substantial differences among languages: translation, though sometimes difficult, is in fact possible. But this possibility depends on the existence of at least some minimal degree of universality with regard to the stock of signifiers—what Peirce called the "community" of interpretants.[11] The problem is to understand how the semantic databases of different individual brains can be harmonized by culturally variable signifiers serving the common interest of mutual comprehension.

Mention needs to be made, finally, of a very important process of cerebral plasticity peculiar to human beings. It plays a major role in the communication of meaning and has made it possible to extend neurally stored databases *outside* the human brain: the use of writing. The invention of writing, a crucial event in the history of humanity, seems to have occurred about 3500 B.C. in Mesopotamia and Egypt, probably rather later (about 1500 B.C.) in China, but in any case long after the earliest documented presence of *Homo sapiens sapiens* (more than 100,000 B.C.). We know that specific neuronal circuits responsible for reading and writing exist in the brains of literate adult subjects (see Chapter 6). The relevant predisposition is already present in the brain of the newborn, though, of course, its development depends on circumstances of birth and upbringing. Persons who, like their earliest human ancestors, reach maturity without learning to read and write also have this predisposition, but it serves different functions. The neuropsychologists Rosaleen McCarthy and Elizabeth Warrington, as well as Tim Shallice, have shown that in the absence of specific training the relevant neural pathways for reading and writing are spontaneously utilized both in phonological processing of speech and in associating visual forms with semantic representations.[12] This predisposition therefore came to be diverted from its original purpose by epigenesis and subsequently amplified with the invention of writing.

The epigenetic diversion of preformed neuronal pathways in literate brains gave rise to a considerable extension of human knowledge, which henceforth could be stored in nonbiological media. It dramatically enlarged the databases of individual brains, now united in a network of shared meanings through the use of language. In Diderot and d'Alembert's *Encyclopédie,* this common semantic network assumed the form of cross references at the end of each article to other essays. Today these interconnections enjoy material existence on a planetary scale thanks to the World Wide Web—a vast network of subsidiary networks implemented by electronic devices and systems distributed throughout the world.

By connecting the semantic databases of individual brains with one another, the epigenetic plasticity of neural networks made possible the pooling and sharing of knowledge and beliefs at the level of the social group. We need next to try to understand how the neural bases of human communication came to be established.

Syntax and Understanding

The theories of the linguistic sign developed by Peirce and Saussure invited a legitimate objection, namely that language is not simply a collection of names and meanings stored in memory. John Hughlings Jackson, a contemporary of Broca, stressed that the essence of language resides in the production of propositions.[13] As Wittgenstein put it in the *Tractatus Logico–Philosophicus* (1921), “Science is not a system of words but of statements.”[14]

The brain’s capacity to create syntactic order by spontaneously combining words and sentences gave language a new dimension—one that had existed only in a very rudimentary way, or not at all, in the ancestors of human beings. Syntax is not limited to the ordering of isolated words possessing appropriate and complementary meanings. It also reflects the manner in which propositions and complete sentences can assume different meanings as a function of context. Certain rules—I will come back to this point—govern the meaning of words in the context of the sentence. The complexity of these morphological rules varies across languages. Moreover, the recursive properties of syntax permit us to describe objects in a potentially infinite number of different ways and levels of self-referentiality. They also make it possible, as we shall see, to attribute a potentially infinite number of mutually embedded mental states to others. (One thinks of sentences such as “He thinks that he knows that I know that . . .”[15]) The problem, then, is to discover which neuronal mechanisms are utilized in generating meaningful propositions. How can such propositions be shared at the level of the social group? And how is their adequacy in capturing the reality of the external world to be judged?

Here again, clinical research in neuropsychology contributes crucial information. The brain lesions that provoke aphasia do not simply alter the usage of words. They also affect the capacity of patients to understand and produce sentences. We know, for example, that patients suffering from Broca’s aphasia can produce isolated words, albeit with difficulty. Indeed, the words spoken by Le Borgne—“tan, tan, . . .”—formed the subject of Broca’s historic paper. These patients do not succeed in forming well-constructed propositions or grammatically correct phrases, saying instead things like “Well though; long time ago; ah, not really; it’s not said, is it?; bicycle; oh, bah the pig,” or “Sir, suitcase, to walk.”[16] Nonetheless they preserve a fairly good ability to understand simple nouns. But they have trouble understanding sentences with subordinate clauses using active and passive constructions. Their “generative capacity” to produce and understand an infinite number of linguistic expressions is profoundly impaired. Moreover, as we have seen, the great many verbalizations produced by patients suffering from Wernicke's aphasia lack syntactic structure. A distinction is also made between aphasic patients who are no longer able to arrange the words of a sentence in the correct order and those who produce words with anomalous endings (or without endings at all). Still more subtle distinctions have been proposed between these different forms of agrammatism and other deficits in sentence comprehension and production. Imaging studies confirm and extend the conclusion that neural pathways are selectively involved in syntactic processing.[17]

Detailed analysis by functional magnetic resonance imaging and electroencephalography unambiguously illustrates the dissociation between syntax and semantics in sentence comprehension (Figure 27).[18] In one test the subject had to decide whether or not two very similar sentences differed in meaning. To bring out the semantic aspect, a word was replaced by a synonym or by a different word ("the *prosecution* questioned the witness" vs. "the *defense* questioned the witness"); to isolate the syntactic aspect, the voice of the sentence was changed from active to passive, altering the word order ("the policeman arrested the thief" vs. "the thief was arrested by the policeman"). The corresponding brain images plainly showed that patterns of neural activity differ depending upon whether the information being processed is syntactic (this involves a part of Broca's area) or semantic (the left anterior frontal gyrus).

Brain imaging has made it possible to go still further in the analysis of the processing of language at a higher level of organization, where the distinction made by Hughlings Jackson between "propositional speech" and "automatic speech" (or mere word production) manifests itself. Blood flows in the brain have been compared in French-speaking subjects under widely varying conditions of linguistic comprehension. These persons listened to a story in Tamil, a language unknown to them; a list of words in French that they understood; sentences containing pseudo-words or semantically anomalous words that they therefore found difficult to understand; and, finally, a story in French that was easy for them to understand. The images obtained revealed very striking differences. Subjects listening to a story in Tamil showed an activation of the primary and secondary auditory areas (left and right superior temporal sulci) but nothing more—they simply heard

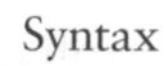

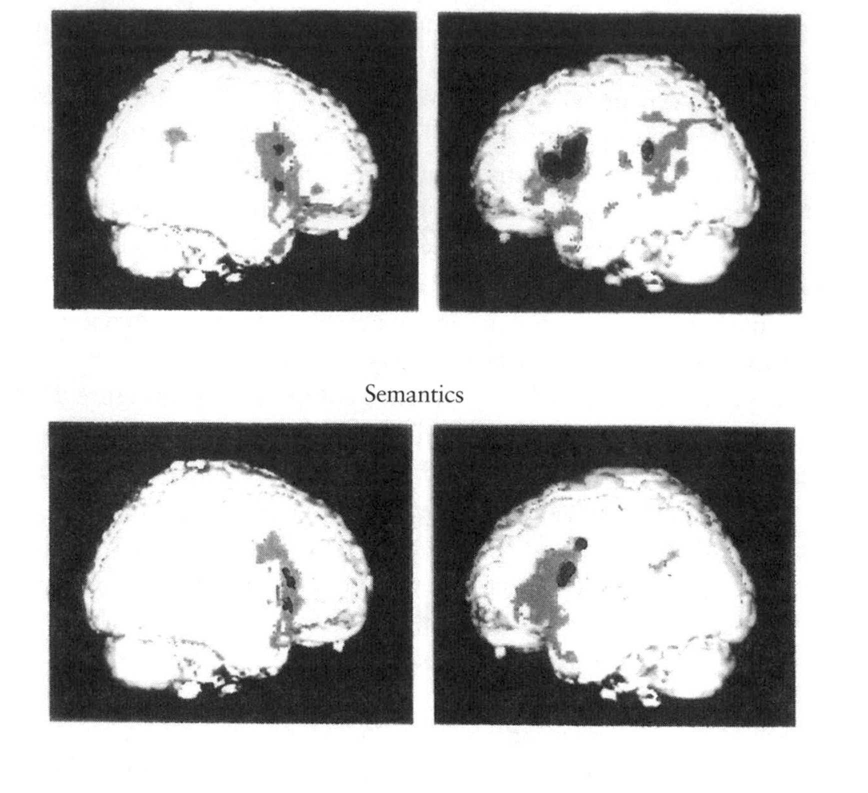

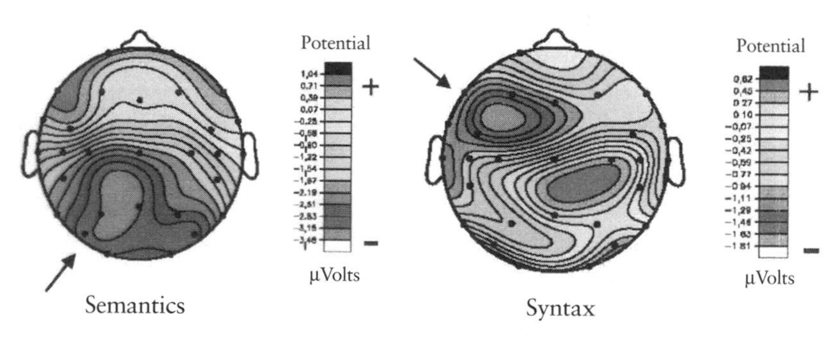

Figure 27. Syntactical vs. semantic processing. The brains of subjects carrying out linguistic tasks that clearly distinguish between syntactic and semantic parameters are examined *(top)* by functional magnetic resonance imaging and *(bottom)* by electroencephalography. An item of syntactic information typically mobilizes Broca's area of the left hemisphere.

the sounds of a language they did not understand. The list of French words produced a more extensive pattern of activations, now including the inferior frontal gyrus, but exclusively on the left side. The sentences containing pseudo-words or semantically anomalous words activated, in addition to the auditory areas, both temporal poles, though the activity was more pronounced on the left than the right side. The story in French yielded a spectacular image: perfect comprehension mobilized by far the greatest number of areas of the cerebral cortex, in particular the left prefrontal region.[19]

The mobilization of the prefrontal cortex under conditions of complete understanding suggests that efficient communication of contextualized knowledge involves the concerted activity of many more cortical areas than the "language areas" identified by Broca and Wernicke. Disorders associated with lesions of the prefrontal cortex also illustrate the contribution of this very recent region of the human encephalon to the processing of language: one notes profound disturbances of speech, marked by incoherence, lapses of attention, and a tendency to stereotypical expression. Both the organization and formation of knowledge that underlie the production of speech are altered, as well as its comprehension.

The word "comprehension" is composed of two Latin roots, *cum* and *prehendere:* literally, to take with, or together. The comprehension of a story does not arise simply from the accumulation of words and sentences without a definite train of thought. To the contrary, it involves a sequence of expectations that recruits and binds together multiple cerebral territories. When speech is incomprehensible, this binding fails to occur. The activation of the prefrontal areas is evidence, in my view, of the mobilization of neuronal networks linking processing units distributed over the whole of the cerebral cortex. The agreement with the neuronal workspace hypothesis described in the last chapter is obvious. The workspace neurons, by means of their long axons, unite topologically distinct processes throughout the brain. These neurons are particularly abundant in the frontal cortex, which therefore does indeed contribute to the "mental syntheses" that the psychiatrist and neurologist Leonardo Bianchi spoke of in the late nineteenth century.[20]

The contribution of definite areas of the prefrontal cortex to sentence processing supports the idea that the workspace neurons play a major role in a particularly developed form of human communication: propositional speech. In the previous chapter I argued for the view that the workspace neurons generate time-ordered sequences, or "melodies," of mental representations. With syntax, language melodies are able to exploit the vast combinatory possibilities offered by the neuronal network of the workspace—thus making infinite use of finite means.

The development of a system of neurons specially adapted to the purposes of syntactic communication suggests that propositions and structured speech can be seen as evolutionary phenomena accompanying the expansion of the prefrontal cortex. This anatomical development, as we shall see, represents a critical genetic step forward in the evolution of human cognitive capacities and, in particular, of man's conscious workspace.[21]

The Sharing of Knowledge

The immense diversity of sentences produced by individuals within a social group raises the equally formidable problem of understanding new sentences and of determining their truth value—this in addition to the problem of variability among individuals. The combinatorial explosion that results from the use of syntax requires new modes of perception and of processing if efficient comprehension among members of a social group is to occur.

Inferential Communication

Up to now I have implicitly assumed that linguistic communication is to be understood in terms of the standard empiricist view that interacting brains behave as input-output processing machines and that words are bearers of discrete meanings, nothing more. These assumptions, which underlie the mathematical theory of communication elaborated in the late 1940s by Claude Shannon and Warren Weaver, are still very widely endorsed today in computer science, artificial intelligence, and even linguistics.[22]

On this theory, signals encoding a message travel along a physical channel in the form of acoustic or electrical impulses that are decoded by a receiver at the other end. A series of letters forming a text, for example, may be coded by a precise set of electrical signals, each of which corresponds to a particular letter. The constraints of this mode of communication are many. In order for successful communication to take place, the same code must be used at both ends of the channel. What is more, this form of communication is vulnerable not only to distortion ("noise") but also to the least error in the transmission of the signal, even an isolated one. The omission or substitution of a single sign in an electronic address, for example, renders it inoperative. This model, though it is perfectly adequate for the purposes of telecommunications, is insufficient to account for verbal (and nonverbal) communication among human beings, in particular the communication of "thoughts."[23] The brain is not an ordinary computer, fed with digital messages. Since, as Dan Sperber and Deirdre Wilson have shown,[24] neither sender nor receiver is a simple encoding device, it follows that the communication and comprehension of thoughts by means of language cannot be reduced to the decoding of a linguistic signal.

The great Russian psychologist Lev Vygotsky pointed out that rational and intentional communication of experience and thought is impossible without some mediating expression: "Communication by means of expressive movements, observed mainly among animals, is not so much communication as spread of affects."[25] Human communication, while it shares this affective dimension, is more complex, in large part because it takes place in a specific context shaped by the sharing of knowledge. Sperber and Wilson have argued that communication involves an intention to modify the "cognitive environment" of another person, which is to say the "set of assumptions which the individual is capable of mentally representing and accepting as true."[26] In order to maximize the efficiency of communication, the listener tries to anticipate—to infer—the speaker's intention in advance. In other words, the listener forms a preliminary idea of the possible content of the message about to be communicated, which constitutes a subset of his or her assumptions about the world. These ideas include information about the physical environment, but also scientific hypotheses, religious beliefs, political opinions, and any relevant suppositions about the mental state of the speaker. Linguistic communication therefore does not conform to a simple input-output model. The speaker,

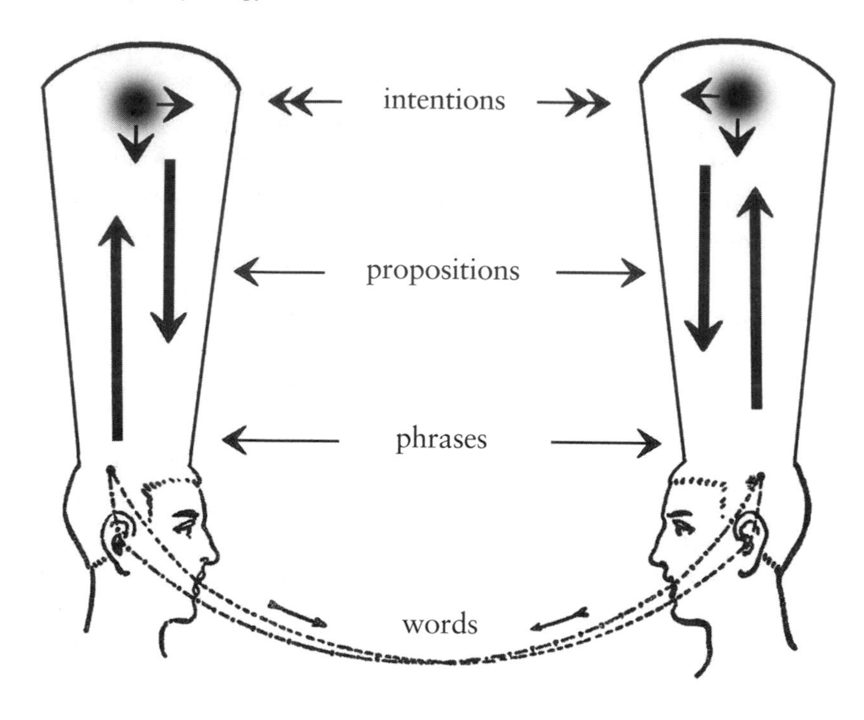

Figure 28. A schematic drawing incorporating Saussure's scheme of verbal communication and Sperber and Wilson's model of inferential communication. The traditional conception of communication through transmission of a coded message is modified to reflect the fact that interlocutors share the intention of communicating within a cognitive context of hypotheses and questions about the world.

meanwhile, tries to project the framework of his or her own thoughts into the mind of the hearer. The ability of interlocutors to attribute intentions to one another, as a consequence of the brain's projective use of contextualized pre-representations, makes communication possible even in the absence of code.[27] Communication requires cooperation between speakers and listeners, enabling them to recognize a common aim—a common intention. Such cooperation is established through conversation (Figure 28).

It should also be noted, by the way, that this inferential model agrees with Noam Chomsky's thesis that linguistic communication requires relatively little in the way of stimulus—certainly much less than the wealth of internal knowledge found in the minds of interlocutors.[28]

Even a very brief utterance—for example, "Watch out!"—can have considerable evocative impact on the representations present in conscious space. How is it that such a modest signal is able to trigger a cascade of long-term memories? Sperber and Wilson showed that, in any given conversation, a certain amount of information is already contained in the picture that the individual has of the world. Other pieces of information are new, but unrelated to these older representations. The union of old and new data in a process of inference—and of production of pre-representations—generates additional items of information. When this multiplicative effect occurs, Sperber and Wilson say that such pieces of information are "relevant." The greater the multiplicative effect, the higher the degree of relevance. In conversation, the cognitive goal of each speaker is to maximize the relevance of the information processed. In seeking to attract the other's attention to certain pieces of information, each hopes to establish a common intentional framework within which communication can take place.

In neural terms, this framework can be conceived as a set of long-lasting and global representations that are formed at the summit of the hierarchy of cerebral networks.[29] These naturally include the high-level pre-representations found in the neuronal workspace, whose combinatorial properties are preserved and acted upon by what I have called the generator of mental diversity. Prolonged anticipatory activity imposes top-down constraints on the underlying sensory, motor, and mental operations, however. The pre-selection of a set of processing units within a given intentional framework, by limiting the number of combinatorial possibilities, thus facilitates the recognition and processing of the immense number of propositions that are in principle accessible to the human brain.

Mirror Neurons and the Communication of Intentions

The discovery of "mirror neurons" by a team of researchers led by the neurophysiologist Giacomo Rizzolatti has greatly assisted the search for a plausible neural mechanism supporting communication within a common intentional framework.[30] These neurons were discovered in the ventral premotor cortex, an area of the prefrontal cortex involved in the preparation of movement. Exploring the function of this particular region, Rizzolatti and his colleagues noticed that firings of individ-

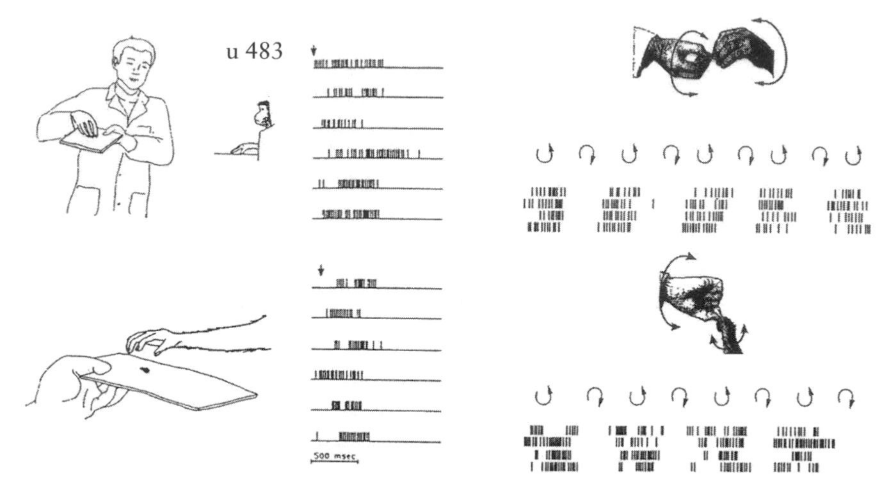

Figure 29. Mirror neurons and imitation. Recordings of individual neurons in the premotor area (area 6) of the frontal lobe of the monkey. *Left:* These mirror neurons are activated *(top)* when the monkey watches the experimenter pick up a peanut; and *(bottom)* when the monkey itself reaches for the peanut and brings it to its mouth. *Right:* They are also activated *(top)* when the monkey watches the experimenter rotate his hands around a grape; and *(bottom)* when the monkey makes the same movement jointly with the experimenter. Note that in both cases the neuron responds when the rotation is performed in a counterclockwise direction, but not in a clockwise direction.

ual neurons occur in an alert monkey during voluntary movements of the hand and of the mouth—for example, when the monkey reaches for a peanut and brings it to its mouth. Moreover, these firings are correlated with the global gesture rather than with its component movements. The researchers identified a "neuronal vocabulary" of six basic motor acts: grasping with the arm and mouth, grasping with the hand, holding, snatching, reaching, and carrying to the mouth and body.

In the course of their experiments they made an unexpected discovery. Some of the neurons that fired when the monkey grasped or manipulated objects were also activated when the monkey observed the experimenter making the same gesture (Figure 29)—as if they were both motor neurons and sensory neurons! The correlation of the activity of these mirror neurons not only with the production of motor actions but also with their sensory representation suggested to Rizzolatti and his team that these neurons were involved both in imitating movements and in understanding them—which is to say in recognizing the actions of another individual, telling them apart from other actions, and adapting behavior accordingly. It therefore seems plausible to suppose that mirror neurons (or their analogue in humans) play a role in the inferential communication of intentions.

There was another cause for surprise as well. Anatomists had long suspected that the ventral premotor cortex of the monkey is homologous with Broca's area in man. Both imaging studies and transcranial magnetic stimulation confirmed the presence of a system of mirror neurons (or neurons having very similar properties) in just this region of the human brain. Broca's area is not exclusively devoted to language. It also is involved in the recognition of actions and contains representations of the hand as well as of the muscles involved in movements of the hand and the pronunciation of words. The discovery of motor neurons in this area led Rizzolatti to suggest that mirror neurons play a role in speech recognition. It may therefore be plausibly supposed, then, that the activation of Broca's area during the observation of a gesture is connected with the recognition not only of sounds produced by persons engaged in verbal communication but also of phonetic movements of the mouth and face. Experimental evidence of a close link between the recognition of actions and inferential communication is in any case consistent with the arguments advanced by Sperber and Wilson.[31]

Intentions and the Theory of Mind

In the early part of the twentieth century the British philosopher Samuel Alexander inquired into "the empirical existence of the mind and of its neural bases," and the question of the empirical existence of other minds, in a novel and penetrating way.[32] How does it happen that we recognize ourselves as conscious subjects? This ability does not seem to exist in animals such as dogs, which do not reason. Reflective consciousness of ourselves, Alexander argued, develops in and through our consciousness of others, which is to say in relation to social life—and, more specifically, to a "social instinct" (thus we are conscious of others as well as of ourselves). A kind of satisfaction occurs when there is reciprocated action, whether through cooperation or rivalry. Recent studies of childhood cognitive development support Alexander's strikingly prescient insight. High-level processes of inferential communication have in fact been identified in children with the aid of ingenious tests that bring out their capacity to "consciously" understand and manipulate the mental states of others, and in this way to modify the behavior of other persons.[33] The terms "theory of mind" and "intentional stance" have been used by the ethologist David Premack and the philosopher Daniel Dennett, respectively, to designate this capacity to attribute mental states to others. It represents the fourth and last stage in the evolution of human consciousness.[34] This capacity does not consist simply in predicting what a person is going to do on the basis of a true belief, that is, one that has been found to agree with reality. The critical test of "mentalization" in this sense consists in being able to calculate how another person is likely to act on the basis of a *false belief*.[35]

The ability to attribute intentions develops gradually, around the age of four years, out of underlying and more primitive predispositions to create simplified images of one's own body and to relate them to images of other bodies. This type of representation appears very early, as we saw in the last chapter: babies are capable of imitation from the age of a month and a half.[36] Next, toward the end of the second year, a true consciousness of oneself develops, with reflective consciousness appearing between two and a half and three years. It is following this stage that the theory of mind begins to operate. Simon Baron-Cohen and his colleagues devised a now-classic test of the acquisition of this theory. Known as "the Sally-Ann task," it demonstrates the child's ability to recognize false beliefs.[37] In a series of comic strips, Ann is shown moving a ball belonging to Sally: she takes it out of a basket and puts it in a box. Then Sally enters the room. The child is asked, "Where is Sally going to look for her ball?" The child realizes that Sally, not knowing that the ball has been moved, will wrongly suppose that it is still in the basket. False beliefs play an important role in everyday life, and are deliberately exploited by cultural and religious systems in the early schooling of young children. The teaching of science and exposure to the habits of critical thought on which it depends will later offset this influence to some degree, but only very selectively.

Children themselves become acquainted with false beliefs at a very early age in playing "make believe" and in trying to deceive others about their true identity and intentions. The development of the theater in ancient Greece was also founded on the ability to attribute mental states to others, arousing the empathy of the spectators for the role assumed on stage by the actor. If the cognitive mechanisms at work in what Diderot called the "actor's paradox" are still poorly understood, it is clear that the actor manages to assume the role of another person without actually identifying himself with it. By the artful use of speech and mimicry of facial and bodily movements, he leads the audience to attribute characteristics to him that have nothing to do with his real "self." In the conscious workspace of the actor's brain there is a splitting of representational schemas between what pertains to his true identity and what pertains to the role he plays. From what I have said so far about conscious space in the brain, it may not be unreasonable to suggest that this disposition depends on both "recursive" consciousness (the capacity to keep in mind two distinct representations at once) and a theory of mind. From role-playing in the theater to games such as poker, political deception, and the manipulation of beliefs through propaganda, our capacity for judging truth also enables us to betray the truth in more or less harmful ways.

Certain pathological alterations of the predisposition to form a theory of mind have been identified in autistic children. In these children the ability to imagine the mental states of others fails to develop normally. Typically they display high levels of intelligence but are incapable of understanding other persons, whom they tend to regard as inanimate objects. Many autistic children fail at the Sally-Ann task, even in adolescence. The delusions of persecution typical of schizophrenia, a disease that manifests itself in adulthood, may be viewed as false inferences about the intentions of others. Schizophrenics overproduce mistaken expectations, as it were.[38] In the case of both autism and schizophrenia it seems plausible to suppose that differential alterations of gene expression during development interfere with the stabilization of a kind of neuronal balance in the brain. The relevant networks are still insufficiently understood, but it is clear that they involve the prefrontal cortex and serve to regulate the evaluation of representations of oneself vis-à-vis others.

Patients suffering from lesions of the prefrontal cortex, especially in the orbital and medial regions, exhibit serious problems of social behavior. They are incapable of medium- or long-term planning that involves relations with others.[39] Imaging studies show that the medial frontal cortex is also activated when subjects are asked to monitor and describe their own mental states (Figure 30).[40] In these subjects one also notes activations in the regions of the temporo-parietal and lateral inferior frontal cortex.

The capacity for attribution derives from a set of dispositions that are encountered among primates as well.[41] In the monkey, for example, individual neurons have been recorded in the temporal sulcus that distinguish between living beings and inanimate objects. There is also evidence of neurons that are activated when the monkey trains its attention in following the gaze of another. Mirror neurons, though they provide a neural basis for the representation of the aims of others, do not distinguish between the self and others. Recordings have been made of nerve cells in the temporal cortex, on the other hand, that respond to sounds produced by others, but not to sounds produced by the subject.[42] The neurons of the cingulate cortex and the medial prefrontal-anterior cortex, which become active when there is an anticipation of self-initiated movement, are responsible for subjective mental states and aims.[43]

The neurobiologist Marc Jeannerod has proposed a network of motor action simulation that includes both momentary perception and a theory of mind.[44] On this model, representations of observed action (associated with mirror neurons) and self-produced representations of contemplated action (associated with parietal cortex neurons) occur in the brains of interacting agents. The latter representations remain below the threshold required for activation until their evaluation in the conscious workspace—often in a reiterated manner—produces a voluntary decision. It is likely under these circumstances that a functional dissociation is consciously made between contemplated action and the evaluation of representations of the self in relation to others: trickery becomes possible. The evaluations of long-term memory are nonetheless more robust than those of the conscious space—so much so that they may occur involuntarily. But we are still far from a coherent theory of the neural bases of lying!

The implication of this research—that attribution and the planning of action at the level of the social group mobilize the prefrontal

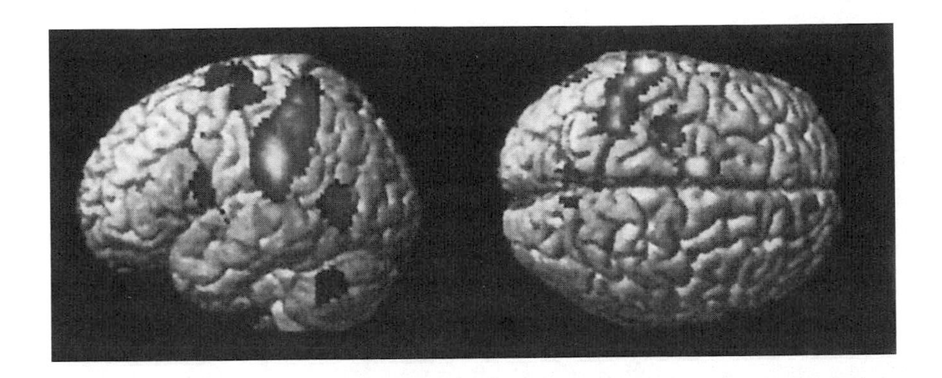

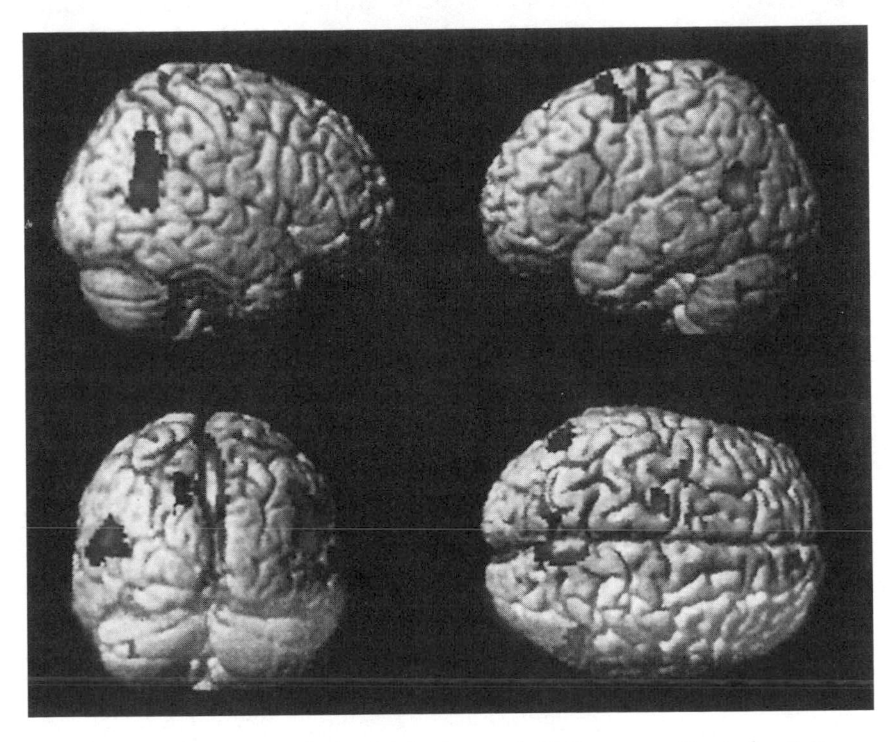

Figure 30. Subjective simulation in the first and third persons. Cortical activity recorded by positron emission tomography in voluntary subjects *(top)* when the subject imagines the experimenter using familiar objects—a razor, a shovel, and a ball—of which he is shown photographs; and *(bottom)* when the subject imagines using the same objects himself. In both cases, various motor areas are activated: the supplementary motor area, the precentral gyrus, the precuneus, and visual area MT/V5. The third-person perspective more heavily involves the right inferior parietal cortex, the precuneus, the posterior cingulate cortex, and the frontopolar cortex.

cortex—is consistent with the neuronal workspace hypothesis. The relationship between these processes of mentalization and the role played by the frontal lobe in decisionmaking remains to be worked out in detail, however.

Having a theory of mind makes it possible for interlocutors not only to recognize one another's informative intentions but also to assess these intentions. The advantages for social life are obvious. Certain standards of cooperation in the communicating knowledge now come into play.[45] In the words of Paul Ricoeur, the subject can "put himself in the place of others" and "see himself as another."[46] He will recognize discrepancies and similarities between his own mental states and those of others, and thus will be able to act toward others in ways that are consistent (or inconsistent) with the norms of the social group. The ability to attribute intentions permits the sharing of the contents of individual workspaces through conversation, discussion, and debate. In this way new means for judging the truth of ideas become available. Testing veracity is no longer simply a matter of individual cognitive games; it is a matter of "games and combats" (in André Lwoff's phrase),[47] now conducted on a social scale.

Signs, Symbols, and Shared Rewards

The ancient Greek word *symbolon* meant both "to throw together" and "to put back together." A symbol was a token of recognition constituted by two halves of a broken object that was handed down within families as proof of ancient bonds of hospitality. The sense of the word "symbol" does not coincide exactly with that of Saussure's linguistic "sign." But the metaphor of the reunion of two separate fragments fits nicely with the hypothesis that neural connections between signifier and signified are epigenetically formed during language learning. This hypothesis nonetheless runs up against several major difficulties. I have frequently mentioned the variability of the brain's organization, which contrasts with the sharing of common—perhaps universal—meanings. There is also, to use Saussure's terms once more, the arbitrary and culturally variable character of the relationship between signifier and signified. How can these two parts of the linguistic symbol be put back together by means of a universally observed convention? A few examples will help us think about these questions. The first has to do with monkeys, the others with the development of the human infant.

Dorothy Cheney and Robert Seyfarth devote a chapter of their important study of African vervet monkeys *(Cercopithecus aethiops)* to vocal communication as a mode of transmitting knowledge about the world.[48] Their careful observations in the field have revealed that monkeys utter distinct cries of alarm in response to at least three distinct categories of predators: leopards, eagles, and snakes (Figure 31). A loud barking noise signals a leopard: on hearing this noise, monkeys on the ground quickly climb to safety in the trees. By contrast, the vervets give a short two-syllable cough when they perceive the presence of two predatory species of eagle: the martial eagle and the crowned eagle. At this signal the monkeys scurry into the bush. The third type of alarm cry is given on encountering snakes: Cheney and Seyfarth call it "hissing" because it mimics the sound made by snakes. On hearing it, the monkeys assume an upright position and inspect the surrounding grass.

These cries of alarm do not signal a general alert. Nor do they reflect different levels of fear. Monkeys use them to communicate to other monkeys what is happening around them and to signal what needs to be done in response. Yet there is no synchronization of response—no monitoring or integration of the reactions of other members of the group. These cries refer to a definite object in the sense that they substitute for the object and generate a representation of it in the brains of the other members of the social group. But, unlike humans, monkeys are incapable of reproducing and transmitting it to their fellow creatures.

Cheney and Seyfarth studied the three main components of the cry of alarm: the correct *utterance* of the cry, the *vocal marking* of a particular event, and the *behavioral response*—Peirce's "energetic interpretant"—appropriate to the cry's utterance. The cries of alarm issued by young monkeys are identical to those of older monkeys and, what is more, produce the same reactions in adults.

The hissing that signals the presence of snakes is spontaneously produced without explicit learning, as in many other species of verte-

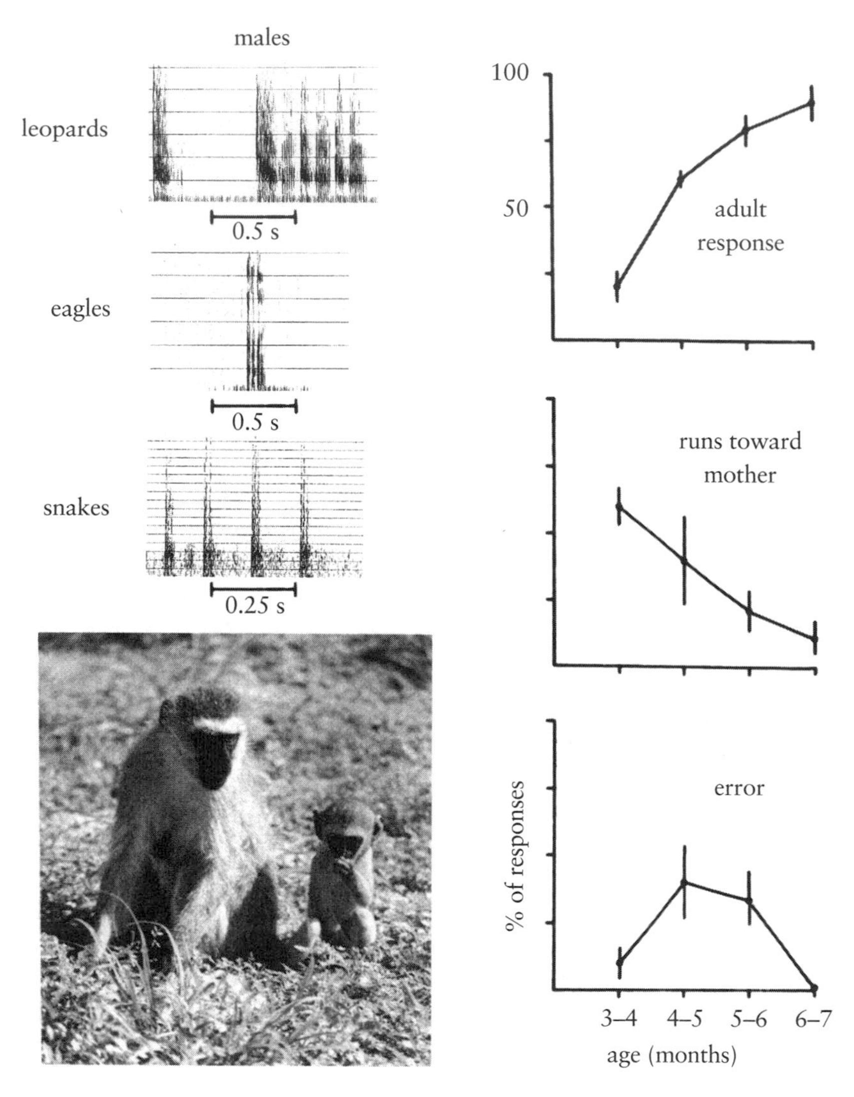

Figure 31. Learning of the cry of alarm in the African vervet monkey *(Cercopithecus aethiops). Top left:* Cries of alarm uttered by adult males in the presence of a leopard, an eagle, and a snake. *Bottom left:* An adult female and her two-month-old male offspring. *Right:* Response of a baby monkey to a cry of alarm as a function of age. The spontaneous response of the newborn (running toward its mother) gradually gives way to the adult-type response after a period of trial and error.

brates. Snakes seem to arouse a sort of innate universal fear, which probably developed fairly early in the course of the evolution of the higher vertebrates. This fear, already present in birds, left its trace in the genetic envelope of humans, with the consequence that inborn patterns of functional neural connection indispensable to survival were specified in a reproducible manner from one individual to another. There is a strong chance, after all, that the first bite of a venomous snake that a monkey experiences will also be the last.

On the other hand, experience is necessary in order to recognize certain predators. Young monkeys often make mistakes. They let out cries of alarm at the sight of things that pose no danger to them—a flock of pigeons, for example, or falling leaves. In systematically analyzing the types of stimuli that provoke cries of alarm specifically related to dangerous birds, Cheney and Seyfarth discovered that very young monkeys (less than a year old) react to predators and nonpredators in the same manner. Between one and four years of age, young monkeys begin to distinguish these categories more accurately. Newborn monkeys react to any form that flies in the air, which is to say to the class of birds as a whole. Then, gradually, a selective stabilization of the response to the shape of dangerous species takes place.[49] But how exactly does this occur? Knowing the answer to this question is important, for it may furnish us with clues to more general selection mechanisms whose operation establishes a connection between image and concept—between signifier and signified—within a social group.

The answer lies in the relationship that the infant forms with the older monkeys (Figure 32). If the first cry of alarm is sounded by one of the young, the nearest adult looks up. If it sees a harmless bird, it does not react. But if the young monkey has spotted a martial eagle, the adult reacts by emitting a cry of alarm that confirms the presence of danger. The selection of appropriate responses is carried out, then, through interaction between adults and their young. In a recent course of lectures at the Collège de France I suggested that this selection operates by means of a process of shared reward.[50] The adult's cry of alarm validates a pertinent relationship between shape and sound that is established in the brain of the young monkey. The neural mechanisms of reward that I described earlier in connection with individual cognitive games may well also be involved in these interactive exercises. None-

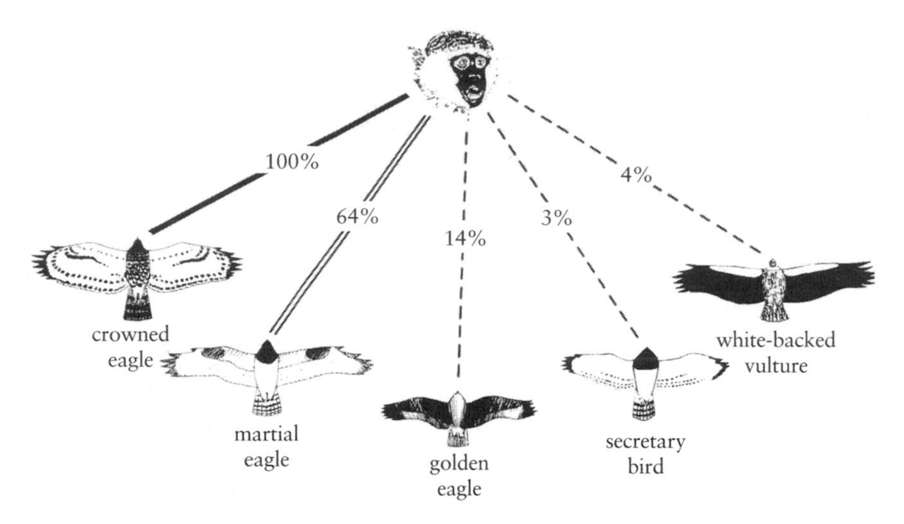

Figure 32. Learning to recognize birds of prey. At first the infant monkey responds indiscriminately to various types of birds of prey. If the mother repeats the baby's cry of alarm, the recognition of a dangerous type is validated. The percentages indicate the probability of a second cry of alarm by the mother following the infant's cry. Note the great morphological similarity between the martial eagle and the secretary bird, which the monkeys nonetheless are able to distinguish.

theless, nothing allows us to say that these adults, strictly speaking, educate the young and monitor the knowledge they acquire. A simple sharing of rewards at the social level suffices to select a pattern of connections correctly linking shape with sound in the brain of the young monkey. An authentic pedagogy, which seems on the whole to be peculiar to man, does not need to be assumed at this stage.

Language Games and Social Consciousness

In humans the situation is far more complex. To begin with, words can no longer be seen as the elementary building blocks of language. The notion of a simple verbal connection between signifier and signified must give way to a more subtle and contextualized interpretation of inferential communication, which will allow us to see how the relation between sound and sense gradually comes to be established in the child through an interlocking sequence of language games and shared selections (Figure 33).

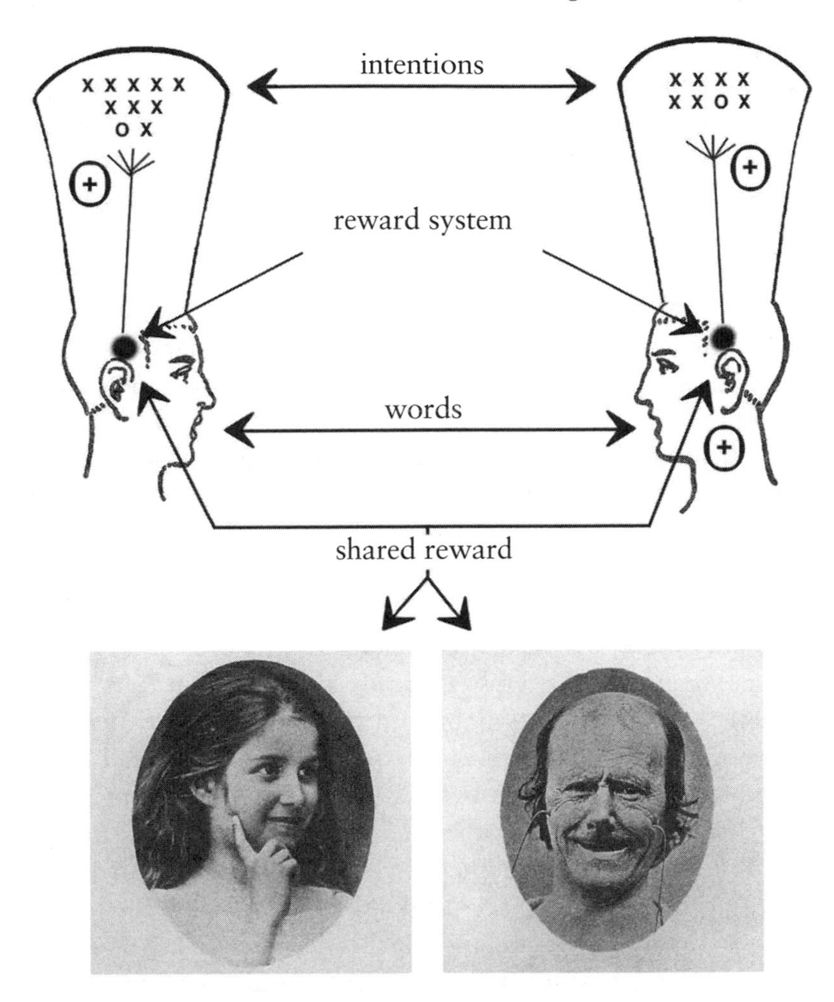

Figure 33. Learning model of the sound-meaning relation through shared reward. This diagram elaborates upon the model represented in Figure 28 by introducing reward neurons within the brains of interlocutors, which underlie the sharing of rewards (expressed, for example, by smiles, as in the photographs below the diagram) in inferential communication.

Production and Perception of Sounds by the Child

From birth, a baby produces a great variety of sounds, not only wails and cries. From four to five months, she devotes herself to vocal play, modulating her sound productions and manipulating the musical envelope of speech: rhythm, stress, and intonation. The child next utters the first consonants—*m, prr, brr*—and the first vowels. At sixteen weeks, she smiles for the first time. At five months, she uses her voice to communicate emotions and begins to imitate the vocalizations of her immediate environment. From four to seven months, the child produces pseudo-syllables such as *arrheu* and *abwa,* then true syllables: *papapa, bababa,* and so on. "Canonical babbling" begins at about seven months, with a combination of consonants and vowels that seems fairly universal. Very quickly, however, the intonation, phonation, and rhythmic organization characteristic of the language of the child's parents is incorporated into her sound productions. The vowels produced by babies of English, French, Algerian, and Cantonese families begin to resemble those of the adults' languages: forward vowels *i, l,* and æ for the English babies; œ and ø for the French; ∂ and *a,* as well as back vowels, for the Cantonese. A kind of cultural babbling thus develops in which innate dispositions are merged with features of the local speech environment.[51]

The child's perceptive capacities undergo a parallel evolution. When still inside its mother the fetus is already able, at about thirty-six or forty weeks, to distinguish syllabic order (*babi* vs. *biba*). After birth, the newborn shows a preference for passages in prose read by her mother during the last weeks of pregnancy. She even recognizes the language spoken by her mother: she distinguishes Russian from French, for example, if her mother is a French speaker. But this capacity is not peculiar to our species. Like the human baby, the tamarin monkey is capable of distinguishing between sentences spoken in Dutch and Japanese—though not if, in a controlled experiment, it is made to listen to the sentence backward.[52] The basic properties of speech recognition therefore rest on the operation of innate processors common to the auditory systems of primates.

At the age of four months, children efficiently recognize a fairly extensive range of syllables. In Japanese, for example, the phonemic contrast between *ra* and *la* does not exist. Japanese adults have a great deal of trouble distinguishing these phonemes in Western languages such as French and English. Japanese babies, on the other hand, manage to discriminate between them as readily as do Western children. Their innate perceptual capacities are more extensive than those of adults. A loss of perceptual capacities therefore occurs in the course of language acquisition.[53] The psycho-acoustic boundaries between perceptual categories are simplified. Boundaries between nonpertinent categories in the mother tongue are eliminated and a selective stabilization of elements compatible with the linguistic environment takes place on the basis of a much larger initial vocabulary.[54] Moreover, the newborn already possesses a hemispheric specialization that is as much anatomical as functional. The left hemisphere is better suited to the discrimination of speech sounds, in particular syllable recognition; the right hemisphere is more effective in distinguishing among musical sounds.

In the course of the infant's postnatal development, the production and the perception of language sounds interact. Children who are deaf from birth babble normally at first, but then exhibit difficulties in producing language. Between nine and twelve months, babbling becomes organized. The baby develops language games, experimenting with the production of speech sounds and patterns of stress. She tests what might be thought of as vocal hypotheses about her family environment and about herself. Progressively, through selection, she manages to adapt her productions and perceptions to the intonation and phonetics of her native language. A process of "syllabic attrition" analogous to the one observed by the ethologist Peter Marler in the young swamp sparrow during song learning[55] takes place in the human child, lending further support to the hypothesis of selective synaptic stabilization.[56]

Language Comprehension and Production

All parents admire (and sometimes dread) their child's intense desire to explore the world around her. The newborn is continually reorienting her gaze, grasping and throwing objects, bringing them to her mouth, experiencing feelings of attachment and rejection, joy and fear. Before mastering language, the infant first learns to correctly recognize objects and changes in their position. She is capable of recognizing the physical existence of objects placed outside her line of sight and of distinguishing very similar sounds from one another.[57] Activation of the brain's main preformed circuits, reinforced by the continuing acquisition of knowledge through the mechanisms of selective learning by reward discussed earlier, causes neural patterns corresponding to particular features of objects and events encountered in exploring the outside world to be stored in long-term memory. In this way a semantic database is gradually constructed in the child's brain.

Word comprehension appears between eight and ten months. Not coincidentally, perhaps, the ability to store representations in memory, and to retrieve them and compare the past with the present—what in the last chapter I called recursive consciousness—emerges between seven and ten months. At this stage the infant is able to carry out Piaget's delayed-response task. It is during precisely this period that connections among the prefrontal cortex neurons are established. The pyramidal and inhibitory interneurons register a sharp increase in rates of growth and differentiation among their axons and dendrites, particularly in layer III, whose long-range connections are posited by the neuronal workspace hypothesis to support conscious mental processes.[58]

The ability to produce words appears later than the ability to understand them, between ten and seventeen months. From then on it constantly grows. The mean number of words learned during the two first years has been placed at 340 (it varies between 20 and 674).[59] From eighteen months to six years, the child learns on average five new words a day. The lexicon undergoes explosive growth.

The socialization of the child plays an essential role in helping her make the connection between sound and meaning. The human child's world of communication differs from that of the young of less social species. She enjoys universal and innate capacities of recognition (particularly of faces), as well as the ability to communicate by means of expressions and gestures. These modes of communication establish connections between a corpus of meanings stored in the brain through cognitive games and the repertory of sound patterns associated with the child's native language, the language of the social group within which she develops. Since inferential communication within the social group is not possible without a certain normalization, or standardization, of acquired knowledge, the reporting of perceptions—even of the feelings ("qualia") evoked by various objects and phenomena of the real world—must be monitored to ensure uniformity.

Very early on, newborns follow their mother's gaze in order to establish emotional contact with her. Communication of affects creates an essential context for the inferential exchange of knowledge: a kind of semantic sharing takes place. In interacting with adults, the infant is attentive to their centers of interest. She manifests what the cognitive psychologist Michael Tomasello calls "joint attention,"[60] but in an increasingly elaborate manner (Figure 34). From nine to twelve months, the infant follows the gaze of the adult and is able to discover the object of the adult's attention, so long as the object is clearly visible. From eleven to fourteen months, she concentrates her own attention on the object of the adult's attention and, presented with two objects, is capable of telling which one the adult is focusing on. Moreover, she begins to learn by imitation. From thirteen to fifteen months, the child actively directs the adult's attention by pointing and uses language to ask the name of the object.

Titian's painting *The Madonna of the Rabbit* (Figure 34) depicts the interplay of gazes between the infant Jesus, his mother, and St. Catherine. The sharing of attention between adults and child and the pointing out of the object suggest a language game in Wittgenstein's sense. Catherine and the infant Jesus fix their attention on the rabbit while the Virgin Mary, following the child's gaze, checks to see that the name she has pronounced has established a link between sound and sense in the mind of her child, who correctly associates the word with the animal.

It seems reasonable to suppose that the neural mechanism of shared reward, discussed earlier in the case of the African vervet monkey, operates in humans as well—only with a supplementary feature, namely shared attention. It goes beyond simple imitation, for it mobilizes a very rich exchange of intentions having a large affective component.

Inferential Communication and the Emergence of Social Consciousness

The development of inferential communication creates a context within which reproducible connections between sounds and meanings can be selectively stabilized, both in the case of a single individual and from one individual to another. Unlike adult vervet monkeys, however, human adults constantly check the soundness of the symbolic bond by looking for signs of disparity between the child's behavior and the social norms to which the child is expected to conform, and

Check attention (9–12 months)

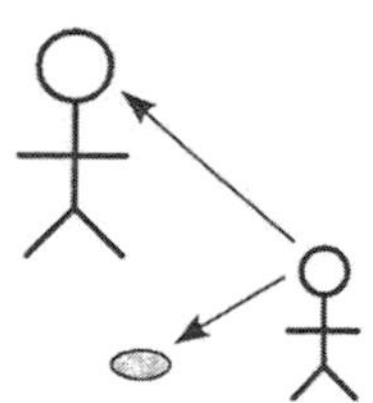

Follow attention (11–14 months)

Direct attention (13–15 months)

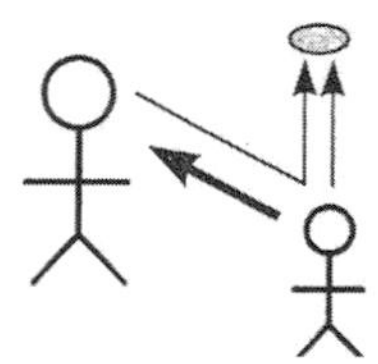

Figure 34. Joint attention. *Top:* Titian's *The Madonna of the Rabbit* (1530). The infant Jesus and St. Catherine look toward the rabbit displayed by the Virgin Mary, who checks to see that their gazes converge. Just a moment before, or so one may imagine, she has uttered the word "rabbit." *Bottom:* Diagrams showing the development of joint attention from the age of nine to fifteen months: from checking attention, to following attention, to directing attention.

acting accordingly. Human adults create a pedagogy for educating their children, which in turn gives rise to a shared social consciousness.

The developmental dynamics of semantic learning, in contradicting the naive conception of vocabulary acquisition as a simple matter of putting signifiers into one-to-one correspondence with signifieds, offer further support for the model of inferential communication. For the child's acquisition of word meaning does not follow a pattern of progressive growth in the number of words learned, then of phrases or groups of words, and finally of propositions. The psycholinguist Peter Jusczyk showed that in fact the very opposite occurs. There is a progressive restriction in what the child understands of the continuous flow of words to which she is exposed in her environment.[61] The central problem facing the child is how to segment the mass of sounds she hears into meaningful units. At five months, she prefers to hear stories containing pauses that fall between sentences. At nine months, she prefers that the pauses come between phrases, though she already understands the words that make them up. Finally, at eleven months, she prefers that the pauses coincide with the boundaries between words.[62] All this suggests that word comprehension and production are closely integrated with a wider intentional context from the beginning. Boundaries appear to develop within the flow of language in an abrupt, nonlinear fashion—as in the case of morphogenesis, which I shall consider in a later chapter—through the cooperative interaction of neighboring nerve cells and widespread patterns of neuronal inhibition.

It is natural to suppose that the progressive specification and restriction of the relations between sound and meaning (together with the relevant neural connections) occur through a process of selection by shared reward. The psycholinguist Luigi Rizzi has presented examples of syntax learning in the child that directly bear upon the question of the learning of epigenetic rules.[63] Rizzi found that once language production gets under way the child explores a great number of possible syntactic rules, rules that are transient and individually variable. Then she "omits" or "forgets"—which is to say, eliminates—constructions that do not agree with basic grammatical knowledge that she has drawn from her immediate social environment. She thus selects the specific grammar of her mother tongue. There is a cultural transmission of the characteristic features of the language from the brain of the adult to the brain of the child through shared selection. This selection is spontaneously and effortlessly carried out by the child in acquiring her mother tongue. In contrast to this are the mechanisms of selection involved in the late learning of a second language, which requires great conscious effort and intense training, possibly because it takes place after the phase of rapid synaptic outgrowth following birth.

A relatively long period of childhood development results in the social normalization of the arbitrary link between sounds and meanings as well as of the network of syntactic and contextual relationships that is necessary for mutual comprehension within a social community. The gradual development of language learning by progressive restriction carries on, over much shorter periods of time, the cultural evolution of the language spoken by the social group and of the body of knowledge the group has accumulated during its history. This process of epigenetic evolution is in any case, as we shall see in the next chapter, orders of magnitude faster than the genetic evolution that took place in the course of the phylogenesis of the human brain.

Recent whole-brain functional magnetic resonance imaging studies of children aged seven to ten years performing effortful visual processing tasks with single words have revealed unexpected differences from adult performances that fit quite well with the hypothesis of the progressive evolution of childhood development. In these children, left secondary visual areas involved in the processing of visual signals display robust activity exceeding that found in adult brains. At the same time, specific regions of the left frontal cortex show variable and systematically smaller activations than in the brains of adults performing the same task—as though the child's brain had not yet incorporated the processing resources of the frontal cortex (and thus of the conscious neuronal workspace).[64]

A great many computational models of neuronal networks have been proposed to explain how the connection between sound and meaning comes to be established. They rest for the most part on associative learning mechanisms that operate by means of explicit instruction.[65] The model I am proposing here, by contrast, assumes that an appropriately contextualized relationship between signifier and signified arises from a process of trial and error. This process depends in turn on a system of rewards that is integrated at the individual level and shared at the social level. The hypothesis of a simultaneously projective and selectionist mechanism consistent with the evolutionary record of human development needs now to be cast in realistic neuronal terms.[66] It may be that babbling, like the syllabic attrition characteristic of song learning in birds, is an instance of the vocal games typical of early childhood development that take place at the level of motor pre-representations. These games can be seen as externalizing inner processes of trial and error[67] that permit sounds and meanings to be appropriately matched.

The child begins to produce two-word combinations between twenty and twenty-four months. Sentence comprehension and production during this period of intense knowledge acquisition increase dramatically. The manipulation of mental objects that are chiefly semantic and motor in origin is not by itself sufficient to connect the child's inner world with the external cultural and social environment: language—and later the use of written symbols—is required as well.

Explicit language games involving direct interaction with the external world, and the rewards that arise from this interaction, develop and expand in an implicit manner within the child's inner world. Soon the infant is capable of making simple causal inferences[68] and can even predict the actions of an agent.[69] The development of mechanisms for generating pre-representations and the tacit self-evaluation characteristic of reflective consciousness make reasoning and analytical thought possible, as we saw in the last chapter. In all these operations, the new ways of processing mental objects made possible by the use of symbols have major consequences for testing the veracity of propositions about the world. First, thought experiments comparing perceptions with stored memories in respect of adequacy and coherence now consist of a much larger repertoire of operations than the simple cognitive games and memory recall I discussed earlier. These experiments also offer new opportunities in later life for comparing one's own knowledge of the world with that of others through private conversation and public discussion. The communication of personal experiences and the critical examination of different opinions make it possible not only to determine how far they are shared, but also to dispel illusions and unsupported judgments. In this way the free individual examination of ideas is converted into a joint process of careful and candid scrutiny.

The verification of the validity of claims about the world makes use of linguistic symbols that were originally devised for the purpose of social communication. But language also gives access to new modes of mental computation. Some philosophers, such as Donald Davidson, have gone so far as to assert that thought is exclusively a matter of interpreting the speech of others.[70] Indeed, for the analytical school of Anglo-American philosophy, as Daniel Dennett has remarked, the only proper subject matter for analysis is language.[71] In fact there is considerable evidence that thought without language exists as much in animals as in humans.[72] Nonetheless, the use of symbols—and what, more generally, I call "epigenetic rules"—adapts the conscious workspace of the human brain to new procedures for checking the truthfulness of ideas, both at the level of the individual and at that of the social group.

Epigenetic Rules and Cultural Transmission of Knowledge

Let us take, as a first example, mathematics. Since Galileo it has been a commonplace that mathematics, by making it possible to describe the universe, gives access to truth about the physical world.[73] Yet birds, rats, and other animals share with the young of the human race the capacity to detect small numbers of objects and events, up to five and sometimes more. This ability is associated with what Stanislas Dehaene and I have called a "numerosity detector," as well as with inborn neural systems for manipulating numbers. An artificial organism exhibiting numerical capacities that closely resemble those of the child has even been designed, and its behavior simulated on the computer.[74] But it does not suffice to explain the full development of mathematics.

A second mechanism of computation makes it possible to carry out approximate, though not exact, numerical calculations. This ability is also found in several animal species. It is independent of language, mobilizes the parietal lobes of the brain in particular, and makes possible the "intuitive" evaluation of large quantities of substances, volumes of liquids, and so on. The capacity to determine whether a glass is half full or a third full does not depend on the exact measurement of the volume of the liquid in cubic centimeters.[75]

Humans possess a third very important source of mathematical processing that relies on these two systems but requires the symbolism of language in order to produce *exact* calculations. This computational ability furnishes new and essential tools for describing reality, now in a quantitative manner. Certain brain lesions create a dissociation between the neural pathways employed in approximate and exact calculation. One patient with a serious injury to the left hemisphere could not decide whether two plus two makes three or four. He was unable to do sums correctly, but consistently preferred three to nine. The capacity for approximate evaluation had therefore been preserved, but the ability to perform exact calculation had been lost.[76]

Techniques for precisely representing numerical quantities developed in the evolution of human societies with the emergence of spoken, and especially written, language. At first, use was made of tangible notations—fingers, notches in pieces of wood, or knots (as in the thin cords of the Inca *quipus*). These gave way to written notations relying on additive or multiplicative principles, and finally to positional notations such as Arabic numbering.[77] The child learns numerical concepts and systems of notation at the same time as language.

Moreover, once the child knows how to represent large numbers precisely, he can perform addition, subtraction, multiplication, division with these quantities. Culturally selected epigenetic rules—the rules and tables associated with the principal operations of mental calculation that children acquire by learning—serve to forestall a combinatorial explosion of possibilities. The acquisition and use of abstract rules to grasp the reality of the world begins very early: by the age of seven months infants are capable of representing, extracting, and generalizing algebraic rules.[78]

In Chapter 2 we looked at several neural network models incorporating rules that organize the behavior of an artificial organism in the simulation of a cognitive learning task such as the Wisconsin card-sorting test and the Tower of London test. The neural architecture of such an organism makes it possible to select from among high-level abstract representations of the color, form, and number of objects that have been presented to it. Here the clusters of rules coding for these representations have been built into the neural network. In actual human brains, of course, defined patterns of connectivity are established in the conscious workspace through the selection of prerepresentations produced by an endogenous diversity generator, with or without an external source of stimulation.[79] Connectionist architectures that store and produce temporal sequences of representations by selection have been devised that simulate, for example, song learning in birds as a function of syllabic attrition.[80] These artificial organisms can serve as elementary neuronal models of context-dependence. (The relative position of a note, for example, is essential in the recognition of melody.) More generally, such models illustrate how simple rules for processing knowledge can be socially acquired through epigenetic selection. They may plausibly be extended even to include more abstract categories or rules selected at higher levels of the conscious workspace that help mediate social interactions.

Another implication of the concept of epigenetic rules at the social level has to do with their embodiment in stable material form. The peculiarly human capacity to create what the psychologist Ignace Meyerson called "*œuvres*"—works, especially tools—is obviously useful in the first place to the person who creates them.[81] But artifacts may also be intended for the use of other members of the social group. They may operate recursively as well: by contributing to the manufacture of other objects, they are the source of technology. These "prostheses" of the mental activity of the human brain have radically changed the nature and quality of human life, as much with respect to the social world as to the natural world (see Chapter 8).

From a philosophical point of view, the notion of epigenetic rules (or "social operators," as they might also be called) may provide a solution to the paradox pointed out by Donald Davidson concerning the "normative" character of the regularities of human behavior. Davidson opposed the rules governing social life to the laws of the natural sciences, which he saw as immutable and existing independently of human minds.[82] The capacity of the human brain to produce epigenetic rules, subject them to the scrutiny of reflective consciousness, store them in memory, and share them among the members of the social group works to break down a whole system of automatic reflexes and opens up new possibilities for testing the truth of representations and beliefs. Human beings—like other animal species, but at a far higher level—possess an instinctive ability to learn, to generate and apply rules that introduce new regularities in human conduct. These culturally acquired norms belong to the natural world by virtue of their neuronal character, and therefore are susceptible to objective examination. Through the use of cognitive tools, and as a consequence of their own nature, humans have created a new environment for themselves that in principle can be explained by the laws of science. If indeed there exist bridge laws linking physical and mental events, surely one of them will have to be sought at the level of epigenetic rules.

Mathematical objects, by virtue of their recursivity and generative character, are a classic example of epigenetic rules. But the implications of these rules for human behavior extend far beyond the world of mathematics in the search for truth. All kinds of rules for correct reasoning—from the laws of Aristotelian logic to Frege's "ideography"—are epigenetic instances of the innate *regulae* of Descartes. Moral rules, to which I shall turn in due course, can be seen as schematic instructions for socially appropriate behavior: they prevent individuals from engaging in conduct that threatens both their own well-being and that of their neighbors.[83] It should not come as a surprise, then, that the struggle for truth, which will occupy us in the following chapters, turns out to be related in part to this harmonization of social life. Epigenetic rules are, in any case, essential components of the cultural traditions that have been selected and accumulated in the course of human history. They permit obvious economies of time and energy in learning about the world, conferring upon those societies that discovered how to produce and use them an exceptional selective advantage. The appearance and development of scientific knowledge—a moment of decisive consequence for the evaluation of the truth of representations and beliefs—plainly depended upon this ability to generate epigenetic rules.

From Genes to Brain

5

The functioning of the human brain as a sort of truth apparatus, among individuals and within the social group, raises important questions that neurobiologists are now able to address from both a theoretical and an experimental point of view. The evolutionary origins of brain structure and function nonetheless remain deeply puzzling. Happily, recent developments in molecular biology offer new material for reflection and, above all, new avenues for experiment.

The sequencing of the human genome is now complete.[1] It will take years to interpret the result, that is, to understand the function of its constituent genes and of the regulatory mechanisms associated with them. Even so, the broad overview we now possess will enable us to settle an ancient debate about the nature of the brain. Is it endowed with an innate structure that accounts for human intellectual capacities? Or is it initially a *tabula rasa,* a blank slate on which knowledge is inscribed through experience alone? Will we ever know what the "initial state" of the brain of the newborn baby really is? Noam Chomsky, referring in particular to the human infant's endowment with the faculty of language, has described this state, without further explanation, as "an expression of the genes comparable to the initial state of the human visual system."[2]

In humans, as we shall see, the regulation of gene expression in most, if not all, cases requires specific interactions with the physical or social environment, or both. It is nonetheless obvious that the monkey's brain and the human brain are two quite different objects; and, moreover, that a great number of behavioral traits distinguish human beings from monkeys. These species-specific differences are genetic in origin, the product of mechanisms encoded in chromosomal DNA. Indeed, these genetic mechanisms set limits to development, creating a "genetic envelope" within which both the prenatal and the postnatal evolution of the human brain and of its predispositions take place.

In addition to humans (about 30,000 genes), we now have at our disposal the full genomic sequences of five major organisms: a yeast, *Saccharomyces cerevisiae* (6,144 genes);[3] a plant, *Arabidopsis thaliana* (25,706 genes);[4] a worm, *Caenorhabditis elegans* (18,266 genes);[5] a fly, *Drosophila melanogaster* (13,338 genes),[6] and a mouse, *Mus musculus* (between 27,000 and 30,500 genes).[7] This basic information makes it possible to compare the complete genetic patrimony of species that are very far removed from each other and, in principle, to identify the gene sequences that govern the manufacture of cells, the manner in which they are assembled to form a multicellular organism, and, more specifically, the development of the central nervous system. We are now in a position to decipher the signature of human nature, as it were; to solve the riddle of what distinguishes humankind from its nearest ancestors. We have now, therefore, arrived at a crucial juncture in the history of biological thought.

Genomic Complexity and Brain Structure

A first approach to the problem—a simple, even somewhat simplistic one—consists in counting genes. It rests on a commonsensical intuition: an increase in the number of genes ought to correspond to an increase in the complexity of organisms and, in particular, the complexity of their brains. In fact, this is not the case. One runs up against a paradox: although the brain has developed in the course of evolution, and although the number and variety of the cells of which it is composed increase in multicellular organisms, the growing complexity of the nervous system, from the fly to the mouse and then to human beings, is not simply the result of a linear increase in the number of genes. More, it turns out, does not necessarily mean better.

To begin with, the number of nonredundant proteins coded for by the genomes of multicellular organisms such as the fly (8,065 proteins) and the worm (9,453 proteins) is only twice that of the yeast, a unicellular organism.[8] About 30 percent of the proteins in the fly and the worm are identical, and about 20 percent are common to both fly and yeast. About 1,308 groups of proteins are shared by humans, flies, worms, and yeasts, representing 3,129, 1,445, 1,503, and 1,441 kinds of protein, respectively.[9] These shared proteins possess functions common to all eucaryotes. Known as "housekeeping proteins," they are responsible for the replication and repair of DNA, biosynthesis, the folding and degradation of proteins, and their transport and secretion. They are essential for the life of the cell. But they do not distinguish yeasts from flies or human beings.

Moreover, from the worm *Caenorhabditis* to man, the total number of DNA bases in the genome increases by almost thirty times, rising from 100 million to 2.9 billion base pairs, while the total number of genes is multiplied by not more than three or four. The coding sequences (or exons) represent only 1.1–1.4 percent of the total genomic sequence (Figure 35). By far the larger part of DNA is formed of repeated noncoding sequences whose size increases with evolution. Interestingly, in the Japanese pufferfish *(Fugu rubripes),* these repetitive sequences are about one-tenth as frequent as in humans.[10] And from the mouse to humans, the 14 percent increase noticed in total genome length (from 2.5 to 2.9 billion base pairs) is entirely due to repetitive sequences.[11] It is possible that they are vestiges of paleontological history, but they may also play an active role in the morphological changes undergone by the genome.[12] Systematic comparison of families of genes that have survived over the course of evolution, from very primitive animals up through mammals, suggests that two successive duplications of the entire genome took place between *Amphioxus,* the archetype of all subsequent vertebrates, and the fishes.[13] The human genome is thus an amplified version of a simpler genome, equipped with a set of nonredundant housekeeping proteins not much larger than that of the fly or the worm. The main differences between flies, worms, and humans derive from a group of specialized genes involved in the construction of the body of the organism.

The paradox is still more striking when one compares the genetic heritage of the species I have just mentioned with the structure of their brains. On the one hand, although the total amount of DNA present

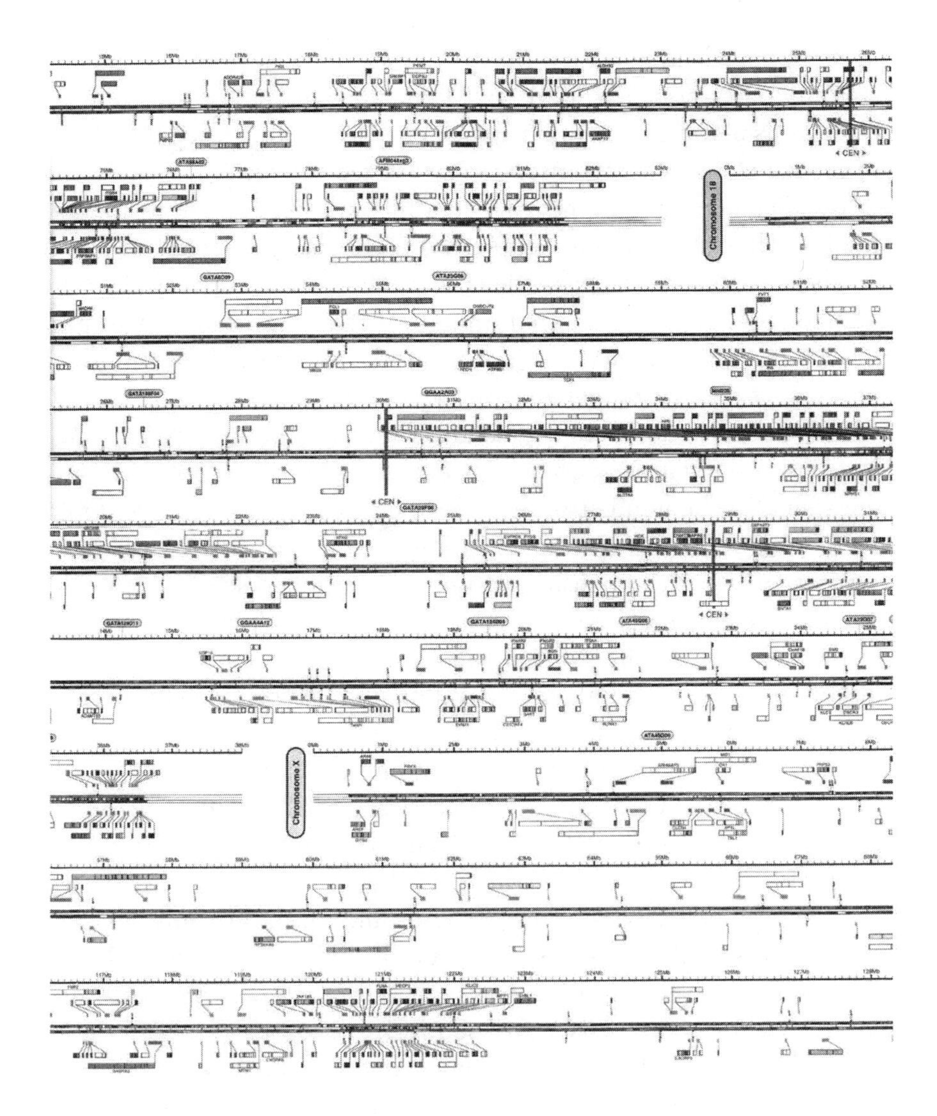

Figure 35. Partial map of the human genome. The double-ruled horizontal line represents the two strands of the DNA molecule, with the genes coded by the DNA shown on either side. The genes shown here constitute between 25.5 and 37.8 percent of the total genome, but the share of coding sequences (exons) represents only 1.1–1.4 percent of the number of base pairs. The chromosomes and the genes themselves contain considerable quantities of noncoding sequences.

in the human genome is on the order of 3 billion base pairs, the genome contains only about 30,000 genes. On the other hand, the total number of neurons in the human brain approaches 100 billion, each one exhibiting distinctive characteristics. Considered in purely quantitative terms, then, the genetic information available for constructing not only the body but also the brain appears to be severely limited.[14]

The second point to be made is that the relation between the total number of genes and the evolution of brain structure reveals a surprising absence of linearity.[15] The genome of the worm *C. elegans* and that of the fruit fly *Drosophila* are comparable in size, containing roughly 18,000 and 13,000 different genes, respectively. But there are only 302 neurons in the worm's nervous system, and about 250,000 in that of the fruit fly. The number of genes in the flowering plant *Arabidopsis* is higher (25,706)—even though it has no nervous system! Still more surprisingly, from bony fish to laboratory mice and so on up to man, the number of genes is roughly constant. And yet, despite the increase in the number of cells (from 40 million in the mouse to 50 or 100 billion in man), mammalian cerebral anatomy evolved from a rather smooth brain, with a cortex divided into only ten to twenty areas (functionally adapted to sight, hearing, motor control, and so forth), to a brain with a very large relative cortical surface, containing at least a hundred areas integrated within a system of parallel and hierarchical levels.[16]

Comparative analysis of the chromosomes of orangutans, gorillas, chimpanzees, and humans discloses certain constant patterns.[17] Moreover, between the chimpanzee and man, 98.3 percent of the sequences containing noncoding DNA are identical, and probably on the order of 99.5 percent in the case of coding sequences. Nonetheless, certain transpositions and inversions of DNA strings have been observed, for example on chromosomes 4, 9, and 12.[18] Comparative maps of human and chimpanzee genomes reveal differences restricted to a limited number of positions (two clusters on human chromosome 21, for example) rather than a wholly random distribution of base pair changes.[19] The genetic distance between the chimpanzee and man is only a bit more than twenty-five times greater than between existing human populations. From a genetic point of view, then, the chimpanzee and man are quite close. Yet the differences between them are very pronounced if one considers the structure and, above all, the function of the brain.[20]

Chimpanzees possess the equivalent of Broca's and Wernicke's language areas, only without the wealth of connectivity that characterizes the processing of language in human beings.[21] In the millions of years from *Australopithecus* to *Homo sapiens,* the volume and morphology of the brain have changed considerably (Figure 36). Three major reorganizations have taken place.[22] First, the parietal lobe—a cortical area concerned with visual attention, spatial relationships, and the coordination of bodily movements—grew in size by comparison with the rest of the brain. This area is directly responsible for the individual's physical relationship to the environment and, more particularly, the manual production and use of tools. Second, the differentiation between right and left hemispheres became more pronounced. Finally, and most importantly, a rapid expansion of the frontal lobe occurred *prior* to the major augmentation in brain volume. The number of genetic events needed to produce such remarkable changes of form seems astonishingly small.

A cursory examination of the structure of the human genome therefore does not give an immediate answer to the question of the origins of the brain—what some philosophers call its "emergence" in the course of evolution.[23] One might even say that the paradox has only been sharpened. The genes of the mouse are very close, if not identical, to those of man. What, then, accounts for the obvious differences between the two?

Genetic Parsimony

Given that the gene sequences themselves hardly differ from one mammal to another, what distinguishes their genomes needs to be sought in the expression and regulation of these genes. We know that, from one cell to another in a given organism, not all genes are simultaneously expressed. Consider, for example, a muscle fiber, a red blood cell, and a visual receptor of the retina. All these cells express the genes that code for the housekeeping proteins, which are indispensable to cellular life. But they also selectively express specific proteins (such as

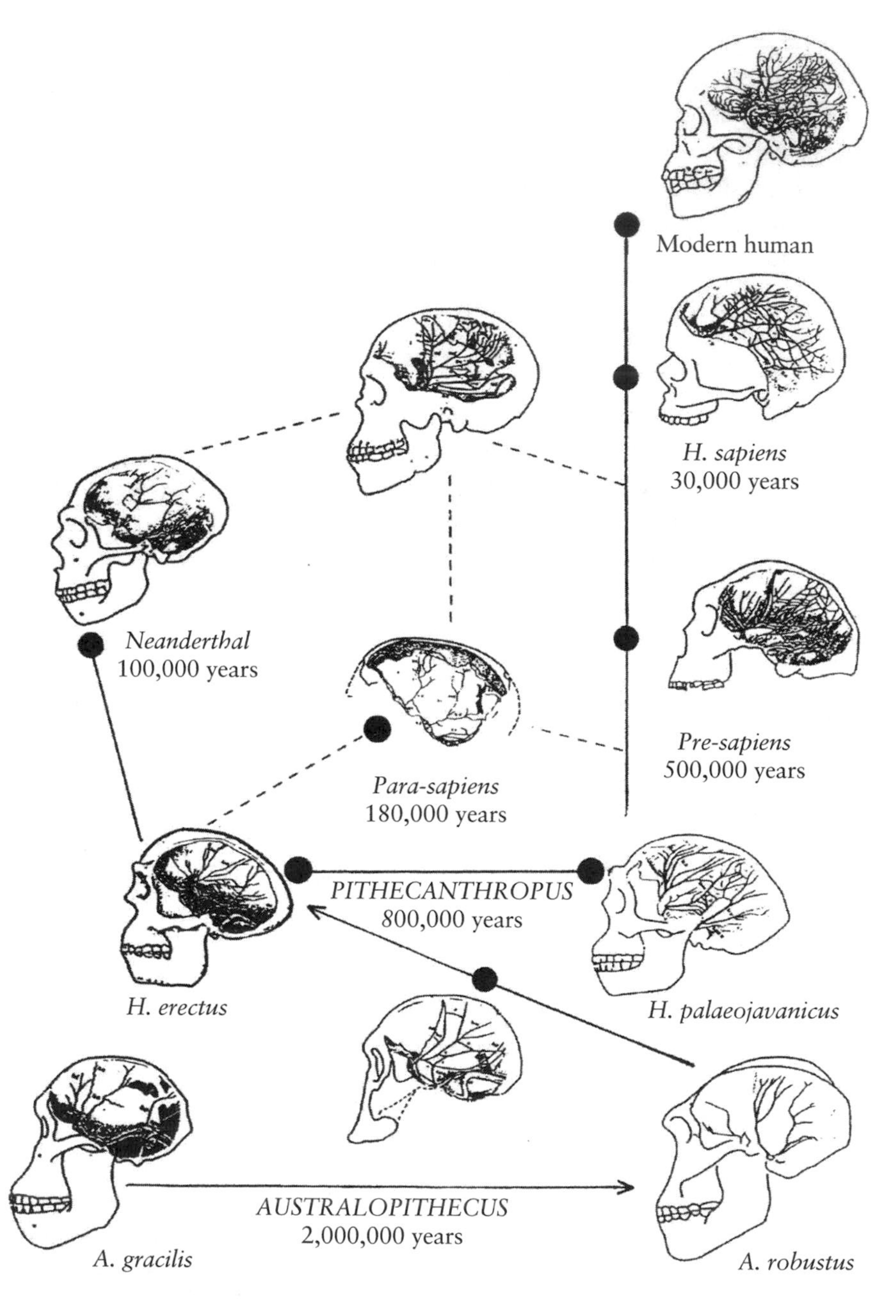

Figure 36. Evolution of the brain in human ancestors. Cerebral evolution is depicted here on the basis of the intracranial imprints of the meningeal vessels.

myosin, hemoglobin, or the visual pigment rhodopsin) that are directly related to their function. Gene expression is therefore regulated in the course of cell differentiation during embryonic development. The passage from gene to protein—the expression of the gene—occurs in several successive stages. First, the stable sequence of the gene's deoxyribonucleic acid (DNA) is transcribed into a complementary labile sequence of ribonucleic acid (RNA). DNA alone is not capable of replicating RNA. The messenger RNA that results from the transcription of the gene must then itself be translated into a sequence of amino acids, that is, proteins. The map of genes expressed in messenger RNA thus constitutes a preliminary sketch of the differentiated state of the cell. The source not only of the diversity of cell types in an organism—particularly with respect to its neurons—but also of the variable character of the organism itself during embryonic development and over the course of evolution is therefore to be sought at the level of transcriptional regulation.

The molecular genetics of the early stages of embryonic development in the fruit fly, the chick, and the mouse provide important clues for unraveling the paradoxes associated with both genetic parsimony and the nonlinear evolution of brain structure by comparison with the evolution of the genome.

In *Drosophila,* a great many genes have been identified that determine the morphology of the embryo, the segmentation of the body, and the identity of its segments. These developmental genes include the homeotic Hox genes, which control body segmentation. Their mutation in the fly, for example, is responsible for the transformation of antennae into legs. Moreover, in the fly's genome, these genes are arranged on the chromosomes in a linear order that reproduces the sequence of their expression along the antero-posterior axis—from the head to the tail—in the course of the development of the embryo (Figure 37).[24]

Quite surprisingly, very similar genes are also found in vertebrate embryos. For example, there are 160 homeobox domains in man, 100 in the fly, 82 in the worm, but only 6 in the yeast.[25] The nonaccidental resemblance of these genes, like that of embryonic vertebrate shapes, suggests a common evolutionary origin of the body plans of these organisms—and therefore of the coordinates of their nervous systems as well.[26]

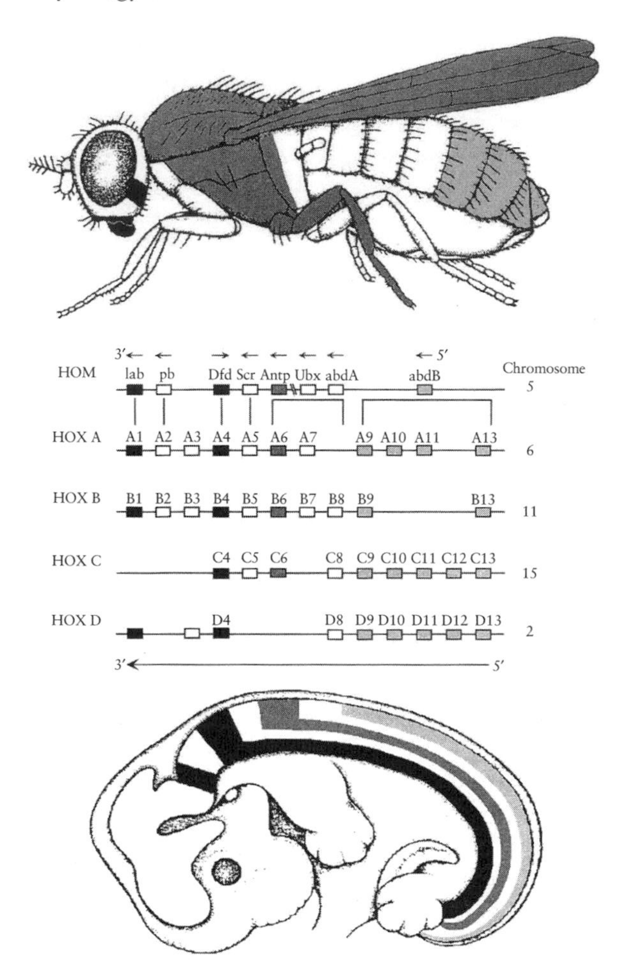

Figure 37. Comparison of the pattern of homeotic developmental gene expression in the fly and the mouse. This diagram illustrates the parallelism between the linear distribution of the genes on the chromosome and that of their product along the axis of the body of the adult *Drosophila* and of the mouse embryo. The overall plan of gene expression is preserved to a remarkable degree from *Drosophila* to the higher vertebrates.

In *Drosophila,* the Cartesian coordinates—head-tail, back-stomach, right-left—of the embryo are established very early, before the mother lays her eggs. In mammals, they are formed later, after the first divisions of the fertilized egg. In the mouse, this occurs after the implantation of the embryo in the mother's uterus, roughly six days following fertilization. At this stage, the cell aggregate (or *conceptus*) resulting from the segmentation of the egg resembles a closed cylinder. One half will form specialized tissues, such as the placenta, which serve to implant the embryo in the mother's uterus, while the other half will become the actual embryo. Within the wall of the uterus, a rotation of the cellular structure leads to the differentiation of the antero-posterior axis. A small set of embryonic cells that make up what is called the visceral endoderm marks the placement of the head of the embryo.[27] It is interesting to note that such precursor cells, as they are known, express developmental genes (such as Otx2 in the mouse) that are also found in the fruit fly embryo (the orthodenticle gene). What is more, mutation of these genes in the mouse produces an embryo that fails to develop a normal antero-posterior axis, with the result that the head itself does not form. Genes such as Otx2 and its homologues are therefore necessary for the formation of the head in both the mouse and the fly. Despite differences in timing and topological detail, the patterns of gene expression in the course of early development in insects and vertebrates are strikingly similar.[28]

Comparative molecular embryology confirms this observation. Careful study of the early stages of development of the neural tube in the fruit fly and the frog has shown that the longitudinal distribution of embryonic nerve cells, or neuroblasts, exhibits a similar striped pattern: three parallel bands on both sides of the midline.[29] Detailed analysis of the genes expressed in the different cell types that form in these columns likewise reveals remarkable resemblances. The genetic mechanisms establishing the general features of the nervous system have been preserved in the course of evolution, from invertebrates to vertebrates, all the way to man. This constitutes a first answer to the paradox of genetic parsimony: a vertebrate brain did not have to be constructed *de novo* out of entirely new genes. The great French paleontologist Geoffroy Saint-Hilaire was the first to formulate this idea, referring to a "unity of plan."[30] The human genome preserves a large number of structural determinants from the genetic heritage of man's invertebrate ancestors.

Yet differences between invertebrate and vertebrate nervous systems are evident. Whereas in invertebrates the neural tube runs along the ventral side, in vertebrates it is located on the dorsal side. Ultimately, vertebrates are nothing more than invertebrates that walk on their backs. Close examination of the pattern of genes expressed in very early stages of embryonic development, in particular at the moment known as gastrulation, once more reveals important similarities; but a complete inversion of the relevant territory of the nervous system has taken place, from the ventral to the dorsal position. Only a small number of genetic events—perhaps only a single event, as we shall see—were needed to bring about a fundamental reorganization of the nervous system.[31]

A second set of differences between invertebrates and vertebrates concerns the segmentation of the body, and therefore of the nervous system as well. Crustaceans, insects, and spiders are often referred to as "articulated" creatures because of the division of their bodies into rigid segments linked by flexible articulations, or joints. In vertebrates, this segmentation (marking off the spinal cord, for example) is much less pronounced. Under the influence of "segment polarity" genes that govern early development, transverse rows of expressed genes are formed in *Drosophila,* but this pattern is lost in vertebrates, where homologous genes produce longitudinal columns.[32] Finally, in vertebrates, one notices a striking asymmetry of the organs of the body (liver, heart, and so on) and of cerebral hemispheres (in mammals and particularly in man). Isolated genes such as *"lefty"* in the mouse and *situs inversus* in man, together with their protein product (a molecule called dynein that is involved in flagellar movement), determine the right-left asymmetry of the body.[33]

In all these instances, a few distinct genetic events dramatically alter an overall pattern of expression of developmental genes, which, by determining the three-dimensional plan of the body, determines the structure of the brain as well. Whereas most patterns of gene expression are preserved, a few genes undergo sudden, all-or-nothing transformations. We need now to examine what such nonlinearity involves.

Nonlinear Networks of Gene Regulation

The development of embryonic forms can be understood as the result of the differential expression of developmental genes in space and time. Let us take as a measure of the complexity of an organism the number of theoretically possible states resulting from the expression of *n* genes that constitute the organism's entire genome. Assuming that each gene has only two possible states (on and off), the total number of possible states is 2^n.[34] The difference in complexity between man and the worm would then be $2^{30,000}$ divided by $2^{20,000}$, or $10^{3,000}$. This is a very large number indeed—larger than the total number of particles in the entire universe. There is no reason in principle, then, why the three-dimensional structural differences among embryos and the differentiation of various types of embryonic cells—or, for that matter, of the neurons and synapses of the adult brain—could not result from the combinatorial expression of a one-dimensional sequence of a limited number of genes. But things are not so simple. An organism is not a random collection of gene states. After all, it possesses a form.

Turing's Model

Relatively few mathematicians and theoretical biologists have addressed the fundamental problem of the emergence of biological form, or morphogenesis. The English mathematician Alan Turing, in a famous article published in 1952, gave the problem its classic statement. In the course of evolutionary development, Turing noted, one starts with a sphere—the egg—and winds up with an organism having a characteristic form: a head, a tail, and four legs. The question arises whether the genesis of this form can be explained solely on the basis of physical and chemical forces. Turing suggested that "a system of chemical substances, called *morphogens,* reacting together and diffusing through a tissue, is adequate to account for the main phenomena of morphogenesis."[35] He went on to demonstrate this principle mathematically. The example he chose is well known and extremely simple: the formation of the tentacles of *Hydra* from a continuous mouth ring. Turing showed that in the initial state—a sphere or ring—the system can be treated as a set of chemical reactions distributed in space in a homogeneous fashion. Then, in the course of development, the system spontaneously develops a structure, a form, as a consequence of instabilities triggered by random events. Turing asserted that morphogenesis occurs only if the chemical reactions that make up the system interact with one another. But this is not a sufficient condition. A reaction-diffusion system must include large-scale autocatalytic reactions, cross-signaling between chemical reactions, and feedback loops through which information about these exchanges is distributed throughout the system, causing nonlinear processes to occur. These processes give rise to "symmetry-breaking," which in turn creates new structures that may be stabilized even under conditions that are far from thermodynamic equilibrium.[36]

Is there a connection between this analysis and the patterns of gene expression that ultimately determine the structure of the brain? I have already mentioned events of the all-or-nothing type that create, for example, boundaries between territories, striped patterns, and right-left asymmetries. It seems reasonable to regard these sharp and stable discontinuities as instances of symmetry-breaking in Turing's sense. The "chemical substances" referred to in the 1952 paper may be seen as the products of the specialized genes expressed in the early stages of embryonic development that I discussed earlier, together with the signaling systems that regulate their expression. The 30,000 genes of the human genome are not all activated simultaneously at the onset of embryonic development. Nor are they independently expressed, one after another. Their activation (or inactivation) occurs in a concerted and gradual fashion—sometimes with the reuse of certain genes—that exhibits well-defined spatial and temporal patterns. Gene expressions are linked to one another, not physically through strands of DNA, but by the diffusion of signals that establish a temporary form of communication between genes spread out along the chromosomes. In this way *signaling networks* among genes are formed, within which nonlinear effects emerge as a result of the operation of local autocatalytic mechanisms and long-distance inhibitory signals[37]—thus providing a material basis for the "interactions" postulated by Turing in his system of chemical reactions. Considerable progress has been made in recent decades in identifying the various components of these gene regulatory networks.

The pioneering work of Jacques Monod and François Jacob on the control of gene expression in bacteria pointed to the essential role played by specialized segments of DNA known today as "promoters." These regulatory sequences directly activate (or repress) the transcription of the DNA of a neighboring gene into messenger RNA.[38] Typically they are situated adjacent to a "structural" gene, whose transcription they laterally control by means of specialized and diffusible allosteric proteins, known as "transcription factors," which serve as signaling molecules.[39] These factors bind to specific elements of DNA in the promoters and, depending on their conformation, trigger or inhibit the transcription of the adjacent gene.[40] A specialized enzyme (technically, a supramacromolecular enzyme complex) named polymerase functions as a catalyst for the transcription of the gene into messenger RNA. The transcription factors trigger (or block) transcription by activating (or inhibiting) the action of polymerase. Many of these transcription factors have been identified. They form very large supramacromolecular assemblies with the polymerase and are anchored to the DNA regulatory sequences found in the vicinity of the gene (see Figure 40C later in this chapter).[41]

An interesting question is whether transcription factors serve as connecting pieces in the construction of intracellular gene regulatory networks. The efficiency of these networks is itself controlled by systems responsible for the production and transmission of signals within cells and between cells. Michel Kerszberg and I have tried to resolve the question on a mathematical basis, with reference to three situations of increasing complexity: the formation of a boundary; the development of a definite pattern of gene expression boundaries; and, finally, the morphogenesis of the central nervous system.

Boundaries of Gene Expression

The simplest case involves the formation of a sharp boundary in gene expression by means of an all-or-nothing mechanism of gene transcription. For experimental purposes we chose an elementary case: the development of the junction between a motor nerve and a skeletal muscle fiber, known as the motor endplate (Figures 38A, 38B).[42] The neurotransmitter of this classic synapse, acetylcholine, binds to a specific receptor on the postsynaptic side of the junction. This receptor is, as we have seen, a much-studied allosteric membrane protein that is traversed by an ion channel.[43] In the adult, the acetylcholine receptor is uniquely found under the motor nerve ending, where it forms a dense and stable cluster. The situation is not the same in the early stages of development, when the acetylcholine receptor is found dispersed over the entire surface of the muscle fiber. The embryonic muscle fiber pos-

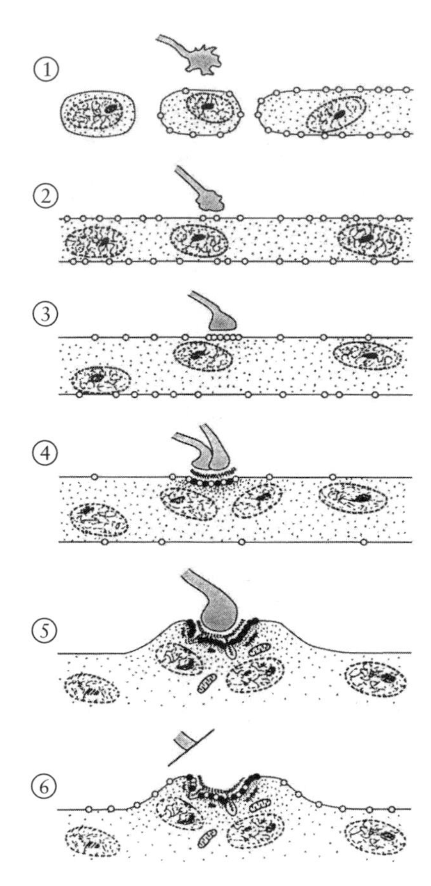

Figure 38A. Evolution of the biosynthesis and the distribution of acetylcholine receptors in embryonic and postnatal development. These diagrams illustrate the successive stages of the development of the synapse between a motor nerve and a skeletal muscle fiber. The embryonic muscle fibers express the receptor (white dots) in mobile and labile form over their entire surface. Contact between the growth cone of the motor nerve and the muscle fiber leads to the aggregation of the receptor molecules under the nerve ending and the elimination of the receptor outside the synapse. By the fourth stage, several nerve endings converge at the synapse, but only one ultimately persists (see Figure 44). In the adult synapse, the receptor is present exclusively under the nerve ending in a stable form (black dots). The electrical activity of the muscle, which begins with the contact between nerve and muscle, represses the biosynthesis of the receptor protein outside the synapse, whereas biosynthesis is preserved *under* the synapse owing to the influence of neural factors such as AGRIN and ARIA.

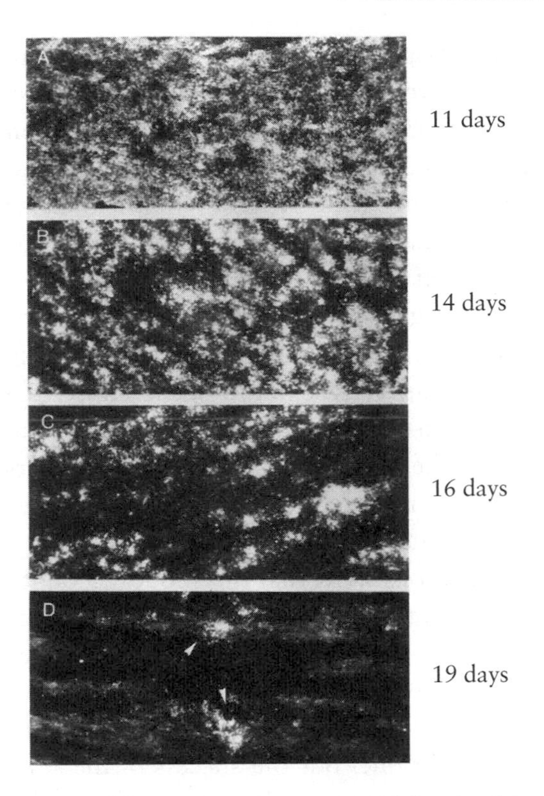

Figure 38B. Evolution of the transcription pattern of the nicotinic receptor α subunit gene at 11, 14, 16, and 19 days of embryonic development in the chick (corresponding to stages 2, 3, and 4 in Figure 38A). The white grains signify the presence of messenger RNA. There is a progressive restriction of the transcription that in the adult is confined solely to the nuclei situated under the nerve ending. This elementary morphogenesis of a singular transcription compartment in the middle of the muscular fiber delimited by sharp boundaries is hypothesized to be produced by a nonlinear response of transcription factors acting at the level of the gene promoters (see Figure 39).

sesses many nuclei, all of which express the several genes responsible for the biosynthesis of the acetylcholine receptor. In the adult, by contrast, only the few nuclei that are located under the motor nerve ending express the receptor genes. A sharp discontinuity in gene transcription therefore develops between the muscle nuclei located at the junction and those located outside it. The pattern is even simpler than that of the hydra's tentacles studied by Turing: a single band of gene expression in the middle of the muscle fiber. Our hypothesis is that a molecular switch—an all-or-nothing mechanism involving at least one transcription factor—governs the transcription of the receptor genes in such a way that a boundary forms on each side of the motor endplate.

This mechanism is postulated to involve a particular transcription factor—known as a myogenic protein—that activates the expression of the receptor genes. It consists essentially of an autocatalytic feedback loop operating at the level of the gene that codes for the transcription factor. The myogenic protein activates its own transcription by binding itself to elements of DNA present in its promoter, triggering an explosive, nonlinear increase in local gene transcription. Moreover, this on-off mechanism is regulated either in a positive fashion by neural factors released by the nerve—thus activating transcription under the nerve ending—or in a negative fashion by electrical signals propagated in the muscle fiber—halting transcription outside the synapse.[44]

Computer simulations show that this model accounts at least in formal terms for the developmental dynamics of the focal expression of acetylcholine receptor genes by endplate nuclei, as a result of which a single gene expression band forms in the middle of the muscle fiber.[45] This, of course, does not mean that the mechanism we have proposed is necessarily the right one. But the success of the simulations shows that the regulation of gene transcription by a minimal number of simple components (Turing's "chemical substances"), including both positive and negative feedback loops, suffices to account for a fundamental process of embryonic morphogenesis: the formation of a sharp boundary.[46] This is not only a theoretical point of departure but an experimental one as well.

Reading a Morphogenic Gradient

The second situation to be considered—the formation of the body plan of the embryo—is more complex. It involves the "reading" of a diffusion gradient for a morphogen that produces a sharp boundary of gene transcription at a well-defined position along the gradient. This process is responsible for the segregation of the embryo into its principal parts: head, thorax, and abdomen (Figure 39). Very early in the history of embryology, gradients of morphogenic substances were assumed to govern the development of such embryonic forms.[47] It is only recently, however, that experimental evidence has been obtained in support of

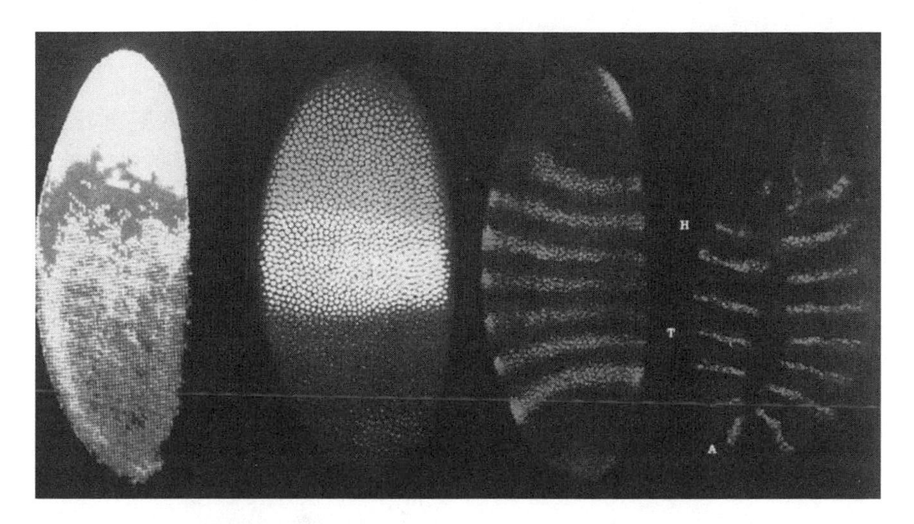

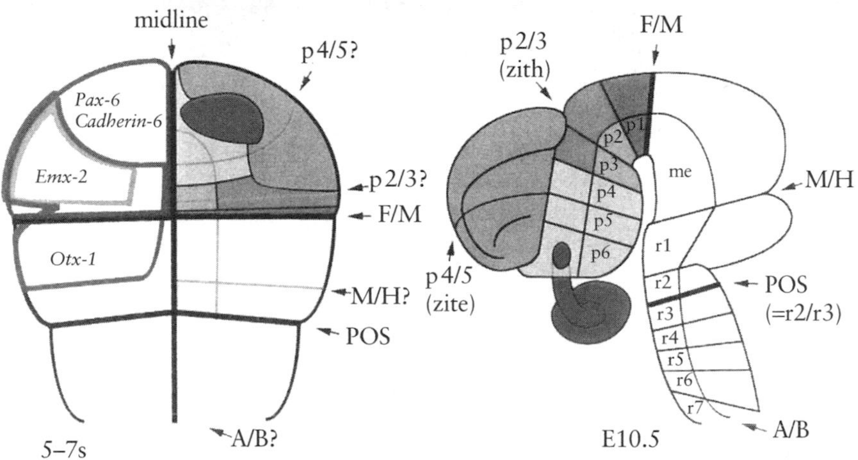

Figure 39. Boundaries and compartments of gene expression. *Top:* In the *Drosophila* embryo, boundaries of gene expression are formed at critical positions at definite moments of development, followed by band patterns corresponding to the segmentation of the body. *Bottom:* In the mouse embryo, the neural plaque is shown at the very beginning (stages 5–7) of the development of the nervous system *(left)*. The neural tube subsequently forms and then, ten and a half days after fertilization, the brain with its successive vesicles *(right)*. The expression of the p4/5 gene marks the presumptive compartment of the cerebral cortex. The regulation of the expression of some developmental genes in this area may be regarded as governing the development of the cerebral cortex in mammals up through humans.

the existence of gradients of diffusible proteins in the course of embryogenesis.

The *Drosophila* embryo resembles a muscle fiber to the extent that, in very early stages of development, it possesses many nuclei within a single cytoplasm having no membrane barrier. But, as one would expect, the embryo exhibits an additional dimension of complexity. While muscle fibers have two equivalent extremities with a synapse in the middle, the *Drosophila* embryo seems to display a head and a tail. This head-tail polarity in the fruit fly is already present in the mother's ovary through the distributed product of particular developmental genes: bicoid and dorsal proteins. Moreover, these morphogens regulate the expression of genes along the antero-posterior axis of the embryo according to a well-defined spatial pattern. The central problem, then, is to identify the mechanism by which a sharp boundary of gene expression systematically emerges at a given position on the gradient, splitting the body, for example, into its principal segments.[48] The model Kerzsberg and I have proposed to account for the reading of such a gradient incorporates the basic elements of the motor endplate model and posits, moreover, the existence of a morphogen that forms a smooth gradient extending from the head to the tail of the embryo.[49] The gradient is read by the nuclei in the cytoplasm of the embryo as a sudden increase in gene expression. Our conjecture is that this mechanism involves, in addition to the molecular switch mentioned in the first model, a new kind of interconnection at the transcription factor level that causes the gradient to be read at one position rather than another.

In the first place, we have tried to link the activation (or inhibition) of genes dispersed throughout the genome by connecting them in a coherent fashion *within* a given nucleus. But links must also be established *between* the nuclei, within the cytoplasm of the embryo, so that a pattern of bands with distinct boundaries can develop. A signaling network is then established via the transcription factors. These molecular "partners" jointly form a complex of several transcription factor units in which, for example, a morphogen molecule from the gradient is associated with a transcription factor that now is coded by a gene expressed in an embryonic nucleus. In other words, a connection is established between components of the gradient and the embryonic

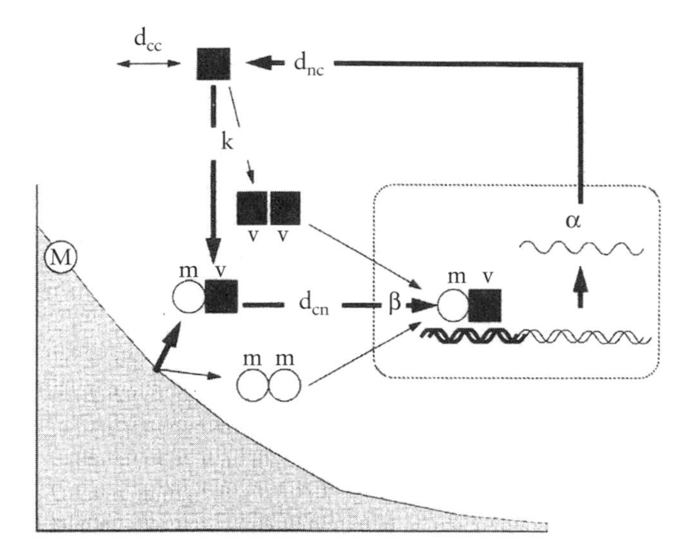

Figure 40A. The model devised by Kerszberg and Changeux seeks to explain how a sharp boundary of gene expression is formed at a definite position within an embryonic territory. The model assumes, first, the existence of a concentration gradient of a morphogenetic substance (M). This substance, assumed here to be a transcription factor (indicated by a white circle), binds as a dimer to a specific sequence of the promoter (double helix in thick lines) of a gene (double helix in thin lines), which itself codes for a transcription factor known as vernier (V, indicated by a black square). As a consequence, an autocatalytic loop may form in the regulation of the transcription of the V-gene and of all the other genes controlled by V. This nonlinearity in the expression of V is postulated to be responsible for the formation of a sharp boundary of gene expression (see Figure 40B).

The model also provides for a boundary-positioning mechanism by assuming that the morphogen and the vernier form a supramacromolecular assembly that connects the expression of the V gene with the local concentration of M. If the dimers MV and MM act upon the promoter, gene expression will occur up to the point where, M having become too weak, only the inactive dimer VV will be present. In this way the boundary is positioned along the gradient.

nucleus. Nonlinear relationships between the concentration of transcription factors and morphogens may then develop as a result of the combinatory operation of all-or-nothing switches analogous to those postulated in the simple case of the neuromuscular synapse. Differing combinations of transcription factors at the promoter level create sharp boundaries of gene expression at definite positions on the morphogen gradient (Figures 40A, 40B, and 40C). Partners, one might say, make patterns.[50]

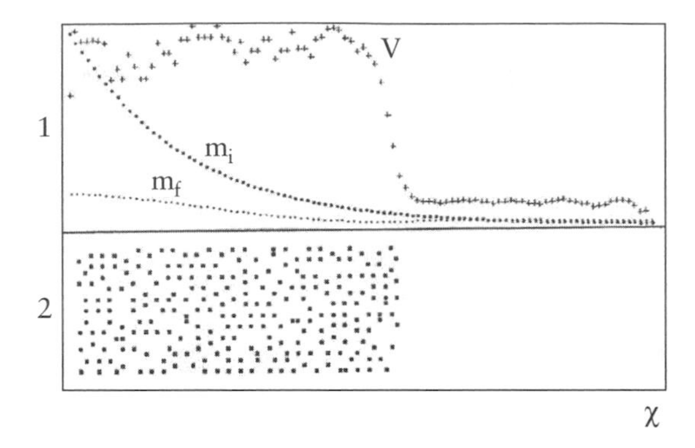

Figure 40B. Gradient reading by the autocatalytic protein V. *Top:* Protein concentrations, denoting the initial gradient of morphogen M_i along coordinate χ of the embryo, its final (late times) concentration M_f, and the final vernier distribution V. *Bottom:* A representation of nuclei in the simulated two-dimensional embryo. Only those nuclei are shown in which V transcription is turned on at late times. A sharp boundary is seen in their distribution.

Transcription of the gene encoding V is induced by the MV dimer, and this cooperativity gives rise to a sharp boundary in V expression. The boundary is first located at that threshold M concentration, M_1, for which the amplification factor (gain) of the V regulation loop is precisely 1. Because of diffusion of the involved substances, it then moves somewhat toward the low-M region. When the morphogen is scarce, its depletion may result in a countergradient which reduces this later motion and stabilizes the boundary.

Computer simulations confirm that the mathematical model accounts for the formation of sharp and stable boundaries and, additionally, predicts the formation of bands at well-defined positions along the gradient. The model thus furnishes a possible explanation for the emergence of embryonic forms.[51]

The existence of such nonlinear and combinatory transcription

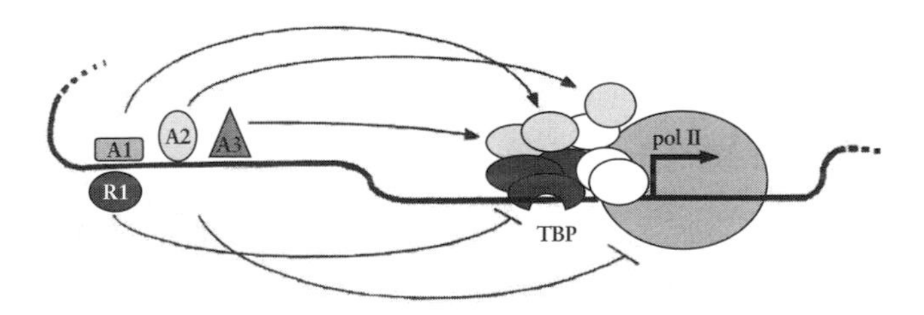

Figure 40C. A plausible representation of the formation of a transcription complex (see Figure 40A), with several factors associated with the enzyme that regulates the transcription (polymerase II).

factor networks has been experimentally confirmed in *Drosophila*.[52] Among other predictions, the model accounts for the displacement of band patterns of gene expression observed experimentally in the fruit fly embryo when transcription factor levels are varied.[53] It shows that the activation of a given gene may depend on the "context" of genes expressed through the network of transcription factors that links them together. The suspicion that concerted regulation of gene expression may be mediated by interactions among proteins has also given rise to systematic (though still rather "functionally blind") studies of such interactions at the level of the genome. These studies constitute a major part of the new research that has been made possible by the complete sequencing of the human genome.[54] Similar studies are under way with the sea urchin embryo.[55] Considerable work remains to be done if we are to understand the specific macromolecular networks of transcription factors established as a consequence of the differential expression of roughly 30,000 human genes during embryonic and fetal development.

Other components of these networks have to be taken into consideration as well.[56] I mentioned earlier that the efficiency of transcription factors and their interaction at a distance may be mediated or regulated (or perhaps both) by systems of first and second messengers responsible for the propagation and transduction of signals (along with their associated receptors, kinases, phosphatases, and G-proteins)[57] within and among embryonic cells. Such networks of diffusible metabolic circuits may themselves include feedback loops and autocatalytic reactions that produce nonlinear effects. These processes, together with other nonlinear processes arising from the operation of gene transcription and translation mechanisms, can be seen as embodying the mathematical rules and chemical reactions postulated by Turing in his model of morphogenesis.

The sequencing of the genome provides important new information about the types of genes required, on the one hand, to construct a multicellular organism and, on the other, to create a large brain. First, a comparison of the genome of a unicellular organism, the yeast, with that of a multicellular organism, the worm, reveals the appearance of new genes and the expansion of already existing genes through gene duplications. These genes code for transcription factors (including 270 nuclear hormone receptors), protein interaction (156 POZ areas), and signal transduction (11 phosphotyrosine binding areas).[58] Second, a still more spectacular expansion of genes coding for transcription factors occurs in humans: the number of factor areas known as C2H2 zinc fingers increases from 771 in the fly to 4,500 in man. Consistent with our hypothesis concerning the formation of nonlinear transcription factor networks, many of these networks contain areas involved in the assembly of transcription factors. Some of these areas, such as KRAB and SCAN, are absent from the genomes of the fly and the worm; others are produced by the reorganization or accretion of protein areas belonging to the genes of already existing invertebrates.[59] It is probable that this increase in gene domains is accompanied by an increase in combinations of transcription factors—the molecular partners I referred to earlier. In my book *Neuronal Man* I referred to genes of this type as "communication genes." They serve, in effect, to regulate the regulatory genes, coordinating the cellular interactions that underlie the formation of the body map of the organism.[60]

Neurogenesis

A large number of these genes are expressed in the nervous system. The concepts employed in connection with the development of the form of the body may therefore also be applied to the morphogenesis of the brain, particularly to the very early formative stages known as "neurulation." This crucial step in the development of the nervous system is the object of a third model that Michel Kerszberg and I have devised.[61]

The process of neurulation appears in different aspects in vertebrates and invertebrates. In both cases the nervous system originates in the differentiation of the outer layer of the embryo, the neural ectoderm. In invertebrates, the first embryonic cells that form the nervous system, the neuroblasts, detach themselves from the neural ectoderm and fuse in a vertical chain of nerve ganglia. In vertebrates the embryonic nerve cells remain bound together, forming a compact neural plate. This plate then wholly closes in upon itself, creating a hollow dorsal tube that has played a decisive role in the course of evolution. It is difficult to increase the volume of a compact ganglion without encountering problems of oxygen supply, and therefore of vascularization. Even if the cerebroid ganglia of the octopus contain several hundred million neurons, this appears to be a limit. By contrast, the formation of a tube permitted an unlimited increase in surface area and an efficient means of vascularization. This expansion is observed in vertebrates, from cyclostomes to mammals and from primates to man. Simple and decisive though it is, this evolutionary transition is not yet entirely understood at the molecular level. Once again, the model that Kerszberg and I have proposed requires only a very small number of genetic modifications, principally affecting the regulation of developmental gene transcription—which includes nonlinear switches and feedback control—for the transition to be achieved.[62]

At the rather advanced stage of embryonic development when the neural plate is differentiated, we suspect that the behavior of embryonic cells noticeably changes. Minimal modification of the switching mechanism at the transcription-factor level would suffice to regulate cell movement[63] as well as cell adhesion.[64] Two possibilities present themselves, at least in theory: either the individual cells do not move, remaining bound to each other to form a dense, compact, and continuous nerve tissue, the neural plate, which then folds in upon itself to form the neural tube in vertebrates; or the individual neuroblasts independently detach themselves from the neural epithelium and subsequently reassemble to form a chain of compact ganglia, as in invertebrates. The mathematical model of neurulation we have devised has been successfully tested against computer simulations. Despite the plausibility that such success confers, the model remains quite hypothetical. Nonetheless it demonstrates once again, at least in principle, that a few discrete modifications of the regulatory systems of gene expression can give rise to a critical point of divergence between invertebrate and vertebrate nervous systems: the formation of a tube whose surface is capable of dramatic increase, from the brain of the lamprey to the human brain with its highly convoluted cortex.

Another example—which, despite its exceptional importance, remains even less well understood—is the rapid surface expansion of the cerebral cortex that occurred in the course of vertebrate brain evolution.[65] The cerebral cortex of mammals is made up of vertical columns of neurons arranged side by side. The number of neurons per cortical column is approximately the same in the brains of all mammals.[66] Accordingly, the total surface area of the cortex—that is, the number of columns—appears to have been the primary target of evolutionary change.[67] If the surface area of the cortex in insectivores is taken as the unit index of cortical expansion, the corresponding area in monkeys equals 25, in chimpanzees 58, and in human beings 156. Over a period of about 6 million years, from *Sahelanthropus tchadensis*[68] and *Australopithecus* to *Homo sapiens,* the frontal lobe and the parieto-temporal areas underwent rapid expansion, with a dramatic increase in the rate of expansion occurring in the past 2 million years, from *Homo habilis* to *Homo sapiens.* It seems plausible to suppose that this expansion was the result of the effects of a small number of developmental genes, producing a rapid increase in surface area through the multiplication of cortical columns (Figure 41).[69] Mapping of the anterior part of the neural plate in the mouse reveals a lateral expansion of the territories of the future cerebral cortex by comparison with those of more primitive vertebrates (Figure 39).[70] Identification of these gene products is currently being undertaken. An interesting candidate is a protein called β-catenin that is involved in the formation of junctions between cells. Genetically modified mice that overexpress this protein in neural precursors develop enlarged brains marked by an increase in the overall surface area of the cerebral cortex and folds resembling the sulci and gyri of higher mammals.[71]

Our models have shown, among other things, that slight variations in the concentration of morphogens may dramatically shift the boundary of gene expression in the course of development. Similarly, as I noted earlier, a single gene—known as "lefty" in the mouse, *situs inversus* in man—controls the right-left asymmetry of the body plan; similar (if not actually the same) genes may also determine the asymmetry of the brain's hemispheres. We have a plausible—albeit still very tentative—idea, then, of the genetic mechanisms that have contributed to the rapid evolutionary development of the human brain by comparison with the brains of its nearest relatives. These mechanisms may also explain, in a more general way, the nonlinear relationships observed in the evolution of the complexity of the anatomical structure of the brain by comparison with the complexity of the genome.

The brain's capacity to form and to communicate conscious representations of the world, and to test their veracity, is therefore circumscribed by a genetic envelope that is fixed in a discrete manner in our

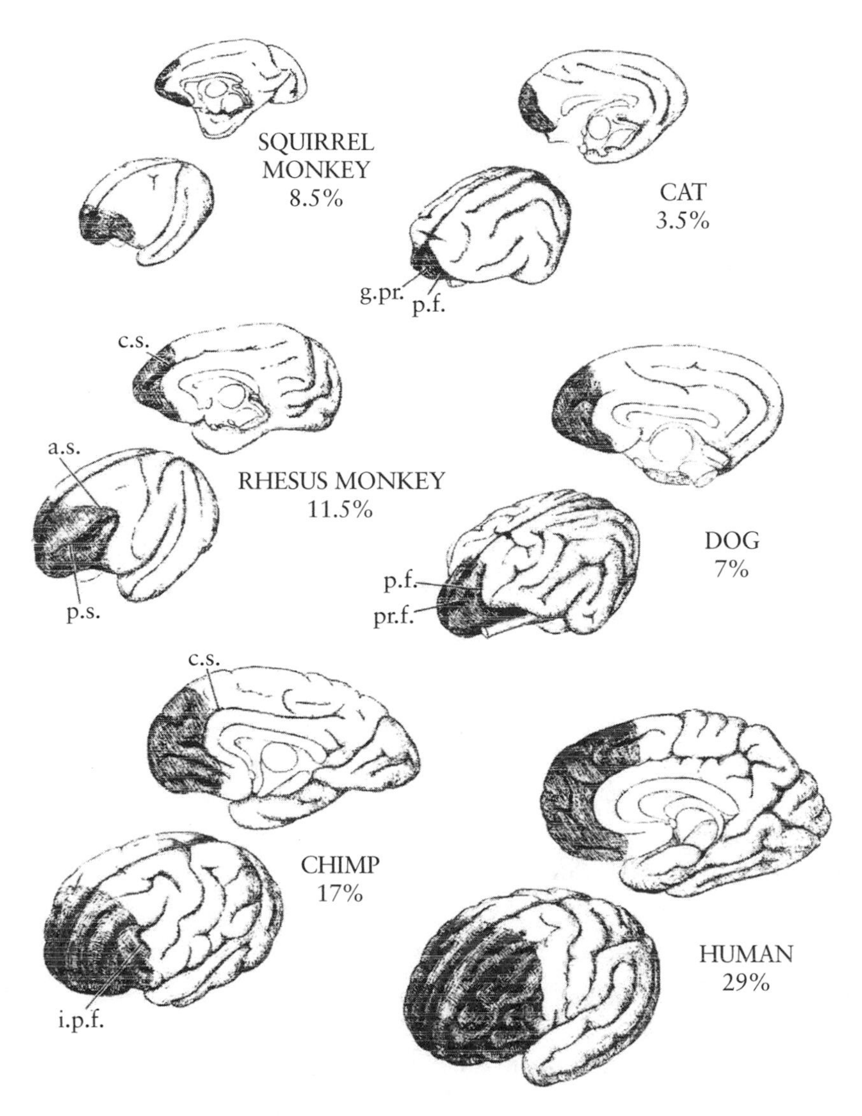

Figure 41. Evolution of the relative surface area of the prefrontal cortex in the higher mammals. Note the dramatic increase from cat and dog to monkey, and then to human, in a territory of the brain that is crucially involved in cognitive functions: the frontal lobe (shaded in black). The percentages indicate the surface area of the prefrontal cortex as a proportion of the total cortical surface area.

chromosomes, particularly at the level of regulatory sequences. This set of genes is common to human beings the world over: from Greece to China, from America to Japan.[72] An initial stage of agreement between brain states and external reality was therefore reached in the course of genetic evolution through natural selection prior to the appearance of *Homo sapiens.* Those species which were capable of using their genetic capital to form sufficiently accurate—sufficiently true—representations of their environment to ensure their homeostasis, and their reproduction, survived.

Genes and Cognition

We do not at present know exactly which families of genes made our brain "human" during the course of the evolution of species. Comparing the human genome with that of invertebrates, one finds that only 7 percent of the total number of gene families are unique to vertebrates, and of these only 12 percent are thought to concern the brain. Many genes whose alteration is responsible for neurological disorders in man have prior homologues in *Drosophila,* including the genes that create a predisposition to Tay-Sachs disease, Duchenne muscular dystrophy, lissencephaly, and "fragile X" mental retardation.[73] Genes associated with amyotrophic lateral sclerosis and adrenoleukodystrophy are present even in the yeast. Only a few such genes appear to be unique to humans (or vertebrates)—the genes responsible for Creutzfeldt-Jakob disease, for example, or Charcot-Marie-Tooth disease. The fraction of genes in the human genome that are peculiar to man turns out to be surprisingly small.

Among the genes that distinguish vertebrates from invertebrates are ones that play a role in inflammation and immunity, homeostasis, development, cell death, and, of course, the structure and function of the nervous system. From the worm and the fly to humans, there is an increase in the number of proteins involved in the development of the nervous system and neural signaling.[74] In addition to genes coding for transcription factors, one finds for example, genes involved in axon guidance (ephrins and their receptors) and the establishment of neural connections, the formation of adhesion molecules (such as proteoglycans), nerve growth factors (NGF), and trophic factors (neuregulins). Similarly, the genes that code for the proteins that constitute the cytoskeleton (such as actins and spectrins) develop at the same time as the proteins that make up the myelin sheath. In other words, there is a marked expansion of the proteins involved in the formation of treelike branchings of axons and dendrites, and of their interconnections. This is also the case with the molecules involved in the propagation of electrical signals (ion channels) and chemical signals (opioid peptides, which are present only in vertebrates).

But there can be no straightforward relation between genes and neuronal phenotype. As I have said, multiple interlocking networks of gene interaction develop during the course of the formation of the body and the brain. Patterns of both convergence and divergence are created, as in neuronal networks. The action of an isolated gene may consequently have a "pleiotropic" effect on the phenotype, affecting various aspects of the functional organization of the brain (and even the body) of the organism. Conversely, the activation of a given gene may require, as we have seen, the joint action of the products of several regulatory genes. The expression of a given gene will inevitably be context-dependent, differing from one tissue or organ to another and also as a function of the stage of development in which it occurs. So great is the complexity that one may well wonder whether expressions such as "intelligence genes" or "language genes" ought not to be banished from the vocabulary of science.

It may be helpful to examine a few specific cases that illustrate the sorts of difficulty encountered in trying to relate genes, neuronal phenotype, and behavior to one another. Let us begin with an example that at first sight appears to be very simple. The human genome contains a gene coding for rhodopsin, a visual pigment that belongs to the class of membrane molecules known as metabotropic receptors. Rhodopsin is the first target of photons. The hit of a single photon produces an allosteric change in molecular conformation that triggers a cascade of enzyme reactions and ultimately produces an electrical signal. The nerve signal is then propagated by a series of steps from the retina to the cerebral cortex. The mutation, or disappearance, of this gene is responsible for congenital blindness, in which the range of vision lost corresponds to the spectrum of the missing pigment.[75] Inactivation of the gene suppresses the function of the receptor that it encodes.

This much suggests that the relation between gene and perceptual behavior is direct. And, indeed, in one sense it is quite simple: a peripheral deficit in sensory receptors causes blindness. Yet the cells and molecules that make up the human nervous system are not assembled independently of one another, like the component parts and prewired circuits of a computer. The question therefore arises whether a deficit at the level of the retina can create disturbances that work their way back into the brain and, more specifically, the cortical areas concerned with vision. As we shall see in the next chapter, the answer is yes. In the congenitally blind subject, rearrangements of neuronal networks are in fact observed at this level. A very simple genetic alteration expressed at the retinal level is accompanied by secondary effects in the central nervous system that cause the reorganization of cortical pathways observed in persons who are blind from birth.

A second example, also involving membrane receptors, concerns the social behavior of small rodents.[76] It is known that the receptor of the hormonal peptide arginine-vasopressin affects the reproductive and social behaviors of the males of several vertebrate species. In the prairie vole, injection of arginine-vasopressin leads to an increase in affiliative behaviors, including olfactory exploration and grooming. Whereas the prairie vole is highly socialized and monogamous, its mountain cousin is relatively asocial and promiscuous. Experimental analysis of the genetic differences between the two has been done in the laboratory using mice, which lend themselves to the *in vivo* application of recombinant DNA technologies. The mouse ordinarily behaves like the mountain vole. Once implanted with the arginine-vasopressin receptor gene from the prairie vole, however, its social behavior becomes that of the prairie vole. The transfer of a single gene seems therefore to create a new social behavior in the mouse.

But this does not mean that a complex behavior is exclusively determined by *one* gene. To the contrary, the "social" response to arginine-vasopressin is very probably only one element of a multigenic set of behavioral components that fails to be activated so long as the receptor concentration remains below a certain threshold. The most likely interpretation is that when the receptor gene is widely expressed at high levels of concentration it has the effect of binding these elements together in a stable social behavior that generates monogamy. On this view, a minor *quantitative* change involving a single chemical component of the brain suffices to *qualitatively* modify the behavior of the organism. As we saw earlier, the introduction of a new component amounts to much more than simply adding an isolated piece to the system. It gives rise instead to an amplifying effect: the larger the effect, the greater its relevance to the functioning of the organism.[77] In this case one might say that the product of the vasopressin-receptor gene has very high relevance for the functioning of the complex circuits in which it becomes incorporated. Singular effects of many genes whose action is known to alter cerebral development and associated behaviors may be interpreted in similar terms.

The concept of relevance in relation to the action of individual genes may also be useful in analyzing the formidably complex phenomenon of knowledge acquisition. Let us take the case of dyslexia, which selectively affects the ability to read in otherwise normal children. At first sight this condition appears much more complicated than visual deficits in the congenitally blind or the sexual behavior of voles. The invention of writing took place about 5,000 years ago. Although the ability to read and write is a classic example of a culturally acquired behavior, there exist specific familial reading disabilities that have been attributed to localized alterations in the histocompatibility region (21.3) of chromosome 6p, and perhaps also in chromosome 15.[78] Brain imaging reveals a characteristic reorganization of cortical pathways in such cases. The very process of learning to read produces modifications in connectivity that I shall examine in the next chapter. For the moment it is important to emphasize that the present state of neurobiological knowledge does not permit us to speak of a "reading gene" that is altered in the case of dyslexia, as Steven Pinker is a bit too eager to do with regard to everything associated with language.[79]

What one can say is that the yet-unknown effect of this particular gene (among many others) contributes to the reorganization observed in literate brains, triggering a cascade of events that culminates in the construction of a complex neuronal network receptive to the acquisition of written language. The same logic applies in the case of a recently discovered mutation of the FOXP2 gene (encoding a transcription factor of the forkhead class), which causes a speech and language disorder characterized by severe articulation difficulties and impairment of the ability to produce grammatical constructions. The trait is monogenic (it maps on region 7q31 on chromosome 7) and dominant,[80] its locus having evolved from the mouse to the chimpanzee to humans.[81] The mutation, on the other hand, is rare. In a recent study, none of the 240 four-year-old children selected from a representative community of 18,000 children suffering severe language impairment showed a mutation of the FOXP2 gene.[82] The production of speech and language is controlled by the joint action of many genes, and discrete alterations may cause extensive defects. This should not come as a surprise—any number of local malfunctions may prevent an automobile engine from running properly!

We know that the genetic evolution of the brain of *Homo sapiens sapiens* from that of its Australopithic ancestors was very rapid. It took about 3 million years, or roughly 100,000 generations. Our detailed knowledge of the genomes of chimpanzees and humans, and more particularly of the regulatory sequences of gene expression, may be expected to yield a fuller and more exact understanding of the genetic mechanisms governing the evolution of the human brain, not only in its many conservative aspects, but also with regard to its relatively rare, but essential, capacity for innovation.[83] For the time being we are far from understanding the genetic mechanisms that determine the many species-specific dispositions in the human infant. These include the nipple-sucking reflex, indispensable to the survival of the newborn baby; the palmar reflex, a grasping movement triggered by stimulation of the palm of the hand that permits the newborn to cling to its mother; the spontaneous crying that signals the infant's distress to family members; and various elements of the child's perceptual knowledge of his or her immediate environment.[84] At a median age of five minutes, for example, newborns respond to an artificial and simplified facial stimulus—a sort of crude caricature of a face—by movements of the eyes and the head. Given the choice between realistic images and random arrangements of facial parts, they prefer faces that look human.[85]

Newborns also possess a basic sort of physical knowledge that can be tested in a simple way by presenting them with objects of various kinds. The duration of focused attention is consistently longer when infants are shown incoherent and surprising events. This makes it possible to estimate the degree of plausibility they attach to a particular physical event. They are capable of distinguishing persons from inanimate objects, and also human movement from the motion of inanimate objects. Presented with an object such as a stone or a toy, neonates perceive it as a bounded body that preserves both its solidity and its contours when it is in motion.[86] Three-and-a-half-month-old infants recognize the permanence and distinctness of individual objects.[87]

As we saw earlier, not only do children possess physical knowledge at a very early age, they also develop the ability to attribute experiences, emotions, and intentions to others.[88] Moreover, newborns exhibit characteristics that anticipate the verbal communication of adults. They are capable, for example, of distinguishing phonetic differences that at the outset are universal but that very rapidly become specific to particular languages.[89] Newborns produce a range of sounds and vocalizations—a "canonical" babbling that, once again, is universal at the beginning of life, no matter what the child's family and cultural background may be.[90]

In the course of biological evolution the brain's innate capacities for representing the world came to be considerably enlarged, from the immediate physical and biological environment to an almost unlimited domain of social and cultural interactions. Genetic evolution led to the stable storage in memory—that is, in the brain—not only of a large endowment of innate knowledge but also of impressive capacities for acquiring, processing, communicating, and testing knowledge obtained from experience of the outside world. But at the present stage of research into the mechanisms underlying the evolution of the human brain, as Richard Lewontin has emphasized, little more than this can be asserted with confidence.[91] For the moment these mechanisms remain beyond the reach of experimental science.

Neuronal Epigenesis and Cultural Evolution 6

The roughly 30,000 genes that make up the genetic endowment of the human species confer upon the brain the universal traits that make us human beings. The architecture of the brain in its main outlines is constrained, as we have seen, by an "envelope" of genes that govern its development. Even so, the human race is distinguished from other species by its remarkable ability to learn and conserve stable traces of past experience. In the course of evolution, this aptitude has grown to an extent unrivaled in the living world. Moreover, vestiges of man's evolutionary past are still perceptible in the early stages of the brain's development.

In this chapter I wish to argue that the formation of the million billion synapses found in the adult brain escapes control by the genes to a limited extent, and that, to this extent, it is properly regarded as an epigenetic evolutionary process characterized by variation and selection that begins during embryonic development and continues after birth.[1] The word "epigenetic" is composed of two Greek roots: *epi,* which means "on" or "upon," and *genesis,* which means "birth." Although the second term furnished the title of the first book of the Bible—the account of the creation of the world, of animals, and of man, as well as of the development of life on earth—the use of the word "genetics" to designate the science of heredity is recent.[2]

"Epigenetic," in the sense in which I use the term, combines two meanings: the idea of superimposition upon the action of the genes, chiefly as a result of learning and experience; and the notion of coordinated and organized development. The neural systems of the brain are not in fact—I repeat the point because it is important—assembled after the fashion of a computer, with prefabricated parts fitted together in accordance with a blueprint that exactly specifies the nature and purpose of each circuit and switch. If this were the case, an error in even the smallest detail of the implementation of a program could have catastrophic consequences. As against an exclusively genetic conception of the brain as the embodiment of a strictly predetermined genetic inheritance, the epigenetic model postulates that the connections between neurons are established in stages, with a considerable margin of variability, and are subject to a process of selection that proceeds by means of trial and error. At certain critical stages of development, the connectivity of the network is refined in a way that exploits the elementary properties of plasticity described earlier. The state of activity of the developing network, whether spontaneous or evoked, works to regulate this process.

The epigenetic hypothesis suggests an alternative approach to the problems of genetic parsimony and the nonlinear evolution of cerebral structure examined in the previous chapter, without ruling out other, possibly complementary solutions. What is more, as we shall see, it gives fresh insight into the mechanisms of memory, the retrieval of stored information, and the acquisition, testing, and transmission of new knowledge—in a word, into the appearance of culture, which, in the case of humans, developed in an exceedingly brief period of time.

Before taking up a number of theoretical issues, I would like to quickly review the experimental data that constitute the basis for current debate and future speculation.

Variability of the Brain

The variations in size, shape, and weight of the human brain are well documented, even if the functional and behavioral significance of this diversity is not altogether clear.[3] Careful anatomical and functional studies of Brodmann's areas show that the topology of the cerebral cortex is not strictly identical from one individual to another. For example, the dimensions of the primary visual area, as measured by functional imaging, exhibit variations on the order of 5 millimeters.[4] This individual variability is often attributed to heredity. Yet both ana-

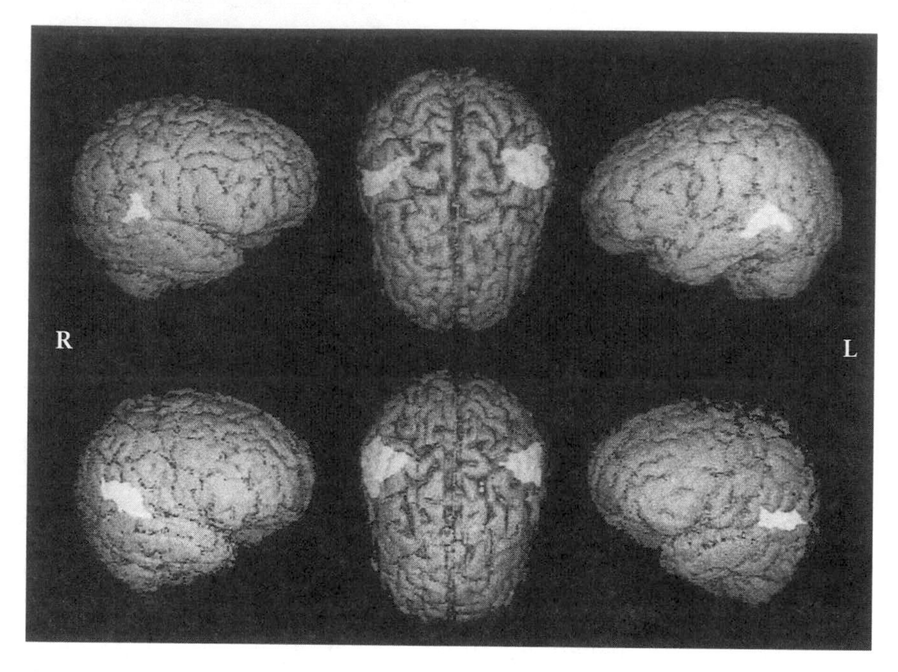

Figure 42A. Variability of the planum temporale, which is involved in language processing (at the level of the temporal lobe) in identical (monozygotic) twins who are opposite-handed. The brain shown at the top is that of a young right-handed woman; the one below it is that of her left-handed twin sister. The difference between the two areas is much more pronounced in the right-handed twin than in the left-handed twin.

tomical and behavioral studies of genetically identical individuals—known as monozygotic (or "identical") twins since they issue from the same fertilized egg (or zygote)—clearly demonstrate that their brains are not in fact identical. Differences in manual preference have been discovered between monozygotic twins, which by itself constitutes a sign of behavioral variance. Moreover, two convergent methods of investigation have succeeded in bringing out this variance more precisely: *in vivo* measurements, using magnetic resonance imaging, of the surface of the language area (known as the planum temporale); and analysis of specific manual tasks in right-handed and left-handed monozygotic twins.[5] Both methods revealed that right-handed subjects display a degree of hemispheric asymmetry (in this case left-side dominance) not found among left-handed subjects (Figure 42A). The reasons for this variability are not well understood. It is thought that

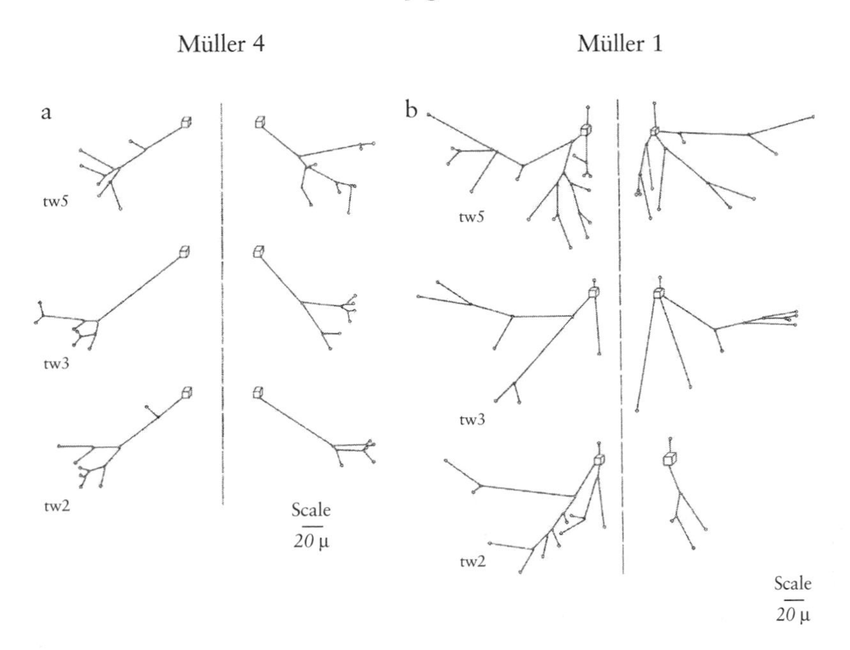

Figure 42B. Variability of the dendritic branching of two identifiable motor neurons (Müller cells M1 and M4) in genetically identical individuals, or clones (TW_2, TW_3, TW_5), of the Amazonian parthenogenetic fish *Poecilia formosa.*

very early epigenetic events, possibly coinciding with the establishment of right-left asymmetry in the embryo, introduce a significant difference in the anatomical and functional lateralization of the two hemispheres. More general kinds of epigenetic variability have been observed between identical twins as well, although this variability is less than that observed between pairs of identical twins.[6]

On the neuronal and synaptic scale, significant variations in connectivity have been detected among neurons in genetically identical (or "isogenic") individuals. In isogenic members of the small invertebrate species *Daphnia magna*—the water flea familiar to all aquarists—the numbers of sensory cells in the eye (175) and neurons in the optical ganglion (110) are preserved, along with the principal categories of synaptic contacts; yet the exact number of synapses and the precise form of the axonal branches vary.[7] Similar observations have been reported with respect to the dendrites of motor neurons—Müller cells—in a parthenogenic fish (Figure 42B).[8] A random element is introduced in neuronal connectivity during development of the adult network. It is reasonable to suppose that this variation is a consequence of the way in which the neurons of the network are assembled, and I believe it represents the stored trace of the trials and errors undergone by their axons and dendrites during their growth phase, as well as of the epigenetic regulation of this expansion. In any case it is plain that significant variability exists in the anatomy of the brain, the topology of the cortical areas, and the details of neural connections—proof that the control exercised by genes is far from absolute.

Formation of Synapses

From the formation of the neural tube to the first stages of embryonic development and up until the maturation of the adult brain, a number of morphological and functional transformations occur, principally under the direction of developmental genes. These transformations include the subdivision of the neural tube into a series of vesicles and the splitting of the foremost vesicle into two compartments, each of which will form a cerebral hemisphere.

Initially, the wall of the neural tube is made up of a single layer of cells. These cells rapidly divide and, in a few months, produce tens of billions of cells. At certain moments as many as 250,000 new cells are formed per minute. The area of the cerebral vesicles increases, and at the same time their walls gain in thickness. At this point six layers of the cerebral cortex can be distinguished, and it is interesting to note that the deepest layers, V and VI, are laid down first, while two of the three layers nearest the surface, II and III—containing cells that, as I have argued, are vital to the operation of the brain's conscious workspace—assume their definitive positions only later. This very organized sequence of development of the cortical layers, and of the synapses that are formed within them, may coincide with the establishment of the hierarchical and parallel systems of the neuronal network described in Chapter 1.

The synapses begin to be formed with the gradual subdivision of the cerebral cortex into areas, or maps. Recently discovered surface proteins called ephrins, which are distributed along continuous gradients that help guide the axons toward their cortical targets, play a major role.[9] Other molecules, such as the so-called slit proteins, are crucially important in the regulation of axonal branching and guidance as well.[10] The cellular architecture of the cerebral cortex, the main lines of which are established *before* birth, is largely determined by developmental genes and by genes responsible for the formation of nerve connections and the propagation of signals, whose considerable growth from the genome of *Drosophila* to that of man, both in number and in nature, I have already discussed.

Even so, quantitative electron microscopy shows that the formation of synapses is far from complete at birth.[11] In humans, about half of all adult synapses are formed *after* birth, and their number continues to change, rising and then falling off, until death. Although the length of the gestation period is roughly comparable in chimpanzees and humans (224 days and 270 days, respectively), the postnatal development of the brain lasts considerably longer in man. Cranial capacity increases 4.3 times after birth in humans, as against 1.6 times in the chimpanzee. Moreover, cranial capacity reaches 70 percent of the adult volume after three years in humans but after only one year in the chimpanzee. This striking aspect of human cerebral development is of great importance since language learning and acquaintance with social conventions and moral rules take place during the first years following birth. The exceptionally prolonged development of the human brain after birth is one of its most distinctive features, predisposing it to the acquisition and testing of knowledge (Figure 43).

The global evolution of synaptic density in the cerebral cortex of both the monkey and humans includes a rapid phase in which 90 percent of all synapses are formed, at a rate of about 40,000 per second—more than 2 million each minute![12] Birth occurs in exactly the middle of this rapid phase. There follows a longer phase, lasting until puberty, in which this rate of growth levels off, subsequently declining until the total number that will be preserved during adulthood is reached. This number then abruptly falls off in old age. In human beings, interestingly, the duration of the rapid phase is shorter in a sensory area such as the visual cortex, where it lasts about two or three years after birth, than in an association area such as the prefrontal cortex, where it lasts up to ten years. This observation has great importance from a functional point of view since the prefrontal cortex—which, incidentally,

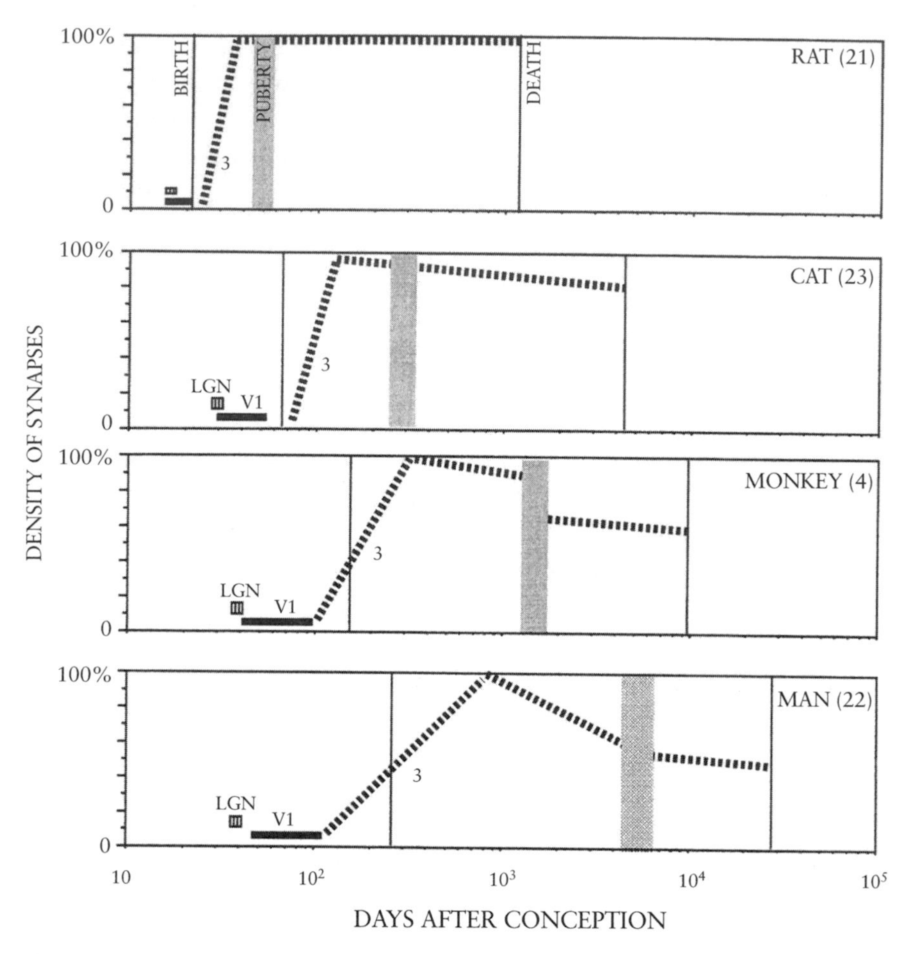

Figure 43. Evolution of synaptic density over the course of development of the primary visual cortex in various species of mammals. The number 3 indicates the phase of rapid growth of the number of synapses. The bold horizontal bars indicate the phase of neuronal proliferation, or neurogenesis, in the lateral geniculate nucleus (LGN) and the primary visual cortex (V1). Note the lengthening of the phase of synaptic proliferation from the rat to man.

is very rich in neurons found in layers II and III—plays a central role in cognitive functions and, more particularly, in consciousness.

It is therefore utterly wrong to suppose that synaptogenesis in the cerebral cortex is a synchronous process that takes place in a single step. The reality is that not all synapses are formed at once. The average values I have mentioned describe a global envelope of multiple, successive, and overlapping waves of synapse formation that differ from one cortical layer to another. Moreover, comparison of the rapid phase in the rat, the cat, the monkey, and man reveals a progressive increase in duration, rising from 14 days in rats to 400 days in humans (Figure 43). The human infant therefore displays a correspondingly greater number of synaptic combinations that may be shaped by epigenetic interactions with the outside world in its physical, social, and cultural aspects, which in turn give rise to a series of interlocking critical periods of development through which the newborn and young child pass before reaching adulthood.[13] This circumstance may also help explain the nonlinear relationship between genetic and cerebral complexity.

Regressive Phenomena

Since the pioneering work of Wilhelm Preyer in the late nineteenth century, it has been known that regressive phenomena attack the emerging cellular and synaptic assembly of the central nervous system in the course of development.[14] Viktor Hamburger, in a classic study, found that about 40 percent of the motor neurons of the spinal cord of the chick embryo die between the sixth and ninth days of the life of the embryo.[15] Similar results have been obtained in the case of the cerebral cortex of the mouse. Cell death is neither a passive nor an accidental process; it is the result, instead, of the activation of specialized molecular mechanisms. Programmed cell death involves protein-degrading enzymes such as caspase 3 and caspase 9, which must be turned on for a cell to die. Inactivating the genes that code for caspases in the mouse reduces cell death, enlarges the population of founder cells and precursor cells, and, by increasing the number of radial columns in the cortex, increases the number of cortical neurons. The surface of the cortex expands as a result.[16] And yet the genetically modified mouse does not appear to have been made more intelligent by this addition of neurons. To the contrary, it presents serious pathological signs—epileptic seizures, for example. In the course of the normal development of the cerebral cortex, there is a dramatic decrease in the number of nerve cells. Analysis of the human genome confirms that caspase proteins are among the essential elements of cerebral plasticity. From the fly and the worm up through man, the number of domains involved in programmed cell death undergoes a spectacular increase. In the human genome, for example, there are sixteen caspase recruitment domains as against only two in the worm and none in the fly.[17]

The influence of the activity of the developing nervous system on this type of cell death is still a matter of dispute. It is known that the massive inflow of Ca^{++} ions into nerve cells causes their death. These ions are present in the fluids that occupy the spaces between cells, and flow into them as a result of electrical or chemical nervous activity. The activation of the glutamate receptor, for example, may open up its channel to Ca^{++} ions and, as a consequence, cause cell death.[18] (This is the source of the so-called Chinese restaurant syndrome.) Although a connection may plausibly be asserted between cell death and nervous activity, a great deal of further research will be needed to identify the precise regulatory mechanisms.

Regressive phenomena also occur at the level of synaptic connections and, more specifically, nerve endings. In the previous chapter I discussed the example of the neuromuscular junction to illustrate the discrete expression of genes coding for the acetylcholine receptor in the muscle nuclei located under the motor nerve ending. This is an instance of an epigenetic phenomenon in which a neural trophic factor and the electrical activity of a muscle fiber combine to differentially regulate the pattern of gene expression under the motor nerve and beyond the synapse. Epigenetic regulation occurs on the presynaptic side of the junction as well. In the adult rat, each muscle fiber is innervated by a single motor nerve ending. In the newborn rat, by contrast, each muscle fiber receives four or five functional motor axon terminals. When the rat begins to walk, the number of these active terminals progressively decreases; after a few days, only one remains (Figure 44). This process of elimination is therefore controlled by the state of activity of the innervated muscle.[19]

Similar cases of synaptic elimination occur in other systems, such as the sympathetic ganglia[20] and the Purkinje cells of the cerebellum. In the latter case, genetic mutations that alter signal transduction act

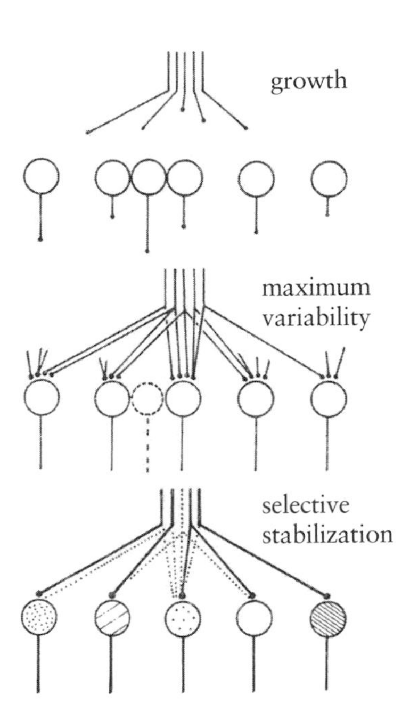

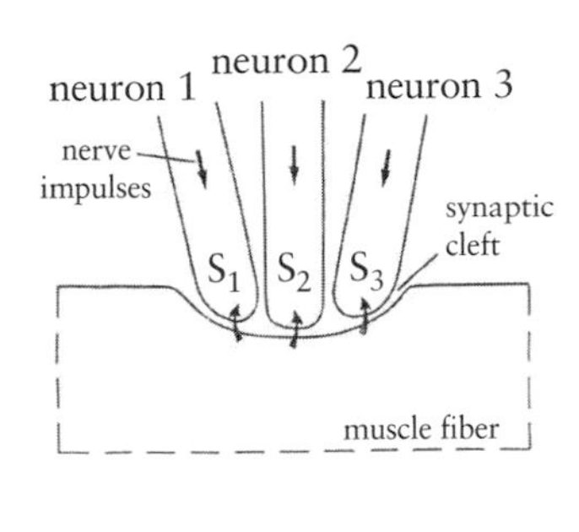

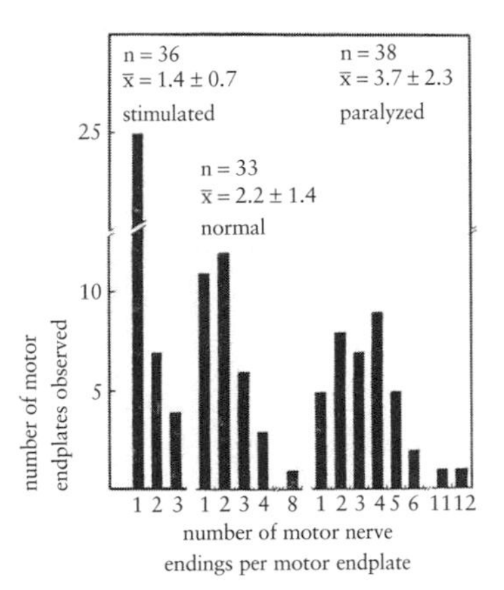

Figure 44. Theory of the epigenesis of neuronal networks by selective stabilization of synapses. *Left:* Schematic illustration of the stages of neuronal growth, maximum variability ("synaptic exuberance" or "transient redundancy"), and selective stabilization through spontaneous or evoked activity. *Top right:* A detailed model of selection by competition of nerve endings for a retrograde growth factor (μ) produced by the muscle fiber. *Bottom right:* Effect of the state of activity of motor innervation during muscle development in the chick embryo. The values marked on the vertical axis correspond to the number of neuromuscular junctions where 1, 2, 3, or more nerve endings converge. The continuous electrical stimulation of the spinal cord produces an acceleration of synaptic elimination whereas the paralysis of the muscle by a synthetic form of curare (Flaxedil) slows synaptic elimination.

to slow the rate of decrease in the innervation of these cells by climbing fibers.[21]

There are many well-documented examples of spontaneous regressive phenomena that affect the development of the nervous system both at the cellular level and the synaptic level. In several cases it has been clearly demonstrated that the state of activity of the network itself controls the evolution of these phenomena.

Outgrowth and Regeneration

The elimination of dendritic and axonal prolongations is offset by a simultaneous process of growth and ramification that leads to a dramatic increase in branching and an expansion of the area covered by these new projections. Torsten Wiesel and David Hubel, in a series of celebrated studies, demonstrated the importance of visual experience in determining the innervation of the visual cortex in some species.[22] They also demonstrated the irreversible character of the lesions caused by experimental manipulation of the visual environment, for example in inducing temporary blindness in one eye. Electrophysiological recordings showed that, in the normally developed visual cortex, stimulation of one or the other eye arouses a pattern of response in alternate columns of neurons. Closing one eye by suturing the eyelid during the first six weeks of the postnatal life of the monkey, for example, was discovered to have lasting effects in the adult animal: the columns corresponding to the closed eye narrow while those associated with the other eye widen. These results unambiguously established the existence of a critical (or sensitive) period during which disruptions of sensory stimulation cause permanent damage to cortical connectivity. Little or no regeneration takes place.

A great many studies have been carried out since, at the cellular and synaptic levels, to assess the relative contributions of growth, elimination, and regeneration of nerve processes in the developing visual cortex. At various critical stages in the maturation of the visual system, the exuberant proliferation of axonal branching (involving retinogeniculate and thalamocortical neurons as well as pyramidal cortical neurons) is accompanied by the limited, but nonetheless decisive, elimination of collateral ramifications in different parts of the visual pathways.[23] Episodes of regenerative outgrowth are known to occur, with lasting effects, even in the adult visual system. There is evidence that these instances of plasticity are controlled by the state of activity of the developing network, though the respective shares of spontaneous and evoked activity differ from one species to another. The precise pattern of activity seems also to play an essential role in fixing the synaptic connections that will persist into adulthood.[24] In the absence of adequate stimulation, as I have said, the cerebral network suffers irreversible injury.

As we saw in the last chapter, investigation of the human genome has disclosed an expansion in the number and type of genes coding for factors stimulating the process of neural branching, such as the nerve growth factor (NGF) discovered by the renowned embryologist Rita Levi-Montalcini. These factors very probably contribute to epigenetic plasticity.[25] In the case of the suturing of the eyelid in rats, for example, the lesions caused by the shift of ocular dominance to the normally functioning eye can be avoided by the *in vivo* introduction of various growth factors in the cortex. These factors also differentially regulate the formation of ocular dominance columns in the course of normal development.[26]

In addition to their effect on nerve extension, growth factors modulate synaptic efficiency in transmitting nerve signals. This result has been achieved experimentally by the exposure of neuromuscular synapses cultivated *in vitro* to a growth factor for several minutes.[27] Further evidence comes from studies of transgenic mice that produce an excess of a factor known as GDNF. In these mice, the elimination of supernumerary motor axons is slowed.[28] Finally, it has been shown (both *in vivo* and *in vitro*) that the synthesis of growth factors and their release through dendritic pathways are regulated by neuronal activity.[29] All these observations support the more general claim that growth factors contribute to the epigenetic regulation of synaptic development.

It therefore seems reasonable to suppose that an equilibrium is established between outgrowth and elimination of nerve connections throughout the life of the organism. The activity of the neuronal network, both spontaneous and evoked, regulates this balance more directly during certain critical periods of development than at other times, however, and the circuits involved in this regulation, as well as the number and the duration of the critical periods, vary from one species to another.

Spontaneous Activity

Earlier I drew attention to the spontaneous firing of nerve cells as an integral part of the functioning of the brain, particularly in connection with cognitive games played by infants. The nervous system is besieged by intense spontaneous activity even before birth, first in the embryo and then in the fetus; following birth, this activity is enriched by interaction with the external world.[30] The role of spontaneous nervous activity has long been the object of debate. Recently, however, the results of a possibly decisive experiment were reported in which a genetic lesion was introduced in the mouse that selectively blocks the secretion of neurotransmitters.[31] The mutant embryo remained immobile and showed no sign of neurotransmitter release. The few action potentials that were recorded failed to propagate through the network. The mutant mice died at birth, but their brains had nonetheless developed in the mother's uterus with the normal stratification of the cortex into six layers and an extensive formation of synaptic contacts. Cerebral development is therefore able to occur in the absence of synaptic activity.

But a mature and stable brain cannot be created simply by assembling its various component parts. Indeed, in these mutant mice, massive degenerative phenomena began to destroy the cerebral edifice from the moment construction began. Such phenomena appear first in those regions that are the earliest to be formed. The spontaneous activity of the embryo, though it is not indispensable to the morphogenesis of the brain as a whole, turns out to be necessary to stabilize and maintain nerve connections up until adulthood. It would be premature to extend these results directly to the development of the human brain. The results so far obtained on various animal subjects nonetheless demonstrate that, although a large number of brain structures are preformed or innate, the spontaneous activity of the nervous system during development is no less essential to their subsequent evolution than the evoked activity that occurs following birth.

The main features of species-specific cerebral organization are determined, as we have seen, by a genetic envelope that controls the division, migration, and differentiation of cell types, the formation of an extensive network of synaptic connections, the amplification of nerve cell processes (in particular the behavior of the growth cone and the recognition of target cells), and the onset of spontaneous activity. This envelope also determines the structure of the molecules that form the synapse, the basic element of the brain's connective architecture, as well as the rules governing the assembly of these molecules and, subsequently, their plastic modification by the activity of the neuronal network. Epigenetic processes take place within the envelope of the developing network, assuming both the progressive and regressive forms I have just mentioned.

During critical periods of development, then, the extensive but transient diversification of synaptic contacts is followed by the selective stabilization of some labile contacts and the elimination of others. At the same time, episodes of growth and regeneration continue to occur. The addition and subtraction of synaptic connections persist beyond childhood and adolescence, producing a stable balance during adult life. The equilibrium becomes more fragile as the organism ages, however, and shifts in favor of regression in the final phase of senescence that lasts until death.

Selective Stabilization of Synapses

Not all of these observations are new. Ramón y Cajal expressed rather similar views at the beginning of the twentieth century. But only in recent years has it been possible to describe the epigenetic evolution of neuronal connectivity in a mathematically rigorous way.

The simple model that Philippe Courrège, Antoine Danchin, and I originally proposed describes synaptic evolution at its stage of maximum diversity in at least three defined states: labile, stable, and degenerated.[32] The fundamental idea is that the evolution of the connective state of a given synapse is controlled within a precise time frame by the totality of the message constituted by the signals arising from spontaneous and evoked activity in the postsynaptic cell. In other words, the activity of the postsynaptic cell regulates the stability, regression, and—in some cases—regeneration of the nerve ending in the presynaptic cell by means of a "trophic signal" that is propagated in a direction opposite to that of the nerve impulse, which is to say in a *retrograde* manner. The characteristic connectivity and biochemical composition of a given nerve cell—what I have called its singularity or individuality[33]—is thus the result of selective stabilization by the activity of a particular distribution of synaptic contacts from among all the contacts that are present at the moment when diversity is greatest.

The theory was initially worked out in detail at the elementary level.

Biochemical mechanisms were proposed to explain the synaptic competition that takes place during the critical phase of exuberant growth. Emergent nerve endings, for example, may be thought of as competing with one another for a limited quantity of retrograde growth factor.[34] The activity of the postsynaptic cell and its afferent connections regulates the amount of the factor available, or the active assimilation of the factor by the individual nerve endings, or both. The ending that most efficiently captures the retrograde factor, finally reaching a certain threshold value, wins the competition. The others fall short of this threshold, and so are condemned to die out.[35]

Additionally, microscopic learning rules were formulated in mathematical and biochemical terms to more precisely describe these elementary changes in synaptic efficiency as a function of experience. The most famous of these rules was introduced in 1949 by the Canadian psychologist Donald Hebb, whose name I mentioned earlier in connection with neuronal assemblies. Hebb stipulated that the "strength" of a given connection increases when there is a temporal coincidence between pre- and postsynaptic activities. This amounted to a restatement of the principle advanced in the mid-eighteenth century by David Hume, in an empiricist context, to account for the association of ideas. For Hume, it will be recalled, the "gentle force" that combines or associates ideas rests on "the quality of contiguity in time or place" of stimuli. This is nothing other than an early version of Hebb's rule.[36]

The physicist Leon Cooper and his colleagues subsequently devised more sophisticated microscopic learning rules to account for the elementary changes in synaptic strength that occur in the cerebral cortex as a result of visual experience.[37] Their algorithm describes change in synaptic efficiency as a function of the firing rates of the target nerve cell. Not only has the pattern of evolution predicted by the model (from a lower "depressed" level to a higher "potentialized" level) been recorded in the developing visual cortex by electrophysiological methods under various experimental conditions, it has been shown to be the result of a change, itself a function of the system's state of activity, in the biosynthesis of two kinds of glutamate receptors having different functional properties.[38]

Larger-scale models were later proposed to account for the formation of functional maps[39] and, in particular, to specify the characteristic architectural features of the visual areas.[40] We know that in the brain, generally speaking, networks of inhibitory neurons coexist with networks of excitatory neurons (which are often wrongly supposed to be dominant in the brain). Inhibitory neurons, by their number and physical size, manage in fact to achieve a balance with excitatory neurons. Computer models of mixed populations of excitatory and inhibitory neurons, whose connectivity is fixed at the outset in a largely stochastic fashion, show that they undergo remarkable changes in form as a function of the innervation they receive.[41] In other words, the morphological rules formulated by Turing with regard to embryonic development can legitimately be extended to the formation of patterns of neuronal connections.

Experimentally, it is easy to investigate the contribution of inhibitory neurons to epigenetic plasticity, for example by modifying the synthesis and release of GABA, the principal inhibitory neurotransmitter. Quite remarkably, switching off the gene coding for the enzyme that synthesizes GABA in the mouse interferes with the competition between the pathways leading out of each eye to the visual cortex.[42] Any realistic model of the epigenesis of neuronal networks in the brain will need to take into account not only the interaction of inhibitory and excitatory neurons but also—so far as I know, this has not yet been done—the possible contribution of reward mechanisms similar to the ones I described earlier in connection with rapid changes in synaptic efficiency. In formal terms, this circumstance is already contemplated by our original model since it provides for the possibility that the *whole* of the signal message received by the postsynaptic cell (including reward signals) controls retrograde synaptic selection. It is obvious that the specific role of reward (and punishment) signals in the evolution of cerebral connectivity during development must be more adequately correlated with learning behaviors. We also need to understand the transition from the short-term learning associated with cognitive games to their long-term consolidation in the form of stable patterns of synaptic connections. It is possible, but unproven, that the transfer mechanisms between short-term and long-term memories identified in the sea slug *Aplysia* can be extended to the central nervous system of vertebrates.[43]

These few examples and remarks will serve to illustrate the great variety of synaptic and biochemical mechanisms that may intervene in the epigenetic regulation of the development of neuronal networks.

Epigenesis and the Acquisition of Knowledge

The theoretical consequences of the formal models just discussed need to be specified and developed in greater detail within the very general perspective of the central nervous system and, more particularly, its cognitive functions.[44] The first point to be made is that the pattern of nerve impulses stored as a series of stable traces can be mathematically described in terms of a neuronal graph, whether or not this pattern is part of an existing neural network. Within a developing network of neuronal connections, the model explains how a temporal distribution of nerve signals can be recorded and preserved in latent form.

Courrège, Danchin, and I proved a variability theorem that, more than thirty years later, still seems to me to be of great importance.[45] This theorem states that, for any given neuronal network, a single afferent message can stabilize different patterns of connections while at the same time preserving the same output or behavioral capacity—and this despite the deterministic character of the model. The concept of functional reproducibility in the face of anatomical variation has subsequently been developed by several research teams and remains the subject of lively debate.[46]

Members of an important school of thought in the cognitive sciences known as "functionalism" long resisted all attempts to relate the neuronal organization of the brain to its function. Their objections took one of two forms. Some argued that the neurological data failed to constitute an acceptable scientific description at the neuronal and synaptic level, and that it was therefore preferable to introduce a set of "black boxes" specified in exclusively functional terms (as, for example, in the case of a functional dissociation caused by a particular brain lesion that was insufficiently specified in anatomical terms).[47] Others held that the approach itself was fundamentally mistaken since neurological structures and psychological functions overlap without corresponding to each other: in Philip Johnson-Laird's phrase, the physical nature of the neurophysiological substrate "places no constraints on the patterns of thought."[48] Noam Chomsky went still further, criticizing the very possibility of investigating language from a naturalistic point of view. The biological limitations of our brain make it likely, according to Chomsky, that language—and the generativity that characterizes it—will remain among the ultimate secrets of nature, forever beyond the reach of human understanding.[49]

In fact, the variability theorem casts new light on the paradoxical constancy of brain function that is observed in spite of a striking variability in neuroanatomical organization. The recording of temporal patterns of nervous activity in the form of a connectional geometry that varies from one individual to another while nonetheless producing effectively the same functions, or behaviors, may in fact provide the basis for one of the most important bridge laws that Jerry Fodor insists are required if the results of neurology are one day to be placed in correspondence with those of psychology.[50] Nonetheless it raises an additional difficulty for any attempt to naturalize the higher functions of the brain: actually detecting functional invariants within anatomically variable networks.

From an experimental point of view, the theory accounts for the differences that are observed between neuronal phenotypes, even in genetically identical organisms. It also agrees with the view that, in the course of evolution, the genetic envelope governing the formation of synapses during the peri- and postnatal period has become more susceptible to environmental influence. Additionally, the theory provides an interpretation in functional terms of the regressive phenomena commonly observed during development, as well as their control by the network's state of activity, and illuminates the function of the spontaneous activity that is manifested in the nervous system very early during embryonic and fetal development. All these processes—"dreams of the embryo," as I have called them—play important roles in the formation of the adult brain. They amount to a series of internal dress rehearsals, as it were, that prepare its developing neuronal networks for their interaction with the external world.[51]

In further support of the theory's plausibility I have chosen some examples, related mainly to the learning of language, that clearly show how neuronal traces can be formed, and indeed selected, in an epigenetic manner. The first example, having to do with song learning in certain species of birds, is classic. Peter Marler and his colleagues demonstrated in the swamp sparrow *(Melospiza georgiana)* that the "crystallization" of the adult song, which contains no more than two types of syllables, is accompanied by the loss of more than three-quarters of the syllables produced by the "babbling" of the young bird.[52] During this process of syllabic attrition, however, a substantial element of variability is incorporated into the song of the adult sparrow as a result of improvisation—and also imitation (which occurs even in response to computer-synthesized "model" songs).

One notes a similar phenomenon of attrition in the case of language learning in humans.[53] Japanese babies of two or three months are capable of distinguishing between the phonemes *ra* and *la,* as we saw earlier, but Japanese adults have great difficulty doing this. The acquisition of adult language is accompanied by a loss of perceptual capacity in the course of development.[54] Patricia Kuhl and her colleagues have shown that this phenomenon extends to the discrimination of *i* vowels in American and Swedish babies.[55] Before the age of six months, the acoustic space of babies is divided up according to universal psychoacoustic boundaries. After six months, however, this space is reorganized and simplified to accommodate the particular languages that babies hear spoken around them. Recent developmental studies suggest that the child's brain may have a more expansive lexical processing system than the adult brain.[56] However this may be, selective stabilization of internally generated brain patterns takes place as a function of the linguistic environment (Figure 45).

We have already considered the more complex case of babbling in human infants. Babbling begins between six and ten months. So-called canonical babbling is characterized by simple syllables produced by the majority of children, though even within a given linguistic community one notices individual differences. Bénédicte de Boysson-Bardies's careful analysis of the babbling of eight-month-old babies from different countries reveals not only striking points of resemblance but also certain differences related to their respective linguistic environments: hard attacks and stressed syllables in Arabic-speaking Algerian children, softer modulations in French children, numerous small variations in pitch in Cantonese children. These changes correspond to the evolution of the infant's perception of sounds. The interaction between

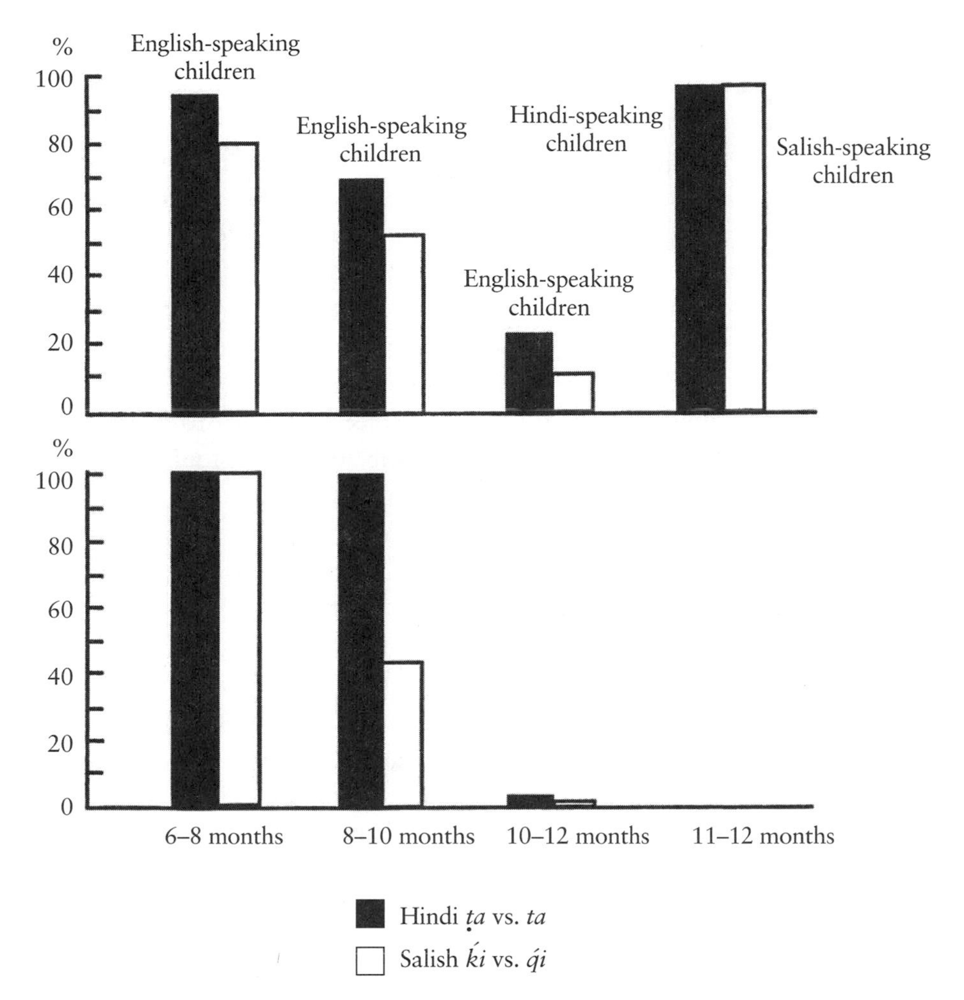

Figure 45. Effect of linguistic environment on the infant's ability to discriminate between phonetic contrasts. The upper part of this diagram represents different groups of children of English-speaking parents who at the onset of language learning perceive the indicated phonetic contrasts of Hindi and Salish. The lower part represents a longitudinal study of children raised in an Anglophone environment who perceive the contrasts between six and eight months but then gradually lose this ability between eight and twelve months.

motor performance and perception contributes to the organization of babbling through selection until twelve months.[57]

A person may learn more than one language. Acquiring a second language after the age of seven to twelve years, however, is more difficult and requires greater effort than learning one's native tongue. Early experiments relying on electrical stimulation of the cortex, as well as certain very localized cerebral lesions, suggested that different cortical areas are utilized in the use of native and second languages in late bilingual subjects. These differences have been confirmed and illustrated through functional magnetic resonance imaging (fMRI) of the brains of late bilingual (French-English) subjects listening to stories in their native and second languages. In all the subjects, listening to the mother tongue systematically activated the same set of areas, particularly ones in the left temporal lobe. By contrast, listening to the second language mobilized quite variable patterns, depending on the subject, not only in left *and* right temporal areas, but also in frontal areas (sometimes exclusively in the right hemisphere).[58]

In another series of experiments using the same method, the bilingual subjects were asked to produce sentences in the first and second languages without uttering them. Once again, cortical territories such as Broca's area were activated in different ways by the two languages.[59] These studies provide a clear anatomical demonstration of the epigenetic neuronal trace associated with language learning and help account for the fact that after a certain age one does not speak a second language with the same ease as one's mother tongue.

My second example has to do with illiteracy, a severe handicap whose incidence in Western populations, to which I shall confine myself here, is still surprisingly high. From the behavioral point of view, the use of spoken language is very similar in persons who know how to read and write and in those who do not. But illiterates exhibit an unexpected difference with respect to a very particular phonological processing task. Though they readily repeat meaningful words, they experience considerable difficulties doing this with words devoid of meaning ("pseudo-words"). Positron emission tomography reveals very clear differences between the brains of literates and illiterates when asked to repeat pseudo-words, but only insignificant discrepancies when asked to repeat actual words (Figure 46A). The cortical terri-

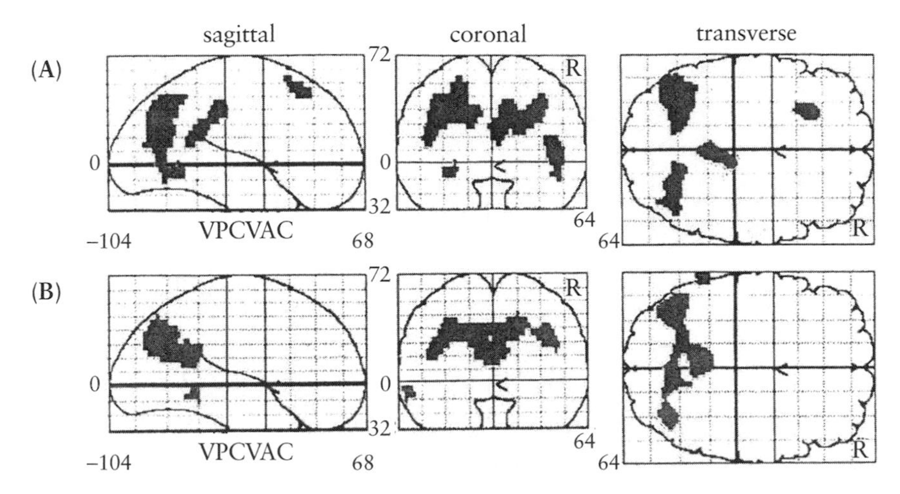

Figure 46A. Modification of cerebral organization by the ability to read and write. Brain images obtained by positron emission tomography in *(top)* subjects who know how to read and *(bottom)* subjects who do not. Both groups were asked to repeat meaningful words and meaningless pseudo-words. The illiterate subjects have difficulty repeating the latter class of words.

tories more strongly activated by real words than by pseudo-words in literate subjects by comparison with illiterate subjects include the right frontal operculum and anterior insula; the left anterior cingulate cortex; the left putamen and pallidum, the anterior thalamus and hypothalamus; and the medial cerebellum.[60]

Similarly, the part of the corpus callosum crossed by parietal fibers linking the left and right hemispheres appears narrower in illiterate subjects.[61] Whether or not one learns to read and write during childhood therefore has a considerable impact on the functional organization of the adult brain.[62]

The acquisition of literacy exploits the epigenetic capacities of the developing brain to memorize new skills. Lesion studies, in particular, have brought out the strong interaction between processing of oral and written language in the adult—as though the act of writing tacitly mobilizes the pathways of oral language (Figure 46B).[63] Reading, too, mobilizes the pathways involved in processing oral language, including those concerned with the phonological processing of new words. Interestingly, a continuing inability to read alters the selective stabilization of these particular phonological pathways. Learning to read and write

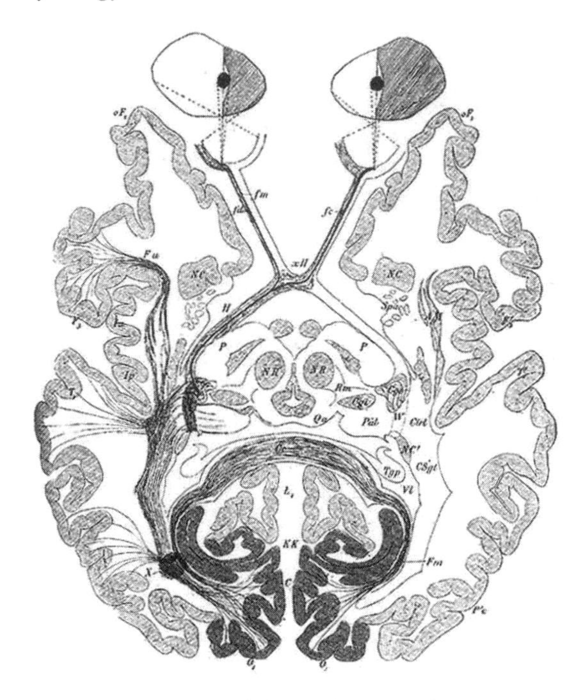

Figure 46B. Déjerine's illustration of the localization of a lesion (black dot) that produces a "pure verbal blindness" accompanied by a selective loss of the ability to read.

leaves profound epigenetic traces in the child's brain that persist until adulthood.[64]

The idea of communicating with the blind and the deaf using new forms of language involving the hands first received attention in France through the efforts of the Abbé de l'Épée in the late eighteenth century. The reading strategy subsequently devised by Louis Braille requires extreme sensitivity and precision in the fingertips in order, first, to distinguish between patterns of raised dots and, then, to transform this spatial code into meaningful information. In certain cases of early blindness, brain imaging reveals a significant enlargement of the parietal somatosensory cortex of the left hemisphere—an area particularly important for the tactile perception of space—after one year of intensive training in Braille. The trace is stable and persists for several years. But functional imaging also reveals something quite unexpected, namely a strong activation of the primary and secondary visual areas of the occipital cortex, which are responsible for processing visual information in sighted persons.[65] With the learning of Braille, the visual areas of blind subjects become capable of receiving and processing tactile information.

Moreover, transcranial magnetic stimulation—a new technique used to reversibly inactivate specific areas of the cortex—dramatically interferes with reading in Braille when applied either to the somatosensory cortex or to the striate visual cortex in the partially sighted. In the first case, the detection of words in Braille is disturbed, regardless of the meaning of these words. In the second case, subjects detect the Braille text but are unable to say whether it is meaningful or not. In both cases, the learning of Braille produces a marked change in cerebral connectivity. The most plausible and parsimonious (though not therefore the only) explanation for these remarkable results assumes that functional connections already exist at birth between the somatosensory and visual cortices as well as between the nonvisual thalamus and the visual thalamus. Braille training has the effect not only of selecting these preexisting pathways for purposes of tactile reading but also, through the outgrowth of additional axon terminals, of amplifying them.[66]

Even though none of these results by itself constitutes a definitive demonstration of the model of selective stabilization of developing synapses—the resolution of the anatomical data is still far too low—taken together they are consistent with it. Since the model's original formulation more than thirty years ago, only one minor assumption has been added, namely the reinforcement of selected connections through local outgrowth of axon terminals.[67]

The Neuronal Habitus

The analysis of the preceding pages, though it by no means puts an end to the debate over nature and nurture, does place it in a new perspective. From now on it will no longer be possible to speculate about the relative importance of innate endowment and acquired experience without taking into account the sequencing data of the human genome, the pattern of gene expression in the course of development, and the epigenetic evolution of neural connectivity in its anatomical, physiological, and behavioral aspects. Taking all these things into account may appear very difficult, indeed almost impossible—above all in the case of the human brain. Yet the conception of gene expression and epigenetic evolution as interrelated, nonlinear, and highly contextualized phenomena exposes the fallacy underlying two very influential views of human intelligence. The first, which postulates the existence of a specialized gene for intelligence, omits epigenesis; the second, which insists on the exclusive influence of environmental factors in mental development, neglects genetics.

The opening up of the genetic envelope to epigenetic variability and to evolution by selection is made possible, as we have seen, by the incorporation of a random component in synaptic development within cascading and nested sequences of synaptic outgrowth that begin in the earliest stages of embryogenesis and last until puberty. Each successive wave of connections, whose type and timing are very probably determined by the genetic envelope, is correlated with the acquisition of particular skills, but also with the loss of certain abilities (possibly due to top-down processes of selective inhibition).[68] Innate knowledge and epigenetic learning are closely associated during pre- and postnatal development. This period is marked by a series of crucial events: the infant's first applications of practical knowledge; the emergence of reflective consciousness and, subsequently, of a theory of mind; and the learning of language, epigenetic rules, and social conventions. Epigenesis makes possible the diversification, transmission, and evolution of culture. A sound education ought to supplement these developmental patterns with an appropriate basis for learning and experience. The individual character of each person is thus constructed as a function of what the sociologist Pierre Bourdieu called "habitus"—a unique synthesis of one's genetic endowment, circumstances of birth and upbringing, and subjective experience of the social and cultural environment in which one has grown up.

Both innate knowledge and the innate disposition to acquire further knowledge—and to consciously test its truth—developed through the genetic evolution of species. The exceptionally long period of epigenetic evolution undergone by the human brain enabled it to incorporate information about the external world that is unobtainable by genetic mechanisms. This process also made possible the production of a cultural memory that is not directly subject to the intrinsic limitations of the brain, and so can be epigenetically transmitted at the level of the social group. In view of the considerable variability that epigenesis introduces in the neuronal network, however, the question arises how invariant and universal truths have been able to be discovered despite the multiplicity of personal experience and the diversity of human cultures—how, in a word, science is possible.

Before taking up this question, and the nature of scientific research, which is properly seen as the highest stage of cultural evolution, let us pause for a moment to take stock of the current state of biological knowledge regarding the brain and its productions, always keeping in mind that our knowledge is provisional and our ignorance immense.

Comparative genomic analysis of vertebrates suggests that a very small number of genetic determinants—localized perhaps in regulatory sequences of transcription factors or in the transcription factor genes themselves, or both—governed the development of the brain of *Homo sapiens* over the last few million years. A remarkable and nonlinear transformation occurred in the morphogenesis and connectional complexity of the human cerebral phenotype on the basis of a relatively stable genetic endowment. This evolution was marked, first, by the striking development of the brain's conscious workspace, which gave access to a new inner universe of mental objects, linked together in a process of unlimited combination, whose capacity to truthfully represent the world could now be examined and evaluated. The evolution of the human brain was marked also by an epigenetic opening up of cerebral connectivity to the external world during the years following birth and continuing into adulthood. In bringing about an expansion—once again wholly nonlinear—of the brain's capacity for representing the world, this permitted both the long-term storage of acquired knowledge and its transmission to succeeding generations, and ultimately the creation of an enduring culture. Moreover, the epigenetic development of synaptic contacts created a stable link between genes, whose mutability manifests itself over generations, and consciousness, whose elusive and evanescent character is perceived in psychological time.

The joint and mutually reinforcing evolution of genetic capacity and the epigenetic products of cerebral activity—of the innate and the acquired—no doubt was selected for by virtue of the considerable evolutionary advantage that it conferred on the human species, both in multiplying the brain's functions and, as a consequence of this, increasing man's power to act upon the world. The mechanisms of this socio-epigenetic evolution are still very poorly understood. It is nonetheless clear that the differentiation of language areas and pathways of the conscious workspace, and the theory of mind this made possible, equipped the brain with new capacities by creating a sort of mental solidarity, or community, at the level of the social group.

A small number of essentially quantitative changes in the genotype and cerebral connectional phenotype were sufficient, then, to bring about qualitatively new changes in human brain function. May one therefore join philosophers such as John Searle in speaking of consciousness as an "emergent" phenomenon? Yes—which is to say that it emerges from the processes of cerebral organization contemplated by Gaston Bachelard's informed materialism.

Scientific Research and the Search for Truth 7

By virtue of our ability to extract, store, and evaluate knowledge, to communicate it, and to discuss it at the social level, the search for truth stands out as the supreme emblem of human intelligence. We are in some sense, as Karl Popper remarked, "natural scientists."[1] And yet the rise of organized scientific inquiry as we know it today, with its elaborate institutionalized rules and practices, is a rather recent event in human history.

In 1794, under the threat of death at the height of the Terror, the Marquis de Condorcet, one of the most eminent representatives of the Enlightenment in France and the first thinker to propose placing the analysis of social behavior on a mathematical basis, wrote *Esquisse d'un tableau historique des progrès de l'esprit humain.*[2] Published posthumously the following year, its concluding chapter described the flowering of science as the final stage in the development of civilization. More than a century earlier, Fontenelle, in *Entretiens sur la pluralité des mondes* (1686),[3] had explicitly asserted an analogy between the history of science and human mental development. Condorcet adopted the idea and developed it further: the "ancient pagans" and "savages" lived in the passive world of early childhood; "barbarians" remained at the stage of adolescent imagination; and "civilized peoples" had managed to reach adulthood thanks to the boundless growth of reason. Historical evolution took over from individual development, enlarging and intensifying it. Condorcet saw no limit to the growth and development of human wisdom. It is important to remember that his doctrine of the "indefinite perfectibility" of the human race had its origins in the rational and secular search for truth that in the following century inspired the Constitution of the United States and, in France, the Declaration of the Rights of Man.

In the nineteenth century, Auguste Comte, the father of both sociology and positivism, carried this analysis further with his celebrated law of the three stages of scientific knowledge.[4] In the "theological" (or "fictive") state, the human mind in its infancy seeks the "final ends" of phenomena: it finds them in the "intentions" that it attributes, first, to animate objects and living beings (animism, or fetishism), then to the action of supernatural beings (polytheism), and finally to the will of a divine creator (monotheism). This is what, on Comte's view, explains man's susceptibility to anthropocentrism. In the "metaphysical" state, the human mind in its adolescence substitutes for the gods of the theological age abstract general principles (such as Spinoza's system of Nature, Leibniz's *Dieu calculateur,* or Diderot's conception of Matter). The mind frees itself from anthropocentrism by producing more rational explanations of the origin of the world, while continuing to search for first causes. On reaching maturity in the "positive"—scientific or industrial—state, the human mind abandons absolute theological and metaphysical explanations, replacing them with the method of the experimental sciences.

There is much to be said against Comte. His religion of humanity and certain of his political views, as well as his obsession with arithmetic, have been severely criticized. More disturbingly, he attached scarcely any importance at all to biological evolution, and saw the growth of society as the result of a law of predetermined development. But there is also much to be said in his favor. Despite the rigid and schematic outlook of positivism, it attracted the support of a number of the most eminent thinkers of the period, among them Hippolyte Taine, Émile Littré, Claude Bernard, and, outside France, John Stuart Mill. Comte exercised a considerable influence on the development of republican parties and trade unions throughout the world, including the United States and South America, notably in Brazil. In France he also inspired the legislation sponsored by Jules Ferry in 1881–1882, establishing a universal, obligatory, and secular system of public education that emphasized scientific literacy. At a time when the bias of religious education against freedom of individual judgment leaves a deep mark on young children, predisposing them to embrace violent conflict in later life, the principles underlying the tradition of secular humanism need to be reaffirmed.[5] We owe these principles to August Comte.

Since Darwin, the success of evolutionary thought has caused the law of the three states to be forgotten. Yet several important elements of Comte's philosophy have survived: the ideas that organized and institutionalized scientific inquiry in its modern form is a quite recent human activity having a history of its own; that if truth exists, it can only be found by means of scientific inquiry; and that the various branches of science can themselves be ordered and submitted to rational examination. Anticipating the tragic perversions of the twentieth century, Comte subordinated the acquisition of scientific knowledge to the interests of humanity, and insisted that certain directions of research be abandoned or reconceived.[6] This is precisely the view adopted by commissions on bioethics today—a point to which I shall recur (Figure 47).

In seeking to understand how human beings manage to acquire knowledge of the natural world and society, we have been led to distinguish three interlocking evolutionary processes that operate by variation and selection at the level of the gene, at the level of synaptic connectivity, and at the level of socially shared (or cultural) representations. Biological evolution, in exploiting nonlinear networks of genetic expression, has given rise to a range of cognitive capacities that are further modified by the operation of epigenetic rules. The storing of objects, events, concepts, and rules as selected neural patterns is accompanied by a combinatory and recursive generation of new concepts in the conscious workspace, which in turn are subject to constant evaluation by the brain. Finally, meanings are related in a conventional and arbitrary manner to sounds and shared among individuals within a social group through language, making possible the cultural retention and transmission of ideas across generations.

We are now in a position to ask how such "natural" predispositions converged during the course of recent history to produce organized scientific activity. A considerable literature has grown up in the past century concerning the metaphysical, economic, and political origins

Figure 47. Pierre-Paul Prud'hon, *La Sagesse et la Vérité* (1796). Truth, led by wisdom, is shown descending from the heavens, dispelling the darkness that shrouds the earth.

of modern science. To this may now be added the contribution of the cognitive sciences, which cast new light on a question that since Comte's time has been unjustly neglected: how the motivated search for truth, this remarkable expression of the higher functions of the human brain, led to a mode of knowledge that aims to be at once universal and objective—in a word, *scientific.*

The Savage Mind

Contemporary oral societies can hardly be regarded as supplying reliable evidence about the prehistoric evolution of human civilizations.

The reality is that the infant discipline of cognitive archaeology will forever be limited by a scarcity of empirical data. Nonetheless, anthropologists are intrigued by the fact, noted by Claude Lévi-Strauss in *La Pensée sauvage* (1962), that the vocabulary used by the members of such societies is very rich in both concrete and abstract words.[7] Their systematic inventory of the animate and inanimate world is impressive, to say the least. The Hanunoo of the Philippines, for example, are able to distinguish 461 types of local fauna, among them 75 birds, 12 snakes, 60 fish, 103 insects (including 13 types of ant), 60 sea molluscs, and 4 leeches—not all of which are necessarily useful or dangerous.[8] The botanical lexicon of the Hanunoo numbers about 2,000 names; among some tribes in Gabon it reaches 8,000. The distinctions between plants may be based on their general appearance, but also on their shape, size, or texture. These distinctions correspond to what earlier I called a pattern of selected traits, which may include their usefulness for human beings. And yet this systematic and rational classification is not based solely on alimentary or medicinal usage.

Comparing the traditional methods of botanical classification among the Hanunoo of the Philippines with those of the Tzeltal Maya of southern Mexico, Brent Berlin noticed that plant names exhibit a great degree of regularity in the two languages.[9] In both systems, the principal types of plants constitute a taxonomic hierarchy organized around three general concepts: trees, vines, and grasses. The fact that individuals belonging to very different cultures manage to classify a great variety of distinct species in very similar ways suggests the existence of a common way of perceiving and organizing the natural world. There may, of course, have been direct contacts between the populations of the Philippines and Mexico; but the most plausible and the most parsimonious interpretation of this convergence is that the human brain, through a combination of common innate predispositions and habits of learning by trial and error, extracts regular features from perceptual experience of the natural world and organizes them as a series of basic conceptual categories.

The respective contributions of innate dispositions and acquired abilities have long aroused passionate debate among anthropologists. As we know from our earlier discussion of cognitive games, certain major human categories such as the distinction between living beings and inanimate objects, or between animals, fruits, and vegetables, are associated with cortical territories that correspond to areas found in the brain of the monkey, probably in innate form. But what are we to make of much more specific names, for example of colors? Are they merely products of linguistic arbitrariness, varying from one culture to another? Berlin and Paul Kay traveled throughout the world with 329 color samples and investigated the color vocabularies of 20 different populations, all speaking different languages.[10] Each person was asked to name the basic colors in his or her language. Their responses pointed to the existence of eleven principal categories of basic colors. No evidence was found of random distribution or shifting conceptual boundaries, as the doctrine of linguistic relativism insists. To the contrary, strong agreement was observed between color vocabularies and spectral boundaries: white, black, red, green, yellow, blue, brown, purple, pink, orange, and gray.

There exists, then, a remarkable regularity—indeed, universality—in the use of color terms across cultures. These data agree with psychophysical recordings, which distinguish responses to red, green, yellow, blue, black, and white. This selectivity is based in turn on the spectral properties of three pigment molecules (allosteric membrane proteins of the rhodopsin family) that are expressed in three distinct types of photosensitive cells in the retina. But it also depends on patterns of connection within the retina and in the brain that ensure its constancy at the cerebral level.[11] Despite differences of language, color vocabularies in widely separated cultures developed in agreement with a common set of neural predispositions. One may therefore speak of an "innate truth" of color, even if the names of specific colors vary as a function of cultural epigenesis. This process subsequently gave rise to new and more subtle categories of terms designating the immense diversity of shades, from pastel to carmine, from Veronese green to Prussian blue. "Natural categories" thus came to be enriched by cultural constructions that incorporated them (Figure 48).

"Any classification is superior to chaos," Lévi-Strauss remarked, "and even a classification at the level of sensible properties is a step towards rational ordering."[12] As a consequence of this common impulse to order the world, individual memories preserve a primary category of "first-order," or basic, cultural representations.[13] These repre-

Figure 48. The Five Sacred Colors of Maize. This Huichol Indian tapestry is woven of wool of five colors (white, yellow, red, blue, and apple green), each of which is personified by a corn goddess (represented by a stalk of corn). The five are daughters of the Mother Goddess Kukuruku, represented here as a white dove. Tapestries of this kind are woven after the annual pilgrimage to the high desert of Wirikuta in Mexico, where the Huichol commune with their gods after eating peyote, a cactus rich in hallucinogenic substances that, like LSD, act principally on serotonin receptors in the brain. These tapestries illustrate the visions they experience.

sentations convey factual, empirical knowledge, much of it essential to the individual's survival or well-being.

Nonetheless, the content of these epigenetic memories is limited, and their transmission from one generation to another through education is vulnerable to disruption. The invention of techniques for making incisions or marks in various materials—wood, stone, bone, clay—

enabled human beings to free themselves from dependence upon the restricted storage capacity of individual brains and to preserve memories over long periods of time, while also accelerating the processing and analysis of large amounts of new information. Among the immediate precursors of Sumerian writing are the clay envelopes and bullae found at Susa, dating from about 3300 B.C., covered with authenticating seal impressions in the form of animals and geometric figures and marked with notches corresponding to the number of tokens or counters *(calculi)* they contained. These notations very probably represented contractual agreements between two parties for the purchase and sale of goods.[14] The majority of early pictographic writings found at the ancient Sumerian city of Uruk (ca. 3700–2900 B.C.) likewise filled useful commercial (rather than religious) functions.[15]

The numbering of animals and commodities in these systems not only throws light on the basic problems of accounting encountered in trade more than five thousand years ago; it may also constitute evidence of the earliest development of arithmetic and a theory of numbers. Similarly, pictographic references to the surveying and irrigation of fields can plausibly be interpreted as indicating the beginnings of geometry. In China, by contrast, such references are found on oracular bones from the Shang Dynasty (twelfth century B.C.) in which characters are engraved in the vicinity of randomly distributed cracks that were used by soothsayers to predict the future—a striking example of the human brain's capacity to give meaning to things that otherwise have none.[16] I shall come back to this point.

Yet in both cases the brain can be seen to function in a projective manner. It generates a constant flow of conjectures and hypotheses about a world that is perceived to be changeable, irregular, and capricious, imposing order upon it through the application of tentative categories, or pre-representations. The scientific impulse grows out of precisely this spontaneous propensity for producing a surplus of meaning, as it were; for entertaining a wide range of possibilities and unproven assumptions prior to settling upon a course of action. The deceptively simple gesture of inscribing such conjectures on a solid and stable substrate provided the human brain with the crucial ability—amounting, one might say, to a prosthesis—to extend the reach of cerebral memory, making it possible to preserve and transmit mental categories of animals, inanimate objects, and natural phenomena over the long term. Not only did the invention of writing improve communication. For the first time it allowed comparisons to be made between types of knowledge that are difficult to hold simultaneously in the working memory of the brain's conscious workspace. And in reassigning the task of communication from the auditory to the visual domain, writing reorganized knowledge in ways that made it accessible to larger numbers of people.[17]

What Lévi-Strauss called "la pensée sauvage" nonetheless involves much more than a systematic description of the physical world. Very early, perhaps even from the beginnings of *Homo sapiens,* mythic and religious thought were important elements of the search for truth. The purpose of mythic imagining is not to ensure the immediate survival of the individual but to respond to basic questions that every child asks but that no adult is able to answer. Can the future be predicted with certainty? How did the world—and especially its peoples—come into being? What sense is to be made of death? These questions take in more than the life of the individual: they concern the social group as a whole.

Mythic thought protests against an absence of meaning by creating a meaningful world populated by spirits and gods having magical powers. Plants, animals, inanimate objects, and meteorological phenomena are endowed with motivation and intentionality, and in their turn impose rules of behavior and rituals—symbolic substitutes for human mastery of natural processes and phenomena. This impulse recalls the remarkable tendency of children to attribute intentions to physical objects.[18] Their theory of mind, which I mentioned earlier, leads them spontaneously to form beliefs about gods, ghosts, robots, Santa Claus, and other agents with supernatural powers. At four or five years of age they understand that what adults call "God" cannot be thought of as having false beliefs in the way that human beings do.[19] Even adults seem to find concepts that are contrary to intuition and common sense acceptable in a mythical or religious context. Nor is the failure of predictions an obstacle to belief. Any number of unnatural or counterintuitive tales come to mind: the burning bush of the Old Testament, the resurrection of the dead in the New Testament, various doctrines of reincarnation, assorted "miracles" that contradict the most elementary laws of physics.

Throughout human history societies have credited imaginary explanations of the world that, far from being based on objective truth, are often wholly at variance with it. In oral tradition, a sort of "sensory pageantry" assists memory by associating unnatural concepts with events such as initiation rites that intensify normal emotions, using sights, sounds, and smells to create far more powerful feelings than those experienced in everyday life.[20] The primary purpose of myths is not to discover objective knowledge but to reinforce group solidarity and confidence, and to facilitate the acceptance of moral rules through easily memorized and propagated signs of recognition.[21]

Earlier I referred to the brain as an open, motivated, and self-organizing neuronal system. The genesis of myths by means of what Lévi-Strauss called "bricolage," or tinkering, nicely captures the fundamentally projective character of the brain, and displays an obvious similarity with the cognitive games mentioned earlier in connection with the mental development of the child. This evolutionary process can therefore be seen as a direct expression of the brain's combinatory and recursive properties as well as of its capacity for generalization. The materials used to construct a mythical model of the world are often prefabricated, and the process of construction itself is a source of gratification, both intellectually and aesthetically. Myths and rituals form part of the cultural memory of the social group, which is transmitted from generation to generation by epigenetic mechanisms at critical periods in childhood development. Through a process of very early education, reinforced by reward mechanisms, this memory comes to be deeply and almost irreversibly rooted in the system of the emotions.[22]

These higher-order cultural representations, though they often disagree with common sense and the laws of physics, are nonetheless stable within the social group. Indeed, they still actively perpetuate themselves today in many parts of the world, in the West no less than in the East. But they have to a considerable extent been transformed or replaced in the course of recent cultural history by a new type of representation—scientific ideas—which, as we shall see, do in fact work better when it comes to explaining reality and acting upon it.

The Agora and the Library

The high degree of sophistication with which prehistoric human beings painted the caves of Lascaux and Chauvet, using a very rich palette of colors, and the ease with which they erected megalithic structures, some of them colossal, are proof of an exceptional level of objective knowledge and technical skill. Yet ancient Greece is usually considered the birthplace of natural philosophy and scientific inquiry. Even if this claim to preeminence might in certain respects be challenged by China or Egypt, the reasons customarily given for the success of the Greeks seem to me to be of particular importance from the point of view of cognitive neuroscience.

This awakening is undoubtedly associated with religious myths and beliefs. Indeed, the mythology of ancient Greece, unlike that of Egypt or Mesopotamia, did not constitute a body of dogmas and rites so structured and rigid as to prohibit criticism or even outright rejection. There is nothing about the heroes and gods in Homer that bears comparison with the almighty power of a Jehovah, for example, or a Marduk. The Greek gods were often immoral and inconstant, to the point that some philosophers were driven to preach atheism for moral reasons.[23] It is not unreasonable to suppose that these circumstances may have favored the appearance of a more rigorous mode of reasoning that caused the propriety of traditional myths to be called into question.

A second reason is perhaps to be sought in the very nature of the Greek city-state. At the center of the city stood a space enclosed by a colonnade with a gallery where citizens gathered: the agora, or public square. The geometrical arrangement of this space expressed a political conception founded on the freedom of citizens to engage in mutual discussion, to exchange opinions and actively participate in a common public life (Figure 49). By encouraging communication, the agora made it possible to test and validate competing representations, or views, of the world. Public debate concerned both legal and political matters, after the example of the law courts and political assemblies. The agora thereby created a common "workspace" of individual brains in which social representations could be jointly and critically examined. It is a well-known paradox of Greek democracy that the considerable place occupied by slavery in the economy of the city-state

Figure 49. Vitruvius's conception of the agora. The public meeting place, or agora, was a square in the ancient Greek city, surrounded by colonnaded porticos with raised galleries. Its dimensions were to be "proportionate to the number of the people." The basilica was part of the colonnade, "situated in the hottest place" in the agora so that the people gathered inside it would not suffer from "the discomfort of the season." This drawing and commentary, by the architect Vitruvius, pertain to the Roman counterpart of the Greek agora—the forum.

permitted citizens to devote themselves to leisurely debate and discussion in the agora.

Despite its class system, the public life of ancient Greece was characterized by a remarkable sense of tolerance among its citizens. The right to active participation in open and free debate enjoyed by representatives of different schools of thought and cultural traditions gave rise to reasoned argument and logical demonstration. The historian Geoffrey Lloyd has pointed out that the Greeks never embraced a single, exclusive concept of truth. Emphasis was placed instead on accuracy in stating premises, reliability of observation, correction for the relativity of individual judgment, and a skeptical attitude toward all claims on behalf of a hidden reality.[24] What mattered was that debate be properly conducted and that the conclusions adopted at any given time be reexamined later in the light of the most recent information. Several of the unwritten norms that underlie the standards of scientific inquiry today—collaborative research, universal access to its results, and a habit of skepticism—seem already to have been at work in the agora.[25]

The rise of rational medicine with the appearance of the Hippocratic school offers an impressive example of this evolving custom of analysis and debate. Ancient medicine in Greece had formerly appealed to supernatural spirits and magic rituals. Disease was considered a divine punishment for the sins committed by human beings. Illness was treated through incantations, prayers, votive offerings, and other propitiatory measures. This does not mean that the medications used by traditional physicians were uniformly ineffective. But the Hippocratic school, in a radical departure from traditional practice, postulated at the outset that illness was a natural rather than a supernatural phenomenon.[26] Epilepsy, for example, was not a "sacred disease" (as it was commonly known) or a "divine visitation"; it resulted instead from natural dysfunctions of the brain. It had "specific characteristics and a definite cause" that until then had been ignored. The advances made by Hippocratic medicine led to a clear distinction between professional physicians and priests.[27] Its most important achievement was the formulation of a method that proceeded from diagnosis, based on the observation of symptoms, and led to the recommendation of a treatment relying on active pharmacological agents rather than magical solutions. The *pharmakos,* or expiatory victim offered up by the city to the gods, thus gave way to the physician. It is interesting to note that the Hippocratic school had no intention of abolishing traditional medicine.[28] The two schools continued to coexist in Greece, as they still do today: witness the continuing popularity of homeopathy and various "natural" or "alternative" medicines, which prosper despite the immense achievements of scientific medicine.

A third, very important factor that fostered the birth of scientific inquiry is the importance the Greeks attached to natural philosophy and to systematic analysis of the grounds for our ability to understand the physical world and human affairs. They sought above all to determine the most reliable method for acquiring sound knowledge, as remarkable developments in pharmacology and surgery subsequently demonstrated. Among the leading figures of the first millennium of the common era were Dioscorides (first century A.D.) and Galen (129–199) at Rome and later the Persian physicians al-Razi (known in the West as Rhazes, 865–925) and Ibn Sina (known as Avicenna, 980–1037). The Renaissance in the West represented the revival not only of the arts but of medicine and the sciences as well (Figure 50).[29] To examine the development of scientific method that followed in the second millennium would fall outside the scope of this book. It has in any case already been extensively described by many authors. I shall present here only a few aspects of the matter, which seem to me to anticipate the subsequent rise of modern science.

Mathematics forms a corpus of statements, propositions, and abstract representations—what I have called epigenetic rules. Its primary aim, at least historically, was to describe as accurately—truthfully—as possible the regularities of our physical world. In the sixth century B.C., Pythagoras asserted that "all things are number." His attempt to represent physical regularities in numerical terms was a crucial advance in the development of scientific inquiry. Astronomy seems to have been the first science of nature to develop quantitative methods for measuring time, devising calendars, and plotting the position of the constellations. Aristotle, an experienced marine biologist among other things, dissented from Plato in placing mathematics in the second rank and privileging observation over theoretical speculation. In the *Historia animalium* he brought together a wealth of observations unequaled for more than two thousand years. What is more, he sought to organize these observations in a hierarchical system of classification. This comprehensive natural history was not to be challenged until the rise of evolutionary biology in the nineteenth century with Lamarck and Darwin.[30]

The history of Greek philosophy illustrates two essential aspects of scientific investigation: the collection of data through observation, and the use of formal rules, or theory, to organize and interpret them. Each of these two approaches assumes a high degree of projective activity on the part of the human brain: on the one hand, exploring the external world, comparing perceptions with one another, noting inconsistencies

Figure 50. Two ancient manuscripts illustrating the cultural universality of scientific knowledge. *Top:* Arabic translation of the *De materia medica* of Dioscorides with illustrations of the buttercup and loosestrife (left) and comfrey (right). Upper Mesopotamia, twelfth century. *Bottom:* Manuscript written in Hebrew, with arabesques and tracery influenced by Arabic calligraphy, of the medical maxims of Ibn Sina (Avicenna) and Hippocrates. Spain, fifteenth century.

and detecting patterns; and, on the other, conducting internal "experiments" with a view to comparing memories of prior events, examining representations for internal consistency, and evaluating their logical implications. Over time, the harmonization of these two approaches, combined with the selection process of public debate, generated a sizable corpus of public knowledge. The record of such shared mental experiments becomes part of the brain's long-term memory, where it is accessible by the conscious workspace, and serves as a building block for the acquisition of further knowledge.[31] Notwithstanding its epigenetic character, the conceptual development of science resembles to some extent the biological evolution of species by natural selection.[32]

The storing of this orally transmitted knowledge in the form of written texts in which observational evidence and theoretical conjectures were combined in an organized, rational way marked a decisive change. By making knowledge literally more visible and presenting it in an ordered fashion, writing enabled human understanding of the world to grow. Signs drawn in the sand, or inscribed on clay and wax, gave way to signs marked on papyrus with ink that made it possible to preserve accumulated knowledge. The storing of increasingly large numbers of scrolls *(volumen)* in libraries constitutes perhaps the first sign of the institutionalization of scientific learning.[33] The most celebrated library was in Alexandria. The shelves *(bibliothekai)* of this library were arranged beneath the porticoes of the Temple of the Muses—or Museum *(Mouseion)*—where collections of natural objects and artifacts were interspersed with works of art. Scholars capable of reading, reflecting upon, and discussing the written knowledge contained in the scrolls of the library lived in the Museum. What is more, they were paid for their work (though scholarship, judged a trivial and empty pursuit by popular opinion, was already much criticized). Here, then, was a further sign of the institutionalization of science: the emergence of a class of professional scholars.[34] The Alexandrian model was later widely imitated by universities and other academic institutions.

During the Renaissance and the centuries that followed, the ancient debate between empiricism and rationalism was renewed. The empiricist position, first formulated by Aristotle, was taken up once more and argued by Bacon, Locke, and Hume (and, more recently, by Ernst Mach). The rationalist conception, descended from Plato, was developed in radically new ways by Descartes and Kant. These two modes of philosophical thought reflect, in my view, two distinct styles of the functioning of the brain, both strongly conditioned by education and the cultural environment.

For Francis Bacon, author of the *Novum organum* (1620), observation was the point of departure for all scientific inquiry. Bacon argued that theories are reliable only insofar as they have an empirical foundation. Scientific method proceeds in the first instance by an exhaustive, often "blind," analysis of empirical data aimed at distinguishing and identifying natural forms. Only once this preliminary phase of categorization has been completed may theories be formulated by induction. "True induction," Bacon asserted, "derives axioms from the senses and particulars, rising by a gradual and unbroken ascent, so that it arrives at the most general axioms last of all."[35] Mach went further, holding that "theoretical entities" are nothing more than useful fictions, provisional tools that assist prediction.[36] This position is still widely endorsed in the world of biochemistry and neuroscience. Theory, if it comes at all, must come only *after* the facts!

Descartes, by contrast, insisted that theory comes first.[37] It involves constructing internally consistent deductive systems—an artificial world analogous to reality—in which simplified automata simulate living organisms and processes. Kant, for his part, anxious to find a way out from the dead end into which he believed the empiricists had led philosophy, affirmed that human knowledge reflects the structure of the *categories* of the mind. Man, in questioning nature, imposes a preorganized conceptual structure on the data of the senses and renders nature intelligible by means of systematic and coherent theories. In other words, the senses are primary in our relation to the world, but we are obliged to make use of preexisting mental frameworks—what I have called contextualized pre-representations—to order what our senses reveal. As Kant famously expressed the matter, concepts without intuitions are empty: by themselves they tell us nothing about the world. But intuitions without concepts are blind: our intellect does not draw its laws from nature, but imposes its laws on nature.[38]

On the first view, theory can be deduced only from empirical observations. On the second, theory anticipates observation, structuring and orienting it. The history of the sciences displays a dialectical alternation between these two modes of apprehending the external world. From the point of view of modern neurobiology, they correspond to bottom-up and top-down processes that simultaneously develop in the brain as it explores the world: nerve impulses travel, on the one hand, from the sensory organs upward to the "processors," and thence to the conscious workspace; and, on the other, downward from the conscious workspace to the processors. In the first case, relative (though not exclusive) priority is given to the senses, which in the limiting case are vulnerable to illusions of various sorts. In the second, theory is dominant, and carries with it the risk of falling into uncontrolled fantasy and dogmatism. The scientific approach—the path to truth—is no doubt to be sought in an unstable equilibrium between these two motions.

From Instruction to Selection

It comes as something of a surprise to note that the first investigations of the cognitive processes underlying scientific thought were carried out by mathematicians. Long before psychologists (such as Jean Piaget and Max Wertheimer) and evolutionary epistemologists (such as Karl Popper and Donald Campbell) took an interest in the matter, Henri Poincaré and his student Jacques Hadamard had carefully examined the sources of scientific imagination. For Poincaré, imagination had nothing to do with the fanciful flights of mind evoked by the Romantics; it involved the capacity to perceive an argument as a whole in the form of a visual, or "sensual," image.[39] Kant had anticipated this view at the end of the *Critique of Pure Reason,* where he identified imagination as the faculty that unifies reason and sensibility. Many mathematicians, Hadamard in particular, have noted that once a first conscious definition of a problem has been given, the creative process consists of a long period of unconscious labor in which a very large number of connections among ideas are made. The sudden "illumination" provoked by the right combination of ideas then fills what I have called the conscious workspace. Afterward it needs to be explicitly verified.[40] Invention, Poincaré maintained, is selection. But the intuitions that guide the mathematician in his work are extremely subtle and delicate: a special sensibility—"a sort of aesthetic emotion"—helps him separate out that which is "harmoniously arranged" and filled with "elegance" and "beauty."[41] Poincaré's "sensual imagery," exactly like Einstein's "muscular image," contains a strong perceptual—empirical—component. Perhaps it is not going too far to consider Euclidean geometry and the Ptolemaic conception of the universe in similar terms, as direct inferences drawn from immediate visual perception.

Einstein argued that mental images may be created as a consequence of sense impressions, but that they do not amount to thought. Scientific thought comes into being with the operation of an "ordering" element that connects these images among themselves.[42] Jacques Monod, for example, recounted his surprise at discovering that, in concentrating on a certain problem, he actually imagined that he was a protein molecule.[43] This particular type of subjective perception—Poincaré's "expérience imaginaire," Einstein's "Gedanken Experiment"—constitutes the starting point for a process by which the imagined object is detached both from ordinary perception and from the self. The selected features of the mental object are now subjected to internal evaluation and incorporated as part of the body of previously evoked memories held in the conscious workspace. A kind of melody develops in the workspace as a consequence of constantly comparing and reconciling the material of inner reality with the data of the outside world. In this way the neural self is placed in correspondence with present, past, and future events, while at the same time standing apart from them.

Current models of such a process are still quite primitive. At a rather low level, neurophysiological correlates exist for the illusory but coherent completion of discontinuous images by the brain.[44] The fact that when we walk or move our heads we have a global perception of a stationary outside world provides additional evidence that the brain constructs a coherent and unified model of the world that is constantly adjusted by feedback signals traveling from motor to sensory pathways.[45] It is tempting to suppose that the coherence and resonance generated in this fashion are exploited in both artistic and scientific creation. Contemporary neuroscience is still far from being able to give a definitive answer.

Rational thought depends in large part on epigenetic rules—notably those of logic and mathematics—that have been selected in the course of cultural evolution and acquired through personal experience.

Changes of mental perspective may nonetheless take place in an all-or-nothing manner, with the result that the egocentric perspective of the scientist becomes "decentered" (to use Piaget's term). Historically, such changes in conceptual orientation have had decisive consequences for the evolution of scientific knowledge; indeed, they may be the source of some of the "paradigm shifts" described by Thomas Kuhn.[46] In the case of the Copernican revolution, for example, it is possible that the traditional picture of the motion of the sun and the planets, arising from "naive" sensory perception, one day suddenly acquired a privileged position in the global workspace of Copernicus's brain so that it could be viewed objectively, that is, as an object on its own account. This moment of liberation from direct perception produced a spectacular reversal of the observer's point of view. One might say that the neural circuits representing the object switched from an egocentric perceptual mode to a detached allocentric perspective.[47]

Similar departures from direct perception are found in the history of biology. The description and classification of living species in terms of a *scala naturae* or hierarchical ordering of creatures (whose history as an idea runs from Aristotle to Linnaeus) is a good example of Baconian empiricism in the sense that theorizing attempts only to define formal relationships a posteriori, among immediately visible forms of living organisms.

A first major detachment occurred when Lamarck introduced the idea that species, rather than occupying a fixed place in a cosmos whose harmony is the product of divine design, "descended" from one another. Living creatures, including human beings, form a branching tree of distinct lineages that descended from one another over geological time scales. Once again, the self-regarding perspective of the scientific observer was discarded in favor of an autonomous and spontaneous process whose natural mechanism remained to be identified. On this view, Lamarck's theory of the heredity of acquired characters amounts to a sort of naive testimony of the senses.

In the fifty years that followed, a further change of mental perspective led to the rationalist interpretation expounded by Darwin in *Origin of Species* (1859). Within natural populations, Darwin held, variations occur that are hereditary from the start, free from all environmental influence: the constitution of those individuals who survive the rigors of an implacable "struggle for existence" therefore carries with it a selective advantage. This is the doctrine of natural selection, which triumphed over Lamarck's illusory hypothesis. Paradoxically, the transition from an "instructivist" model to a "selectionist" paradigm went against the grain of dominant national philosophical traditions—Cartesian rationalism in France, Scottish empiricism in Great Britain.

Many other examples in the history of biology illustrate a similar evolution in thinking. Proteins, for example, take their name from the Greek sea god Proteus, who was endowed with the power to change form at will. These molecules were initially regarded as "colloids" existing in an unstable state characteristic of "living matter."[48] Even after the discovery of the peptide bond, and of the fact that proteins are composed of amino acids that are covalently linked into polypeptide chains stabilized by weak bonds, they were still conceived as "protean" objects possessing multiple configurations. The diversity and specificity of antibodies, whose structure seemed magnificently well adapted to the form of any antigen whatever, posed a formidable problem. The celebrated chemist Linus Pauling suggested that antibody specificity resulted from an "unstable configuration impressed on the molecule by its environment (influence of the antigen) during its biosynthesis."[49] X-ray diffraction studies of protein crystals have shown that, generally speaking, proteins are neither as versatile nor as flexible as physical chemists supposed as recently as the 1960s: they possess a stable three-dimensional structure down to the atomic level. No longer considered to be plastic (or "statistical") spherical objects, they are now regarded as rather rigid bodies.[50]

The instructivist paradigm nonetheless long remained influential among immunologists concerned to explain the diversity of antibodies and their apparently exquisite adjustment to the structure of the antigen. Monod himself thought that "the antigen's impression" on the immunoglobulin molecule was responsible for the molecule's remarkable capacity for adaptation.[51] Decades went by before Susumu Tonegawa persuasively argued that antibody diversity is strictly genetic in origin and results from a reshuffling of immunoglobulin genes prior to any interaction with the antigen.[52] Instead, the antigen selects the complementary antibody from a rich population of diverse molecules.

Tonegawa's selectionist model was subsequently verified and accepted by the scientific community, displacing another mistaken instructivist theory.

An analogous debate continues today over the regulation of enzymes and receptors by chemical signals. How can a neurotransmitter such as acetylcholine trigger the opening of an ion channel located at a relatively great distance (on the molecular scale) from the acetylcholine binding site on the receptor protein? The same question was raised in the early 1960s with regard to regulatory bacterial enzymes whose catalytic activity is controlled by metabolic signals having a structure very different from that of the enzyme substrate.[53] Two theories came into conflict. In line with Pauling's views, Daniel Koshland proposed that the binding substance, or ligand, "induces a fit"—a Lamarckian "impression"—on a suitably flexible protein molecule.[54] Monod, Jeffries Wyman, and I argued to the contrary that the ligand selects one of a small number of rigid, discrete, and mutually convertible conformations of the protein molecule to which it preferentially attaches itself, thus triggering the transduction of the signal.[55] Today the experimental evidence leans toward the selectionist mechanism,[56] even if local instances of conformational adaptation do demonstrably occur. In the case of neurotransmitter receptors, the instructivist model—which assumes that the ion channel opens only *after* the binding of the neurotransmitter—does not account for a great many observed phenomena, particularly the spontaneous opening of the channel in the absence of a neurotransmitter, which can readily be explained in terms of a selection mechanism that operates among preexisting conformational states.[57]

All these examples illustrate the influence exerted by "sensible impressions" on the brain of the scientist before a rationalist "detachment" from immediate perception takes place, producing a mental object that can be critically examined. The release of this object into the brain's conscious workspace enlarges the potential scope for examination, allowing it to be tested against both inner and external reality in ways that are relatively, if not completely, free from the subjective bias of the observer. As a result, there is an increased awareness of one's own consciousness of "thinking about thinking itself."[58]

Objective Knowledge and Mythic Thought

Émile Durkheim, in *Les Formes élémentaires de la vie religieuse* (1912), argued that the major institutions of human social life, apart from economic activity, have their roots in religion, and that religious life expresses in condensed form the whole of collective experience.[59] For want of an objective explanation of the natural world, or of the relations of human beings with this world and among themselves, primitive *Homo sapiens* created a system of supernatural forces. These forces are a product of the natural function of the human brain to project meaning onto the world and to idealize reality—that is, to substitute for reality an imaginary world to which access is possible by means of thought.

Pascal Boyer has analyzed the various impulses that have been associated with the origin of religion: a desire to explain natural phenomena such as death, dreaming, violence, and suffering that appear mysterious; to provide comfort in the face of solitude, anxiety, and distress; to give a foundation for morality and social order; to gain power over simple and credulous minds.[60] These explanations, in Boyer's view, do not suffice. He sees myths, instead, as "cognitive gadgets"—inferential instruments produced by the brain that are decoupled from both the evidence of the senses and rational analysis. The violations of intuitive expectations and elementary physics that give myths their supernatural quality also favor their retention in memory and, subsequently, their epigenetic transmission.

An alternative, but complementary, interpretation involves the reward mechanisms that figured prominently in my earlier discussion of cognitive games. The imaginary world of myths created in the brain's conscious workspace—myths concerning human origins, the survival of the soul after death, divine blessings assuring an eternally happy life—profits individuals by giving them a feeling of serenity and inner peace that, for the faithful, amounts to a sort of experimental proof of their beliefs. In other words, mythic thought is a source of substantial and shared mental rewards, despite—or perhaps owing to—the very impossibility of validating them.[61] It brings a sense of inner calm, hope, and confidence through the activation of reward systems (particularly ones concerned with expectation of reward that involve neuromodulators such as dopamine and the opiates) whose effects are felt on the scale of populations rather than of individuals. The fact that placebo effects are associated with the release of dopamine, triggered by the patient's anticipation of relief from his suffering,[62] suggests that myths may be interpreted as a kind of institutionalized social placebo. Considered in this light, Marx's famous characterization of religion as "the opium of the people" suddenly acquires neural plausibility.

Durkheim laid emphasis on the notion that religious beliefs have effect only to the degree that they are shared. Religious practice he saw as strengthening cooperation and reinforcing solidarity by providing a common language of belief. The selection and retention of myths depend on their ability to reinforce social bonds rather than on their adequacy as descriptions of objective reality. By providing adherents with practical, social, and motivational benefits, they contribute to "group selection."[63] But the great difference between myths and scientific theory, as François Jacob observed, is that myths are "frozen." The special utility of myths consists in the fact that they "apply in all domains and answer all questions"[64] and, once imagined, are "considered the only possible explanation of the world."[65] They therefore readily lend themselves to all manner of fundamentalist dogma.

The distinguishing characteristic of a scientific theory, by contrast, is that it is constantly modified and amended in the light of new evidence. The critical skepticism to which theories are subjected depends on a particular set of social and political conditions—free discussion, intellectual competition, an atmosphere of tolerance, institutions devoted to research, uncensored publication of results, and so on—that inevitably bring scientific investigation into conflict with religious belief.[66] In the Greek agora, critical debate among persons of differing beliefs hastened the emergence of an objective and collective form of knowledge that was more effective than mythical thought in explaining the natural world. Scientific knowledge was therefore born of a dual process of detachment, not only from sensory perception of the external world, but also from the imaginary world—no less profoundly anchored in the sense of self—of myths and the social structures in which they are embedded.

Yet the mythic style of thought is not likely to die out in the near future. The eternally fragmentary, ephemeral, and incomplete character of scientific research, as well as the inevitable difficulties of monitoring its social use and abuse, will continue to favor the survival of mythic thought. Indeed, despite the immense progress made by science over the last few centuries, religious fundamentalism is stronger today than it has ever been. Neurobiologists and researchers in the cognitive sciences therefore seem to me to have a duty, working in concert with scholars in anthropology, sociology, and the history of religion, to establish and develop an authentic science of mythic thought, building on the work of Durkheim, Marcel Mauss, and Lévi-Strauss, so that the operation of irrational belief may be compared with the rational search for truth that descended from it.

The Humanity of Science 8

"The principal human problem," Auguste Comte wrote in the *Catéchisme positiviste* (1852), "is to subordinate egoism to altruism . . . and to live for others."[1] Paradoxical though it may seem today, the development of scientific knowledge has brought an unexpected response to this problem. In an important essay published in 1972, the eminent French jurist René Cassin, winner of the Nobel Peace Prize and, together with Eleanor Roosevelt, author of the Universal Declaration of Human Rights (adopted by the United Nations in 1948), called attention to "the enormous role played by science in the conception, content, development, and enforcement of human rights."[2] It is a commonplace that the practical inventions of human industry, from the wheel, paper, and the alphabet to the compass, printing, and modern computers, as well as the development of rational medicine, from ancient Greece to the biotechnologies of the present day, have served to lessen the burdens of man. Cassin went further, emphasizing that since the Renaissance and the Reformation the aspiration to freedom of religious belief—and the right to freely examine one's own conscience—has gone hand in hand with the flourishing of free expression, an essential condition of creative thought in the sciences. Indeed, as John Lukacs has written, "the pursuit of truth is life-giving."[3]

The development of science has led, indirectly, to a gradual recognition of human rights: the right to life, to information, to the communication of ideas, to the free movement of persons. Indeed, the Universal Declaration on the Human Genome and Human Rights, proclaimed

Figure 51. René Cassin (1887–1976), awarded the Nobel Peace Prize in 1968, observed that the Universal Declaration of Human Rights was the first ethical document to have been adopted by humanity as a whole: "Now that we possess an instrument capable of lifting or easing the burden of oppression and injustice in the world, we must learn to use it."

by the United Nations in 1997, expressly stipulates that "freedom of research, which is necessary for the progress of knowledge, is part of freedom of thought."[4] In what follows I wish to argue, contrary to an opinion that is often expressed, that scientific progress and freedom of thought are themselves part of a larger struggle for equality and fraternity among human beings. Both the Constitution of the United States and the Declaration of the Rights of Man of 1789 may be seen as consequences of the advances in knowledge achieved during the Enlightenment—a critical moment in history when the sciences, freed from the twin tyrannies of absolute power and religious obscurantism, caused to be brought forth a new idea of human happiness and well-being.[5]

I would like to address in turn three aspects of science as a human enterprise that seem to me to be closely related: the neuronal "tinkering" that takes place in the brain of the scientist in formulating conjectures and hypotheses; the development of experimentation as a method for determining the truth or falsity of scientific models; and the struggle for truth as it unfolds within the scientific community. It can hardly be denied that the consequences of this struggle for society as a whole are neither simple nor always benign. Recognition of the manifest abuses to which scientific progress is inevitably liable will lead to the topic of my Conclusion: the relation of science to the ideal of the good life that has occupied philosophers from ancient times until the present day.

Neuronal Tinkering

I mentioned earlier that Claude Lévi-Strauss first used the term "tinkering" (bricolage) to characterize the generative process of mythological thought in oral and traditional societies. François Jacob later applied this concept to the mechanisms of variation and selection that act upon the genetic endowment of living organisms in the Darwinian evolution of species, stressing the limited character—both in quantity and quality—of the elementary building blocks that such tinkering operates upon. In this book I have sought to extend the notion still further, arguing that evolutionary tinkering may also take place, in an epigenetic manner, both with regard to the processors responsible for the acquisition of semantic and procedural knowledge in the brain and with regard to the neuronal workspace. What I have called the "conscious milieu" is roughly analogous to Claude Bernard's "internal milieu," whose stability, ensured by the homeostatic regulation of bodily functions, Bernard conceived as "the price of freedom."[6] By this he meant that the physiological equilibrium of living organisms allows them to function autonomously in relation to the external world. Similarly, the conscious milieu constitutes an autonomous inner world within which a new form of epigenetic evolution operates through trial and error upon mental objects. The homeostatic regulation of consciousness may therefore be thought of as the price we pay for freedom of thought. Yet the genesis of mental pre-representations in the neuronal workspace of the scientist's brain is not quite as free as one might suppose. It seems to be limited by a number of interlocking processes of epigenetic selection, which include stored long-term memories, each with its own built-in constraints. Even so, the longing for freedom is inarguably one of the most distinctive features of the search for truth.

Cultures and Subcultures in the Sciences

Since the time of the library at Alexandria, scientific knowledge has been preserved in written form in books and specialized journals, and, more recently, in electronic data banks. It has also been perpetuated through the practice of science and transmitted from teacher to student, for the most part orally. The technological applications of scientific research also contribute to the conservation, diffusion, and transmission of a body of knowledge selected by generations of scientists. All these things have helped bring into existence a peculiar kind of culture that is at once universally endorsed and continually challenged.

This does not mean that scientific culture is either homogeneous or uniform. D'Alembert, inspired by Francis Bacon's Tree of Knowledge, had proposed a classification of human knowledge in the *Discours préliminaire de l'encyclopédie* (1751) based upon the three "principal faculties" of human understanding (or, as we would say today, the human brain): memory, reason, and imagination.[7] These faculties find expression in history, philosophy (including both the humanities and the natural sciences), and poetry (representing the arts). Comte's innovation, in the *Cours de philosophie positive* (1830), consisted in giving d'Alembert's cognitive classification both a sociological and a historical dimension. This he based on the proposition that the sciences, having begun as a search for simple, abstract principles, subsequently evolved toward the comprehension of complex and concrete phenomena, passing from mathematics to biology and so, finally, to sociology, which Comte saw as synthesizing the whole of human knowledge and therefore entitled to a preeminent position, not only in the world of learning, but also in the conduct of human affairs.

Yet the various disciplines identified by Comte do not form coherent fields of knowledge. Matters are further complicated by the rapid development of scientific research since Comte's time, which has introduced additional subdivisions and overlapping specialties. The biological, physical, and mathematical sciences all exhibit internal cultural differences that work to hinder communication. Moreover, the emergence of new disciplines blurs existing boundaries, rendering them counterproductive and obsolete.

In the sciences of the nervous system, the distinction between anatomy and physiology drawn by Claude Bernard in *Introduction à l'étude de la médecine expérimentale* (1878) was challenged by Du Bois-Reymond, Helmholtz, and Bernstein, who laid emphasis on the electrical properties of nervous tissue.[8] The study of the pharmacology and biochemistry of the nervous system developed simultaneously, though as separate subfields.[9] Quite remarkably, these long-standing cleavages still persist today. The reliance on specialized techniques, the use of distinctive vocabularies, and the insistence on exclusive conceptions of the proper approach to theory and experiment all contributed to the survival of these divisions, while at the same time deepening them.

Electrophysiology, for example, has until recently limited itself to describing electrical signals in terms of voltage, currents, and capacitance, seldom making reference to work in biochemistry on proteins and other topics.[10] Molecular biology and biochemistry, by contrast, favored collaborative research that drew upon a wide range of techniques (including those of electrophysiology) and analyzed data with a view to establishing pertinent relationships between structure and function, particularly at the molecular level. Nor was a priori theoretical speculation excluded from the research tradition in molecular biology—no doubt owing to the influence of the many physicists it attracted in the early days. The famous clash between Bernard Katz and David Nachmansohn in the 1950s is a good illustration of the sort of conflict among subcultures that I have in mind: whereas for Katz the interpretation of nerve signaling in terms of ion currents and electrical circuits was crucial for a complete understanding of bioelectrical phenomena, Nachmansohn argued (correctly, as it turned out, though the evidence he adduced was sometimes a source of controversy) that biochemical and molecular data needed to be taken into account as well. The much-discussed "conversion" of Sir John Eccles in the same decade, from a wholly electrical conception of signal transmission between neurons in the central nervous system to a mixed chemical and electrical interpretation, is similarly revealing for the light it sheds upon the confrontational atmosphere that developed during the period between electrical ("dry") and chemical ("wet") subcultures.[11]

These two examples from the field of neurobiology must stand for a great many others in the world of science as a whole. Far from being a homogeneous population of like-minded researchers who subscribe to a single style of thought, science constitutes a complex network of individuals, many with strong personalities, who do not always see eye to eye, and institutions, which have their own identities, shaped by the crosscutting influences of culture, economics, and politics.

The Necessity of Models

The young scientist who enters a well-equipped laboratory for the first time—well equipped not only in the physical sense, but also because it has the intellectual atmosphere required for carrying out important research—has not merely entered a particular set of rooms. His formal training at school and college, the discussions with his first supervisor, his earliest experiences in a research institution, the community of scientists that he has joined by becoming a member of this institution—all these things leave profound and lasting traces in the neural circuits of his brain. These traces exhibit a specifically cultural character that in certain respects may be compared with the ones produced by his family environment, his native language, and the system of norms and values of his community. The young scientist very quickly receives the epigenetic imprint of a certain scientific subculture, often without even being aware of it. He acquires what, following Pierre Bourdieu, I have called a scientific habitus. The simple act of setting foot in a particular laboratory constitutes a fateful step in the career of the young scientist. As André Lwoff used to say, the most important thing is to choose the right supervisor, in the right laboratory, at the right moment!

No scientist today could even imagine adopting a strictly empirical method, confining himself to the simple analysis of facts, free from all preconceived notions, in the manner recommended by Bacon. There is always an implicit theoretical context underlying his scientific activity, preserved in long-term memories, that tacitly organizes the conscious play of conjecture and hypothesis. An important part of the scientific process, in my view, consists in making this context explicit.

Most scientists proceed by tinkering with a model, which is to say with a minimal, internally consistent representation (expressed in mathematical form if possible) of the object or phenomenon being examined.[12] How is this model constructed? Jacques Hadamard identified a first phase in mathematical work, which he called "preparation," that corresponds to what Henri Poincaré called the effort to "govern the unconscious" and what Alain Connes describes as an attempt to "concentrate upon on a very precise object of thought" and to "focus on preparing the groundwork."[13] The sort of groundwork Connes refers to is typically bound up with a research program, whose standard expression is found in grant applications.[14] Already at this early stage the political and economic constraints associated with the subvention power of public agencies and private enterprises begin surreptitiously to impinge upon the scientist's thinking, which is to say upon the activity of his brain.

The focusing of attention upon a precisely stated problem creates an "intentional framework" that leads to the next stage in Hadamard's scheme: incubation. During this period, the scientist's conscious workspace is filled with transient mental objects—what I have called pre-representations—produced in a combinatory and recursive manner. An element of randomness introduces novelty and the unexpected into the structure of these objects; indeed, certain arrangements of new mathematical ideas, owing to their accidental character, have been compared to genetic mutations.[15] In this case, however, the mutations are epigenetic in nature. Often, too, scientists deliberately work around a problem—wandering, as Connes puts it, into an adjacent field from which the problem can be explored indirectly. They deviate from the straight and narrow paths of conventional analysis, bypassing the problem at hand, circling around it—in order finally to take it by surprise.[16] From a neurobiological point of view, these cognitive wanderings may be thought of as mobilizing the long-axoned neurons of the workspace that establish connections with other neurons located in topologically separate processing areas. In this way unforeseen links come to be created between previously stabilized concepts, giving rise to incongruous juxtapositions of ideas, "unnatural" fantasies, and the like. The imagination is at work.

There are many anecdotes of scientists who report that their most original ideas suddenly came to them in a dream. One of the best known is that of Otto Loewi, who claimed to have conceived the experimental demonstration of the mechanism of chemical synaptic transmission while dreaming. Even if the accuracy of such subjective accounts invites critical examination (since the later incorporation of false memories cannot be excluded), it is probable that the generator of mental diversity is particularly active during the REM phase of sleep, introducing random associations—a surplus of variability, one might say—between very distant and unrelated representations.

The transient mental sketches that collectively link dispersed nonconscious memories and immediate sense-data are subject to some degree of internal control. First, the actual organization of the brain itself, which has been shaped since early childhood by nested series of sophisticated cognitive games and language games, imposes constraints on the genesis of such pre-representations. The specific language of the scientific subculture, including not only its vocabulary but also the epigenetic rules absorbed during training that structure research in a given field, also comes into play. After a period of trial and error marked by tentative formulations and discarded hypotheses, the chance encounter with some new observation or combination of formal rules causes previously dispersed pre-representations to bind together, taking over the conscious workspace. This is the "illumination" mentioned by Hadamard, the overwhelming sense of beauty experienced by Poincaré.

The inner perception of this novel and harmonious integration—a sort of neural *consensus partium*—appears to be correlated with very powerful positive rewards whose effect is felt with intense emotion. Poincaré's metaphorical reference to beauty may in fact be based upon a profound and very real analogy between mathematical apprehension and aesthetic appreciation, whose common features unite the True, the Beautiful, and the Good. The unfolding sequence of representations in the conscious space of the brain may be likened, as I suggested earlier, to a melody: each "note" resulting from the concomitant mobilization of distinct processes is held on-line in working memory until a moment of convergence or resolution is reached. Indeed, the composer André Jolivet used to recommend testing the quality of a melody's "composition" by playing its component tones on the piano as a chord.

There may also be a deep connection between the perception of music and language. Electrophysiological correlates have been identified for meaningful (as opposed to unmeaningful) sentences and for melodies played in key (rather than out of key).[17] Well-formed sequences of various kinds—a chain of logically connected propositions constituting a coherent line of argument, for example, or a pleasingly congruent series of geometrical forms—may be thought of as producing an inner resonance, an organized and pervasive response in the brain corresponding to the perception of what Matisse called the "harmonie d'ensemble" in a painting.

This consonance, or accord, of mental representations, either among themselves or with the objects of the external world, plays a crucial role in the workings of the scientist's brain. The neural mechanisms of evaluation and reward involved are still very poorly understood. In the case of scientific creativity they intervene with decisive effect in the assessment of the plausibility of a tentative model, which is to say the degree to which it agrees with reality; and also, more generally, in the struggle to obtain intellectual rewards, which even scientists themselves recognize as one of their chief motivations—a vital source of curiosity and competitiveness alike.

Poincaré stressed that science does not live by illuminations alone. Hallucinations and delusions, misconceptions, ideas that appear true at first sight but on closer examination turn out to be false—all these have their place in scientific research. How many distinguished mathematicians before Andrew Wiles thought they had proved Fermat's theorem! Whence the necessity of the last phase insisted upon by Hadamard: verification. As many mathematicians and scientists are prepared to testify, this phase can be very painful.[18] Demonstrating a theorem or a conjecture requires considerable effort—further rounds of reasoning, deduction, and evaluation, always proceeding by trial and error. These inner experiences have great importance in creative scientific work. They are seldom reported in the periodical literature and, indeed, are systematically repressed by the public memory of scientists themselves. But not infrequently these experiences—even, or perhaps especially, when they are unhappy ones—bring about a change in the scientist's view of the world and his way of thinking about it.

Some scientists, as I have said, prefer to maintain a discreet silence about their work, fearing that the chance that their model may turn out to be false will limit their freedom in carrying out future experimental work and, and above all, harm their reputation—and thus their chances of obtaining funding—in the scientific community. Others, especially in physics but increasingly in biology as well, remain attached to the Cartesian rationalist ideal and concern themselves solely with the construction of formal models. In neuroscience, for example, research traditions differ in their attitude toward modeling. Hodgkin and Huxley's model for the interpretation of the action potential in terms of Na^+ and K^+ currents is a classic and splendid example of an a posteriori model that closely fits the experimental data. In molecular biology and biophysics, in contrast, it is customary to give freer rein to speculation about high-level neurobiological functions such as learning,[19] cognition,[20] and consciousness.[21]

In my view the advantages of a priori formal modeling offset the risk of error. Let us take the example of the neuronal mechanisms involved in a cognitive task such as the Wisconsin card-sorting test. This test is commonly used by neurologists, as we have seen, to detect lesions of the frontal lobe. A wealth of experimental data, mostly neurophysiological and pharmacological, is available concerning the execution of similar tasks by the monkey. It seemed a sensible idea, then, to try to organize this information in the form of a theoretical model uniting neuronal activity and behavior.

The first step was to define a minimal set of architectural elements necessary to carry out the task: multiple and overlapping levels of organization, a diversity generator operating upon the artificial neuronal network specified by the model, reward systems that regulate learning by selection, and so on. The second step was to use the properties of the artificial network to create a computer program that would simulate the behavior of the natural system. Simulation makes it possible, by comparing the model's predictions with the experimental data, to assess its adequacy in reproducing molecular or neuronal phenomena. The simplicity of a model, though not itself a criterion of truth, is useful in confirming or falsifying its predictions. The third, and final, step was to introduce a "lesion" in the artificial network and compare the behavioral consequences with those produced in patients displaying actual lesions. It is interesting to note in this connection that the selective lesions of the artificial network lead to pathological behaviors (perseverance in error, liability to distraction, and so on) similar to those observed as a consequence of lesions to the prefrontal cortex in human beings. The testing of the model by means of a simulated experiment completes the procedure by furnishing important evidence of the model's validity: its capacity to reconstruct the object or the phenomenon studied.

An additional advantage of mathematical models arises from the intrinsic generative power of their formalism. This is obvious in the case of pure mathematics, where theorems are systematically constructed on the basis of prior ones. The same thing occurs in modeling biological objects and processes. Thus, for example, the elementary formalism devised by Warren McCulloch and Walter Pitts to capture the essential features of neuronal activity inspired a great many mathematical models of neuronal networks.[22] Epigenetic rules are particularly important in this connection. They enrich the recursive and combinatory properties of the brain through the addition of a sizable number of new operators (in the mathematical sense) that result from a stringent selection among procedures recognized to have been effective in the past. Very considerable economies of thought suddenly become possible.

Language plays an essential role in the formulation of scientific models as well. Its importance was stressed by Rudolf Carnap, a leader of the Vienna school of logical positivism, who ventured to assert that statements about the logic of science are in fact propositions about the logical syntax of language, and, moreover, that "all psychological statements can be translated into physical language."[23] From a neurocognitive point of view, this means that scientific statements are in no way exceptional: they do no more than exploit innate dispositions and syntactic rules, together with rules selected during the learning of language in the infant's brain. A great many mathematicians—one thinks particularly of Gottlob Frege—disagree. For them, the logical rules that are fundamental to mathematics belong to a Platonic universe of ideal forms. My own view is that there is no longer any justification for assuming the existence of an immaterial and eternal world independent of human minds. The most parsimonious hypothesis, as I argued earlier, is that logical rules constitute a definite population of innate and epigenetically selected operators coexisting in long-term memory with semantic and symbolic representations.

The Limits of Models

A model may be defined, then, as a minimal and internally consistent set of mental objects devised to solve a particular scientific puzzle within a very broad context of theories, observations, and ongoing experiments, a context that is subject to the sociological forces that shape scientific research as a whole. Nonetheless, because even the formalized written expressions of a model—its mathematical form—belong to the category of brain representations, it is a physical object, albeit a physical object of a very special kind that is the product of a particularly rigorous process of selection.

The "substance" of the mental objects that make up a model—a constellation of both stable and dynamic molecular traces distributed throughout the neuronal network—differs in important respects from that of the object or process in the external world to which the model refers. But this melody (ultimately resolved as a chord) of spatiotemporal patterns of nerve impulses, synaptic efficiencies, and firing thresholds is nonetheless the same kind of substance. Descartes was led to suppose that thought *(res cogitans)* is composed of a different substance than physical objects *(res extensa)*. Yet the dualism associated with his name has no basis in fact: body and soul are made of the very same matter, only this matter is *organized* in extremely different ways in space and in time, so that it exhibits different properties or functions. It is not impossible, by the way, though conclusive evidence is lacking, that the young Descartes himself may have secretly shared this physicalist point of view.[24]

No scientific model or algorithm—no matter adequate it may appear to be, and despite its long epigenetic history and the extensive process of mental selection to which it has been exposed—can be expected to supply an exhaustive description of external reality. Nor is a model, however perfect, to be confused with the object or the process that it seeks to reproduce. Mathematicians and physicists are so fond of speaking of the "unreasonable effectiveness" of mathematics in describing physical reality[25] that the distinction between mathematical theory and physical object is sometimes lost, and the immense mental effort made by the scientific community to produce successful models forgotten.

Mendel's laws, for example, give a rigorous description of the way genetically determined "characters" (such as the colors of pea blossoms) are transmitted from one generation to another. But in no sense do they give a complete account of the properties of the underlying mechanisms of heredity. The role of chromosomes was discovered only later (by Thomas Hunt Morgan), together with their principal component, DNA (by Oswald Avery, Colin McLeod, and Maclyn McCarty) and the double-helix structure of the DNA molecule (by James Watson and Francis Crick). But none of these major discoveries, though they are in perfect agreement with—even subsumed by—Mendel's laws, could have been derived from them. Mendel's laws failed to exhaust the reality of the material substrate of heredity.

A model must be seen instead as a mental tool: a crude sketch, an approximate neural embodiment of external reality. Models are provisional instruments whose fate is to be abandoned or revised. Some of them, being more adequate and more fertile than others, survive the test of time. Science is reductionist by necessity. But reductionism has nothing to do with the content of what is represented; it is a method—a very demanding one—for describing reality in a comprehensible and communicable form. Nor can science escape being reductionist simply because it uses language to demonstrate and transmit its results.

Experimentation

Agreement between a theoretical model and observational data no more suffices to establish the model's validity than does the internal coherence or beauty of its elements. In order to attain the desired *adaequatio rei et intellectus,* it is necessary to go beyond the purely intellectual approach insisted upon by Descartes and to operate directly upon reality by means of experiments designed to test the adequacy of models.

Wittgenstein distinguished between certainty and knowledge. Certainty, he argued, involves much more than merely seeing if a proposition is true; it can only be achieved by *acting* upon the world.[26] In the natural sciences, one cannot imagine attaining certainty without experimentation. This is particularly true in the life sciences, where there can be no hope whatever of attaining it without a constant passing back and forth between theory and experiment. Experiment, in its turn, requires that endosomatic experience—the inner world of memories and current perceptions—be mobilized to select and structure action upon the external world, to actually solve concrete problems. Thus Wittgenstein and Popper are reconciled within the brain's neuronal workspace![27]

Successful experimentation is possible only if at least three conditions are satisfied. The first requirement is that a definite link be established between the theoretical predictions of the model and the observable characteristics of the object or phenomenon being examined. This is not always easy to do, but it is essential for the purpose of quantifying action on the world—that is, of *measuring*. In this connection it is useful to recall the case of signal transduction and allosteric proteins (which, as we have seen, may involve regulatory enzymes, transcription factors, or neurotransmitter receptors) and the distinction between instructivist and selectionist models that I discussed in the previous chapter. Here the problem was to devise an experiment capable of deciding between two interpretations: either a protein molecule is infinitely malleable, like a ball of wax, or it is a rigid object with an internal mechanism, like that of a lock, that is either in an active or an inactive state under conditions of reversible equilibrium.[28]

The first step was to give an explicit statement of the two possibilities in mathematical form. This yielded what then was a novel distinction between the structural, or conformational, state of the protein molecule (the "state function") and the actual presence of the regulatory ligand at the binding site (the "binding function"). In the instructivist model, with its assumption of an "induced fit," the two functions coincide. In the selectionist model, by contrast, the state function is assumed to be independent of the binding function. Hence the need to design experiments that would differentiate the observable structural features of the protein and the observable binding properties of the regulatory signal. Early studies of the bacterial enzyme aspartate transcarbamylase unambiguously demonstrated that, in this system at least, the state and binding functions are in fact distinct.[29] The observation, previously mentioned in the case of the acetylcholine receptor, that the ion channel can be opened in the absence of a neurotransmitter lent further support to the selectionist model.[30]

The second condition, which plainly follows from the first, is the development of new observational techniques and measuring instruments that will make a reality that is particularly difficult to apprehend more visible. Biology, and in particular neuroscience, has made immense advances in this regard, and promises to make further progress thanks to new imaging technologies.[31] There are many examples, ranging from the invention of the glass microelectrode to optical and electron microscopy and scanographic methods of brain imagery, to say nothing of the enormous impact of genetic engineering technologies.

The third and final requirement has to do with the reproducibility of observations and measurements. Stochastic elements are often an integral part of the process being studied. This is the case, for instance, with the release of neurotransmitters at nerve endings in the brain.[32] Reliable observation requires statistical analysis of a great number of trials until significant regularities become apparent. Statistical methods also play an essential role in the medical sciences, notably in the diagnosis of disease.[33]

The difficulty appears still more formidable when the variability of individual brains is taken into account, particularly in the case of pathologies. The epigenetic development of nerve connections can, as we have seen, give rise to very different patterns of organization, even in genetically identical individuals, whose brains implement alternative connective strategies in carrying out the same task or solving the same problem. Analysis of individual cases, in combination with statistical analysis of populations, is therefore crucial in trying to understand the neural mechanisms underlying behavior and associated dysfunctions.

If experimentation serves to test theoretical models and their predictions in order to improve our understanding of the world, it also plays another, quite different role. Experimentation not only makes it possible to detect deviations from the predictions made by the model but also yields new and unexpected observations. This kind of fortuitous discovery has made a great impression on the general public since the earliest days of modern science: Alexander Fleming's discovery of the antibiotic action of penicillin is only one of many examples. Whence the widespread but fallacious notion that science moves steadily forward from one spectacular discovery to another. Science advances instead by means of the arduous work of thousands of scientists around the world—through an immense ferment of ideas, endless waves of experimentation and observation, the failure of a vast number of hypotheses and the success of a few—which opens new directions of research while closing off others. The evolutionary dynamic of scientific inquiry is impressive indeed.

The revolution brought about by computers in the acquisition and processing of data—especially experimental data—is comparable in its importance for the growth of human knowledge to the invention of writing. Modern information technologies give unimaginably rapid access to huge databases and permit the efficient comparison and integration of experimental results. Computerized analysis holds particular promise for interpreting the sequencing data of the human genome in order to identify genetic predispositions (at the level of populations) to diseases such as diabetes, for example, or to develop a genetic profile (at the level of individuals) that will form the basis of a person's medical record. The time may not be far off when doctors will be able to draw upon virtually unlimited reserves of knowledge in order to prescribe, in a few fractions of a second, treatment that is appropriate to a patient's biological typology and his individual history—treatment, it may be hoped, that will at last be truly effective.

More generally, the development of experimental technique in the natural sciences, in combination with theoretical analysis, has yielded increasingly detailed access to external reality and, as a consequence of this, has progressively improved our understanding of the world. Advances in experimental method have also made it possible to develop more satisfactory procedures for verifying hypotheses; that is, to construct increasingly adequate (and therefore true) models of physical reality—which includes the reality of our brains. The attempt to make sense of the world is, ultimately, a quest for objectivity.

Truth and the Scientific Community

Scientists as individuals are central to scientific inquiry. Though they sometimes hold themselves aloof from the world, not infrequently they seek publicity, even celebrity, not only to call attention to their personal achievements but also to secure the funding on which their research depends. It may nonetheless be wondered whether the individual search for knowledge is capable by itself of producing scientific objectivity. The popular view of the history of the sciences as a sort of a genealogical tree populated by geniuses and eminent figures encourages such an opinion. In most cases, however, it amounts to nothing more than a convenient social fiction.

The reality of scientific inquiry is both more complex and more prosaic. Advances in knowledge result from the combined efforts of a great many researchers who constitute what is rightly called the scientific community. Scientists are not dwarves standing on the shoulders of giants, as Newton modestly claimed in his own case; they are dwarves standing on the shoulders of a vast population of dwarves.

The Advantages of Joint Research

Scientific inquiry cannot rest solely on the isolated contributions of individual scientists, no matter how numerous or distinguished. The scientist's personal history, his political and religious beliefs, the social and economic pressures brought to bear upon him by the environment in which he works, the profound emotional investment and exceptionally strenuous mental effort required by theoretical analysis and experimental work—all these things are apt to undermine the objectivity of scientific research.

The working lives of scientists are filled with accidental and nonreproducible observations, errors of interpretation, conscious or nonconscious manipulations of data, illusions—even hallucinations! Scientific objectivity requires an act of depersonalization that many scientists, wrapped up in their own work, find almost impossible (Monod's sense of actually being a protein molecule, which I mentioned earlier, is a striking exception). It is for this reason that the quest for truth necessarily becomes the concern of the community of scientists as a whole—a state of affairs that is obscured by the current tendency to overpersonalize scientific research. The function served by the agora in ancient Greece remains critical for scientific inquiry today. We know very little about the sociological mechanisms by which scientific knowledge is acquired through joint and coordinated effort. Further investigation is needed.

Working as part of a team is a common way to overcome the isolation of the lone scientist and the tendency to self-centered attachment to one's own work. Famous partnerships are a familiar feature of the history of the natural sciences: one thinks of Pierre and Marie Curie, James Watson and Francis Crick, Michael Brown and Joseph Goldstein, David Hubel and Torsten Wiesel, François Jacob and Jacques Monod, and many others. The shared experience of devising and testing conjectures makes it easier to eliminate residual elements of subjectivity, which in turn enlarges the combinatory possibilities for constructing and analyzing models. It also offers the opportunity to bring together scientists from neighboring disciplines. Thus the structure of the DNA molecule was discovered as a consequence of joint research by specialists in crystallography, biochemistry, and genetics. Similarly, the fundamental mechanisms regulating gene expression were discovered as a result of the convergence of work in genetics, biochemistry, and bacterial physiology, until then independent fields.[34] New subcultures are apt to develop out of the fusion of older ones as well. Molecular biology is a notable instance of this tendency.

These examples suggest that scientific progress may be conceived as a sort of cognitive network—an extended "conversation" between individual brains—that continually expands, as much through cooperation as through competition. The appearance of new cleavages alongside new connections breaks down old objects, as Claude Debru observed, and replaces them with new ones.[35] The connections that are established within the network are for the most part transient. But turning points do occur from time to time: almost irreversible transitions in conception of a given problem; discontinuities in the blind evolution of scientific knowledge by trial and error. These singularities are called "discoveries" or "inventions," depending on whether their content is observational or derives, instead, from theory and imagination. The exchange of ideas and points of view produces that sudden moment of insight Hadamard called illumination—only now it is not restricted to the individual brain, but instead is distributed over a population of interacting brains, with the result that the intellectual reward of scientific discovery is shared by a team (or teams) of scientists working together on a problem. This supplanting of individual gratification by a collective sense of satisfaction is the price to be paid not only for a rapid acceleration of conceptual innovation but also for the detachment from egoistic motivation that I mentioned a moment ago—the freedom from narrow self-interest that is indispensable if objective knowledge is to be obtained. The feeling of triumph that arises from discovery and invention is no longer the exclusive property of a single brain, but belongs instead to the network of individual neuronal workspaces whose interaction yields novel and nonlinear connections.

This notion of an evolving network of individual brains also helps illuminate one of the most distinctive characteristics of the growth of scientific knowledge, namely the constant incorporation of new information into an established body of knowledge. The cumulative nature of scientific knowledge is the very condition of intellectual progress and the reason why the search for truth at the level of the scientific community fundamentally differs from mythic thought and religious devotion.

Scientific Controversy and the Universality of Knowledge

Throughout the international community of science, cooperative and competitive exchanges of ideas develop with regard to both theory and experiment. In this regard the critical examination of models, data, and interpretations is of particular importance. It occurs in three ways: through imitation (scientists seek to meet a standard of achievement set by the other members of the scientific community); competition (each scientist tries to criticize models proposed by others); and innovation (each tries to propose new models that are superior to their rivals). The freedom to publish fair and uncensored criticisms, rather than having to retreat into a broad and inarticulate skepticism, is therefore an essential element in the struggle for truth. Public controversy leads, if not always to the survival of the fittest model, then at least to a finely calibrated index of acceptability among competing theories.[36]

At the international level, it is true, the search for truth is often biased by nonscientific constraints. I have already noted the influence of economic forces, marked by fierce competition for patents and research support. Other constraints are less visible: the editorial decisions of journals, where national preferences and economic interests are continually in play, and the political power of various lobbies, which operate surreptitiously both within and among nations. Yet the convergence of differing theoretical and experimental approaches to a common problem, together with the capacity to modify or abandon one interpretation in favor of another, shows that we are not prisoners of our cognitive faculties. Quite the opposite is true, in fact: theories and evidence are mercilessly put to the test in the debates that take place in our planetary agora. Once confirmed, models that have shown themselves to be the most adequate sooner or later become independent of their creators, acquiring a life of their own. One might even say that this detachment from both empirical perception and the ego of individual scientists, by conferring upon models an autonomous and anonymous character, constitutes a criterion of scientific legitimacy.

Newly validated explanations are propagated from brain to brain throughout the world of science by means of articles and books as well as graduate seminars and international conferences. This "epidemiology" of scientific ideas[37] (or, as Richard Dawkins calls them, "self-replicating memes")[38] is the source of another distinctive feature of scientific knowledge: its universality. Access to truth spreads throughout the world in a way that is unmatched by any other human activity. The free, public, and worldwide examination of hypotheses requires that scientists be prepared to undergo frequent (and sometimes painful) changes of opinion. Even if such changes are sometimes slow to take effect, the recognized authority of proof makes the abandonment of discredited hypotheses unavoidable. It is a remarkable feature of the scientific mentality—one not found in other intellectual communities—that not all opinions are equally respectable. A point of view that has been shown to be incorrect instantly ceases to be of interest. No one talks any longer about phlogiston.

And yet it is striking, from a historical point of view, how seldom this freedom of thought has been welcomed by human societies. From Galileo to Darwin there have been many instances of violent opposition provoked by the changes in mankind's conception of the world—and of mankind itself—that accompany scientific progress. In our own time one thinks of the controversy surrounding embryonic stem cell research and gene therapy. Perhaps the best-known modern examples of the power of ideological and political forces to obstruct freedom of biological research are Lysenkoism in the former Soviet Union and creationism in the United States. Looking to the future, it is not unreasonable to suppose that the abandonment of the idea of an immortal soul, which is a natural consequence of research into the structure and function of the human brain, may lead to an upheaval in traditional

Western thinking that will prove to be at least as important as the Copernican revolution. But the selection of myths at the social level often comes into conflict with the search for scientific truth, as we have seen, acting as a brake on the emergence and acceptance of new ideas.

The Rise of Technology

No scientist has the right to assert, even in a restricted domain of research, that he or she has attained absolute truth. Systematic skepticism, which applies to established facts and theories, confers upon scientific inquiry a "dignity" (to recall Francis Bacon's term) that places it above other human activities, in particular those that claim to transmit some kind of revealed Truth. From the incessant combat against error, illusion, and irrationality one must be careful, however, not to conclude that scientific research is a destructive—much less a self-destructive—process. As Saint-Simon and other utopian theorists pointed out more than a century ago, science inspires and hastens the development of technologies—and thus of industries—that benefit humanity. Practical applications not only constitute the clearest test imaginable of the truth of scientific knowledge; they also serve to bridge the gap that separates the scientific community from the rest of society (Figure 52).

The list of technical and industrial applications of basic science that have improved the standard of living and the health of human beings over the past centuries is immensely long—so long, in fact, that a return to the conditions of life of the eighteenth or nineteenth century is scarcely conceivable. Consider but two examples. In the eighteenth century the rate of infant mortality in France was 30 percent; today it is less than 1 percent. In 1872 the average life expectancy in France was forty-three years; today it is seventy-nine. Is there anyone in the developed world today who would seriously contemplate doing without electricity, the telephone, or high-speed transport? Anyone who would welcome the return of widespread famine and epidemic disease? Ultimately, it is technology that gives science its most human face.

And yet the enormous benefits that science and technology bring are not universally regarded as unmixed blessings. Bitter, sometimes violent attacks have been launched in recent years against the perceived evils of "technoscience," seen as a sort of Frankenstein's monster

Figure 52. Fernand Léger, *Le Remorqueur* (1920). This painting celebrates the beauty of man united with machine in a balanced, light-hearted, and optimistic spirit.

whose power, amplified by alliance with malign economic forces, escapes the control of its creators. Jean-Jacques Rousseau was only the first of many writers who feared that technology would turn out to be totalitarian and even antihumanist.[39] There is no doubt whatever that the vigorous development of technologies often has disturbing consequences, arousing a sense of alienation that reflects the difficulty we feel as human beings in adjusting to new ways of looking at the world and acting upon it. But neither is there any doubt that scientific knowledge provides more effective remedies to human suffering than does divination or prayer. The solution therefore does not lie in a wholesale rejection of technology. It resides instead in the development of a culture that is more harmoniously adapted to the realities of the world.

Conclusion

René Cassin, like others of his generation, was keenly aware of the tragic events that had occurred in Europe, Japan, and the rest of the world since the nineteenth century, particularly the massacres of whole civilian populations that were made possible by willful diversion of the resources of science and technology from their intended purpose. There is nothing in the least new about this—apart, of course, from the scope of the methods of destruction devised by modern physicists, chemists, and microbiologists. From the first use of cut stone, and then of iron, in making weapons to the domestication of fire and the invention of explosives, humankind over the ages has systematically recast the discoveries of science to suit destructive ends. Alongside a science of life, whose chief purpose is to alleviate the suffering of human beings and to contribute to their happiness, there grew up a gruesomely efficient science of death. The invention of "daisy cutter" bombs (designed to lop off heads rather than the tops of flowers) and the development of exceedingly virulent bacterial and viral strains resistant to treatment by antibiotics are only the most recent signs that the arms race continues unabated, especially in advanced industrial countries, parasitically profiting from the progress of science and technology a bit more every day.

There are good reasons, then, for feeling a profound uneasiness about the course of modern civilization, even for doubting the worth of scientific inquiry itself. No matter that some degree of risk inevitably accompanies any technological innovation or industrial application, scientific advance carries with it a far greater chance of harmful consequence today than in the past. Indeed, the secondary dangers of technological development on a worldwide scale—unknown in previous centuries, when humans had to defend themselves against nature—are so great that the natural world must now be protected against destruction by humankind.

Scientific research is motivated primarily, as I have argued, by a desire to acquire knowledge whose veracity is universally recognized. Yet the benefits of scientific research are very unequally distributed throughout the world. More than a billion people have access neither to health services nor to basic education. No less troubling is the use of the deadliest and most sophisticated weapons against armies recruited from the poorest populations on the planet, whether in Tibet, Afghanistan, Chechnya, Palestine, or indeed many other places. Within the domain of medical science, the temptation is increasingly great to carry out research on human subjects in the most disadvantaged parts of the world, whose populations will in any case not be the first to enjoy the benefits of such research. The causes of these inequalities in the treatment of human beings are not to be sought within scientific research itself. As everyone knows, the causes are economic and political, and closely associated with activities that escape effective regulation either by states or by supranational organizations, with the result that the forces of unrestrained economic competition in global markets prevail over humanitarian considerations at the local level.

What hope is there of reversing a tide of events that betrays the values of humanity and peace upheld by scientific inquiry? Almost fifty years ago Gilbert Simondon suggested, as a first step, that we revise our understanding of both the possibilities and the obligations of science and technology.[1] Doing this will require a vast program of information and education aimed at bringing about a change in habits of thought and behavior comparable to that achieved in the eighteenth century by the *Encyclopédie* of Diderot and d'Alembert. The new culture I have in mind must be universal, secular, and independent of local beliefs and ideologies. It will require constant public debate and discussion, and, above all, critical examination of the doctrines promoted by political, economic, and religious groups, however powerful they may be, with a view to separating beliefs grounded in reason from ones that are products of mere fantasy.

The philosopher Jacques Bouveresse has pointed out that rationalism, far from exercising the sort of tyranny for which it is regularly reproached, has in fact long been a poorly defended and unpopular position.[2] The influence of myth and legend is, if anything, more widespread today than it was a hundred years ago. Invocations of divine sanction and authority, bellicose appeals to the Bible and the Koran, calls to embark on crusades of Good versus Evil, faith in the prophetic guidance of the stars, the marketing of potions having no active molecular agent as medicines, the search for demons and witches—all these things, quite astonishingly, hold a major place in the political discourse and social practice of nations that call themselves civilized.[3]

Under these circumstances it becomes a matter of urgent necessity to devise new symbolic systems suited to the promise and the dangers of a world of perpetually evolving technologies. This means having to reconsider, not only the relationship between nature and technology, but also the relationship between the individual and the group. At the beginning of the last chapter I cited René Cassin's remark about the great importance of science in helping inspire and direct the campaign for human rights. Cassin laid particular emphasis on the "rights to life (especially in connection with health and reproduction), information, the unimpeded communication of ideas, and the free movement of human beings."[4] It goes without saying that freedom of research is an essential element of the freedom of thought. Surely it is not going too far to suggest that the scientific model might be applied to society no less usefully than to physics, chemistry, and biology. A genuinely comprehensive and integrated anthropology—incorporating neurobiology along with the other cognitive sciences, and treating the epigenetic nature of beliefs and customs as well as their selection, diffusion, amplification, and extinction—would be of inestimable value in helping bring about the lasting reign of peace, justice, and harmony within and among human societies.

Cassin, in hoping for a "new and more pacific culture," was nonetheless firm in his insistence that scientific research should not take precedence over "respect for the rights of man, the fundamental freedoms and dignity of persons or, as the case may be, groups of persons."[5] He proposed that laws be enacted to this effect, after consultation with a permanent or occasional body of scientists, lawyers, and economists. This suggestion gave rise to the various commissions on ethics that have subsequently come into existence throughout the world. The time has come at last, I believe, to contemplate establishing a still more ambitious institution—one that would have worldwide scope and authority.[6]

The obstacles facing any such proposal are formidable, to say the least. It may be helpful to think of differences among social conventions and religious beliefs as analogous to differences among languages. The intercultural dialogue on ethical questions that I envisage will need to proceed on the basis of an act of simultaneous translation, as it were, that will make the world's various philosophical and religious traditions mutually intelligible. The positive ethical debate made possible in this way would amount to a form of "ideal speech," to quote Jürgen Habermas, who imagines an encounter where the terms in which each participant expresses himself are judged acceptable only so long as they are accepted by the other participants as well.[7] Controversy will then naturally develop in an open and pluralist manner. An important aspect of this debate is that participants are free to change opinions and points of view, to invent and adopt new rules, rather than simply having to ratify a minimal overlapping consensus. Ethical innovation of this sort requires, however, that the authorities and institutions that are party to the debate—themselves products of political life, which evolves through them—be open and pluralist as well. The purpose of this joint inquiry goes beyond the interest of science in understanding the nature of the physical and biological world. In seeking to discover and explain the aspirations and beliefs of human beings—in short, their mental states and expectations of reward—it aims at bringing about the good life that all human beings desire.

To do this it will be necessary to reconcile the considerable advantages that the sciences (particularly the biological and medical sciences) offer society as a whole with respect for the dignity and freedom of individuals. A global approach to the ethical problems facing the world cannot content itself with recapitulating positions—many of them in any case contradictory—that have already been stated; it must try to identify the shared interests of humanity. Arriving at genuine agreement, as Paul Ricoeur and I have emphasized,[8] is possible only to the extent that a common fund of morality can be drawn upon that is both characteristically human and indispensable not only to the survival of the species but also to the achievement of a more harmonious balance between the rights of the individual and the needs of human society.

The main architectural principles of the human brain are common to all the various representatives of the species. Men and women are not simply rational beings. They are also social creatures. They possess singular traits that are the hallmarks of *humanitas:* innate capacities, not only for reasoning and creativity, but also for attributing knowledge and desires to others and for feeling the "moral" emotions of sympathy and aversion to violence.[9] They also possess an instinct for learning, together with a set of epigenetic dispositions favoring the storage and retrieval of individual memories within a social, or cultural, context. Though naturally inclined to seek personal rewards, they respond no less favorably to shared rewards at the social level. Moral norms can therefore be seen as distinctive expressions of a general disposition to ethical behavior.[10]

The ethical project that I am proposing comes at a moment in our social and cultural history that demands democratic forms of deliberation aimed at devising rules that will be acceptable not only to scientists but also to citizens (which is to say, in the case of biomedicine, to patients). The health and well-being of the human family—as we must begin thinking of ourselves—have to be valued as something entirely independent of the cultural barriers between states, which are arbitrary, contingent, and plainly devoid of moral force.[11] Our frame of reference—our mental coordinates—will then deliberately evolve from the highly emotional, selfish, and ethnocentric ways of thinking that so far have been dominant in human history to a universalist conception of humankind.

My own experience as chairman of the National Advisory Committee on Bioethics in France between 1992 and 1998 has led me to believe that such an inquiry into the ethical foundations of human behavior bears a striking resemblance to scientific research. In both cases the search for truth is enriched by an insistence on respect for individual well-being and, above all, the common good. Moreover, the multicultural character of this search promotes diversity in the construction of epigenetic norms, increasing the likelihood that a more adequate fit with human needs and aspirations will be found. Has progress not in fact been made in the conduct of human affairs, no less than in science, over the past two centuries? In the interval that separates the Declaration of the Rights of Man of 1789 from the Universal Declaration of Human Rights of 1948? From the first session of the International Court of Justice at the Hague in 1946 to the creation of the International Criminal Court by the Rome Statute of 1998? Surely it is not unreasonable, then, to look to the scientific model of free and reasoned debate as a source of inspiration in elaborating universal principles of ethical judgment and practice.

The dangers of a worldwide project of this sort have often been pointed out. Kant, in *Zum ewigen Frieden* (1795),[12] called attention to the difficulties of creating a single world state, which is apt to oscillate between global despotism on the one hand and the fragile authoritarianism of an empire ravaged by permanent civil war on the other. The fact remains that no international committee on ethical standards of scientific research and development that represents the fields of physics, chemistry, computer science, biomedicine and the neurosciences, as well as law and the other social sciences, can hope to be effective unless it is established in direct association with the only existing democratic institution that has some degree of worldwide authority: the United Nations.[13] The powers of such a committee would be purely advisory, to be sure; but appeal could be made to it by national committees, or indeed any group of citizens, public or private, seeking clarification on ethical questions that might arise at the national level. An international body of this sort would be in a position, moreover, to make specific recommendations that would go beyond mere declaration of abstract principles to address the actual causes of human suffering in a detailed and practical way.

Throughout this book I have sought to demonstrate the importance of acquiring objective knowledge about the function of the human brain. The attempt to naturalize what is still quite widely regarded as belonging, now and forever, to the domain of the spiritual—which includes the spheres of ethics and aesthetic contemplation—can scarcely be considered an offense against human dignity. To the contrary, a deeper understanding of what makes us human will favor tolerance and mutual respect on the basis of a recognition of others as persons like ourselves, members of a single social species that is the product of biological evolution.

There are a number of ethical obligations whose force will generally be admitted by all reasonable persons, regardless of cultural, philosophical, or religious background. These include putting an immediate halt to the development of offensive weapons; reducing global levels of industrial pollution; making the benefits of medical research available to all human beings in order to relieve suffering, improve the prospects for health, and raise living standards in the poorest countries; and enforcing observance of the fundamental human rights of both individuals and populations.

All these things recommend themselves as a matter of common sense. Further investigation into the physiology of truth will add to the list of obligations that human beings must recognize that they owe to one another if they wish, not merely to survive, but also to freely exercise their rights to life, liberty, and happiness.

Notes
Credits
Acknowledgments
Index

Notes

Introduction

1. Denis Diderot and Jean Le Rond d'Alembert, eds., *Encyclopédie, ou, Dictionnaire raisonné des sciences, des arts, et des métiers,* 29 vols. (Paris: Briasson, 1751–1772), 17:68.
2. Spinoza, *L'Éthique,* trans. Émile Saisset (Paris: Charpentier, 1842), 44; Henri Bergson, *Matière et mémoire: Essai sur la relation du corps à l'esprit* (Paris: F. Alcan, 1896).
3. René Descartes, *Discours de la méthode pour bien conduire sa raison, et chercher la vérité dans les sciences* (Paris: Théodore Girard, 1668), 44; *L'Homme,* 2nd ed. (Paris: Charles Angot, 1677), 66; *Sixièmes réponses,* in *Œuvres de Descartes,* ed. Charles Adam and Paul Tannery, 12 vols. plus supplement (1896–1913; Paris: Vrin/Centre National de la Recherche Scientifique, 1964–1974), 9:226–227.
4. Democritus, frag. 9, in *Les Penseurs grecs avant Socrate: De Thalès de Milet à Prodicos,* trans. Jean Voilquin (Paris: Garnier Frères, 1941), 170.

1. Thinking Matter

1. Gaston Bachelard, *Le Matérialisme rationnel* (Paris: Presses Universitaires de France, 1953), 20, 10, 8–9, 3.
2. Ibid., 9–10, 3.
3. Voltaire, *Correspondance,* 13 vols., ed. Théodore Besterman (Paris: Gallimard, 1977), 1:447.
4. Denis Diderot, *Le Rêve de d'Alembert* (Paris: Garnier-Flammarion, 1965), 70.
5. F. J. Gall, *Sur les fonctions du cerveau et sur celles de chacune de ses parties,* 6 vols. (Paris: Ballière, 1822–1825).
6. Korbinian Brodmann, *Vergleichende Lokalisationslehre der Groshirnrinde* (Leipzig: J. A. Barth, 1909).

7. Jerry A. Fodor, *The Modularity of Mind: An Essay in Faculty Psychology* (Cambridge, Mass.: MIT Press/Bradford Books, 1983).
8. M. Kerszberg et al., "Stabilization of complex input-output functions in neural clusters formed by synapse selection," *Neural Networks* 5 (1992): 403–413.
9. Bernard J. Baars, *A Cognitive Theory of Consciousness* (Cambridge: Cambridge University Press, 1988).
10. See M. M. Mesulam, "From sensation to cognition," *Brain* 121 (1998): 1013–52.
11. Bachelard, *Le Matérialisme rationnel,* 19–20.
12. Jean-Pierre Changeux, *Neuronal Man: The Biology of Mind,* trans. Laurence Garey, intro. Vernon B. Mountcastle (Princeton: Princeton University Press, 1997), 21–96.
13. Santiago Ramón y Cajal, *Textura del sistema nervioso del hombre y des los vertebrados,* 2 vols. (Madrid: N. Moya, 1899–1904); *Histologie du système nerveux de l'homme et des vertébrés,* 2 vols., trans. L. Azoulay (Paris: Maloine, 1909–1911); *Histology of the Nervous System,* 2 vols., trans. Neely Swanson and Larry W. Swanson (New York: Oxford University Press, 1994).
14. Eric R. Kandel et al., eds., *Essentials of Neural Science and Behavior* (Norwalk, Conn.: Appleton and Lange, 1995).
15. E. A. Nimchinsky et al., "A neuronal morphologic type unique to humans and great apes," *Proc. Nat. Acad. Sci. USA* 96 (1999): 5268–73.
16. See C. Léna et al., "Diversity and distribution of nicotinic acetylcholine receptors in the locus ceruleus neurons," *Proc. Nat. Acad. Sci. USA* 96 (1999): 12126–131.
17. See J.-P. Changeux, "Concluding remarks on the 'singularity' of nerve cells and its ontogenesis," *Prog. Brain Res.* 58 (1983): 465–478; P. Somogyi, "Salient features of synaptic organization in the cerebral cortex," *Brain Res. Rev.* 26 (1998): 113–115.
18. See John C. Eccles, *The Physiology of Synapses* (Berlin: Springer-Verlag, 1964).
19. J. H. Morais-Cabral et al., "Energetic optimization of ion conduction rate by the K^+ selectivity filter," *Nature* 414 (2001): 37–42.
20. Eccles, *Physiology of Synapses.*
21. T. Hökfelt et al., "Peptidergic neurons," *Nature* 284 (1980): 515–521.
22. A. Beaudet and L. Descarries, "The monoamine innervation of rat cerebral cortex: Synaptic and nonsynaptic relationships," *Neuroscience* 3 (1978): 851–860.
23. J.-P. Changeux and S. Edelstein, "Allosteric receptors after 30 years," *Neuron* 21 (1998): 959–980.
24. J. Monod et al., "On the nature of allosteric transitions: A plausible model," *J. Mol. Biol.* 12 (1965): 88–118; M. Perutz, "Mechanisms of cooperativity and allosteric regulation in proteins," *Quarterly Rev. of Biophys.* 22 (1989): 139–236.

25. René Thom, *Paraboles et catastrophes: Entretiens sur les mathématiques, la science et la philosophie* (Paris: Flammarion, 1983), 43.
26. See Michael J. Zigmond et al., eds., *Fundamental Neuroscience* (San Diego: Academic Press, 1999), sec. 2, chs. 3–14.
27. Stanley Finger, *Origins of Neuroscience: A History of Explorations into Brain Function* (New York: Oxford University Press, 1994), 193–205.
28. Ivan Pavlov, *Conditioned Reflex: An Investigation of the Physiological Activity of the Cerebral Cortex* (Oxford: Oxford University Press, 1927).
29. Alain Berthoz, *The Brain's Sense of Movement,* trans. Giselle Weiss (Cambridge, Mass.: Harvard University Press, 2000).
30. Changeux, *Neuronal Man,* 31–33, 77–83.
31. M. Berridge and P. E. Rapp, "A comparative survey of the function, mechanisms, and control of cellular oscillations," *J. Expl. Biol.* 81 (1979): 217–280.
32. Wilhelm T. Preyer, *Spezielle Physiologie des Embryo: Untersuchungen ueber die Lebenserscheinungen vor der Geburt* (Leipzig: Grieben, 1885).
33. K. Ripley and R. Provine, "Neural correlates of embryonic reality in the chick," *Brain Res.* 45 (1972): 127–134.
34. R. Bergstrom, "Electrical parameters of the brain during ontogeny," in R. J. Robinson, ed., *Brain and Early Behaviour Development in the Fetus and Infant* (London: Academic Press, 1969), 15–42.
35. H. Berger, "Über das Elektroenkephalogramm des Menschen," *Archiv für Psychiatrie und Nervenkrankheiten* 87 (1929): 527–570.
36. D. Gusnard and M. Raichle, "Searching for a baseline: Functional imaging and the resting human brain," *Nat. Rev. Neurosci.* 2 (2001): 685–693.
37. See Mark F. Bear et al., *Neuroscience: Exploring the Brain* (Baltimore: Williams and Wilkins, 2000).
38. Immanuel Kant, *Critique of Pure Reason,* trans. Norman Kemp Smith (New York: St. Martin's, 1965), esp. "Transcendental logic."
39. See J.-P. Changeux and S. Dehaene, "Neuronal models of cognitive functions," *Cognition* 33 (1989): 63–109.
40. Bear et al., *Neuroscience;* Semir Zeki, *A Vision of the Brain* (Oxford: Blackwell, 1993).
41. T. Preuss and J. H. Kaas, "Human brain evolution," in Zigmond et al., eds., *Fundamental Neuroscience,* 1283–1311.
42. *The Positive Philosophy of Auguste Comte,* 2 vols., trans. Harriet Martineau (Bristol: Thoemmes, 2001).
43. R. Lorente de Nó, "Analysis of the activity of the chains of internuncial neurons," *J. Neurophysiol.* 1 (1938): 207–244; John F. Fulton, *Physiology of the Nervous System,* 2nd ed. (London: Oxford University Press, 1943); W. S. McCulloch, "A heterarchy of values determined by the topology of nervous nets," *Bull. Math. Biophys.* 7 (1945): 89–93.
44. Gerald M. Edelman and Vernon B. Mountcastle, *The Mindful Brain: Cortical*

Organization and the Group-Selective Theory of Higher Brain Function (Cambridge, Mass.: MIT Press, 1978).

45. D. J. Felleman and D. C. Van Essen, "Distributed hierarchical processing in the primate cerebral cortex," *Cerebral Cortex* 1 (1991): 1–47.
46. M. G. Kryazeva et al., "Visual stimulus-dependent changes in interhemispheric EEG coherence in humans," *J. Neurophysiol.* 82 (1999): 3095–3107; S. Dehaene et al., "A neuronal model of a global workspace in effortful cognitive tasks," *Proc. Natl. Acad. Sci. USA* 95 (1998): 14529–534.
47. L. F. Agnati et al., "Intercellular communication in the brain: Wiring versus volume transmission," *Neuroscience* 69 (1995): 711–726.
48. Ilya Prigogine and D. K. Kondepudi, *Modern Thermodynamics: From Heat Engines to Dissipative Structures* (New York: Wiley, 1998); Élisabeth Pacherie, *Naturaliser l'intentionalité: Essai de philosophie de la psychologie* (Paris: Presses Universitaires de France, 1993).
49. D. Laplane and B. Dubois, "Autoactivation deficit: A basal ganglia-related syndrome," *Movement Disorders* 16 (2001): 810–814.
50. Henri Bergson, *The Creative Mind: An Introduction to Metaphysics,* trans. Mabelle L. Andison (New York: Philosophical Library, 1946).
51. Empedocles, frags. 58, 59, 62, in *Les penseurs grecs avant Socrate: De Thalès de Milet à Prodicos,* trans. Jean Voilquin (Paris: Garnier Frères, 1941), 128.
52. John Hughlings Jackson, *Selected Writings,* ed. James Taylor, 2 vols. (London: Hodder and Stoughton, 1932–1933).
53. Jacques Monod, *Chance and Necessity: An Essay on the Natural Philosophy of Modern Biology,* trans. Austryn Wainhouse (New York: Random House, 1972); Karl R. Popper, *Objective Knowledge: An Evolutionary Approach,* rev. ed. (1972; Oxford: Clarendon Press, 1983).
54. Changeux and Dehaene, "Neuronal models of cognitive functions."
55. Dan Sperber and Deirdre Wilson, *Relevance: Communication and Cognition,* 2d ed. (1986; Oxford: Blackwell, 1995).
56. Rudolf Carnap, *The Unity of Science,* trans. M. Black (Bristol: Thoemmes, 1995), 93.
57. A. Einstein, "Physics and reality," *Journal of the Franklin Institute* 221 (1936): 313–347.
58. J. Z. Young, *A Model of the Brain* (Oxford: Oxford University Press, 1964), 15.
59. Jean-Baptiste de Lamarck, *Philosophie zoologique, ou, Exposition des considérations relatives à l'histoire naturelle des animaux,* 2 vols. (Paris: Dentu, 1809), 1:281.

2. The Acquisition of Knowledge

1. Johann Gottfried Herder, *Essay on the Origin of Language,* trans. John H. Moran and Alexander Gode (Chicago: University of Chicago Press, 1986).
2. Spinoza, *L'Éthique,* trans. Émile Saisset (Paris: Charpentier, 1842), 85.

3. B. Russell, "The philosophy of logical atomism" (1918), in *Logic and Knowledge,* ed. Robert Charles Marsh (London: Macmillan, 1956).
4. See Peter Marler and Herbert S. Terrace, eds., *The Biology of Learning* (Berlin: Springer-Verlag, 1984); Robert Boakes, *From Darwin to Behaviorism: Psychology and the Minds of Animals* (Cambridge: Cambridge University Press, 1984).
5. E. L. Thorndike, "Animal intelligence: An experimental study of the associative processes in animals," *Psychological Rev.,* suppl. 8 (1898).
6. See, e.g., E. Kandel and L. Tauc, "Mechanisms of prolonged laterosynaptic facilitation," *Nature* 202 (1964): 145–147; Eric R. Kandel et al., eds., *Essentials of Neural Science and Behavior* (Norwalk, Conn.: Appleton and Lange, 1995); T. Bliss and T. Lømo, "Longlasting potentiation of synaptic transmission in the dentate area of the anesthetized rabbit following stimulation of the perforant path," *J. Physiol.* 232 (1973): 331–356.
7. Clark L. Hull, *Principles of Behavior: An Introduction to Behavior Theory* (New York: Appleton-Century-Crofts, 1943); C. B. Ferster and B. F. Skinner, *Schedules of Reinforcement* (New York: Appleton-Century-Crofts, 1957).
8. J.-P. Changeux and A. Danchin, "Selective stabilization of developing synapses as a mechanism for the specification of neuronal networks," *Nature* 264 (1976): 705–712; Jean-Pierre Changeux, *Neuronal Man: The Biology of Mind,* trans. Laurence Garey, intro. Vernon B. Mountcastle (Princeton: Princeton University Press, 1997), 246–249.
9. Boakes, *From Darwin to Behaviorism.*
10. Marler and Terrace, eds., *The Biology of Learning.*
11. D. Denton et al., "Correlation of regional cerebral blood flow and change of plasma sodium concentration during genesis and satiation of thirst," *Proc. Natl. Acad. Sci. USA* 96 (1999): 2532–37.
12. See Jean-Didier Vincent, *Biologie des passions* (Paris: Odile Jacob, 1986), and *La Chair et le Diable* (Paris: Odile Jacob, 1996).
13. J. Olds and P. Milner, "Positive reinforcement produced by electrical stimulation of septal area and other regions of rat brain," *J. Comp. Physiol. Psych.* 47 (1954): 419–427; J. Olds, "Self-stimulation of the brain," *Science* 17 (1958): 315–324.
14. G. Di Chiara, "Drug addiction as dopamine-dependent associative learning disorder," *Europ. J. Pharmacol.* 375 (1999): 13–30.
15. Ibid.
16. See "Le Normal et le pathologique," in *A Vital Rationalist: Selected Writings from Georges Canguilhem,* ed. François Delaporte, trans. Arthur Goldhammer (New York: Zone Books, 1994).
17. G. Koob and M. Le Moal, "Drug abuse: Hedonic homeostatic dysregulation," *Science* 278 (1997): 52–58.
18. M. J. Keopp et al., "Evidence for striatal release during a video game," *Nature* 393 (1998): 266–268.

19. W. Schultz and A. Dickinson, "Neuronal coding of prediction errors," *Annu. Rev. Neurosci.* 23 (2000): 473–500.
20. B. A. Sorg and P. W. Kalives, "Effects of cocaine and footshock stress on extracellular dopamine levels in the medial prefrontal cortex," *Neuroscience* 53 (1993): 695–703.
21. Wittgenstein, *Philosophical Investigations,* trans. G. E. M. Anscombe, 3rd ed. (London: Blackwell, 2001), §27–31, 72.
22. Fred I. Dretske, *Naturalizing the Mind* (Cambridge, Mass.: MIT Press, 1995).
23. See, e.g., Colin McGinn, *The Problem of Consciousness: Essays toward a Resolution* (Oxford: Blackwell, 1991), and *The Mysterious Flame: Conscious Minds in a Material World* (New York: Basic Books, 1999).
24. H. Lissauer, "Ein Fall von Seelenblindheit nebst einem Beitrag zur Theorie derselben," *Archiv für Psychiatrie* 21 (1890): 222–270; Sigmund Freud, *Zur Aufassung der Aphasien* (Vienna: Deuticke, 1891).
25. Rosaleen A. McCarthy and Elizabeth K. Warrington, *Cognitive Neuropsychology: A Clinical Introduction* (San Diego: Academic Press, 1990).
26. J. M. Nielson, "Unilateral cerebral dominance as related to mind blindness," *Archives of Neurology and Psychiatry* 38 (1937): 108–135.
27. McCarthy and Warrington, *Cognitive Neuropsychology.*
28. R. Vandenberghe et al., "Functional anatomy of a common semantic system for words and pictures," *Nature* 383 (1996): 254–256.
29. L. Chao et al., "Attribute-based neural substrates in temporal cortex for perceiving and knowing about objects," *Nat. Neurosci.* 2 (1999): 913–919.
30. Ibid.
31. F. Pulvemüller, "Hebb's concept of cell assemblies and the psychophysiology of word processing," *Psychophysiology* 33 (1996): 317–333.
32. Changeux, *Neuronal Man,* 62–65, 140–144.
33. D. A. Allport, "Distributed memory, modular systems and dysphasia," in Stanton P. Newman and Ruth Epstein, eds., *Current Perspectives in Dysphasia* (Edinburgh: Churchill Livingstone, 1985).
34. John Locke, *An Essay Concerning Human Understanding,* ed. A. C. Fraser (Oxford: Oxford University Press, 1894).
35. McCarthy and Warrington, *Cognitive Neuropsychology;* Tim Shallice, *From Neuropsychology to Mental Structure* (Cambridge: Cambridge University Press, 1988).
36. A. Roskies, "The binding problem," *Neuron* 24 (1999): 7–125.
37. Yves Delage, *Le Rêve: Étude psychologique, philosophique et littéraire* (Paris: Presses Universitaires de France, 1919).
38. David Hume, *A Treatise of Human Nature,* ed. L. A. Selby-Bigge, 2nd ed. (Oxford: Clarendon Press, 1978), 11.
39. See Donald Hebb, *The Organization of Behavior* (New York: Wiley, 1949).
40. Moshe Abeles, *Corticonics: Neuronal Circuits of the Cerebral Cortex* (Cam-

bridge: Cambridge University Press, 1991); C. M. Gray et al., "Oscillatory responses in cat visual cortex exhibit inter-columnar synchronization which reflects global stimulus properties," *Nature* 338 (1989): 334–337; W. Singer and C. M. Gray, "Visual feature integration and the temporal correlation hypothesis," *Annu. Rev. Neurosci.* 18 (1995): 555–586; F. Varela et al., "The brainweb: Phase synchronization and large-scale integration," *Nat. Rev. Neurosci.* 2 (2001): 229–238.

41. E. Vaadia et al., "Dynamics of neuronal interactions in monkey cortex in relation to behavioural events," *Nature* 373 (1995): 515–518.
42. M. Castelo-Branco et al., "Neural synchrony correlates with surface segregation rules," *Nature* 405 (2000): 685–689.
43. M. Shadlen and A. Movshon, "Synchrony unbound: A critical evaluation of the temporal binding hypothesis," *Neuron* 24 (1999): 67–77.
44. P. Roelfsema et al., "Figure-ground segregation in a recurrent network architecture," *J. Cogn. Neurosci.* 14 (2002): 525–537.
45. Changeux, *Neuronal Man,* 77–83.
46. A. Arieli et al., "Coherent spatiotemporal patterns of ongoing activity revealed by real-time optical imaging coupled with single-unit recording in the cat visual cortex," *J. Neurophysiol.* 73 (1995): 2072–93.
47. M. Tsodyks et al., "Linking spontaneous activity of single cortical neurons and the underlying functional architecture," *Science* 286 (1999): 1943–46.
48. Wittgenstein, *Philosophical Investigations,* §7.
49. See Ivan Pavlov, *Le Travail des glandes digestives,* trans. V. Pachon and J. Sabrazès (Paris: Masson, 1901); Kandel et al., *Essentials of Neural Science and Behavior;* Patricia Churchland and Terrence J. Sejnowski, *The Computational Brain* (Cambridge, Mass: MIT Press/Bradford Books, 1992).
50. See Changeux, *Neuronal Man,* 139–141; J.-P. Changeux and S. Dehaene, "Hierarchical neuronal modeling of cognitive function: From synaptic transmission to the Tower of London," *C. R. Acad. Sci. Paris* 321 (1998): 241–247.
51. Changeux, *Neuronal Man,* 169; Gerald M. Edelman, *Neural Darwinism: The Theory of Neuronal Group Selection* (New York: Basic Books, 1987).
52. Michael A. Arbib et al., *Neural Organization: Structure, Function, and Dynamics* (Cambridge, Mass.: MIT Press, 1998).
53. Donald S. Faber and Henri Korn, *Neurobiology of the Mauthner Cell* (New York: Raven Press, 1978).
54. D. Hansel and H. Sompolinsky, "Synchronization and computation in a chaotic neural network," *Phys. Rev. Lett.* 68 (1992): 718–721; P. Faure and H. Korn, "A nonrandom dynamic component in the synaptic noise of a central neuron," *Proc. Natl. Acad. Sci. USA* 94 (1997): 6506–11.
55. S. Dehaene and J.-P. Changeux, "Development of elementary numerical abilities: A neuronal model," *J. Cogn. Neurosci.* 5 (1989): 390–407.

56. O. Sporns et al., "Reentrant signaling among simulated neuronal groups leads to coherence in their oscillatory activity," *Proc. Natl. Acad. Sci. USA* 86 (1989): 7265–69.
57. Tsodyks et al., "Linking spontaneous activity of single cortical neurons."
58. Peter Gärdenfors, *Conceptual Spaces: The Geometry of Thought* (Cambridge: Mass.: MIT Press, 2000).
59. J. Fodor and Z. Pylyshyn, "Connections and cognitive architecture: A critical analysis," *Cognition* 28 (1988): 3–71.
60. D. A. Allport, "Distributed memory, modular systems and dysphasia," in Stanton P. Newman and Ruth Epstein, eds., *Current Perspectives in Dysphasia* (Edinburgh: Churchill Livingstone, 1985); McCarthy and Warrington, *Cognitive Neuropsychology.*
61. Jerome Kagan, *Three Seductive Ideas* (Cambridge, Mass.: Harvard University Press, 1998).
62. Susanna Millar, *The Psychology of Play* (Baltimore: Penguin, 1968).
63. McCarthy and Warrington, *Cognitive Neuropsychology.*
64. Changeux and Dehaene, "Neuronal models of cognitive functions."
65. Changeux, *Neuronal Man,* 142–145; Dehaene and Changeux, "Development of elementary numerical abilities"; S. Dehaene and J.-P. Changeux, "The Wisconsin card-sorting test: Theoretical analysis and simulation of a reasoning task in a model neuronal network," *Cerebral Cortex* 1 (1991): 62–79; O. Sporns et al., "Modeling perceptual grouping and figure-ground segregation by means of active reentrant connections," *Proc. Natl. Acad. Sci. USA* 88 (1991): 129–133; G. Tononi et al., "Reentry and the problem of integrating multiple cortical areas: Simulation of dynamic integration in the visual system," *Cerebral Cortex* 2 (1992): 310–335; Y. Miyashita and T. Hayashi, "Neural representation of visual objects: Encoding and top-down activation," *Curr. Opin. Neurobiol.* 10 (2000): 187–194.
66. S. Dehaene et al., "Neural networks that learn temporal sequences by selection," *Proc. Natl. Acad. Sci. USA* 84 (1987): 2727–31.
67. Changeux, *Neuronal Man,* 246–249.
68. See S. R. Quartz and T. J. Sejnowski, "The neural basis of cognitive development: A constructivist manifesto," *Behav. Brain Sci.* 20 (1997): 537–556.
69. See Jerry A. Fodor, *The Modularity of Mind: An Essay in Faculty Psychology* (Cambridge, Mass.: MIT Press/Bradford Books, 1983).
70. Mark H. Johnson and John Morton, *Biology and Cognitive Development: The Case of Face Recognition* (Oxford: Blackwell, 1991).
71. Locke, *Essay Concerning Human Understanding,* 228.
72. Dehaene and Changeux, "Development of elementary numerical abilities"; Dehaene and Changeux, "Wisconsin card-sorting test"; S. Dehaene et al., "A neuronal model of a global workspace in effortful cognitive tasks," *Proc. Natl. Acad. Sci. USA* 95 (1998): 14529–534; S. Dehaene and J.-P. Changeux, "A

hierarchical neuronal network for planning behavior," *Proc. Natl. Acad. Sci. USA* 94 (1997): 13293–298.

73. C. F. Jacobsen, "Functions of the frontal association areas in primates," *Arch. Neurol. Psychiatry* 33 (1935): 558–569.
74. Ibid.
75. A. Diamond, "Difference between adult and infant cognition: Is the crucial variable presence or absence of language?" in Lawrence Weiskrantz, ed., *Thought without Language* (Oxford: Clarendon Press, 1988).
76. N. Herschkowitz et al., "Neurobiological bases of behavioral development in the first year," *Neuropediatrics* 28 (1997): 296–306.
77. Dehaene et al., "Neuronal model of a global workspace."
78. Edelman, *Neural Darwinism.*
79. Jean-Pierre Changeux and Alain Connes, *Conversations on Mind, Matter, and Mathematics,* trans. M. B. DeBevoise (Princeton: Princeton University Press, 1995), 168–178.
80. T. Heidemann and J.-P. Changeux, "Un modèle moléculaire de régulation d'efficacité d'une synapse chimique au niveau postsynaptique," *C. R. Acad. Sci. Paris* 295 (1982): 665–670; S. Dehaene and J.-P. Changeux, "A simple model of prefrontal cortex function in delayed-response tasks," *J. Cogn. Neurosci.* 1 (1989): 244–261; M. R. Picciotto et al., "Acetylcholine receptors containing beta2-subunit are involved in the reinforcing properties of nicotine," *Nature* 391 (1998): 173–177.
81. Picciotto et al., "Acetylcholine receptors containing beta2-subunit"; M. Cordero-Erausquin et al., "Nicotinic function: New perspectives from knockout mice," *Trends Pharmacol. Sci.* 21 (2000): 211–217.
82. T. Bliss and G. L. Colindridge, "A synaptic model of memory: Long-term potentiation in the hippocampus," *Nature* 361 (1993): 31–39; C. M. Pennartz, "The ascending neuromodulatory systems in learning by reinforcement: Comparing computational conjectures with experimental findings," *Brain Res. Rev.* 21 (1995): 219–245; E. Quinlan et al., "Bidirectional, experience-dependent regulation of N-methyl D aspartate receptor subunit composition in the rat visual cortex during postnatal development," *Proc. Natl. Acad. Sci. USA* 96 (1999): 12876–880; C. D. Rittenhouse et al., "Monocular deprivation induces homosynaptic long-term depression in visual cortex," *Nature* 397 (1999): 347–350.
83. K. Friston et al., "Value-dependent selection in the brain: Simulation in a synthetic neural model," *Neuroscience* 59 (1994): 229–243; Richard S. Sutton and Andrew G. Barto, *Reinforcement Learning: An Introduction* (Cambridge, Mass.: MIT Press, 1998).
84. W. Schultz et al., "A neural substrate of prediction and reward," *Science* 275 (1997): 1593–99.
85. Dehaene and Changeux, "Wisconsin card-sorting test."

86. Sutton and Barto, *Reinforcement Learning.*
87. Dehaene and Changeux, "Wisconsin card-sorting test"; Dehaene and Changeux, "Hierarchical neuronal network for planning behavior."
88. M. Laubach et al., "Cortical ensemble activity increasingly predicts behavior outcomes during learning of a motor task," *Nature* 405 (2000): 567–571.
89. Varela et al., "The brainweb."
90. E. Rodriguez et al., "Perception's shadow: Long-distance synchronization of human brain activity," *Nature* 397 (1999): 430–433.
91. E. Miller and W. Assad, "The prefrontal cortex: Conjunction and cognition," in François Boller and Jordan Grafman, eds., *Handbook of Neuropsychology,* 2nd ed., vol. 8: *The Frontal Lobes* (Amsterdam: Elsevier, 2000); Miyashita and Hayashi, "Neural representation of visual objects"; Laubach et al., "Cortical ensemble activity increasingly predicts behavior outcomes."
92. S. Kosslyn et al., "Neural foundations of imagery," *Nat. Rev. Neurosci.* 2 (2001): 635–642.
93. G. Ganis et al., "Transcranial magnetic stimulations of primary motor cortex affect mental rotation," *Cereb. Cortex* 10 (2000): 175–180.
94. But see B. L. Schlaggar et al., "Functional neuroanatomical differences between adults and school-age children in the processing of single words," *Science* 296 (2002): 1476–79.
95. E. Spelke, "Principles of object perception," *Cognitive Science* 14 (1990): 29–56.
96. Susan Carey, *Conceptual Change in Childhood* (Cambridge, Mass.: MIT Press, 1985).

3. States of Consciousness

1. John R. Searle, *The Mystery of Consciousness* (New York: New York Review of Books, 1997).
2. A. Revonsuo, "Can functional brain imaging discover consciousness in the brain?" *J. Consciousness Studies* 8 (2001): 3–23.
3. Étienne Bonnot de Condillac, *Treatise on the Sensations,* trans. Geraldine Carr (Los Angeles: School of Philosophy, University of Southern California, 1930), I, vi, 3.
4. Immanuel Kant, *Anthropology from a Pragmatic Point of View,* trans. Victor Lyle Dowdell, rev. and ed. Hans H. Rudnick (Carbondale: Southern Illinois University Press, 1996).
5. Jean-Baptiste de Lamarck, *Philosophie zoologique, ou, Exposition des considérations relatives à l'histoire naturelle des animaux,* 2 vols. (Paris: Dentu, 1809), 1:281.
6. Ibid.
7. Herbert Spencer, *The Principles of Psychology* (London: Longman, Brown, Green, and Longmans, 1855).
8. Jean-Pierre Changeux, *Neuronal Man: The Biology of Mind,* trans. Laurence Garey, intro. Vernon B. Mountcastle (Princeton: Princeton University Press,

1997), 264–272; Francis Crick, *The Astonishing Hypothesis: The Scientific Search for the Soul* (New York: Scribner, 1994); Gerald M. Edelman and Giulio Tononi, *A Universe of Consciousness: How Matter Becomes Imagination* (New York: Basic Books, 2000).

9. J. R. Searle, "Consciousness," *Ann. Rev. Neurosci.* 23 (2000): 557–578.
10. L. Descarries et al., "What? Where? When? How? Why?" in Herbert H. Jasper et al., eds., *Consciousness: At the Frontiers of Neuroscience* (Philadelphia: Lippincott-Raven, 1998), xiii–xvi.
11. Henri Ey, *La Conscience* (Paris: Desclée de Brouwer, 1963).
12. See, e.g., W. Sellars, "Foundations for a metaphysics of pure process," *Monist* 64 (1981): 3–90; Thomas Nagel, *The View from Nowhere* (New York: Oxford University Press, 1986); John Searle, *The Rediscovery of the Mind* (Cambridge, Mass.: MIT Press, 1992).
13. Rodolfo R. Llinás, *I of the Vortex: From Neurons to the Self* (Cambridge, Mass.: MIT Press/Bradford Books, 2001); Ey, *La Conscience.*
14. William James, *The Principles of Psychology,* 2 vols. (New York: H. Holt, 1890).
15. Quoted by Ey, *La Conscience,* 153; see also Edelman and Tononi, *Universe of Consciousness.*
16. S. Gallagher, "Philosophical conceptions of the self: Implications for cognitive science," *Trends in Cog. Sci.* 4 (2000): 14–21.
17. Paul Ricoeur, *Soi-même comme un autre* (Paris: Seuil, 1990).
18. Jacques Monod, *Chance and Necessity: An Essay on the Natural Philosophy of Modern Biology,* trans. Austryn Wainhouse (New York: Random House, 1972).
19. F. Varela, "Resonant cell assemblies: A new approach to cognitive functions and neuronal synchrony," *Biol. Res.* 28 (1995): 81–95.
20. Ey, *La Conscience.*
21. Louis Althusser, *Philosophie et philosophie spontanée des savants* (Paris: Maspero, 1974).
22. Pierre Buser, *Cerveau de soi, Cerveau de l'autre* (Paris: Odile Jacob, 1998). See Henri Bergson, *Essai sur les données immédiates de la conscience* (1889), in *Œuvres,* ed. André Robinet (Paris: Presses Universitaires de France, 1959); John Gerald Taylor, *The Race for Consciousness* (Cambridge, Mass.: MIT Press, 1999).
23. John Hughlings Jackson, *Selected Writings,* ed. James Taylor, 2 vols. (London: Hodder and Stoughton, 1932–1933).
24. J. Barresi and C. Moore, "Intentional relation and social understanding," *Behav. Brain Sc.* 19 (1996): 107–154.
25. P. R. Zelazo and P. D. Zelazo, "The emergence of consciousness," in Jasper et al., eds., *Consciousness,* 149–163.
26. Bernard J. Baars, *A Cognitive Theory of Consciousness* (Cambridge: Cambridge University Press, 1988).

27. Michel Jouvet, *Le Sommeil et le rêve* (Paris: Odile Jacob, 1992); B. Jones, "The Neural Basis of Consciousness across the Sleep-Waking Cycle," in Jasper et al., eds., *Consciousness,* 75–94; J. A. Hobson, "Sleep and dreaming," in Michael J. Zigmond et al., eds., *Fundamental Neuroscience* (San Diego: Academic Press, 1999), 1207–27; T. Paus, "Functional anatomy of arousal and attention systems in the human brain," *Progr. Brain Res.* 126 (2000): 65–77.
28. R. Llinás et al., "The neuronal basis of consciousness," *Phil. Trans. Roy. Soc. Lond. B* 353 (1998): 1841–49; A. Rougerel-Buser and Pierre Buser, "Electrocortical rhythms in the attentive cat: Phenomenological data and theoretical issues," in Christo Pantev et al., eds., *Oscillatory Event-Related Brain Dynamics* (New York: Plenum, 1994), 275–293.
29. F. Crick and C. Koch, "Some reflections on visual awareness," *Cold Spring Harbor Symp. Quant. Biol.* 55 (1990): 956–962.
30. H. Jasper, "Diffuse projection systems: The integrative action of the thalamic reticular system," *Electroencephalogr. Clin. Neurophysiol.* 1 (1949): 405–420; M. Steriade and R. Llinás, "The functional states of the thalamus and the associated neuronal interplay," *Physiol. Rev.* 68 (1988): 649–742; Mircea Steriade and Robert W. McCarley, *Brainstem Control of Wakefulness and Sleep* (New York: Plenum, 1990); Jones, "Neural basis of consciousness across the sleep-waking cycle."
31. Llinás, *I of the Vortex.*
32. G. Moruzzi and H. W. Magoun, "Brain stem reticular formation and activation of the EEG," *EEG Clin. Neurophysiol.* 1 (1949): 455–479.
33. Ey, *La Conscience.*
34. Jones, "Neural basis of consciousness across the sleep-waking cycle"; Hobson, "Sleep and dreaming."
35. S. Greenfield, "Mind, brain and consciousness," *Br. J. Psychiatry* 181 (2002): 91–93.
36. C. Léna et al., "Diversity and distribution of nicotinic acetylcholine receptors in the locus ceruleus neurons," *Proc. Nat. Acad. Sci. USA* 96 (1999): 12126–131.
37. Z. Xiang et al., "Cholinergic switching within neocortical inhibitory neurons," *Science* 281 (1998): 985–988.
38. Llinás, *I of the Vortex.*
39. Johann Friedrich Herbart, *A Text-Book in Psychology: An Attempt to Found the Science of Psychology on Experience, Metaphysics, and Mathematics,* trans. Margaret K. Smith (New York: D. Appleton, 1894).
40. E. Pöppel, R. Held, and D. Frost, "Residual visual function after brain wounds involving the central visual pathways in man," *Nature* 243 (1973): 295–296.
41. Lawrence Weiskrantz, *Consciousness Lost and Found: A Neuropsychological Exploration* (New York: Oxford University Press, 1997).
42. A. Cowey and P. Stoerig, "Blindsight in monkeys," *Nature* 373 (1995): 247–249.

43. Hermann Munk, *Über die Funktionen der Grosshirnrinde* (Berlin: A. Hirschwald, 1881), 28–53.
44. S. Dehaene and L. Naccache, "Toward a cognitive neuroscience of consciousness: Basic neuroscience and a workspace of consciousness," *Cognition* 79 (2001): 1–37.
45. S. Dehaene et al., "Imaging unconscious semantic priming," *Nature* 395 (1998): 597–600; L. Naccache and S. Dehaene, "The priming method: Imaging unconscious repetition priming reveals an abstract representation of number in the parietal lobes," *Cereb. Cortex* 11 (2001): 966–974.
46. Jean-Pierre Changeux and Paul Ricoeur, *What Makes Us Think?: A Neuroscientist and a Philosopher Argue about Ethics, Human Nature, and the Brain,* trans. M. B. DeBevoise (Princeton: Princeton University Press, 2000), 128–129.
47. C. M. McLeod, "Half a century of research on the Stroop effect: An integrative review," *Psychol. Bull.* 109 (1991): 163–203.
48. Joaquin M. Fuster, *The Prefrontal Cortex: Anatomy, Physiology, and Neuropsychology of the Frontal Lobe,* 2d ed. (New York: Raven Press, 1989); P. Goldman-Rakic, "Topography of cognition: Parallel distributed networks in primate associative cortex," *Ann. Rev. Neurosci.* 11 (1996): 137–156.
49. R. Knight and M. Grabovecky, "Escape from linear time: Prefrontal cortex and conscious experience," in *Cognitive Neuroscience,* ed. Michael Gazzaniga (Cambridge, Mass.: MIT Press, 1996).
50. Tim Shallice, *From Neuropsychology to Mental Structure* (Cambridge: Cambridge University Press, 1988).
51. F. Lhermitte, "Utilization behavior and its relation to lesions of the frontal lobes," *Brain* 106 (1983): 237–255; A. R. Luria, *Higher Cortical Functions in Man,* trans. Basil Haigh (London: Tavistock, 1966).
52. R. Cooper and T. Shallice, "Contentions scheduling and the control of routine activities," *Cog. Neuropsy.* 17 (2000): 297–338.
53. Quoted in Olivier Sabouraud, *Le Langage et ses maux* (Paris: Odile Jacob, 1995).
54. See K. M. Heilman et al., "Possible mechanisms of anosognosia, a defect in self-awareness," *Phil. Trans. R. Soc. London B.* 353 (1998): 1903–1909.
55. Antonio R. Damasio, *The Feeling of What Happens: Body and Emotion in the Making of Consciousness* (New York: Harcourt Brace, 1999).
56. J. K. Hietanen and D. I. Perrett, "Motion-sensitive cells in the macaque superior temporal polysensory area: 1. Lack of response to the sight of the animal's own limb movement," *Exp. Brain Res.* 93 (1993): 117–128.
57. K. Shima et al., "Two movement-related foci in the primate cingulate cortex observed in signal-triggered and self-paced forelimb movement," *J. Neurophysiol.* 65 (1991): 188–202.
58. C. Frith and U. Frith, "Interacting worlds: A biological basis," *Science* 286 (1999): 1692–95.

59. S. Dehaene et al., "A neuronal model of a global workspace in effortful cognitive tasks," *Proc. Natl. Acad. Sci. USA* 95 (1998): 14529–534.
60. Edelman and Tononi, *Universe of Consciousness.*
61. C. F. von Economo, *The Cytoarchitectonics of the Human Cerebral Cortex* (London: Oxford University Press, 1929); Vernon B. Mountcastle, *Perceptual Neuroscience: The Cerebral Cortex* (Cambridge, Mass.: Harvard University Press, 1998).
62. E. D. Lumer et al., "Neural dynamics in a model of the thalamocortical system, part 1: Layers, loops and the emergence of fast synchronous rhythms," *Cereb. Cortex* 7 (1997): 207–227.
63. Dehaene et al., "Neuronal model of a global workspace in effortful cognitive tasks."
64. Ibid.
65. Z. Pylyshyn, "Is the Imagery Debate Over? If So, What Was It About?" in Emmanuel Dupoux, ed., *Language, Brain, and Cognitive Development* (Cambridge, Mass.: MIT Press, 2001), 59–83.
66. J.-P. Changeux et al., "Learning by selection," in Peter Marler and Herbert S. Terrace, eds., *The Biology of Learning* (Berlin: Springer-Verlag, 1984), 115–133.
67. M. Posner and S. Petersen, "The attention system of the human brain," *Ann. Rev. Neurosci.* 13 (1990): 25–42.
68. S. Dehaene and J.-P. Changeux, "The Wisconsin card-sorting test: Theoretical analysis and simulation of a reasoning task in a model neuronal network," *Cerebral Cortex* 1 (1991): 62–79; S. Dehaene and J.-P. Changeux, "A hierarchical neuronal network for planning behavior," *Proc. Natl. Acad. Sci. USA* 94 (1997): 13293–298.
69. Goldman-Rakic, "Topography of cognition."
70. R. W. Sperry, "Hemisphere deconnection and unity in conscious awareness," *Amer. Psychol.* 23 (1968): 723–733.
71. Llinás, *I of the Vortex.*
72. V. Lamme et al., "Masking interrupts figure-ground signals in V_1," *J. Cogn. Neurosci.* 14 (2002): 1044–53.
73. F. Varela et al., "The brainweb: Phase synchronization and large-scale integration," *Nat. Rev. Neurosci.* 2 (2001): 229–238.
74. Paus, "Functional anatomy of arousal and attention systems"; C. M. Portas et al., "Auditory processing across the sleep-wake cycle: Simultaneous EEG and fMRI monitoring in humans," *Neuron* 28 (2000): 991–999.
75. P. Fiset et al., "Brain mechanisms of propofol-induced loss of consciousness in humans: A positron emission tomographic study," *J. Neurosci.* 19 (1999): 5506–13.
76. Portas et al., "Auditory processing across the sleep-wake cycle."
77. J. D. Cohen et al., "Temporal dynamics of brain activation during a working memory task," *Nature* 386 (1997): 643–651; J. V. Pardo et al., "The anterior

cingulate cortex mediates processing selection in the Stroop attentional conflict paradigm," *Proc. Natl. Acad. Sci. USA* 87 (1990): 256–259.

78. M. E. Raichle et al., "Practice-related changes in human brain functional anatomy during nonmotor learning," *Cereb. Cortex* 4 (1994): 8–26.
79. S. Dehaene et al., "Localization of neural system for error detection and compensation," *Psychol. Sci.* 5 (1994): 303–305.
80. Dehaene et al., "Imaging unconscious semantic priming."
81. Paus, "Functional anatomy of arousal and attention systems."
82. J. Duncan and A. M. Owen, "Common regions of the human frontal lobe recruited by diverse cognitive demands," *Trends in Cog. Sci.* 23 (2000): 475–482; Fuster, *Prefrontal Cortex.*
83. J. Rowe et al., "The prefrontal cortex response selection or maintenance within working memory," *Science* 288 (2000): 1656–60.
84. T. S. Kilduff and C. Peyron, "The hypocretin/orexin ligand-receptor system: Implications for sleep and sleep disorders," *Trends in Cog. Sci.* 23 (2000): 359–365.
85. N. P. Franks and W. R. Lieb, "Anesthetics set their sites on ion channels," *Nature* 408 (1997): 334–335.
86. S. Castner et al., "Reversal of anti-psychotic-induced working memory deficits by short-term dopamine D1 receptor stimulation," *Science* 287 (2000): 2020–22.
87. S. Granon et al., "Nicotinic and muscarinic receptors in the rat prefrontal cortex: Differential roles in working memories, response selection, and effortful processing," *Psychopharmacology* 119 (1995): 139–144.
88. J.-P. Changeux and S. Edelstein, "Allosteric receptors after 30 years," *Neuron* 21 (1998): 959–980.
89. Jouvet, *Le Sommeil et le rêve.*
90. E. Perry et al., "Acetylcholine in mind: A neurotransmitter correlate of consciousness?" *Trends in Cog. Sci.* 22 (1999): 273–280.
91. Ibid.
92. S. F. Berkovic and O. K. Steinlein, "Genetic partial epilepsies," *Adv. Neurol.* 79 (1999): 375–381.
93. M. Cordero-Erausquin et al., "Nicotinic function: New perspectives from knockout mice," *Trends Pharmacol. Sci.* 21 (2000): 211–217.
94. G. Celesia and H. H. Jasper, "Acetylcholine released from the cerebral cortex in relation to its state of activation," *Neurobiology* 16 (1966): 1053–1064.
95. D. A. Silbersweig et al., "A functional neuroanatomy of hallucinations in schizophrenia," *Nature* 378 (1995): 176–179.
96. Daniel L. Schachter, ed., *Memory Distortion: How Minds, Brains, and Societies Reconstruct the Past* (Cambridge, Mass.: Harvard University Press, 1995); Daniel L. Schachter, *The Seven Sins of Memory: How the Mind Forgets and Remembers* (Boston: Houghton Mifflin, 2001).

97. Frederic C. Bartlett: *Remembering: A Study in Experimental and Social Psychology* (Cambridge: Cambridge University Press, 1932).
98. D. L. Schachter et al., "Memory consciousness and neuroimaging," *Phil. Trans. Roy. Soc. Lond. B.* 353 (1998): 1861–78.
99. S. Kosslyn et al., "Neural foundations of imagery," *Nat. Rev. Neurosci.* 2 (2001): 635–642.
100. H. Tomita et al., "Top-down signal from prefrontal cortex in executive control of memory retrieval," *Nature* 401 (1999): 699–703.
101. I. Hasegawa et al., "Callosal window between prefrontal cortices: Cognitive interaction to retrieve long-term memories," *Science* 281 (1998): 814–818.
102. B. Kast, "Decisions, decisions . . . ," *Nature* 411 (2001): 471–488.
103. Cooper and Shallice, "Contentions scheduling and the control of routine activities."
104. O. Houdé et al., "Shifting from the perceptual brain to the logical brain: The neural impact of cognitive inhibition training," *J. Cogn. Neurosci.* 12 (2000): 721–728.
105. T. Gisiger et al., "Computational models of association cortex," *Curr. Opin. Neurobiol.* 10 (2000): 250–259; Immanuel Kant, *Critique of Pure Reason,* trans. Norman Kemp Smith (New York: St. Martin's, 1965), B 87.
106. Zelazo and Zelazo, "Emergence of consciousness."
107. Ibid.
108. Barresi and Moore, "Intentional relation and social understanding."
109. T. Nagel, "What is it like to be a bat?" *Philo. Rev.* 83 (1974): 435–450.
110. Barresi and Moore, "Intentional relation and social understanding."
111. Fuster, *Prefrontal Cortex.*

4. Knowledge and Social Life

1. Wittgenstein, *Philosophical Investigations,* trans. G. E. M. Anscombe, 3rd ed. (London: Blackwell, 2001), §43.
2. *The Collected Papers of Charles Sanders Peirce,* ed. Charles Hartshorne et al., 8 vols. (Cambridge, Mass.: Harvard University Press, 1931–1958), esp. vol. 2: *Elements of Logic,* ch. 2.
3. Ferdinand de Saussure, *Cours de linguistique générale,* ed. Tullio de Mauro (Paris: Payot, 1972).
4. Saussure, *Cours de linguistique générale,* 101.
5. Ibid., 38.
6. F. J. Gall, *On the Functions of the Brain and of Each of Its Parts,* trans. Winslow Lewis (Boston: Marsh, Capen and Lyon, 1835).
7. P. Broca, "Nouvelle observation d'aphémie produite par une lésion de la 3ème circonvolution frontale," *Bull. Soc. Anatomie* 6, 2d ser. (1861): 398–407.
8. Paul Wernicke, *Der Aphasische Symptomenkomplex: Eine psychologische Studie auf anatomischer Basis* (Breslau: Cohn, 1874).
9. Quoted in Olivier Sabouraud, *Le Langage et ses maux* (Paris: Odile Jacob,

1995). [This is only one of many imaginable translations of an altogether nonsensical text in the French: "Les costelles qui se frenent, ici un sacrène, deux enfourches à jampié, deux zénes sobe, un chandier qui met le clistone."—Trans.]

10. L. Lichtheim, "Ueber Aphasie," *Deutsches Archiv fuer klinische Medizin* 36 (1885): 204–268; also published in English as "On Aphasia," *Brain* 7 (1885): 433–484.
11. Peirce, *Collected Papers,* 2:2.
12. Rosaleen A. McCarthy and Elizabeth K. Warrington, *Cognitive Neuropsychology: A Clinical Introduction* (San Diego: Academic Press, 1990); Tim Shallice, *From Neuropsychology to Mental Structure* (Cambridge: Cambridge University Press, 1988).
13. John Hughlings Jackson, *Selected Writings,* ed. James Taylor, 2 vols. (London: Hodder and Stoughton, 1932–1933).
14. Wittgenstein, *Tractatus Logico-Philosophicus,* trans. D. F. Pears and B. F. McGuinness (London; Routledge, 1994), 1.1.
15. P. Bloom, "Some issues in the evolution of language and thought," in Denise D. Cummins and Colin Allen, eds., *The Evolution of Mind* (Oxford: Oxford University Press, 1998).
16. Sabouraud, *Le Langage et ses maux.*
17. B. M. Mazoyer et al., "The cortical representation of speech," *J. Cogn. Neurosci.* 4 (1997): 467–479.
18. M. Dapretto and S. Bookheimer, "Formal content: Dissociating syntax and semantics in sentence comprehension," *Neuron* 24 (1999): 427–432.
19. Mazoyer et al., "Cortical representation of speech."
20. L. Bianchi, "The functions of the frontal lobes," *Brain* 18 (1895): 497–530.
21. M. Novak et al., "The evolution of syntactic communication," *Nature* 404 (2000): 495–498.
22. Claude E. Shannon and Warren Weaver, *The Mathematical Theory of Communication* (Urbana: University of Illinois Press, 1949). On the influence of this theory see Jean-Pierre Dupuy, *The Mechanization of the Mind: On the Origins of Cognitive Science,* trans. M. B. DeBevoise (Princeton: Princeton University Press, 2000).
23. Jean-Pierre Changeux and Paul Ricoeur, *What Makes Us Think? A Neuroscientist and a Philosopher Argue about Ethics, Human Nature, and the Brain,* trans. M. B. DeBevoise (Princeton: Princeton University Press, 2000), 132–133.
24. Dan Sperber and Deirdre Wilson, *Relevance: Communication and Cognition,* 2d ed. (1986; Oxford: Blackwell, 1995).
25. L. S. Vygotsky, *Thought and Language,* ed. and trans. Eugenia Hanfmann and Gertrude Vakar (Cambridge, Mass.: MIT Press, 1962); quoted by Sperber and Wilson, *Relevance,* 6.
26. Sperber and Wilson, *Relevance,* 46.

27. See H. P. Grice, "Meaning," *Philosophical Rev.* 66 (1957): 377–388.
28. Noam Chomsky, *Cartesian Linguistics: A Chapter in the History of Rationalist Thought* (New York: Harper and Row, 1966).
29. J.-P. Changeux and S. Dehaene, "Neuronal models of cognitive functions," *Cognition* 33 (1989): 63–109.
30. G. Rizzolatti et al., "Neurons related to reaching-grasping arm movements in the rostral part of area 6 (area 6a)," *Exp. Brain Res.* 82 (1990): 337–350; G. Rizzolatti and M. A. Arbib, "Language within our grasp," *Trends Neurosci.* 21 (1998): 188–194.
31. Rizzolatti and Arbib, "Language within our grasp."
32. Samuel Alexander, *Space, Time, and Deity: The Gifford Lectures at Glasgow, 1916–1918,* 2 vols. (London: Macmillan, 1920). I thank Anne Fagot-Largeault for having called this book to my attention.
33. C. Frith and U. Frith, "Interacting worlds: A biological basis," *Science* 286 (1999): 1692–95.
34. J. Barresi and C. Moore, "Intentional relation and social understanding," *Behav. Brain Sc.* 19 (1996): 107–154.
35. Daniel C. Dennett, *The Intentional Stance* (Cambridge, Mass.: MIT Press/ Bradford Books, 1987); Frith and Frith, "Interacting worlds."
36. P. R. Zelazo and P. D. Zelazo, "The emergence of consciousness," in Herbert H. Jasper et al., eds., *Consciousness: At the Frontiers of Neuroscience* (Philadelphia: Lippincott-Raven, 1998), 149–163.
37. S. Baron-Cohen, "Mechanical, behavioral and intentional understanding of picture stories in autistic children," *Brit. J. Dev. Psychol.* 4 (1986): 113–125.
38. Frith and Frith, "Interacting worlds."
39. Antonio R. Damasio, *The Feeling of What Happens: Body and Emotion in the Making of Consciousness* (New York: Harcourt Brace, 1999).
40. P. Ruby and J. Decety, "Effect of subjective perspective-taking during simulation of action: A PET investigation of agency," *Nat. Neurosci.* 4 (2001): 546–550.
41. Frith and Frith, "Interacting worlds."
42. J. K. Hietanen and D. I. Perrett, "Motion-sensitive cells in the macaque superior temporal polysensory area: 1. Lack of response to the sight of the animal's own limb movement," *Exp. Brain Res.* 93 (1993): 117–128.
43. K. Shima et al., "Two movement-related foci in the primate cingulate cortex observed in signal-triggered and self-paced forelimb movement," *J. Neurophysiol.* 65 (1991): 188–202; Frith and Frith, "Interacting worlds."
44. M. Jeannerod, "Neural simulation of action: A unifying mechanism for motor cognition," *Neuroimage* 14 (2001): 103–109.
45. See H. P. Grice, "Logic and Conversation," in Peter Cole and Jerry L. Morgan, eds., *Syntax and Semantics,* vol. 3: *Speech Acts* (New York: Academic Press, 1975): 41–58.

46. Paul Ricoeur, *Soi-même comme un autre* (Paris: Seuil, 1990).
47. André Lwoff, *Jeux et combats* (Paris: Fayard, 1981).
48. Dorothy L. Cheney and Robert M. Seyfarth, *How Monkeys See the World: Inside the Mind of Another Species* (Chicago: University of Chicago Press, 1990).
49. J.-P. Changeux and A. Danchin, "Selective stabilization of developing synapses as a mechanism for the specification of neuronal networks," *Nature* 264 (1976): 705–712.
50. J.-P. Changeux, "Cours: Jeux de langage et épigenèse neuronale," *Annuaire du Collège de France,* 2001.
51. Bénédicte de Boysson-Bardies, *How Language Comes to Children: From Birth to Two Years,* trans. M. B. DeBevoise (Cambridge, Mass.: MIT Press/Bradford Books, 1999).
52. F. Ramus et al., "Language discrimination by human newborns and by cotton-top tamarin monkeys," *Science* 288 (2000): 349–351.
53. P. D. Eimas, "Auditory and phonetic coding of the cues for speech: Discrimination of the [r-l] distinction by young infants," *Perception and Psychophysics* 18 (1975): 341–347.
54. P. Kuhl et al., "Linguistic experience alters phonetic perception in infants by six months of age," *Science* 255 (1992): 606–608; A. J. Doupe and P. Kuhl, "Bird song and human speech: Common theories and mechanisms," *Annu. Rev. Neurosci.* 22 (1999): 567–631.
55. P. Marler and S. Peters, "Developmental overproduction and selective attrition: New process in the epigenesis of bird song," *Dev. Psychobiol.* 15 (1982): 369–378. See also Jean-Pierre Changeux, *Neuronal Man: The Biology of Mind,* trans. Laurence Garey, intro. Vernon B. Mountcastle (Princeton: Princeton University Press, 1997), 242–244; S. Dehaene et al., "Neural networks that learn temporal sequences by selection," *Proc. Natl. Acad. Sci. USA* 84 (1987): 2727–31; Doupe and Kuhl, "Bird song and human speech."
56. J.-P. Changeux et al., "A theory of the epigenesis of neural networks by selective stabilization of synapses," *Proc. Natl. Acad. Sci. USA* 70 (1973): 2974–78; Changeux and Danchin, "Selective stabilization of developing synapses."
57. E. S. Spelke and S. J. Hespos, "Continuity, competence, and the object concept," in Emmanuel Dupoux, ed., *Language, Brain, and Cognitive Development: Essays in Honor of Jacques Mehler* (Cambridge, Mass.: MIT Press, 2001), 325–341; Bloom, "Some issues in the evolution of language and thought."
58. N. Herschkowitz et al., "Neurobiological bases of behavioral development in the first year," *Neuropediatrics* 28 (1997): 296–306; Herschkowitz et al., "Neurobiological bases of behavioral development in the second year," *Neuropediatrics* 30 (1999): 221–230.
59. Ibid.

60. Michael Tomasello, *The Cultural Origins of Human Cognition* (Cambridge, Mass.: Harvard University Press, 1999).
61. P. W. Jusczyk et al., "Perception of acoustic correlates of major phrasal units by young infants," *Cog. Psych.* 24 (1992): 252–293; Peter W. Jusczyk, *The Discovery of Spoken Language* (Cambridge, Mass.: MIT Press/Bradford Books, 1997).
62. Boysson-Bardies, *How Language Comes to Children;* Alec Marantz, *No Escape from Syntax* (Cambridge, Mass.: MIT Press, 1997).
63. L. Rizzi, "Learning by Forgetting in Syntax," in Dupoux, ed., *Language, Brain, and Cognitive Development.*
64. B. L. Schlaggar et al., "Functional neuroanatomical differences between adults and school-age children in the processing of single words," *Science* 296 (2002): 1476–79.
65. Patricia Churchland and Terrence J. Sejnowski, *The Computational Brain* (Cambridge, Mass: MIT Press/Bradford Books, 1992).
66. I am currently working on this problem in collaboration with Michel Kerszberg.
67. Dehaene et al., "Neural networks that learn temporal sequences."
68. A. M. Leslie, "The perception of causality in infants," *Perception* 11 (1982): 173–186.
69. D. Premack, "The infant's theory of self-propelled objects," *Cognition* 36 (1990): 1–16.
70. Donald Davidson, *Essays on Actions and Events* (Oxford: Oxford University Press, 1980).
71. Dennett, *Intentional Stance.*
72. Lawrence Weiskrantz, ed., *Thought without Language* (Oxford: Clarendon Press, 1988).
73. Michel Blay, *Reasoning with the Infinite: From the Closed World to the Mathematical Universe,* trans. M. B. DeBevoise (Chicago: University of Chicago Press, 1998).
74. S. Dehaene and J.-P. Changeux, "Development of elementary numerical abilities: A neuronal model," *J. Cogn. Neurosci.* 5 (1989): 390–407.
75. S. Dehaene and L. Cohen, "Two mental calculation systems: A case study of severe acalculia with preserved approximation," *Neuropsychologia* 29 (1991): 1045–47.
76. Ibid.
77. Georges Ifrah, *Histoire universelle des chiffres* (Paris: Seghers, 1981); Stanislas Dehaene, *La Bosse des maths* (Paris: Odile Jacob, 1997).
78. G. F. Marcus et al., "Rule-learning in seven-month-old infants," *Science* 283 (1999): 606–609.
79. S. Dehaene et al., "A neuronal model of a global workspace in effortful cognitive tasks," *Proc. Natl. Acad. Sci. USA* 95 (1998): 14529–534.
80. Dehaene et al., "Neural networks that learn temporal sequences."

81. Ignace Meyerson, *Existe-t-il une nature humaine?* (Paris: Les Empêcheurs de Penser en Rond, 2000).
82. Davidson, *Actions and Events.*
83. See Changeux and Ricoeur, *What Makes Us Think?,* 212–222.

5. From Genes to Brain

1. See reports of the International Human Genome Sequencing Consortium: J. C. Venter et al., "The sequence of the human genome," *Science* 291 (2001): 1304–51; E. Lander et al., "Initial sequence and analysis of the human genome," *Nature* 409 (2001): 860–921.
2. Noam Chomsky, "Language and the Brain," paper delivered at a conference on cognitive science in Siena, Italy, 1999.
3. A. Goffeau et al., "Life with 6,000 genes," *Science* 274 (1996): 546, 563–567.
4. H. Schoof et al., "MIPS *Arabidopsis thaliana* Database (MAtDB): An integrated biological knowledge resource based on the first complete plant genome," *Nucleic Acids Res.* 30 (2002): 91–93.
5. *C. elegans* Sequencing Consortium, "Genome sequence of the nematode *C. elegans:* A platform for investigating biology," *Science* 282 (1998): 2012–18.
6. M. D. Adams et al., "The genome sequence of *Drosophila melanogaster,*" *Science* 287 (2000): 2185–95.
7. A. Bradley et al., "Mining the mouse genome," *Nature* 420 (2002): 512–514, 520–562.
8. Goffeau et al., "Life with 6,000 genes"; "Genome sequence of the nematode *C. elegans";* Adams et al., "Genome sequence of *Drosophila melanogaster.*"
9. Venter et al., "Sequence of the human genome"; Lander et al., "Initial sequence and analysis of the human genome."
10. S. Aparicio et al., "Whole-genome shotgun assembly and analysis of the genome of *Fugu rubripes,*" *Science* 297 (2002): 1301–10.
11. Bradley et al., "Mining the mouse genome."
12. Lander et al., "Initial sequence and analysis of the human genome."
13. R. De Rosa et al., "Hoxgenes in brachiopods and priapulids, and protostomes evolution," *Nature* 399 (1999): 772–776.
14. J.-P. Changeux, "Concluding remarks on the 'singularity' of nerve cells and its ontogenesis," *Prog. Brain Res.* 58 (1983): 465–478.
15. Ibid.
16. Ibid.; Vernon B. Mountcastle, *Perceptual Neuroscience: The Cerebral Cortex* (Cambridge, Mass.: Harvard University Press, 1998).
17. Bernard Dutrillaux, "Chromosomal evolution of the great apes and man," in R. V. Short and Barbara J. Weir, eds., *The Great Apes of Africa* (Colchester: Journal of Reproduction and Fertility, 1980); J. Yunis and O. Prakash, "The origin of man: A chromosomal pictorial legacy," *Science* 215 (1982): 1525–30.
18. H. Kaessmann et al., "Extensive nuclear DNA sequence diversity among

chimpanzees," *Science* 286 (1999): 1159–62; A. Gibbons, "Which of our genes make us human?" *Science* 281 (1998): 1432–34.

19. A. Fujiyama et al., "Construction and analysis of a human-chimpanzee comparative clone map," *Science* 295 (2002): 131–133.
20. Jean-Pierre Changeux, *Neuronal Man: The Biology of Mind,* trans. Laurence Garey, intro. Vernon B. Mountcastle (Princeton: Princeton University Press, 1997); Marc D. Hauser, *The Evolution of Communication* (Cambridge, Mass.: MIT Press, 1996); F. Aboitiz and R. Garcia, "The evolutionary origin of the language areas of the human brain: A neuroanatomical perspective," *Brain Res. Rev.* 25 (1997): 381–396.
21. J. P. Rauschecker et al., "Processing of complex sounds in the macaque nonprimary auditory cortex," *Science* 268 (1995): 111–114; Aboitiz and Garcia, "Evolutionary origin of the language areas of the human brain"; Terrence W. Deacon, *The Symbolic Species: The Co-Evolution of Language and the Brain* (New York: Norton, 1997).
22. R. L. Holloway, "Toward a synthetic theory of human brain evolution," in Jean-Pierre Changeux and Jean Chavaillon, eds., *Origins of the Human Brain* (Oxford: Oxford University Press, 1995); Hauser, *Evolution of Communication.*
23. See A. Fagot-Largeault, "L'Émergence," in Daniel Andler et al., *Philosophie des Sciences,* 2 vols. (Paris: Gallimard, 2002), 2:939–1048.
24. Peter A. Lawrence, *The Making of a Fly: The Genetics of Animal Design* (Boston: Blackwell, 1992); W. Driever and C. Nüsslein-Volhard, "The bicoid protein determines position in the *Drosophila* embryo in a concentration-dependent manner," *Cell* 54 (1988): 83–93.
25. Venter et al., "Sequence of the human genome."
26. D. Arendt and K. Nübler-Jung, "Comparison of early nerve cord development in insects and invertebrates," *Development* 126 (1999): 2309–25.
27. R. Beddington and E. Robertson, "Axis development and early asymmetry in mammals," *Cell* 96 (1999): 195–209.
28. Arendt and Nübler-Jung, "Comparison of early nerve cord development."
29. Ibid.
30. Geoffroy Saint-Hilaire, *Philosophie anatomique* (Paris, 1818), 18–19.
31. D. Arendt and K. Nübler-Jung, "Dorsal or ventral: Similarities in fate maps and gastrulation patterns in annelids, arthropods, and chordates," *Mechanisms of Development* 61 (1997): 7–21.
32. Arendt and Nübler-Jung, "Comparison of early nerve cord development."
33. Beddington and Robertson, "Axis development and early asymmetry in mammals."
34. J.-M. Claverie, "What if there are only 30,000 genes?" *Science* 291 (2001): 1255–57.
35. A. Turing, "The chemical basis of morphogenesis," *Phil. Trans. Roy. Soc. B.* 237 (1952): 37–72.

36. Ilya Prigogine and D. K. Kondepudi, *Modern Thermodynamics: From Heat Engines to Dissipative Structures* (New York: Wiley, 1998).
37. R. Meinhardt and A. Gierer, "Application of the theory of biological pattern formation based on lateral inhibition," *J. Cell Sci.* 15 (1974): 321–346; M. Freeman, "Feedback control of intercellular signalling in development," *Nature* 389 (2000): 334–335.
38. J. Monod and F. Jacob, "Concluding remarks: Teleonomic mechanisms in cellular metabolism, growth, and differentiation," *Cold Spring Harbor Symp. Quant. Biol.* 26 (1961): 389.
39. J. Monod et al., "Allosteric proteins and cellular control systems," *J. Mol. Biol.* 6 (1963): 306–329.
40. C. Bell and M. Lewis, "A closer view of the conformation of the Lac repressor bound to operator," *Nat. Struct. Biol.* 7 (2000): 209–214.
41. M. Mannervik et al., "Transcriptional coregulators in development," *Science* 284 (1999): 606–609.
42. M. Kerszberg and J.-P. Changeux, "A model for motor endplate morphogenesis: Diffusible morphogens, transmembrane signalling and compartmentalized gene expression," *Neural Comput.* 5 (1993): 341–358.
43. J.-P. Changeux and S. Edelstein, "Allosteric receptors after 30 years," *Neuron* 21 (1998): 959–980.
44. L. Schaeffer et al., "Implication of a multisubunit Ets-related transcription factor in synaptic expression of the nicotinic acetylcholine receptor," *EMBO J.* 17 (1998): 3078–90.
45. Kerszberg and Changeux, "Model for motor endplate morphogenesis."
46. Freeman, "Feedback control of intercellular signalling."
47. See Charles Manning Child, *Patterns and Problems of Development* (Chicago: University of Chicago Press, 1941).
48. Lawrence, *Making of a Fly;* Driever and Nüsslein-Volhard, "Bicoid protein determines position in the *Drosophila* embryo."
49. M. Kerszberg and J.-P. Changeux, "A model for reading morphogenetic gradients: Autocatalysis and competition at the gene level," *Proc. Natl. Acad. Sci. USA* 91 (1994): 5823–27; M. Kerszberg and J.-P. Changeux, "Partners make patterns in morphogenesis," *Current Biol.* 4 (1994): 1046–47.
50. Kerszberg and Changeux, "Partners make patterns in morphogenesis"; R. White, "Homeotic genes seek partners," *Curr. Biol.* 4 (1994): 751–758.
51. P. Smolen et al., "Mathematical modeling of gene networks," *Neuron* 26 (2000): 567–580.
52. Mannervik et al., "Transcriptional coregulators"; A. Carmena et al., "Combinatorial signaling codes for the progressive determination of cell fates in the *Drosophila* embryonic mesoderm," *Genes and Development* 12 (1998): 3910–22; M. S. Halfon et al., "Ras pathway specificity is determined by the integration of multiple signal-activated and tissue-restricted transcription factors," *Cell* 103 (2000): 63–74.

53. M. Hoch et al., "Gene expression mediated by cis-acting sequences of the Kruppel gene in response to the *Drosophila* morphogens bicoid and hunchback," *EMBO J.* 10 (1991): 2267–78.
54. See, e.g., M. Fromont-Racine et al., "Genome-wide protein-interaction screens reveal functional networks involving Sm-like proteins," *Yeast* 17 (2000): 95–110.
55. E. Davidson et al., "A genomic regulatory network for development," *Science* 295 (2002): 1669–78.
56. Smolen et al., "Mathematical modeling of gene networks."
57. J. Lisman and J. F. Fallon, "What maintains memories," *Science* 283 (1999): 339–340; Freeman, "Feedback control of intercellular signalling."
58. S. A. Chervitz et al., "Comparison of the complete protein sets of worm and yeast: Orthology and difference," *Science* 282 (1998): 2022–28.
59. Venter et al., "Sequence of the human genome."
60. Changeux, *Neuronal Man,* 264–268.
61. M. Kerszberg and J.-P. Changeux, "A simple molecular model of neurulation," *BioEssays* 20 (1998): 758–770.
62. Ibid.; Freeman, "Feedback control of intercellular signalling."
63. Kerszberg and Changeux, "Simple molecular model of neurulation."
64. Gerald M. Edelman, *Topobiology: An Introduction to Molecular Embryology* (New York: Basic Books, 1988).
65. Changeux, *Neuronal Man,* 263; Mountcastle, *Perceptual Neuroscience.*
66. A. Rockell et al., "The basic uniformity in structure of the neocortex," *Brain* 103 (1980): 221–224.
67. P. Rakic, "Specifications of cerebral cortical areas," *Science* 241 (1988): 170–176.
68. See M. Brunet et al., "A new hominid from the Upper Miocene of Chad, Central Africa," *Nature* 418 (2002): 145–151.
69. Changeux, *Neuronal Man,* 265–266.
70. See T. Inoue et al., "Fate mapping of the mouse prosencephalic neural plate," *Developmental Biology* 219 (200): 373–383.
71. A. Chenn and C. Walsh, "Regulation of cerebral cortical size by control of cell cycle exit in neural precursors," *Science* 297 (2002): 365–369.
72. L. Luca Cavalli-Sforza et al., *The History and Geography of Human Genes* (Princeton: Princeton University Press, 1994).
73. G. M. Rubin et al., "Comparative genomics of the eukaryotes," *Science* 287 (2000): 2204–15.
74. Lander et al., "Initial sequence and analysis of the human genome"; Venter et al., "Sequence of the human genome."
75. J. Nathan et al., "Molecular genetics of human colour vision: The genes encoding blue, green and red pigments," *Science* 232 (1986): 193–202.
76. L. Young et al., "Increased affiliative response to vasopressin in mice expressing the V_{1a} receptor from a monogamous role," *Nature* 400 (1999): 766–

768; T. Insel and L. Young, "Neuropeptides and the evolution of social behavior," *Curr. Op. Neurobiol.* 10 (2000): 784–789.

77. Dan Sperber and Deirdre Wilson, *Relevance: Communication and Cognition,* 2d ed. (1986; Oxford: Blackwell, 1995).
78. S. E. Fisher et al., "A quantitative-trait locus on chromosome 6p influences different aspects of developmental dyslexia," *Am. J. Hum. Genet.* 64 (1999): 146–156; J. Gayán et al., "Quantitative-trait locus for specific language and reading deficits on chromosome 6p," *Am. J. Hum. Genet.* 64 (1999): 157–164.
79. See Steven Pinker, *The Language Instinct* (New York: William Morrow, 1994).
80. C. S. Lai et al., "A forkhead-domain gene is mutated in a severe speech and language disorder," *Nature* 413 (2001): 519–523.
81. W. Enard et al., "Molecular evolution of $FoxP_2$, a gene involved in speech and language," *Nature* 4181 (2002): 869–972.
82. E. Meaburn et al., "Language-impaired children: No sign of the FOXP2 mutation," *NeuroReport* 13 (2002): 1075–77.
83. B. Wood, "Human evolution," *BioEssays* 18 (1996): 945–954.
84. N. Herschkowitz et al., "Neurobiological bases of behavioral development in the first year," *Neuropediatrics* 28 (1997): 296–306.
85. Mark H. Johnson and John Morton, *Biology and Cognitive Development: The Case of Face Recognition* (Oxford: Blackwell, 1991).
86. Elizabeth Spelke et al., "Infant's knowledge of object motion and human action," in Dan Sperber et al., eds., *Causal Cognition: A Multi-Disciplinary Approach* (Oxford: Clarendon Press, 1995), 44–78.
87. M. D. Hauser and S. Carey, "Building a cognitive creature from a set of primitives," in Denise D. Cummins and Colin Allen, eds., *The Evolution of Mind* (Oxford: Oxford University Press, 1998), 51–106.
88. A. M. Leslie, "A theory of agency," in Sperber et al., eds., *Causal Cognition,* 121–149; D. Premack and A. J. Premack, "Intention as psychological cause," ibid., 185–200.
89. P. Kuhl et al., "Linguistic experience alters phonetic perception in infants by six months of age," *Science* 255 (1992): 606–608.
90. Bénédicte de Boysson-Bardies, *How Language Comes to Children: From Birth to Two Years,* trans. M. B. DeBevoise (Cambridge, Mass.: MIT Press/Bradford Books, 1999).
91. R. Lewontin, "An invitation to cognitive science," in Daniel N. Osherson and Edward E. Smith, eds., *Invitation to Cognitive Science,* vol. 3: *Thinking* (Cambridge, Mass.: MIT Press, 1990).

6. Neuronal Epigenesis and Cultural Evolution

1. See J.-P. Changeux et al., "A theory of the epigenesis of neural networks by selective stabilization of synapses," *Proc. Natl. Acad. Sci. USA* 70 (1973): 2974–78; Gerald M. Edelman and Vernon B. Mountcastle, *The Mindful*

Brain: Cortical Organization and the Group-Selective Theory of Higher Brain Function (Cambridge, Mass.: MIT Press, 1978); J. Lichtman and H. Colman, "Synapse elimination and memory," *Neuron* 36 (2000): 269–278.

2. The term "genetics," first proposed by William Bateson in 1905, was formally adopted two years later on the occasion of the first international congress of researchers in this field.
3. See Stephen J. Gould, *The Mismeasure of Man* (1981; rev. and exp. ed., New York: Norton, 1996).
4. M. K. Hasnain et al., "Intersubject variability of functional areas in the human visual cortex," *Human Brain Mapping* 6 (1998): 301–315.
5. H. Steinmetz et al., "Brain asymmetry in monozygotic twins," *Cereb. Cortex* 5 (1995): 296–300; M. J. Traino et al., "Brain size, head size and intelligence quotient in monozygotic twins," *Neurobiology* 50 (1998): 1246–52; D. W. Kee et al., "Multi-task analysis of cerebral hemisphere specialization in monozygotic twins discordant for handedness," *Neuropsychology* 12 (1998): 468–478.
6. I. E. Sommer et al., "Language lateralization in monozygotic twin pairs concordant and discordant for handedness," *Brain* 125 (2002): 2710–18; M. A. Eckert et al., "The epigenesis of planum temporale asymmetry in twins," *Cereb. Cortex* 12 (2002): 749–755; T. White et al., "Brain volumes and surface morphology in monozygotic twins," *Cereb. Cortex* 12 (2002): 486–493; P. M. Thompson et al., "Genetic influences on brain structure," *Nat. Neurosci.* 4 (2001): 1253–58.
7. E. Macagno et al., "Structural development of neuronal connections in isogenic organisms: Variations and similarities in the optic system of *Daphnia magna*," *Proc. Natl. Acad. Sci. USA* 70 (1973): 57–61.
8. F. Levinthal et al., "Anatomy and development of identified cells in isogenic organisms," *Cold Spring Harbor Symp. Quant. Biol.* 40 (1976): 321–331.
9. V. Drescher et al., "*In vitro* guidance of retinal ganglion cell axions by RAGS: A 25 kDa tectal protein related to ligands for Eph receptor tyrosine kinases," *Cell* 82 (1995): 359–370; D. O'Leary et al., "Molecular development of sensory maps: Representing sights and cells in the brain," *Cell* 96 (1999): 255–269.
10. K. Brose and M. Tessier-Lavigne, "Slit proteins: Key regulators of axon guidance, axonal branching and cell migration," *Curr. Opin. Neurobiol.* 10 (2000): 95–102.
11. J.-P. Bourgeois and P. Rakic, "Changes in synaptic density in the primary visual cortex of the macaque monkey from fetal to adult stage," *J. Neurosci.* 13 (1993): 2801–20; J.-P. Bourgeois, "Synaptogenesis in the neocortex of the newborn: The ultimate frontier for individuation," in Hugo Lagercrantz et al., eds., *The Newborn Brain: Neuroscience and Clinical Applications* (Cambridge: Cambridge University Press, 2002); P. Huttenlocher and A.

Dabholkar, "Regional difference in synaptogenesis in human cerebral cortex," *J. Comp. Neurol.* 387 (1997): 167–178.

12. J.-P. Bourgeois, "Synaptogenesis, heteronomy, and epigenesis in the mammalian neocortex," *Acta Paediatr. Suppl.* 422 (1997): 27–33.
13. M. Barinaga, "A critical issue for the brain," *Science* 288 (2000): 2116–19.
14. Wilhelm T. Preyer, *Spezielle Physiologie des Embryo: Untersuchungen ueber die Lebenserscheinungen vor der Geburt* (Leipzig: Grieben, 1885).
15. V. Hamburger, "Cell death in the development of the lateral motor column of the chick embryo," *J. Comp. Neurol.* 160 (1975): 535–546.
16. K. Kuida et al., "Decreased apoptosis in the brain and premature lethality in CPP32-deficient mice," *Nature* 384 (1996): 368–372; K. Kuida et al., "Reduced apoptosis and cytochrome c-mediated caspase activation in mice lacking caspase 9," *Cell* 94 (1998): 325–337.
17. J. C. Venter et al., "The sequence of the human genome," *Science* 291 (2001): 1304–51.
18. P. Nicotera et al., "Neuronal cell death: A demise with different shapes," *Trends Pharmacol.* 20 (1999): 46–51.
19. P. Benoît and J.-P. Changeux, "Consequences of tenotomy on the evolution of multi-innervation in developing rat soleus muscle," *Brain Res.* 99 (1975): 354–358; P. Benoît and J.-P. Changeux, "Consequences of blocking nerve activity on the evolution of multi-innervation at the regenerating neuromuscular junction of the rat," *Brain Res.* 149 (1978): 89–96; Lichtman and Colman, "Synapse elimination and memory."
20. D. Purves and J. W. Lichtman, "Elimination of synapses in the developing nervous system," *Science* 20 (1980): 153–157.
21. F. Crépel et al., "Evidence for a multiple innervation of Purkinje cells by climbing fibres in the immature rat cerebellum," *J. Neurobiol.* 7 (1976): 567–578; J.-P. Changeux and M. Mikoshiba, "Genetic and 'epigenetic' factors regulating synapse formation in vertebrate cerebellum and neuromuscular junction," *Prog. Brain Res.* 48 (1978): 43–64; M. Kano et al., "Persistent multiple climbing fiber innervation of cerebellar Purkinje cells in mice lacking mGluR1," *Neuron* 18 (1997): 71–79.
22. T. N. Wiesel and D. Hubel, "Effects of visual deprivation on morphology and physiology of cells in the cat's lateral geniculate body," *J. Neurophysiol.* 26 (1963): 978–993.
23. L. C. Katz and C. J. Shatz, "Synaptic activity and the construction of cortical circuits," *Science* 274 (1996): 1133–38; D. W. Sretavan and C. J. Shatz, "Prenatal development of retinal ganglion cell axons: Segregation into eye-specific layers within the cat's lateral geniculate nucleus," *J. Neurosci.* 6 (1986): 234–251.
24. Katz and Shatz, "Synaptic activity and the construction of cortical circuits."
25. R. Levi-Montalcini, "The nerve-growth factor: 35 years later," *Science* 237

(1987): 1154–62; Y. A. Barde, "The nerve-growth factor family," *Progr. Growth Factor Res.* 2 (1990): 237–248; H. Thoenen, "Neurotrophins and neuronal plasticity," *Science* 270 (1995): 593–598; L. I. Zhang et al., "A critical window for cooperation and competition among retinotectal synapses," *Nature* 395 (1998): 37–44.

26. L. Maffei et al., "Nerve growth factor (NGF) prevents the shift in ocular dominance distribution of visual cortical neurons in monocularity-deprived rats," *J. Neurosci.* 12 (1992): 4651–62; R. J. Cabelli et al., "Inhibition of ocular dominance column formation by infusion of NT4/5 or BDNF," *Science* 267 (1995): 380–400.
27. A. M. Lohof et al., "Potentiation of developing neuromuscular synapses by the neurotrophins NT-3 and BDNF," *Nature* 363 (1993): 350–353.
28. Q. T. Nguyen et al., "Hyperinnervation of neuromuscular junctions caused by GDNF overexpression in muscle," *Science* 279 (1998): 1725–29.
29. Thoenen, "Neurotrophins and neuronal plasticity"; A. F. Schinder and M.-M. Poo, "The neurotrophic hypothesis for synaptic plasticity," *Trends in Cog. Sci.* 23 (2000): 639–645.
30. Jean-Pierre Changeux, *Neuronal Man: The Biology of Mind,* trans. Laurence Garey, intro. Vernon B. Mountcastle (Princeton: Princeton University Press, 1997), 220–223, 248–249.
31. M. Verhage et al., "Synaptic assembly of the brain in the absence of neurotransmitter secretion," *Science* 287 (2000): 864–869.
32. Changeux et al., "Theory of the epigenesis of neural networks"; Changeux, *Neuronal Man,* 227–228; M. Kerszberg and J.-P. Changeux, "A model for reading morphogenetic gradients: Autocatalysis and competition at the gene level," *Proc. Natl. Acad. Sci. USA* 91 (1994): 5823–27. See also A. E. Harris et al., "A model of ocular dominance column development by competition for trophic factors," *Proc. Natl. Acad. Sci. USA* 94 (1997): 9944–49; T. Elliott and N. R. Shabold, "Competition for neurotrophic factors: Mathematical analysis," *Neural Computation* 10 (1998): 1939–81; K. Miller, "Equivalence of a sprouting-and-retraction model and correlation-based plasticity models of neural development," *Neural Computation* 10 (1998): 529–547.
33. Changeux, *Neuronal Man,* 65.
34. J.-P. Changeux and A. Danchin, "Selective stabilization of developing synapses as a mechanism for the specification of neuronal networks," *Nature* 264 (1976): 705–712; J.-L. Gouzé et al., "Selective stabilization of muscle innervation during development: A mathematical model," *Biol. Cybern.* 46 (1983): 207–215; Nguyen et al., "Hyperinnervation of neuromuscular junctions"; P. R. Montague et al., "Spatial signalling in the development and function of neural connections," *Cereb. Cortex* 1 (1991): 199–220.
35. Schinder and Poo, "Neurotrophic hypothesis for synaptic plasticity."
36. David Hume, *A Treatise of Human Nature,* ed. L. A. Selby-Bigge, 2nd ed. (Oxford: Clarendon Press, 1978), 11.

37. E. Bienenstock et al., "Theory for the development of neuron selectivity: Orientation specificity and binocular interaction in visual cortex," *J. Neurosci.* 2 (1982): 32–48.
38. E. Quinlan et al., "Bidirectional, experience-dependent regulation of N-methyl D aspartate receptor subunit composition in the rat visual cortex during postnatal development," *Proc. Natl. Acad. Sci. USA* 96 (1999): 12876–880.
39. M. Kerszberg et al., "Stabilization of complex input-output functions in neural clusters formed by synapse selection," *Neural Networks* 5 (1992): 403–413.
40. R. Durbin and G. Mitchison, "A dimension-reduction framework for understanding cortical maps," *Nature* 343 (1990): 644–647; O. Sporns et al., "Reentrant signaling among simulated neuronal groups leads to coherence in their oscillatory activity," *Proc. Natl. Acad. Sci. USA* 86 (1989): 7265–69; G. Tononi et al., "Reentry and the problem of integrating multiple cortical areas: Simulation of dynamic integration in the visual system," *Cerebral Cortex* 2 (1992): 310–335; E. D. Lumer et al., "Neural dynamics in a model of the thalamocortical system, part 1: Layers, loops and the emergence of fast synchronous rhythms," *Cereb. Cortex* 7 (1997): 207–227.
41. Kerszberg et al., "Stabilization of complex input-output functions."
42. T. Hensch et al., "Local GABA circuit control of experience-dependent plasticity in developing visual cortex," *Science* 282 (1998): 1504–08.
43. E. Kandel and L. Tauc, "Mechanisms of prolonged laterosynaptic facilitation," *Nature* 202 (1964): 145–147.
44. See Changeux, *Neuronal Man,* 229–249.
45. Changeux et al., "Theory of the epigenesis of neural networks."
46. See Gerald M. Edelman and Giulio Tononi, *A Universe of Consciousness: How Matter Becomes Imagination* (New York: Basic Books, 2000).
47. Tim Shallice, *From Neuropsychology to Mental Structure* (Cambridge: Cambridge University Press, 1988).
48. Philip N. Johnson-Laird, *Mental Models: Towards a Cognitive Science of Language, Inference, and Consciousness* (Cambridge: Cambridge University Press, 1983), 9; see also Jerry A. Fodor, *The Language of Thought* (Cambridge, Mass.: Harvard University Press, 1979).
49. N. Chomsky, "Language and nature," *Mind* 104 (1995): 1–61.
50. Jerry A. Fodor, *The Modularity of Mind: An Essay in Faculty Psychology* (Cambridge, Mass.: MIT Press/Bradford Books, 1983).
51. Changeux, *Neuronal Man,* 220–223.
52. P. Marler and S. Peters, "Developmental overproduction and selective attrition: New process in the epigenesis of bird song," *Dev. Psychobiol.* 15 (1982): 369–378.
53. A. J. Doupe and P. Kuhl, "Bird song and human speech: Common theories and mechanisms," *Annu. Rev. Neurosci.* 22 (1999): 567–631.

54. P. D. Eimas, "Auditory and phonetic coding of the cues for speech: Discrimination of the [r-l] distinction by young infants," *Perception and Psychophysics* 18 (1975): 341–347.
55. P. Kuhl et al., "Linguistic experience alters phonetic perception in infants by six months of age," *Science* 255 (1992): 606–608.
56. W. D. Gaillard et al., "Cortical localization of reading in normal children: An fMRI language study," *Neurology* 57 (2001): 47–54; W. D. Gaillard et al., "Functional anatomy of cognitive development: fMRI of verbal fluency in children and adults," *Neurology* 54 (2000): 180–185.
57. Bénédicte de Boysson-Bardies, *How Language Comes to Children: From Birth to Two Years,* trans. M. B. DeBevoise (Cambridge, Mass.: MIT Press/Bradford Books, 1999).
58. S. Dehaene et al., "Anatomical variability in the cortical representation of first and second language," *NeuroReport* 17 (1997): 3775–78.
59. K. Kim et al., "Distinct cortical areas associated with native and second languages," *Nature* 388 (1997): 171–174.
60. A. Castro-Caldas et al., "The illiterate brain," *Brain* 121 (1998): 1053–63.
61. A. Castro-Caldas and A. Reis, "Neurological substrates of illiteracy," *Neuroscientist* 6 (2000): 475–482.
62. Castro-Caldas et al., "The illiterate brain."
63. Shallice, *From Neuropsychology to Mental Structure.*
64. Castro-Caldas et al., "The illiterate brain."
65. N. Sadato et al., "Activation of the primary visual cortex by Braille reading in blind subject," *Nature* 380 (1996): 526–528.
66. R. Hamilton and A. Pascual-Leone, "Cortical plasticity associated with Braille learning," *Trends Cog. Sci.* 2 (1998): 168–174.
67. Lichtman and Colman, "Synapse elimination and memory."
68. J. Mehler, "Connaître par désapprentissage," in Edgar Morin and Massimo Piattelli-Palmarini, eds., *L'Unité de l'homme: Invariants biologiques et universaux culturels* (Paris: Seuil, 1974), 187–319.

7. Scientific Research and the Search for Truth

1. K. Popper, "Natural selection and the emergence of mind," *Dialectica* 22 (1978): 339–355.
2. See Marquis de Condorcet, *Sketch for a Historical Picture of the Progress of the Human Mind,* trans. June Barraclough (London: Weidenfeld and Nicolson, 1955).
3. See Bernard Le Bovier Fontenelle, *Conversations on the Plurality of Worlds,* trans. H. A. Hargreaves (Berkeley: University of California Press, 1990).
4. August Comte, *Système de Politique positive,* 4 vols. (Paris: L. Mathias, 1851–1854).
5. See Jean-Pierre Changeux and Paul Ricoeur, *What Makes Us Think?: A Neu-*

roscientist and a Philosopher Argue about Ethics, Human Nature, and the Brain, trans. M. B. DeBevoise (Princeton: Princeton University Press, 2000), 259–272.

6. See Juliette Grange, *Auguste Comte: La politique et la science* (Paris: Odile Jacob, 2000).
7. Claude Lévi-Strauss, *The Savage Mind* (Chicago: University of Chicago Press, 1966).
8. Harold C. Conklin, "The relation of Hanunoo culture to the plant world" (doctoral thesis, Yale University, 1954).
9. Brent Berlin et al., *Principles of Tzeltal Plant Classification: An Introduction to the Botanical Ethnography of a Mayan-Speaking People of Highland Chiapas* (New York: Academic Press, 1974).
10. Brent Berlin and Paul Kay, *Basic Color Terms: Their Universality and Evolution* (Berkeley: University of California Press, 1969).
11. See Semir Zeki, *A Vision of the Brain* (Oxford: Blackwell, 1993); Margaret Livingstone, *Vision and Art: The Biology of Seeing* (New York: Abrams, 2002).
12. Lévi-Strauss, *The Savage Mind,* 15.
13. D. Sperber, "Anthropology and psychology: Toward an epidemiology of representation," *Man* 20 (1985): 73–89.
14. See Denise Schmandt-Besserat, *Before Writing,* vol. 1: *From Counting to Cuneiform* (Austin: University of Texas Press, 1992).
15. See Annie Caubet and Patrick Pouyssegur, *L'Orient ancien: Aux origines de la civilisation* (Paris: Terrail, 1997).
16. See Changeux and Ricoeur, *What Makes Us Think,* 42–43.
17. Jack Goody, *The Domestication of the Savage Mind* (Cambridge: Cambridge University Press, 1977).
18. See David Premack and Ann J. Premack, "Intention as Psychological Cause," in Dan Sperber et al., eds., *Causal Cognition: A Multi-Disciplinary Approach* (Oxford: Clarendon Press, 1995), 185–200.
19. J. L. Barrett, "Exploring the natural foundations of religion," *Trends in Cog. Sci.* 4 (2000): 29–34.
20. Ibid.
21. See Pascal Boyer, *Et l'homme créa les dieux* (Paris: Robert Laffont, 2001).
22. See Jaak Panskepp, *Affective Neuroscience: The Foundations of Human and Animal Emotions* (New York: Oxford University Press, 1998); Edmund T. Rolls, *The Brain and Emotion* (Oxford: Oxford University Press, 1999); Joseph LeDoux, *Synaptic Self: How Our Brains Become Who We Are* (New York: Viking, 2002).
23. See Jean-Pierre Vernant, *Les Origines de la pensée grecque* (Paris: Presses Universitaires de France, 1962); G. E. R. Lloyd, *Magic, Reason, and Experience: Studies in the Origin and Development of Greek Science* (Cambridge: Cambridge University Press, 1979).
24. G. E. R. Lloyd, "Les concepts de vérité en Grèce et en Chine ancienne: Per-

spectives et implications comparatives," in Jacques Bouveresse and Jean-Pierre Changeux, eds., *La Vérité dans les sciences* (Paris: Odile Jacob, 2003), 49–60.

25. See Robert K. Merton, *The Sociology of Science: Theoretical and Empirical Investigations,* ed. Norman W. Storer (Chicago: University of Chicago Press, 1973).
26. Jacques Jouanna, *Hippocrates,* trans. M. B. DeBevoise (Baltimore: Johns Hopkins University Press, 1999).
27. Hippocrates, *The Sacred Disease,* trans. W. H. S. Jones (Cambridge, Mass.: Harvard University Press, 1992).
28. G. E. R. Lloyd, *Early Greek Science: Thales to Aristotle* (London: Chatto and Windus, 1970).
29. See Jouanna, *Hippocrates.*
30. See Ernst Mayr, *The Growth of Biological Thought: Diversity, Evolution, and Inheritance* (Cambridge, Mass.: Harvard University Press, 1982).
31. See John Lukacs, *Historical Consciousness: The Remembered Past* (New Brunswick, N.J.: Transaction, 1994).
32. See Stephen Toulmin, *Human Understanding* (Oxford: Clarendon Press, 1972); Karl R. Popper, *Objective Knowledge: An Evolutionary Approach,* rev. ed. (1972; Oxford: Clarendon Press, 1983); D. Campbell, "Blind variation and selective retention in creative thought as in other knowledge processes," *Psychological Reviews* 67 (1960): 380–400; David L. Hull, *Science as a Process: An Evolutionary Account of the Social and Conceptual Development of Science* (Chicago: University of Chicago Press, 1988).
33. See Juliette Blamont, *Le Chiffre et le Songe* (Paris: Odile Jacob, 1993).
34. See Luciano Canfora, *The Vanished Library,* trans. Martin Ryle (Berkeley: University of California Press, 1990).
35. Francis Bacon, *The New Organum,* ed. Lisa Jardine and Michael Silverthorne (Cambridge: Cambridge University Press, 2000).
36. Ernst Mach, *The Science of Mechanics,* trans. Thomas J. McCormack, 6th ed. (La Salle, Ill.: Open Court, 1974); Mach, *Popular Scientific Lectures,* trans. Thomas J. McCormack (La Salle, Ill.: Open Court, 1986).
37. René Descartes, *Meditations on First Philosophy: With Selections from the Objections and Replies,* trans. and ed. John Cottingham (New York: Cambridge University Press, 1996).
38. Immanuel Kant, *Critique of Pure Reason,* trans. Norman Kemp Smith (New York: St. Martin's, 1965), B 186.
39. Henri Poincaré, *Science et méthode* (Paris: Flammarion, 1908).
40. See Jean-Pierre Changeux and Alain Connes, *Conversations on Mind, Matter, and Mathematics,* trans. M. B. DeBevoise (Princeton: Princeton University Press, 1995), 75–81.
41. Poincaré, *Science et méthode,* 60–61.

42. See Jacques Hadamard, *An Essay on the Psychology of Invention in the Mathematical Field* (1945; Princeton: Princeton University Press, 1996); Arthur I. Miller, *Imagery in Scientific Thought: Creating 20th-Century Physics* (Cambridge, Mass.: MIT Press, 1986).
43. Jacques Monod, *Chance and Necessity: An Essay on the Natural Philosophy of Modern Biology*, trans. Austryn Wainhouse (New York: Random House, 1972).
44. E. Peterhans and R. von der Heydt, "Mechanisms of contour perception in monkey visual cortex: I. Lines of pattern discontinuity; II. Contours bridging gaps," *J. Neurosci.* 9 (1989): 1731–63.
45. Alain Berthoz, *The Brain's Sense of Movement*, trans. Giselle Weiss (Cambridge, Mass.: Harvard University Press, 2000).
46. Thomas S. Kuhn, *The Structure of Scientific Revolutions* (1962; Chicago: University of Chicago Press, rev. ed. 1968).
47. See Berthoz, *The Brain's Sense of Movement.*
48. Jacques Duclaux, *Recherches sur les substances colloïdales* (Paris: Laval, 1904).
49. L. Pauling and C. Niemann, "The structure of proteins," *J. Am. Chem. Soc.* 61 (1939): 1866.
50. Claude Debru, *L'esprit des protéines: Histoire et philosophie biochimiques* (Paris: Hermann, 1983).
51. Monod, *Chance and Necessity.*
52. S. Tonegawa, "Somatic recombination and mosaic structure of immunoglobulin genes," *Harvey Lect.* 75 (1980): 61–83; Tonegawa, "Somatic generation of antibody diversity," *Nature* 302 (1983): 575–581.
53. J.-P. Changeux, "The feedback control mechanism of biosynthetic L-threonine desaminase by L-isoleucine," *Cold Spring Harbor Symp. Quant. Biol.* 26 (1961): 313–318; J. Monod et al., "Allosteric proteins and cellular control systems," *J. Mol. Biol.* 6 (1963): 306–329; J. Monod et al., "On the nature of allosteric transitions: A plausible model," *J. Mol. Biol.* 12 (1965): 88–118.
54. D. Koshland et al., "Comparison of experimental binding data and theoretical model in protein containing subunits," *Biochemistry* 5 (1966): 365–385.
55. J.-P. Changeux and S. Edelstein, "Allosteric receptors after 30 years," *Neuron* 21 (1998): 959–980.
56. M. Perutz, "Mechanisms of cooperativity and allosteric regulation in proteins," *Quarterly Rev. of Biophys.* 22 (1989): 139–236; C. P. Macol et al., "Direct structural evidence for a concerted allosteric transition in *Escherichia coli* aspartate transcarbamylase," *Nat. Struct. Biol.* 8 (2001): 423–426.
57. Changeux and Edelstein, "Allosteric receptors after 30 years."
58. Lukacs, *Historical Consciousness*, 353.
59. Émile Durkheim, *The Elementary Forms of the Religious Life*, trans. Joseph Ward Swain, 2nd ed. (London: George Allen and Unwin, 1976).

60. Boyer, *Et l'homme créa les dieux.*
61. See Changeux and Ricoeur, *What Makes Us Think,* 286–292.
62. R. de la Fuente-Fernández and A. J. Stoessel, "The placebo effect in Parkinson's disease," *Trends in Neuroscience* 25 (2002): 302–306.
63. See David Sloan Wilson, *Darwin's Cathedral: Evolution, Religion, and the Nature of Society* (Chicago: University of Chicago Press, 2002).
64. François Jacob, *Le Jeu des possibles: Essai sur la diversité du vivant* (Paris: Fayard, 1981), 27.
65. François Jacob, "L'Évolution sans projet," in *Le Darwinisme aujourd'hui,* ed. Émile Noël (Paris: Seuil, 1979), 145.
66. See Georges Minois, *L'Église et la science: Histoire d'un malentendu,* 2 vols. (Paris: Fayard, 1990–1991).

8. The Humanity of Science

1. Auguste Comte, *Catéchisme positiviste* (Paris: Garnier, 1852), 48–50.
2. René Cassin, "La Science et les Droits de l'Homme," *Impact: Science et Société* 22, no. 4 (1972): 359–369.
3. John Lukacs, *Historical Consciousness: The Remembered Past* (New Brunswick, N.J.: Transaction, 1994), 358.
4. Universal Declaration on the Human Genome and Human Rights (Paris: UNESCO, 1997), Article 12b.
5. See F. Ewald and D. Lecourt, "Les OGM et les nouveaux vandales," *Le Monde* (4 Sept. 2001).
6. Alain Prochiantz, *Claude Bernard: La Révolution physiologique* (Paris: Presses Universitaires de France, 1990).
7. Jean Le Rond d'Alembert, *Preliminary Discourse to the Encyclopedia of Diderot,* trans. Richard N. Schwab and Walter E. Rex (Chicago: University of Chicago Press, 1995).
8. See Emil Du Bois-Reymond, *Untersuchungen über thierische Elektrizität,* 2 vols. (Berlin: Reimer, 1848–1884); Jean-Pierre Changeux, *Neuronal Man: The Biology of Mind,* trans. Laurence Garey, intro. Vernon B. Mountcastle (Princeton: Princeton University Press, 1997).
9. See Sir Henry Hallett Dale, *Adventures in Physiology: With Excursions into Autopharmacology* (London: Pergamon, 1953); David Nachmansohn, *Chemical and Molecular Basis of Nerve Activity* (New York: Academic Press, 1959).
10. See, e.g., John C. Eccles, *The Physiology of Synapses* (Berlin: Springer-Verlag, 1964).
11. Ibid.; J.-P. Changeux, "David Nachmansohn: A Pioneer of Neurochemistry," in Jean-Pierre Changeux et al., eds., *Molecular Basis of Nerve Activity* (Berlin: De Gruyter, 1985), 1–32.
12. See Jean-Pierre Changeux and Alain Connes, *Conversations on Mind, Matter, and Mathematics,* trans. M. B. DeBevoise (Princeton: Princeton University Press, 1995), 46; Gérard Radnitsky, *Entre Wittgenstein et Popper. Détours vers*

la découverte: Le vrai, le faux, l'hypothèse (Paris: Vrin, 1987); Jean-Michel Besnier, *Les Théories de la connaissance: Un exposé pour comprendre, un essai pour réfléchir* (Paris: Flammarion, 1996).

13. Jacques Hadamard, *An Essay on the Psychology of Invention in the Mathematical Field* (1945; Princeton: Princeton University Press, 1996); Henri Poincaré, *Science et méthode* (Paris: Flammarion, 1908), 57; Changeux and Connes, *Conversations,* 76.
14. See Imre Lakatos, *Philosophical Papers,* vol. 1: *The Methodology of Scientific Research Programmes,* ed. John Worral and Gregory Currie (Cambridge: Cambridge University Press, 1978).
15. See Charles Nicolle, *Biologie de l'invention* (Paris: Alcan, 1932).
16. Changeux and Connes, *Conversations,* 78–79.
17. M. Besson and D. Schon, "Comparison between language and music," *Ann. N.Y. Acad. Sci.* 930 (2001): 232–258.
18. See Changeux and Connes, *Conversations,* 75–76.
19. See E. Bienenstock et al., "Theory for the development of neuron selectivity: Orientation specificity and binocular interaction in visual cortex," *J. Neurosci.* 2 (1982): 32–48.
20. See S. Dehaene and J.-P. Changeux, "The Wisconsin card-sorting test: Theoretical analysis and simulation of a reasoning task in a model neuronal network," *Cerebral Cortex* 1 (1991): 62–79.
21. See Francis Crick, *The Astonishing Hypothesis: The Scientific Search for the Soul* (New York: Scribner, 1994); Gerald M. Edelman and Giulio Tononi, *A Universe of Consciousness: How Matter Becomes Imagination* (New York: Basic Books, 2000).
22. See Warren McCulloch and Walter Pitts, "A logical calculus of the ideas immanent in nervous activity," *Bull. Mathematical Biophysics* 5 (1943):115–133; Patricia Churchland and Terrence J. Sejnowski, *The Computational Brain* (Cambridge, Mass: MIT Press/Bradford Books, 1992).
23. Rudolf Carnap, *The Unity of Science,* trans. Max Black (Bristol: Thoemmes, 1995), 71.
24. See Jean-Pierre Changeux and Paul Ricoeur, *What Makes Us Think?: A Neuroscientist and a Philosopher Argue about Ethics, Human Nature, and the Brain,* trans. M. B. DeBevoise (Princeton: Princeton University Press, 2000), 33–38.
25. See Changeux and Connes, *Conversations,* 47–51.
26. See Ludwig Wittgenstein, *On Certainty,* ed. G. E. M. Anscombe and G. H. von Wright, trans. Denis Paul and G. E. M. Anscombe (Oxford: Blackwell, 1974), §275, 308.
27. See David Edmonds and John Eidinow, *Wittgenstein's Poker: The Story of a Ten-Minute Argument between Two Great Philosophers* (New York: Ecco, 2001); Karl Popper, *All Life Is Problem Solving,* trans. Patrick Camiller (New York: Routledge, 1999).

28. J.-P. Changeux and S. Edelstein, "Allosteric receptors after 30 years," *Neuron* 21 (1998): 959–980."
29. M. Rubin and J.-P. Changeux, "Allosteric interactions with aspartatetranscarbamylase: Interpretation of the experimental data in terms of the model of Monod, Wyman and Changeux," *Biochemistry* 7 (1968): 553–561.
30. S. J. Edelstein et al., "Single binding versus single channel recordings: A new approach to study ionotropic receptors," *Biochemistry* 36 (1997): 13755–760.
31. See R. G. Shulman et al., "Biophysical basis of brain activity: Implications for neuroimaging," *Quarterly Rev. of Biophysics*, forthcoming.
32. P. Faure and H. Korn, "Is there chaos in the brain? 1. Concepts of nonlinear dynamics and methods of investigation," *C. R. Acad. Sci. Paris, Life Science* 324 (2001): 773–793.
33. See Anne Fagot-Largeault, *Médecine et probabilités* (Paris: Université Paris-XIII/Didier Érudition, 1982); also a forthcoming article based on Fagot-Largeault's 2001–2002 course at the Collège de France, "Logique de la recherche, éthique de la recherche."
34. See J. Monod and F. Jacob, "Concluding remarks: Teleonomic mechanisms in cellular metabolism, growth, and differentiation," *Cold Spring Harbor Symp. Quant. Biol.* 26 (1961): 389.
35. Claude Debru, *L'Esprit des protéines: Histoire et philosophie biochimiques* (Paris: Hermann, 1983).
36. See Karl R. Popper, *Objective Knowledge: An Evolutionary Approach*, rev. ed. (Oxford: Clarendon Press, 1983); D. Campbell, "Blind variation and selective retention in creative thought as in other knowledge processes," *Psychological Reviews* 67 (1960): 380–400.
37. D. Sperber, "Anthropology and psychology: Toward an epidemiology of representation," *Man* 20 (1985): 73–89.
38. Richard Dawkins, *The Selfish Gene* (Oxford: Oxford University Press, 1976).
39. See Jacques Ellul, *La Technique, ou l'Enjeu du siècle* (Paris: Armand Colin, 1954).

Conclusion

1. See Gilbert Simondon, *Du mode d'existence des objets techniques* (Paris: Aubier, 1958).
2. See introduction to Jacques Bouveresse and Jean-Pierre Changeux, eds., *La Vérité dans les sciences* (Paris: Odile Jacob, 2003), 4–10.
3. John Lukacs has argued that truth "responds to a deeper human need than does justice, especially near the end of this age, when we are threatened less by the absence of justice than by the nearly fantastic prevalence of untruth." Lukacs, *Historical Consciousness: The Remembered Past* (New Brunswick, N.J.: Transaction, 1994), 358.
4. R. Cassin, "La Science et les Droits de l'Homme," *Impact: Science et Société* 22, no. 4 (1972): 359–369.

5. Ibid.
6. See J.-P. Changeux, “For a World Ethics Committee,” in Federico Mayor and Roger-Pol Droit, eds., *Taking Action on Human Rights in the Twenty-First Century* (Paris: UNESCO, 1998), 137–144.
7. See Jürgen Habermas, *Moral Consciousness and Communicative Action,* trans. Christian Lenhardt and Shierry Weber Nicholsen (Cambridge, Mass.: MIT Press, 1990); John Rawls, *Political Liberalism* (New York: Columbia University Press, 1993).
8. Jean-Pierre Changeux and Paul Ricoeur, *What Makes Us Think?: A Neuroscientist and a Philosopher Argue about Ethics, Human Nature, and the Brain,* trans. M. B. DeBevoise (Princeton: Princeton University Press, 2000), 272–298.
9. See Antonio R. Damasio, *The Feeling of What Happens: Body and Emotion in the Making of Consciousness* (New York: Harcourt Brace, 1999); J. Greene et al., “An fMRI investigation of emotional engagement in moral judgment,” *Science* 293 (2001): 2105–08.
10. See Changeux and Ricoeur, *What Makes Us Think,* 212–222.
11. See Martha Nussbaum, *Cultivating Humanity: A Classical Defense of Reform in Liberal Education* (Cambridge, Mass.: Harvard University Press, 1997); Martha Nussbaum and Amartya Sen, eds., *The Quality of Life* (Oxford: Clarendon Press, 1993).
12. See Immanuel Kant, *Perpetual Peace,* trans. Lewis Beck (New York: Liberal Arts Press, 1957).
13. See Changeux, “For a World Ethics Committee.”

Illustration Credits

1. Musée d'Orsay, Paris.
2. From Descartes, *L'Homme* (1677).
3. From François Leuret and Pierre Gratiolet, *Anatomie comparée du système nerveux, considéré dans ses rapports avec l'intelligence,* 2 vols. (Paris: Ballière, 1839–1857).

4A. From Michael A. Arbib, Peter Erdi, and Janos Szentágothai, *Neural Organization: Structure, Function, and Dynamics* (Cambridge, Mass.: MIT Press, 1998).

4B. Electron micrographs courtesy of Jean Cartaud.

4C. *Top:* After J. Del Castillo and B. Katz, "Interaction at endplate receptors between different choline derivatives," *Proceedings of the Royal Society of London* 146 (1957): 369–381.
Bottom: After E. Neher and B. Sakmann, "Single-channel currents recorded from membrane of denervated frog muscle fibres," *Nature* 260 (1976): 799–802.

4D. From C. Toyoshima and N. Unwin, "Three-dimensional structure of the acetycholine receptor by cryoelectron miscroscopy and helical image reconstruction," *Journal of Cell Biology* 111 (1990): 2623–35.

5A. Reprinted with permission from *Nature.* K. Brejc, W. J. van Dijk, R. V. Klaassen, M. Schuurmans, J. van Der Oost, A. B. Smit, and T. K. Sixma, "Crystal structure of an ACh-binding protein reveals the ligand-binding domain of nicotinic receptors," *Nature* 411 (2001): 269–276. Copyright 2001, Macmillan Magazines Limited.

5B. Reprinted with permission from *Nature.* J. Morais-Cabral, Y. Zhon, and R. McKinnon, "Energetic optimization of ion conduction rate by the K^+ selectivity filter," *Nature* 414 (2001): 37–42. Copyright 2001, Macmillan Magazines Limited.

6. I. From J. Monod, J. Wyman, and J.-P. Changeux, "On the nature of allosteric transitions: A plausible model," *Journal of Molecular Biology* 12 (1965): 88–118; after J.-P. Changeux, "Sur les propriétés allostériques de la L-thréonine-désaminase d'Eschericia coli K12" (doctoral thesis, University of Paris, 1964).
   II. From S. Iwata, K. Kamata, S. Yoshida, T. Minowa, and T. Ohta, "T and R states in the crystals of bacterial L-lactate dehydrogenase reveal the mechanism for allosteric control," *Nature Structural Biology* 1, no. 3 (1994): 176–185.
   III. From P. F. Egea, A. Mitschler, N. Rochel, M. Ruff, P. Chambon, and D. Moras, "Crystal structure of the human RXR-alpha ligand-binding domain bound to its natural ligand: 9-cis retinoic acid," *EMBO Journal* 19, no. 11 (2000): 2592–2601, by permission of Oxford University Press.
   IV. Reprinted from *Trends in Biochemical Sciences* 26, no. 8, T. Grutter and J.-P. Changeux, "Nicotinic receptors in wonderland," 459–463, copyright 2001, with permission from Elsevier.
7. *Top:* From Ramón y Cajal, *Histologie du système nerveux de l'homme et des vertèbres* (Paris: Maloine, 1909–1911).
   Bottom: Illustration by Nicolas le Novère, Institut Pasteur, Paris, after Linda Amos, "Focusing in on microtubules," *Current Opinion in Structural Biology* 10(2) (2000): 236–241, and Dennis Bray, *Cell Movements: From Molecules to Motility,* 2nd ed. (New York: Garland, 2000).

8A. From C. Mulle, P. Benoît, C. Pinset, M. Roa, and J.-P. Changeux, "Calcitonin gene-related peptide enhances the rate of desensitization of the nicotinic acetylcholine receptor in cultured mouse muscle cells," *Proceedings of the National Academy of Sciences USA* 85 (1988): 5728–32, copyright 1988 National Academy of Sciences USA.

8B. From T. Heidmann and J.-P. Changeux, "Un modèle moléculaire de régulation d'efficacité d'une synapse chimique au niveau postsynaptique," *C. R. Acad. Sci. Paris, Série III, Sc. Vie* 295 (1982): 665–670.

9. From Korbinian Brodmann, *Vergleichende Lokalisationslehre der Groshirnrinde* (Leipzig: J. A. Barth, 1909).
10. Musée Cognacq-Jay, Paris.

11A. *Top left:* Reprinted by permission from J. Olds, "Self-stimulation of the brain," *Science* 127 (1958): 315–324, copyright 1958 American Association for the Advancement of Science.
Top right and bottom: From E. Merlo Pich, C. Chiamulera, and L. Carboni, "Molecular mechanisms of the positive reinforcing effect of nicotine," *Behavioural Pharmacology* 10 (1999): 587–596.

11B. From *The Biochemical Basis of Neuropharmacology,* 5th ed., by Jack Cooper, Floyd Bloom, and Robert Roth, copyright 1970, 1974, 1978, 1982, 1986 by Oxford University Press, Inc.

12. From L. Chao, J. Haxby, and A. Martin, "Attribute-based neural substrates in temporal cortex for perceiving and knowing about objects," *Nature Neuroscience* 2 (1999): 913–919.
13. From D. A. Allport, "Distributed memory, modular systems and dysphasia," in Stanton P. Newman and Ruth Epstein, eds., *Current Perspectives in Dysphasia* (Edinburgh: Churchill Livingstone, 1985).
14A. From F. Varela, J.-P. Lachaux, E. Rodriguez, and J. Martinerie, "The brainweb: phase synchronization and large-scale integration," *Nature Reviews Neuroscience* 2 (2001): 229–238.
14B. From P. Fries, P. R. Roelfsema, A. K. Engel, P. König, and W. Singer, "Synchronization of oscillatory responses in visual cortex correlates with perception in interocular rivalry," *Proceedings of the National Academy of Sciences USA* 94 (1997): 12699–704, copyright 1997 National Academy of Sciences, USA.
15A. From S. Dehaene and J.-P. Changeux, "The Wisconsin card-sorting test: Theoretical analysis and modeling in a neuronal network," *Cerebral Cortex* 1 (1991): 62–79; by permission of Oxford University Press.
15B. From S. Dehaene and J.-P. Changeux, "The Wisconsin card-sorting test: Theoretical analysis and modeling in a neuronal network," *Cerebral Cortex* 1 [1991]: 62–79; by permission of Oxford University Press.
15C. Reprinted with permission from *Nature.* From E. Rodriguez, N. George, J.-P. Lachaux, J. Martinerie, B. Renault, and F. J. Varela, "Perception's shadow: long-distance synchronization of human brain activity," *Nature* 397 (1999): 430–433, copyright 1999 Macmillan Magazines Limited.
16. Reprinted from *Neuroscience* 44, R. Llinás and D. Paré, "Of dreaming and wakefulness," 521–535, copyright 1991, with permission from Elsevier.
17. From S. Dehaene, L. Naccache, L. Cohen, D. L. Bihan, J. F. Mangin, J. B. Poline, and D. Rivière, "Cerebral mechanisms of word masking and unconscious repetition priming," *Nature Neuroscience* 4 (2001): 752–758.
18A. From Santiago Ramón y Cajal, *Histologie du système nerveux de l'homme et des vertèbres* (Paris: Maloine: 1909–1911).
18B. *Left:* From C. F. von Economo, *The Cytoarchitectonics of the Human Cerebral Cortex* (London: Oxford University Press, 1929).
Right: From L. D. Selemon and P. S. Goldmann-Rakic, "Common cortical and subcortical targets of the dorsolateral prefrontal and posterior parietal cortices in the rhesus monkey: Evidence for a distributed neural network subserving spatially-guided behavior," *Journal of Neuroscience* 8 (1988): 4049–68, copyright 1988 by the Society of Neuroscience.
19. From S. Dehaene, M. Kerszberg, and J.-P. Changeux, "A neuronal model of a global workspace in effortful cognitive tasks," *Proceedings of the National Academy of Sciences USA* 95 (1998): 14529–534, copyright 1998 National Academy of Sciences, USA.

20. From S. Dehaene, M. Kerszberg, and J.-P. Changeux, "A neuronal model of a global workspace in effortful cognitive tasks," *Proceedings of the National Academy of Sciences USA* 95 (1998): 14529–534, copyright 1998 National Academy of Sciences, USA.
21. From S. Dehaene, M. Kerszberg, and J.-P. Changeux, "A neuronal model of a global workspace in effortful cognitive tasks," *Proceedings of the National Academy of Sciences USA* 95 [1998]: 14529–534, copyright 1998 National Academy of Sciences, USA.
22. Reprinted from *Neuron,* 30, J. M. Fuster, "The prefrontal cortex, an update: Time is of the essence," 319–333, copyright 2001, with permission from Elsevier.
23. Reprinted with permission from *Nature.* H. Tomita, M. Ohbayashi, K. Nakahara, L. Hasegawa, and Y. Miyashita, "Top-down signal from prefrontal cortex in executive control of memory retrieval," *Nature* 401 (1999): 699–703, copyright 1999 Macmillan Magazines Limited.
24. From O. Houdé, L. Zago, E. Mellet, S. Moutier, A. Pineau, B. Mazoyer, and N. Tzourio-Mazoyer, "Shifting from the perceptual brain to the logical brain: The neural impact of cognitive inhibition training," *Journal of Cognitive Neuroscience* 12 (2000): 721–728, copyright 2000 by the Massachusetts Institute of Technology.
25. From Ferdinand Saussure, *Cours de linguistique générale* (Paris: Payot, © 1916, 1995).
26. *Top:* Modified from Rosaleen A. McCarthy and Elizabeth K. Warrington, *Cognitive Neuropsychology: A Clinical Introduction* (San Diego: Academic Press, 1990).
    Bottom: From Joseph-Jules Déjerine, *Anatomie des centres nerveux* (Paris: Rueff, 1895–1901).
27. *Top:* Reprinted from *Neuron,* 42(2), M. Dapretto and S. Y. Bookheimer, "Form and content: Dissociating syntax and semantics in sentence comprehension," 292–293, copyright 1999, with permission from Elsevier.
    Bottom: Reproduced by permission of Helen Neville.
28. Drawing by the author.
29. *Left:* Reprinted from *Experimental Brain Research,* 82, G. Rizzolatti, M. Gartilucci, R. M. Camarda, V. Gallex, G. Luppino, M. Matelli, and L. Fogassi, "Neurons related to reaching-grasping arm movements in the rostral part of area 6 (area 6a)," 337–350, copyright 1990, with permission from Elsevier.
    Right: Reprinted from *Cognitive Brain Research,* 3, G. Rizzolatti, L. Fadiga, and L. Fogassi, "Premotor cortex and the recognition of motor action," 131–141, copyright 1996, with permission from Elsevier.
30. From P. Ruby and J. Decety, "Effect of subjective perspective-taking during simulation of action: A PET investigation of agency," *Nature Neuroscience* 4 (2001): 546–550.

31. From Dorothy L. Cheney and Robert M. Seyfarth, *How Monkeys See the World* (Chicago: University of Chicago Press, 1984).
32. From Dorothy L. Cheney and Robert M. Seyfarth, *How Monkeys See the World* (Chicago: University of Chicago Press, 1984).
33. Photographs from Charles Darwin, *The Expression of the Emotions in Man and Animals* (London: J. Murray, 1872).
34. *Top:* Musée du Louvre, Paris.
Bottom: From Michael Tomasello, *The Cultural Origins of Human Cognition* (Cambridge, Mass.: Harvard University Press, 1999), copyright 1999 by Michael Tomasello.
35. Map annotated by Celera Genomics on the basis of the complete sequence published as a supplement to *Science* 291 (2001): 5507. Reprinted with permission from J. C. Venter et al., "The Sequence of the Human Genome," *Science* 291 (2001): 1304–51, copyright 2001, American Association for the Advancement of Science.
36. From R. Saban, "Image of the human fossil brain: Endocranial casts of the meningeal vessels in young and adult subjects," in Jean-Pierre Changeux and Jean Chavaillon, eds., *Origins of the Human Brain* (Oxford: Oxford University Press, 1995).
37. From Walter J. Gehring, *Master Control Genes in Development and Evolution: The Homeobox Story* (New Haven: Yale University Press, 1998).

38A. From A. Duclert and J.-P. Changeux, "Acetylcholine receptor gene expression at the developing neuromuscular junction," *Physiological Reviews* 75, no. 2 (1995): 339–368.

38B. After B. Fontaine and J.-P. Changeux, "Localization of nicotinic acetylcholine receptor alpha-subunit transcripts during myogenesis and motor endplate development in the chick," reproduced from the *Journal of Cell Biology* 108, no. 3 (1989): 1025–37, by copyright permission of the Rockefeller University Press.

39. After T. Inoue, S. Nakamura, and N. Osumi, "Fate mapping of the mouse prosencephalic neural plate," *Developmental Biology* 219 (2000): 373–383.

40A. From M. Kerszberg and J.-P. Changeux, "A model for reading morphogenetic gradients: autocatalysis and competition at the gene level," *Proceedings of the National Academy of Sciences USA* 91 (1994): 5823–27, copyright 1994 National Academy of Science, USA.

40B. From M. Kerszberg and J.-P. Changeux, "A model for reading morphogenetic gradients: autocatalysis and competition at the gene level," *Proceedings of the National Academy of Sciences USA* 91 (1994): 5823–27, copyright 1994 National Academy of Science, USA.

40C. Reprinted with permission from M. Mannervik, Y. Nibu, H. Zhang, and M. Levine, "Transcriptional coregulators in development," *Science* 284 (1999): 606–609, copyright 1999 American Association for the Advancement of Science.

41. From Joaquin M. Fuster, *The Prefrontal Cortex: Anatomy, Physiology, and Neuropsychology of the Frontal Lobe,* 2d ed. (New York: Raven Press, 1989).
42A. From H. Steinmetz, A. Herzog, G. Schlang, Y. Huang, and L. Jäncke, "Brain asymmetry in monozygotic twins," *Cerebral Cortex* 5 (1995): 296–300, by permission of Oxford University Press.
42B. From F. Levinthal, E. Macagno, and L. Levinthal, "Anatomy and development of identified cells in isogenic organisms," *Cold Spring Harbor Symposia on Quantitative Biology* 40 (1976): 321–331.
43. From J.-P. Bourgeois, "Synaptogenesis, heterochrony and epigenesis in the mammalian neocortex," *Acta Paediatrica Suppl.* 422 (1997): 27–33.
44. *Left:* From Jean-Pierre Changeux, *L'Homme neuronal* (Paris: Libraire Artheme Fayard, 1983).
Top right: From J.-L. Gouzé, J.-M. Lasry, and J.-P. Changeux, "Selective stabilization of muscle innervation during development: A mathematical model," *Biological Cybernetics* 46 (1983): 207–215, copyright 1983 Springer-Verlag.
Bottom right: Reprinted from *Journal of Developmental Neuroscience,* vol. 4, no. 5, J.-P. Bourgeois, M. Toutant, J.-L. Gouzé, and J.-P. Changeux, "Effect of activity on the selective stabilization of the motor innervation of fast muscle posterior latissimus dorsi from chick embryo," 415–429, copyright 1986, with permission from Elsevier.
45. Modified from Bénédicte de Boysson-Bardies, *Comment la parole vient aux enfants* (Paris: Odile Jacob, 1996).
46A. From A. Castro-Caldas, K. M. Peterson, A. Reis, S. Stone-Elander, and M. Ingvar, "The illiterate brain," *Brain* 121 (1998): 1053–63, by permission of Oxford University Press.
46B. From Joseph-Jules Déjerine, *Anatomie des centres nerveux* (Paris: Rueff, 1895–1901).
47. Städelsches Kunstinstitut, Frankfurt-am-Main.
48. Fine Arts Museums of San Francisco, gift of Mr. Peter F. Young, 74.21.9.
49. From *Les Dix Livres d'architecture de Vitruve* (Paris: J.-B. Coignard, 1673).
50. Bibliothèque Nationale de France, Paris.
51. Reproduced by permission of Mme Hélène Berthoz.
52. Musée de Grenoble.

Acknowledgments

Several years ago I was asked to give a series of three lectures at Harvard University that might be of interest not only to specialists in the natural sciences but also to people working in the humanities and social sciences. These talks, delivered in the fall of 1999 under the auspices of the Mind, Brain, and Behavior Initiative, were entitled "The Good, the True, and the Beautiful: Provocations from the Brain Sciences." I subsequently came to feel that this plan was overly ambitious for a single book, and retained only the topic of the lecture on truth.

I owe thanks in the first place to Anne Harrington at Harvard for having extended the invitation that led to the present work, which originally appeared in French as *L'Homme de vérité* in 2002.

The French edition would not have been possible without the enthusiastic support, criticism, and friendship of Odile Jacob. I take this opportunity once more to express my warmest appreciation to her.

Anne Harrington and Elizabeth Knoll of Harvard University Press very kindly agreed to read an early version of the text. Anne Fagot-Largeault, Stuart Edelstein, Henri Korn, Christian Jacquemin, Pierre-Marie Lledo, and Sylvie Granon commented on later drafts. I am greatly indebted to all of them, as well as to Professor Gerald Weissmann, who arranged for me to have access to the rich library of the Marine

Biological Laboratory in Woods Hole, Massachusetts, during the summers of 2000 and 2001.

Last, but not least, I have Malcolm DeBevoise to thank for his care and diligence in seeking to convey not only the letter, but also the spirit, of the French text in English. He has produced an outstanding translation.

Index